The Writing on the Wall

original size

9.0 × 11.3

. 93%

Encounters with Asia

Victor H. Mair, Series Editor

A complete list of books in the series is available from the publisher.

The Writing on the Wall

How Asian Orthography Curbs Creativity

William C. Hannas

PENN

University of Pennsylvania Press

Philadelphia

10   9   8   7   6   5   4   3   2   1

Published by
University of Pennsylvania Press
Philadelphia, Pennsylvania 19104-4011

Library of Congress Cataloging-in-Publication Data
Hannas, Wm. C., 1946–
    The writing on the wall : How Asian orthography curbs creativity / William C. Hannas.
        p.   cm. (Encounters with Asia)
    ISBN 0-8122-3711-0 (cloth : alk. paper)
    Includes bibliographical references and index.
    1. Creation (Literary, artistic etc.).   2. Creative ability.   3. East Asia—Languages—Writing.
I. Title.   II. Series.
P381.E18 H36   2003
495   dc21   2002075056

for Hà Thị Ánh Thu
whom history spared these
linguistic travails

Contents

Introduction

The following chapters explore language, creativity, the brain, technology transfer, Chinese writing, and the processes that link these elements together. A personal anecdote will help bring the relationship into focus.

In 1997 I sat through a presentation on intracompany "teams," the latest panacea hawked by management consultants for making America more competitive. The facilitator was giving her pitch for the new program and offered the following proof of its superiority.

"Think back four decades ago to Japan," she said. "How would you characterize that country's products then?"

"Cheap." From one of the attendees.

"Imitative." Another voice.

"Do I hear low-tech?"

"Low-tech."

The ritual continued until the facilitator elicited a host of unflattering stereotypes that described the sort of production done in Japan in the immediate postwar period, before its manufacturers adopted a team approach. What came next was mostly predictable:

"And how would you describe Japanese products today?"

"First-rate." "Superior technology." "High value-added." And so on around the room, until one wag blurted out:

"Imitative."

"Imitative?"

"They're still copying from everybody like before."

A lively exchange followed, ending in a consensus among the attendees that creativity is a part of the entrepreneurial act not necessarily served by a team approach, and one that has not been mastered by Japan even now. The conclusion clearly was out of step with the facilitator's agenda, and a year earlier the wag wouldn't have gotten away with it. All indications then were that Japan was satisfying the world's appetite for high-tech novelty better than any other country.

But this was 1997, and signs of trouble were showing. Massive evidence painstakingly compiled by U.S. lawyers and trade experts confirmed what revisionist authors like Prestowitz (1988), van Wolferen (1989), and Fallows (1995) had claimed about Japan's export drive being artificially subsidized by a closed and captive domestic market.[1] Bankruptcies, a falling stock index, and lackluster economic growth—new phenomena in Japan—came to be viewed in some quarters as the outcome of structural problems when repeated attempts at piecemeal reform failed to revive the economy. That something was basically wrong with the world's leading model of economic development had become grimly apparent.

What was true of Japan was also true elsewhere in Asia. On the same day that the facilitator was scribbling outdated descriptions of the Japanese miracle on her flip chart, the Seoul media were reporting the dramatic end to economic prosperity in South Korea, a country that had followed Japan in all particulars. Within a few weeks corporate insolvency quadrupled, the won fell to an all-time low, and the stock market was nearly shattered. A new government, elected to remedy the failed policies, began laying plans for across-the-board fiscal retrenchment mandated by the International Monetary Fund, which had barely rescued the nation from default.

Amid the scramble to meet IMF guidelines, the only program to escape Seoul's budgetary ax was basic science and research.[2] Although product R&D was being slashed, moneys allotted for pure science were kept in place, indicating the importance South Korea now attaches to this area. I have watched this trend toward greater science and technology (S&T) expenditures in Korea with much interest over the past few years. My curiosity was piqued by the fact that these new programs—hosting international research projects, funding local centers of excellence, targeting specific future technologies—are usually announced in paranoid terms that suggest Korea has gone as far as it can with imitation, needs to *create* new technology, and worries that it is unable.

In Japan, too, there is widespread concern that the country lacks the creative skills needed to sustain growth into the twenty-first century. This is evidenced on the one hand by frantic moves to stimulate innovative research and apply new ideas to industrial production through decentralized research facilities, joint university-corporate R&D programs, and interdisciplinary collaboration, and on the other hand by frank admissions that Japan can no longer afford to take its research cues from the United States and Europe and must become "a scientifically and technologically creative nation" in its own right.[3] To cite just one example, the Japan Science and Technology Corporation, a quasi-official scientific support body, reportedly shifted from product-oriented research to "cultivating the seeds of pioneering research" and "promoting creative exploratory research in basic fields" in response to this change in priorities.[4]

Still, there are signs that the "creativity gap" between Japan and the West is not being closed. According to a 1997 Science and Technology Agency report, Japan's basic science expenditures are half those of the United States, with the gap widening. The report noted, "Japan is more dependent on technology than any other major country yet has the strongest tendency to acquire technologies from other countries."[5] Later the same agency publicized the results of another study that found "Europe and the United States pulling ahead of Japan in both basic and applied research and development."[6] That Japan's attempts to be more innovative were going nowhere had become apparent earlier that year, when the powerful Ministry of International Trade and Industry introduced sweeping revisions aimed at building more creativity into its highly touted "Frontier Program" that was started back in 1993 to promote "basic, original research and development and to achieve technological breakthroughs."[7]

China, too, has been engaged in a similar quest for scientific creativity, despite the fact that the country's industrial technology has not yet reached the stage where licensing and imitation are no longer viable means for sustaining a growing economy. Awareness of this issue seems to have penetrated the highest levels of the bureaucracy. For example, in June 1997 Vice-Premier Li Lanqing was quoted as saying that China must focus on basic research and on "cultivating creative scientific personnel" to achieve the breakthroughs needed for competitiveness in the twenty-first century.[8] In August of that year President Jiang Zemin publicly emphasized the need for "major breakthroughs" in basic science to realize China's goal of continuous economic progress.[9] At the opening ceremony of Beijing's

Research Center of Innovation Strategy and Management, Xu Guanhua, vice president of the State Science and Technology Commission, observed similarly "increasing global economic and scientific competition requires that more emphasis be placed on research."[10]

I believe, with many Asians, that the area's present economic difficulties stem in large part from a lack of scientific innovation, of which these countries are acutely aware but that they are addressing with only limited success. In fact, I will go a step further and argue in this book that East Asia's economic development has relied to a great extent on its ability to exploit scientific breakthroughs made in the West and to maintain these advantages by incrementally improving process and product technologies, leaving the real innovative work—with its economic and social costs—to their foreign competitors. These intellectual property transfers, sanctioned in policy, are carried out deliberately, systematically, and even cynically through a variety of mechanisms and metaphors that Westerners richly deserve to know more about. The real victims, however, are East Asians themselves, since imitation holds the seeds of its own demise as Asians run out of things to copy and improve. This is approximately where Japan and South Korea are today, and where China is headed.

Ironically, this thesis will be challenged only in the West, and in the United States especially, where East Asia's technical skills are typically confused with real creativity, and where the people have little clue about the degree to which their creative resources are utilized abroad for commercial profit. Asians themselves are cognizant of how much they depend on Western innovation and, until recently, had not even bothered to hide it. Accordingly, one of this book's tasks is to document the practices used by East Asians to relieve foreign firms and institutions of proprietary technology. My purpose is to convince Westerners inundated with clichés about Asian ingenuity that the truth is almost exactly the opposite and to persuade others who might be sympathetic to the linguistic arguments made later in this book that the creativity gap on which these subsequent arguments are based does in fact exist.

Americans in particular, who tend to imagine international competition as an extension of the fair play they enjoy at home, will find these facts upsetting. But the book's main thesis—that the lack of creativity that inspires all this "borrowing" has *its psychological roots in the Chinese-based writing* used there—will depress Asians even more, who have forsaken much of their past to modernize but have been able to leave this sacred stone of Asian culture mostly untouched. My feeling, which I share with Chinese writer and reform advocate Lu Xun (1881–1936) is that no amount of rational discourse will persuade Asian intellectuals and policy makers to jettison their obsolete systems of writing until progress, as measured in international competitiveness, grinds to a halt.

Westerners will find this part of my thesis less controversial. For years academics have criticized Chinese character-based orthography for contributing to conservatism in Asian society and thought by stifling curiosity, miring people's thinking in process instead of substance, and shoring up a moribund social hierarchy that rewards obedience and conformity.[11] Also, the mirror argument—that alphabetic literacy *promotes* creativity—has been laid out by scholars like Goody (1968), Havelock (1982), Ong (1982), de Kerckhove (1986, 1988), Logan (1986), and Olson (1994). What's missing is a description of how Asian writing affects creativity that takes into account what we already know about the connection between alphabetic literacy and brain processes. Providing such a demonstration is this book's primary task.

There are reasons why a linguistic theory linking Asian writing and Asian conservatism, such as we shall attempt here, did not appear earlier. One, as I have mentioned, is the difficulty Westerners have believing that beneath East Asia's material progress lurks a genuine creativity deficit that cries out for a scientific explanation. Another reason is the reluctance of Western linguists to stray from their familiar model of writing based on letters and words into a world where neither concept applies. A third reason, regrettably, is the mountain of hype and nonsense that has made so much of the literature on Asian writing implausible, such as claims that Chinese writing is ideographic, that unique oriental processing mechanisms are available to East Asian readers or, even more far-fetched, that the systems function independently of sound and hence cannot be compared with alphabetic writing.

Although my treatment of creativity in the main follows that of writers with more specialized backgrounds, I can, perhaps, help clear the way for a better appreciation of its psycholinguistic dimensions, particularly as they apply to Asia, having spent most of my life reading, teaching, translating, and analyzing the major East Asian languages and writing systems. These efforts led to an earlier book on Chinese character-based orthography to which the reader is referred for more detailed explanations of East Asian writing and reform (Hannas 1997). The present volume builds on this work, but focuses more squarely on some contentious issues that I was unable to take up earlier for lack of space and concern over reaction within the academy.

I have arranged this book's chapters to address initially those readers skeptical of the claim that Asia has a creativity problem, since my explanations for the linguistic causes of this problem are unlikely to mean much to those who think this deficit is temporary or imagined. Accordingly, the first three chapters deal extensively with the mechanisms employed by Japan, China, and Korea to transfer science and technology. If this seems like overkill to readers interested in the cognitive aspects of my thesis, please feel free to skip these parts (but you'll miss some insights into realpolitik). Chapter 4 examines the common experiences these countries have had with technology transfer, and weighs them against other material from history and social psychology to support my claim of a relative shortage of scientific creativity among the countries of the "Chinese character cultural sphere."

The remainder of the book attempts to account for this deficit. Chapter 5 explores modern theories of the creative process and integrates these findings into a cognitive model of human creativity. This model is used in Chapter 6 as a basis for explaining the role the alphabet has played in promoting creativity. Although previous scholarship has provided evidence of a link between the rise of scientific thought and the appearance of a fully phonemic alphabet, these arguments need to be backed by a linguistic account of how the two—creativity and alphabets—are related. After reviewing the psycholinguistic features of the alphabet, we proceed in Chapter 7 to an overview of East Asian writing: what it is and how it differs. I will try to show, as DeFrancis (1984) has for Chinese, that *all* East Asian orthographies—Korean *hangul,* Japanese *kana,* and Chinese characters—function primarily as concrete syllabaries, in contrast to phonemic alphabets, which are analytic in nature.

This basic difference between Western alphabetic and East Asian syllabic writing acts on several levels to promote or inhibit creativity, particularly that associated with breakthroughs in science. In Chapter 8 I examine the likelihood that syllabic literacy entails a diminished propensity for abstract and analytical thought. Problems that defy traditional solutions are not broken down into the basic components that are needed for novel re-combinations to emerge. Nor are the analogical recombinations proposed by right-track brain processes subjected to an adequate degree of logical scrutiny, for the same reason. These arguments are extensions of points made by cognitive scientists working within the framework of alphabetic culture. In Chapter 9 we break new ground by suggesting that the analogi-cal processes characteristic of creative thinking depend for their imple-mentation on the ability to dissociate concepts from the linguistic labels that hold them and their elements together. When these labels are per-ceived as a collection of abstract phonemes, which is how they are repre-sented in alphabetically literate minds, the link between address (the internal linguistic sign) and concept is more easily shed than when the lin-guistic sign is concretely and holistically bound to the concept it repre-sents, as is the case with syllable-based literacy.

In Chapter 10 we revisit some traditional explanations of the connection between writing and scientific creativity, such as the interplay between speech and writing, and the effect that rote memorization has on the indi-vidual's disposition toward novel habits of thought. Chapter 11 expands these observations to East Asian society as a whole. I will argue that certain Asian characteristics credited with blocking creativity, such as conservative political and social institutions and group-oriented behavior, derive in part from effects that the orthography has had on the minds of individuals. Fi-nally, in Chapter 12 I take Westerners to task for failing to ensure that their creative accomplishments are fairly compensated (the intellectual prop-erty rights problem) and for assuming, wrongly, that creativity is all that is needed to maintain economic competitiveness. East Asians, for their part, must recognize that overdependence on others for scientific innovation serves neither party's long-term interests. Eliminating the linguistic causes of this dependency will be a key element in escaping the paradigm.

Chapter One
Japan's Creative Imitations

It is very clear that Japan is making money by taking and applying the fruits of science that the West creates at great expense.

—Tonegawa Susumu, Nobel laureate

Thinking About Language and Thought

This is a book about language, especially written language. I shall argue that the mechanism used to write a language significantly affects one's ability to engage in creative thinking. In other words, there is a direct, causal link between the writing system people use and the contributions they make to science.

Establishing this hypothesis will require me to spend some time, indeed several chapters, on what would seem to be an unrelated *political* issue, namely, the transfer of technology between nations. My purpose in doing so is to show that the phenomenon under study—the poor record East Asia has in creative science—is in fact a real issue that cuts across Asia's national boundaries and is serious enough to warrant an explanation beyond what economists and social scientists offer. I am convinced that the root cause of East Asians' endemic borrowing of Western ideas lies in their use of non-alphabetic writing and that their "creativity problem" is linguistic in nature.

Given the central role linguistics will play in this study, I would like to say a few words about language before getting wrapped up in the political dimensions of the problem. The institutions Asia has to transfer Western technology respond to features of Asian psychology that are language-dependent. As we enter this world of political intrigue, I ask you to keep in mind our goal of relating this behavior to its linguistic antecedents.

Language is so much a part of the human condition that we tend to take it for granted. While essential to our livelihood, it is not something we often contemplate. We use language every day of our lives, paying little attention to the structures that support it, assuming that our thoughts will be conveyed independently of the medium itself. The same naiveté extends to writing. No one thinks about *how* a writing system expresses ideas, still less about its *effects* on an individual's thinking, and not at all about how such effects are manifested cumulatively in the *behavior* of whole societies.

But what if it could be shown that language—the mechanism itself—matters? And that the systems we use to form and convey thoughts shape our behavior in subtle but significant ways? There is no a priori basis for assuming, as the more cosmopolitan among us do, that language is neutral about how ideas are conceptualized and strung together. Given the great diversity between languages, and the intimate connection between language and thought, the notion that differences in language and its means of expression equate somehow to differences in thinking would seem tenable. This argument applies not just to comparisons between so-called "primitive," that is, technologically less advanced societies versus more technologically advanced societies, but also to countries like Japan and China, where differences in the two languages have been linked to what some scholars see as analogous differences in behavior.[1]

The notion that language determines thought, formalized in the writings of Benjamin Whorf (1897–1941), has received a bad press in recent decades for being too simplistic, in its strong version at least, and for being out of step with the currently dominant intellectual paradigms. Chomsky's theory of universal grammar (1957, 1965) holds that "surface" distinctions made by different languages disappear at the "deep structure level" where language interacts with thought. Deacon (1997:121), who rejects this nativist hypothesis in favor of an evolutionary model of language convergence, also does not put much stock in Whorf's theory for the same reason: universal deep structure, whether the result of biological or linguistic evolution, has no room for a theory that equates psychological and cultural variation with differences in morphology and syntax.

Whorf's theory also failed certain tests relating to its claims about color terms and Native American verb forms (Foss and Hakes 1978:382–84), which discredited its strong or deterministic version for most linguists. Equally damaging to the theory was its assault on the belief that all humans are alike, notwithstanding the apparent differences. Most of us, on some level, want to believe that humans share the same basic cognitive apparatus that can be relied on to generate shared perceptions of our common condition. Thus it should be no surprise that arguments explaining psychological and cultural differences in terms of different linguistic structures have not been well received.[2]

Although the strong version of Whorf's hypothesis has not won acceptance, a weaker claim that "the lexical items and linguistic structures that a language provides can have an important influence on thought processes even though they do not determine all such processes" (385) has proven more convincing and is enjoying a rebirth in some quarters.[3] Not only do empirical studies support this commonsense view. Replacing hard determinism by a calculus of probabilities is consistent with trends in other sciences. The results would scarcely differ in pragmatic terms from a more deterministic process, particularly for long-established speech groups, where the interaction of millions of individuals over many generations has afforded ample opportunity for these weak tendencies to show an effect.

If linguistic structures are believed to influence, though not dictate, thought and behavior, the opposite claim—that thought patterns at least partly determine language categories—has been put forward by intellectuals from Aristotle onward. Fortunately, there is no need to take sides since the two arguments are complementary. Instead of attributing the structure of language to thought, or vice versa, it makes more sense to view this as a coevolutionary relationship, where one system both effects and is affected by changes in the other,[4] so that a linguistic bias in one speech community toward concrete expressions, for example, *parallels* a similar proclivity in many (but not all) of its speakers' habits of thought.

If this is true of language as spoken, it should also be true of writing, perhaps more so. Whereas the basic psychophysical parameters of speech are common to all humans, writing systems vary enormously in how they represent language. This variation not only impinges on the structures of languages that evolved under a particular writing system's tutelage. It also affects thought, as a consequence of writing's influence on language and through psychological processes attending writing that extend to nonlinguistic aspects of cognition. While derived from speech, or more exactly the linguistic competence that leads to speech, writing occupies a semiautonomous position in the language hierarchy and, in the view of many writing theorists, connects with speech at the level where thought processes are realized as linguistic signs (Amirova 1977:35). Given the gross differences between Western alphabets and the syllabic scripts of Japan and East Asia, the likelihood that these differences, like those of speech, have their correlates in thought and behavior cannot be dismissed.

Japan Bashing and "Absorbing" Technology

Language's bias is also evident on another plane studied at one time under the rubric of "general semantics" (Hayakawa 1949). While this movement to clarify the nuances of terms used to obfuscate sociopolitical realities seems to have run out of steam, the phenomenon itself is quite alive and has an immediate bearing on the issues I raise in this chapter.

Most of us have heard, or even used, the phrase "Japan bashing" (*Nihon tataki*). This term is normally understood to mean unfair criticism of Japan by foreigners envious of Japan's success, but it has also been applied to attacks on Japan's culture. It originated in the early 1980s, when Japan's ascendancy in world markets coincided with a decline in the confidence Americans had in their own products and way of life. Rather than admit their shortcomings, the argument ran, Americans preferred to scapegoat or "bash" Japanese for working harder, studying diligently, restricting their consumption, and investing in the future—in short, for following the practices that Americans held responsible for their own success but had, through laziness, permitted to lapse.

Guilt comes easily to those in the West whose opulent lifestyle permits this luxury. Painful as it was, many Americans accepted the notion that their country's decline was the result of their own bad habits. A few critics did suggest that Japan's mercantilist policies were responsible for this role reversal, but American opinion-makers dismissed the allegation as sour grapes. Other arguments that Japan owed its success to the fruits of U.S. scientific research were also viewed as the complaints of a second-rate producer who had lost the ability to compete.[5]

It is now recognized that behind this deluge of hand wringing and despondency was a massive and well-funded public relations campaign run from Tokyo through American principals hired to silence U.S. critics and present Japan's case in a favorable light.[6] The scope of these efforts, brought out by Michael Crichton in his dramatic but in many ways understated novel *Rising Sun* (1992), has more recently been the subject of a detailed study by Robert Angel, a Japan scholar who played an early role in the U.S. Japan lobby.[7] It was Professor Angel himself, as CEO of the Japan Economic Institute and a registered agent for the Japanese Government, who coined the term "Japan bashing," in his words,

as a means of discrediting credible critics of Japan's policies. It tends to shift attention away from the substance of the charges or assertions made by the critic and toward the critic's personal motives. An effective piece of propaganda.[8]

The criticism of Japan that did emerge centered on bilateral trade, specifically, barriers that frustrated American efforts to sell products in Japan and export subsidies that made Japanese goods more attractive to American buyers. Less attention has been paid to the technology transfers that made Japanese goods competitive in the first place. Even here the tendency has been to describe these transfers—some benign, others downright illegal—positively in terms of Japan's ability to "absorb" foreign technology,[9] as if an aversion to creative enterprise were a national asset instead of the problem that Japanese today acknowledge and are struggling to overcome.

It is this "absorption" by Japan of foreign technology, and of American technology especially, that will be my concern through the remainder of this chapter. And it is hoped that by exposing the origin of "Japan bashing" I will have preempted its application to the present study. It is clear that Japan in the postwar era, and arguably through much of its history, has been reaping one-sided advantages by importing technologies created abroad, contributing few fundamental innovations in return. Efforts to whitewash this fact by praising Japan's skills at adaptation are beside the point. What is sorely needed is a demonstration of Japan's ability to engage consistently and successfully in cutting-edge research or, barring that, a serious effort to determine what prevents Japan from achieving its creative goals.

Language as an Adaptation Model

Japan experienced three great periods of foreign borrowing: (1) when the Japanese state was formed in the seventh century on the basis of innovations brought in from China; (2) in the last half of the nineteenth century, when the process was repeated with Western technology and cultural artifacts; and (3) in the post-World War II era, when the source of borrowing shifted to the United States. These first two stages are well documented in standard histories; I would add only that they represent high points in the process of borrowing and adaptation rather than the whole of it. Japan throughout much of its history kept up with technical developments abroad through overseas missions or contact with foreign intermediaries. When the country was closed to foreigners during the Tokugawa period (1600–1867), Japan continued to import technology through Dutch traders and by allowing certain Japanese (the *rangakusha*, or "specialists in Dutch studies") to pursue foreign learning.

The third stage, which began with postwar reconstruction and continues into the present, has only recently begun to draw attention from journalists and scholars. Clyde Prestowitz in his landmark book *Trading Places*, was one of the first to identify the implications of this latest wave of technology transfers for U.S. competitiveness, noting that "While the United States has sought security by giving away technology, Japan has sought it by hoarding technology, even from the United States, its primary source" (1988:140). According to Prestowitz, "This transfer of technology and its effects cannot be emphasized enough. The major advantage of U.S. firms in their competition with Japan has been their technological level. The Japanese system has always worked as a kind of siphon for this technology" (177).

Peter Schweizer, whose book *Friendly Spies* took the important step of moving the dialogue on technology transfer out of its Cold War context and into today's complex world of economic competitiveness, devotes a large part of his book to East Asia's illicit acquisitions of U.S. technology, of which Japan comes in for the lion's share of criticism. Schweizer observed that Japanese technology information gathering in America had gotten so out of hand by the 1970s that "the State Department, at the encouragement of the FBI, quietly moved to tighten the procedures for granting visas to Japanese citizens" (1993:79). More recently, John Fialka noted in his book *War by Other Means: Economic Espionage in America* that Japan's industrial and high-tech collection efforts against the United States have been so successful that China and Taiwan are adopting them as models (1997:12).

While the gray aspects of Japan's technology transfers have drawn the greatest attention, most acquisitions, as Glickman and Woodward (1989:109) have pointed out, are straightforward.[10] None of the items on Herbig's (1995:81–82) list, for example, including Japan's penchant to "pursue competitive information, conduct widespread technology surveillance, consult foreign specialists, call frequently on suppliers, cull operating manuals, send students to foreign universities, send managers on Western tours, translate technical journals, and attend large numbers of professional meetings in pursuit of foreign technology" are illegal or, individually, unethical. Yet the combination of these incremental efforts to tap the sources of Western creativity has worked the same magic in the area of information gathering as it has in Japan's approach to industrial production. Today Japan can boast of the world's most sophisticated technology transfer network just as it boasts of its accomplishments in trade and industry.

The problem with this approach to technological development, as Japan is discovering, is that it leads to a dead end. Borrowing and adaptation may be effective midterm strategies, but they sap a society of its ability to innovate as the habit takes hold and becomes reinforced in other parts of the culture. Nowhere is this more apparent than in the history of the Japanese language, whose development paralleled that of the technological culture as a whole, both helping to shape it and being shaped by it in turn. Let's look for a moment at how these linguistic borrowings coincide with technology borrowing in general.

In the seventh century, while the Japanese were importing Chinese technology, they simultaneously restructured their own language by introducing Chinese script and the Sinitic vocabulary that came with it. There was nothing natural about this, the two languages having as little in common as Japanese has with English. Faced with the tasks of introducing a foreign writing system *and* thousands of obscure Chinese terms, Japanese had no hope of absorbing the innovations in the usual sense. Rather, they *grafted* Chinese elements onto their original language until they eventually overwhelmed it, crippling its phonology and driving out many indigenous forms and processes.

Although this linguistic infusion may have eased the importation of Chinese culture, it did nothing to stimulate creativity.[11] Instead the borrowing fostered a psychology of looking abroad for sources of innovation that has remained through the ages. It also forced the language into serious dislocations, the worst being the inability of Japanese speech and writing to interact in a normal manner. Arguably an analogous effect occurred in the society, where a borrower's mentality has accentuated the gap between Japan's ability to do basic research and development and what the world expects of a country of Japan's stature. And because of the way these borrowed forms were written—the Sinitic terms in one system and the remnants of Japanese in another—they helped perpetuate a paranoid distinction between "native" and "foreign" that continues to haunt Japan today. This is in addition to everything else I will say later about how Chinese writing affected Japanese cognitive behavior.

In the nineteenth century, when Japan was introducing Western technology, the process was essentially repeated as Japanese scholars and translators dug into the corpus of Sinitic morphemes to assemble hybrid words that mimicked Western vocabulary. These calques or "loan translations" today number in the thousands and (like the shortcuts Japan has taken in its technological development generally) solved the immediate problem of how Japanese would render borrowed concepts but produced long-term contradictions in the language's structure. Although some Japanese claim that these Sinitic combinations provide a natural window to high-level concepts,[12] their chief effect seems to be greater dependency on Chinese writing, with all the problems that connection entails.

Finally, there is the direct borrowing of American English that occurred in the postwar period and continues today. Partly a sociolinguistic phenomenon, partly a result of a breakdown in the language's ability to generate phonetically viable terms, these *gairaigo* or direct foreign loans, like the Sinitic genre that preceded them, are written in a separate *kana* subscript and are literally countless in number.[13] This habit of borrowing language technology, like the analogous practice of borrowing technology in general, has become an ingrained part of Japanese culture.[14] While historians and even linguists have praised Japan for being able to adopt foreign conventions, the time has come to take stock of what this habit costs Japan—and the world—in lost potential.

Cataloging Transfer Venues

We can gauge the magnitude of Japan's reliance on foreign sources of technology by examining the mechanisms used to effect these transfers. Some twenty such venues or techniques have been identified, including access to foreign labs, benchmarking, company buyouts, corporate intelligence networks, database exploitation, direct licensing, foreign-based research institutes, government collection support, imitation, industrial espionage, investment in high-tech foreign firms, involvement in international scientific projects, leveraging institutional inequities, liaisons with foreign universities, membership in professional societies, partnerships and coproduction agreements, patents research, rejection of foreign patent applications (while gleaning their ideas and finding workarounds), reverse engineering, sending researchers abroad, technology offsets, and trading technology for market access.[15]

This formidable list could be expanded by refining individual categories. For example, "liaisons with foreign universities" includes contracting for research; funding labs, chairs, and whole departments; taking advantage of educational and research opportunities; building personal relationships with top scientists; and providing grants to establish goodwill. "Headhunting," or recruitment of foreign scientific talent by overseas-based research institutes, technology brokerage firms, or the overseas branches of Japanese corporations, could also be treated as a separate category. "Database exploitation," an important transfer venue in its own right,[16] is probably too narrow a term for the various information operations used by Japan to access foreign technology and gain advantage over rival firms.

Other transfer venues are omitted here for lack of public documentation. For example, certain East Asian countries run both licit and gray science and technology collection programs from embassies and foreign consulates.[17] It would be unusual and out of character for Japan not to use this opportunity to broaden its collection effort. And unlike China's Ministry of State Security and South Korea's National Intelligence Service, both of which engage actively in covert technology acquisitions in the United States, Japan has no centralized intelligence service. The function is performed on a national level by the Science and Technology Agency (STA)[18] and by the Ministry of International Trade and Industry (MITI)[19] and its affiliates, including the Japan External Trade Organization (JETRO), the Institute for Industrial Protection, and others.

Some collectors cloak their governmental affiliation in harmless sounding titles. James Hansen in his book *Japanese Intelligence—The Competitive Edge* describes a "Japanese Productivity Center" in Washington, D.C. that translates English-language articles in science and engineering into Japanese (1996:114). The Federation of Economic Organizations (Keidanren), which acts as a quasi-official link between corporate Japan and MITI, was identified by *Washington Times* reporter Bill Gertz (1992:A6) as "a key economic intelligence agency. It sets requirements for information collection, formulates policy recommendations for the government and is a collector of information as well." Some Japanese argue that the lack of a centralized facility has impaired foreign intelligence operations. There may be some substance to this complaint, particularly as it applies to analysis and dissemination, but in my view this distributed, multi-agency approach, coupled with prodigious private sector collection, is one of the system's greatest strengths.

Unlike China and South Korea, which rely heavily on expatriate nationals to transfer U.S. high technology, Japan appears to make little use of this venue. It has nothing equivalent to Seoul's Federation of Overseas Korean Scientists and Engineers, Association of Korean Physicists in America, and sundry other expatriate organizations that function, at minimum, as support bodies for Asian S&T development. There are two reasons for this. Whereas the Chinese and South Korean governments regard emigrants, and emigrants' descendants, as nationals of their country of origin despite their actual citizenship and appeal to these "overseas Chinese" (*huáqiáo*) and "overseas Koreans" (*kyop'o*) for support on the basis of ethnicity, Japanese who have acquired foreign citizenship or stayed abroad too long are viewed as having lost their Japaneseness and are no longer trusted. Although I dislike using generalities, this characterization seems to apply. Second, appeals to help "the fatherland" do not command much sympathy in the case of Japan, which has enjoyed more economic security than most of the expatriates' host countries.

Institutional Inequities

Imbalances resulting from social, economic, and political differences confer a tremendous advantage on Japan in its efforts to access and commercialize foreign technology and hence qualify broadly as a transfer "venue" in their own right. Since these institutional inequities also act as facilitators for concrete transfer mechanisms, it will be worthwhile to examine them in some detail. Many such inequities can be cited:

1. The bulk of Japan's national intelligence effort, including programs run by MITI, the STA, and their affiliates, has been directed at economic targets, especially foreign R&D. This information is passed on to Japanese manufacturers. Conversely, U.S. intelligence focuses on military threats and is concerned with technology issues primarily for their impact on national

security, narrowly defined. Although the United States at one time considered passing foreign technological data gleaned incidentally in the course of normal collection activities to American companies, the idea was vetoed for ethical reasons and because there is no way the information can be distributed fairly among competing American firms (Perry 1992:197).[20] Meanwhile the United States shares military intelligence with its Japanese ally and extends an umbrella of protection over Japan, freeing Japan to gather foreign intelligence of commercial value, mostly from the United States.

2. The same is true of R&D in general. Since Japan spends less on its military, and still less on military R&D, the country has been able to devote proportionally more resources to commercial technology (and commercializing foreign technology), enjoying a "free ride" in the exercise of its international responsibilities. During the same decades that Japan experienced its highest rates of economic growth, the United States saw its own wealth and scientific talent derailed into nonproductive military research. The benefits to U.S. industry of military R&D (spin-off) have been exaggerated both absolutely and relative to America's economic competitiveness, since the same U.S.-led breakthroughs are exploited by foreign competitors. The shift underway within the U.S. defense establishment toward adapting commercial off-the-shelf technology instead of initiating its own R&D belies the earlier claim.

3. The imbalance in R&D spending is not limited to the defense sector but applies to scientific research across the board. According to Herbig (1995:60), the United States spends as much on R&D as "Japan, Germany, and France combined." Although Japan claims a research investment that is 3 percent of its gross domestic product (GDP), actual expenditures are overstated by a large multiple because academic salaries are included in the figure. Moreover as Herbig points out, "R&D expenditures represent input, not output," which in Japan's case has been spotty at best. Instead of investing heavily in research, Japan has found it profitable to support mechanisms to transfer and commercialize foreign R&D, often in advance of the country making the discovery.

4. Not only is Japan doing less R&D, absolutely and relative to GDP, than the United States. It focuses its research more narrowly on applied areas closer to the end of the product cycle. Reid and Schriesheim note that Japan spends "nearly half as much per capita on basic research as the

United States," and add "what the Japanese classify as basic research is, in fact, more application oriented and proprietary in character" (1996:127). Herbig estimates that a mere 2.3 percent of Japan's R&D expenditures are in basic research, with 54 percent spent on product development and 43.7 percent on applied research (1995:63). The same disparity is evident in—and in part originates from—higher education, with the United States graduating three to four times as many engineering Ph.D.s as Japan but roughly the same number of engineering bachelors of science.

5. Although Japanese have nearly unlimited access to the best research done in the United States, Americans enjoy little reciprocity. This imbalance is partly caused by Japan's parochial attitude toward foreigners and partly the result of institutional differences. In America, much of the top research is conducted in the public domain at universities open to foreign enrollment and in publicly funded institutes, which Japanese have patronized more assiduously than any other foreign nationality (Reid and Schriesheim 1996:113). By contrast, most Japanese R&D is done inside companies, is proprietary, and is not open to foreign participation. Although Japan does fund national research, these institutes accomplish little, providing instead what Peters calls "a context for building information networks" (1987:199), in other words, a forum through which Japanese companies aligned with the institutes can access the research of participating U.S. firms.

6. Whereas America's technology trade typically involves the exporting of high-tech items to its international competitors, Japan avoids making its high technology available to countries that compete in the same sectors (the term used is "boomerang effect"). Herbig notes that although 85 percent of U.S. technology exports are to advanced countries, "the majority of Japan's technological exports are being sold to developing countries" which do not threaten Japanese manufacturers. That is, Japan exports mature technologies "while importing key portions of new, frontier, state-of-the-art technology from the West (particularly the United States)" (1995:73).

7. Japan also benefits from legal asymmetries in its efforts to obtain and commercialize foreign technology. Loose enforcement of intellectual property rights (IPR) is a continuing problem particularly in computer software. Japanese corporations have also used the U.S. Freedom of Information Act to collect technical information in areas as sensitive as rocketry and satellites (Schweizer 1993:92). There is nothing comparable to this law in

Japan. Since U.S. antitrust law prevents American companies from coordinating licensing activities, Japanese firms are able to play off one U.S. company against another to get needed technology (Prestowitz 1988:36). Justice for American firms seeking relief from patent infringements and broken joint ventures is severely hampered by the difficulty foreign lawyers have practicing in Japan. Finally, approval to sell products in Japan often entails submitting proprietary information, which puts advanced technology in the hands of a U.S. company's most capable competitors.

8. The Japanese patent system offers foreigners little protection. On the one hand, Japanese officials reject for trivial formalities or for no reason at all applications on products patented in other countries. Or they stall applications interminably while "Japanese competitors use the technology to gain new markets" (Yoder and Lachica 1988).[21] Frustrated foreign firms often end up selling technology licenses to their Japanese rivals, which is, of course, the purpose of the delays (Fialka 1997:58). On the other hand, minor changes by Japanese firms in the design of a patented U.S. invention can qualify for patent protection in Japan. Known as "patent flooding," the strategy was used routinely in Japan against U.S. firms prior to the 1995 U.S.-Japan Trade Framework Agreement and is still a significant threat.

9. The content of Japanese and American patents reflects the disparity in the type of research done in the two countries at the same time it demonstrates different attitudes toward technology acquisition. Unlike U.S. patents, Japanese patents are awarded for relatively minor innovations, not major breakthroughs.[22] As Herbig puts it, "The Japanese have applied for and registered more patents than others because the knowledge they seek to protect tends to be less significant technologically and of lower quality, and the Japanese have a greater propensity to seek patents for know-how that others would consider too mundane or short lived to bother about" (1995:59).

10. The notion that patents can protect an innovating country such as the United States from countries such as Japan and South Korea, which are weak innovators but strong in manufacturing, is inherently flawed—a fact American companies and trade officials have been slow coming to grips with.[23] What patents end up becoming are *targets* for exploitation by foreign corporations and governments. Dalton and Genther report that "Since 1957, the Japan Information Center of Science and Technology (JICST), a

branch of Japan's Science and Technology Agency, collects 10,000 foreign and domestic patents each year which are abstracted by 5,000 scientists and engineers" (1991:2). Herbig notes similarly the parallel global patent scanning done by Japanese corporations (1995:88).

This last item leads to the greatest inequity between Japan and the United States in the area of technology transfer, namely, the two countries' perceptions of the exchange process. Whereas Japanese businessmen and officials have no illusions about the nature of their goals and the means they use to attain them, their U.S. counterparts labor under the belief that any type of exchange presupposes benefits in equal proportion. When the fallacy of this approach becomes manifest, as it often does, Americans involved in promoting these exchanges resort to a standard repertoire of excuses to justify their misplaced faith, salvage their worldview, and avoid the unpleasantness of remedial action.

One such justification is that Japanese engaged in joint research or coproduction ventures must have some knowledge of the technology in question to absorb it and that they will share what they know with their American colleagues. Complaints from the latter suggest this is not always the case. Another standard gloss is that Japan contributes process and manufacturing technology in *exchange* for U.S. wellspring technology. While true in itself, the argument ignores the fact that the technology Japan seeks is beyond its ability to create, whereas America's failure to invest in process technology is symptomatic of a decline in its manufacturing industry, brought about in part by Japan's unfair trade practices.

It may have been possible at one time to hope that concessions in the area of technology transfer would bring about benefits later in the form of increased openness, cooperation, and so on. Unfortunately, change in Japan happens at a glacial pace, if at all, while the cost of promoting basic technological change, borne largely by the United States, continues to climb. As Fallows (1995) has argued, the naive faith Americans put in Japan and other East Asian countries to play by the same rules works to neither country's long-term benefit. In the end, it is the psychological difference between a wary Japan, fully cognizant of its limitations in resources and creativity, and gullible Americans that enables Japan to operate the transfer methods we will now discuss.

Intelligence Networks

A detailed treatment of Japan's technology transfer mechanisms would require an entire volume. I will try in the few pages that remain to cover the salient points by condensing the material into broader categories.

Japanese corporate and government entities operate redundant intelligence networks designed to locate foreign scientific and technological innovations before they are commercialized abroad or before they are even patented. Japan's STA, in addition to translating science and technology publications, has been identified by Herbig as a pivotal player in transferring foreign technology to Japanese corporations (1995:32). MITI, for its part, has been likened to a military intelligence service, choosing targets on the basis of national interest and coordinating collection. For example, in 1976 MITI set up a Committee on Information and Acquisitions in its Electrotechnical Laboratory to monitor developments in the American computer industry. According to Schweizer, "Funds were available to the committee for the purchase of information from individuals in the United States who were willing to sell it, whether legally or illegally," through front companies set up by MITI or so-called "consulting" contracts with employees of U.S. computer firms. This information was instrumental in Japan's subsequent ability to dominate the field of microelectronics (1993:78–79). Since the late 1980s, MITI has been running the same type of operation against the U.S. biotech and aerospace industries.

The role of the Japanese External Trade Organization (JETRO) in collecting foreign intelligence is legendary. Created in 1958 as part of MITI's International Trade Administrative Bureau to support foreign trade, its unofficial and major role has been to collect intelligence on foreign business strategies, trade secrets, and new technologies (DeLuca 1988:10). JETRO has eighty overseas offices, eight of which are in the United States, and a worldwide staff of 1,300 who collect information from host country gray and open sources. The information is then made available to Japan's corporations (Kahaner 1996:170).[24] The Japanese government is also involved in sending researchers abroad, sponsoring joint R&D, hosting seminars, and inviting foreign experts to Japan, all aimed at capturing specific technologies or bolstering its S&T intelligence network.

Japan's best information on foreign technology comes not from its government, however, but from corporations. Some Japanese firms ran worldwide intelligence networks before World War II. But the real boom came after the allied occupation in 1945, when former military intelligence officers found new venues for their skills in Japan's consolidated trading companies (*sōgō shōsha*). The largest of these conglomerates maintain field offices in major cities throughout the world. Kahaner notes that a typical *sōgō shōsha* every day "collects about 100,000 pieces of information from its 10,000 employees in about 180 offices worldwide" and spends some $60 million annually to maintain its collection infrastructure (1996:166).[25] By the 1960s, other companies within the *keiretsu* (vertically integrated manufacturers) headed by individual *sōgō shōsha* began setting up their own intelligence networks to supplement what they were receiving from the large trading firms.

These companies' overseas branches or liaison offices methodically collect "gray literature," defined by Meyer as "statistics, documents, brochures, articles from technical and current events magazines, reports delivered at industrial and scientific conferences" (1987:107). Information gleaned locally is passed to the company's home office, where it is circulated, catalogued, stored, and shared among firms within the *keiretsu* and with the government. One such "research" library kept by Toshiba is said to hold 40,000 volumes (Kahaner 1996:168). Overseas offices and individual employees stationed abroad are normally required to submit weekly or monthly reports to their company's intelligence unit on host country technology and other developments. This "technology scanning" is for most Japanese firms the first phase of the development cycle and is the functional equivalent of creative brainstorming in a Western firm.

Many overseas branches of Japanese companies are located near high-technology centers, which in the United States include California's Silicon Valley, the Route 128 corridor in Massachusetts, and the Rockville area of Maryland. Besides helping them keep up with the latest developments in technology, their strategic locations facilitate negotiation of joint ventures with high-tech (and capital-starved) U.S. startups as a means of acquiring promising new technology. It also allows direct recruitment of local scientists, technical experts, and employees of competing firms with inside knowledge of that firm's technology.

Recruitment takes two forms. On the one hand, Japanese companies conduct vigorous hiring campaigns in sectors judged by MITI and the companies themselves to be of importance. For example, in one issue of an industry magazine Toshiba America Electronics Components, Inc., a Silicon Valley subsidiary of the Japanese electronics manufacturer, ran an advertisement asking American semiconductor engineers with three or more years' experience to become part of "the new wave of VLSI technology." A few pages later, Fujitsu Microelectronics in San Jose invited experienced computer engineers to "imagine a world without any boundaries." The ad promised "We're not about to put limits on your creativity, either." In the same issue, HAL Computer Systems, another Fujitsu subsidiary in Silicon Valley, tried to interest U.S. software engineers in joining "The Dawn of a New Era."[26]

On the other hand, Japanese employees of local subsidiaries seek personal relationships with specialists at nearby U.S. companies in a position to provide technical information. Bylinski (1978:74–79) noted that these "liaison officers track executives and engineers as assiduously as intelligence agents watch the movements of an adversary's military personnel. . . . Once they spot a knowledgeable individual, the Japanese tempt him with offers of generous consulting fees . . . which are really attempts to pump dry a source of knowledge about the company he has worked for." Occasionally these efforts to suborn American employees are detected, as for example, when Hitachi and Mitsubishi Electric tried to obtain proprietary technology illegally from an IBM employee through a Silicon Valley-based consulting firm. According to Halamka (1984:127), the attempt "seemed to represent little more than an extension of normal business activities that got out of hand."[27] In another exposed operation, Japanese agents in San Francisco had recruited a midlevel engineer at Fairchild, who between 1977 and 1986 passed some 160,000 pages of research results to the consultants of Japanese companies (Schweizer 1993:38).

Besides establishing a corporate presence in local centers of advanced technology, Japanese companies have a history of sending individual businessmen abroad on technology gathering missions. The effort began in the 1950s with government-subsidized expeditions, primarily to the United States, to scout out and obtain new technologies, and it continues today. Figures as high as 10,000 trips annually have been reported (Schweizer 1993:74; Hansen 1996:36). Collection goals can be generic or technology specific. Also important are the 15,000 Japanese scientists and engineers (Herbig 1995:15) staying in the United States at high-tech companies such as Boeing or U.S. government-funded laboratories at Los Alamos and the

National Institutes of Health under exchange programs or what are described as "codevelopment" projects.[28] As Nakagawa explains it, most of these employees collect information on their U.S. employers as a natural course. "This is as much of a mind set as it is a process" (Prescott and Gibbons 1993:60).

Overseas Research Institutes

In addition to local branches and liaison offices, Japanese companies rely heavily on overseas research labs to "scan" technological developments in the host country and transfer the new technologies. Donald Dalton, a U.S. Department of Commerce economist who tracks U.S.-based foreign research institutes, regards Japanese R&D installations abroad as "the second largest form of technology transfer after royalties and license fees" (Dalton and Genther 1991:15). Dalton counted 224 Japanese research facilities in the United States as of 1995, more than double the number owned by second-ranking Great Britain and more than all other nations combined (Dalton and Serapio 1995:8). Reflecting Japan's dependence on foreign sources for state-of-the-art technology and the shrinking length of product cycles, Japanese spending on U.S. R&D centers has also grown more quickly than that of any other country, from $307 million in 1987 to $1.8 billion in 1993 (11).

Reid and Schriesheim (1996:42) provide similar figures showing an increase in spending by Japanese-owned R&D institutes in the United States from $88 million in 1980 to $1.656 billion in 1992, coinciding with the period when Japanese manufacturers were targeting the computer industry. However, these statistics tell only part of the story. Foreign-based research facilities have two purposes: to adapt a firm's existing products to local markets and to tap local scientific expertise for the benefit of the sponsoring country or corporation. European-owned research labs in the United States emphasize the former function; according to Reid and Schriesheim (55) they are "more heavily oriented toward supporting the technical needs of their US-based manufacturing affiliates." By contrast, the Japanese-owned labs are meant "to support the R&D strategy of the parent company." Most have small research staffs and are "primarily monitoring research and technology developments, not conducting much basic research themselves."

Herbig draws the same conclusion that Japanese overseas labs do "very little actual research or product development. . . . Instead of carrying out research directly, they contract out research to independent laboratories" (1995:217). Most significant in terms of the present book's claim of a shortfall in East Asian creativity is Reid and Schriesheim's observation that the research targeted by these overseas Japanese institutes "is in an area in which the parent company does not yet possess significant capabilities" (1996:55). This fact is in stark contrast to the European practice of conducting overseas R&D in areas where the parent firm already has a strong base. Hansen came to the same conclusion about the purpose of these institutes, noting that "Japanese firms conduct relatively little basic research and their studies may be perceived as lacking originality, analytic depth or thoroughness. But to the Japanese, their goal is not so much to be original, as to serve as information sweepers" (1996:98).

Work done by the Japanese contingent stationed at foreign-based institutes has little to do with research in the usual sense. Instead their primary function is to *transfer* advanced technology out of the host country to the sponsoring Japanese corporation by taking advantage of the collection opportunities that their location provides.[29] The actual creative work is done by American scientists hired for that purpose. Kolata (1990:1, 14), who reported on the role of these labs in the computer industry, noted that U.S. scientists are attracted by salaries substantially higher than what American firms or universities offer. Once hired, they are used to recruit colleagues in the industry and to achieve technological breakthroughs in the name of the Japanese company supporting the research.

The location of these institutes betrays their function. Herbig reports that "every major US research university has at least one Japanese corporate research facility nearby" (1995:219). These labs are in addition to the ones funded by Japanese companies directly on university campuses (see below). Silicon Valley, of course, hosts R&D laboratories for most of Japan's major electronics manufacturers, which vie with Korean- and Chinese-affiliated labs to hire talented American semiconductor and software designers. As traditional sources of technology dry up due to the host country's awareness of the problem and, in Japan's case, the borrowing country's success at penetrating the outer limits of technology, it seems likely that these local R&D facilities will increase in number and importance.[30]

Connecting with Foreign Universities

Japanese companies have been especially adept at seizing and creating opportunities within the U.S. system of higher education to transfer advanced technology. Their success here can be attributed to three factors: (1) the openness of American universities that encourages the types of exchanges the Japanese seek, (2) Japan's appreciation of this resource as measured by its willingness to invest serious funds, and (3) U.S. academic administrators' obsession with revenue and the bottom line.

Japan's presence on American campuses is felt at every level, starting with student enrollment. According to Herbig, over 30,000 Japanese students enroll annually in U.S. universities, which for decades was the highest figure of any foreign country (recently surpassed by China) and more than twenty-five times the number of U.S. students studying at any one time in Japan (1995:219). The balance is skewed further by the technological orientation of the Japanese students' curricula, and by the fact that many of the students are not academics at all but company employees sent to the United States to acquire specific skills (Dreyfuss 1987:84). During their course of studies, they are able to participate in advanced research projects, gaining exposure to leading technologies of which American companies themselves may be unaware. Besides these general opportunities for technology transfer, Japanese students may be asked by their sponsoring organizations to collect information on specific technologies (Kahaner 1996:176).

The Japanese student population is the most visible measure of Japan's use of American higher education, but it is not the only link or even the most important. Japanese companies also affiliate with U.S. universities by agreeing to underwrite research, sending employees to participate in laboratory projects, signing consultancy agreements, and marketing the university's research patents, as the large trading firm Nissho Iwai has done for Georgia Tech (Prestowitz 1988:207). Or the connection may simply be a personal relationship with faculty members, who are invited periodically to Japan to share information or asked to facilitate the placement of Japanese graduate students and researchers. Peters (1993:227) found that 40 percent of the Japanese companies she surveyed had "collaborative activities" of one kind or another with American universities.

Reid and Schriesheim regard foreign participation in American R&D as a win-win exchange for both parties. They point out, however, that Japan has been unusually aggressive in exploiting these opportunities, spending more on American university-based research than any other foreign country (1996:97). This involvement extends to purchasing or outfitting entire research labs, as Hitachi Chemical did for the University of California at Irvine, gaining rights over all intellectual property produced in the laboratory. NEC went a step further for its research lab at Princeton by hiring prominent scientists from outside the university to join the operation.

Japanese corporations, ministries, and government-run foundations also gain influence over American universities by funding chairs and special programs. This funding yields the direct benefit of access to university resources on multiple levels and the important indirect benefit of ensuring that academic criticism of Japanese policies is muted. Examples include the seven professorships endowed at Stanford University by Japanese corporations and thirty-four "affiliation programs" that the respective parties were able to work out (Duggan and Eisenstodt 1990:96). MIT's linkages with Japan are particularly noteworthy. Herbig (1995:222) found that Japanese companies fund 19 of MIT's 54 corporate-endowed chairs. In turn, half of the 100 foreign corporate members of the university's Industrial Liaison Program are Japanese. This liaison program, Herbig notes, "provides access to more than 3,000 research projects, 1,000 faculty members, a full-time research staff of 2,250, and nearly 10,000 elite students." Significantly "only a quarter of the formal visits from industry to MIT are *not* from Japan" (my emphasis).[31]

In fairness to Japan and other East Asian countries, I should point out that their eagerness to establish footholds in American higher education is matched by the willingness of American educators to accept their funds. I have personally heard professors boast of their success at obtaining East Asian money. Indeed, the criteria used in faculty hiring and promotion decisions include candidates' skills in this area ("proven fundraising ability"). Voicing concern over the impact of these programs on America's economic security is not career enhancing.

Foreign Investments and Coproduction Agreements

Foreign high-tech companies, particularly innovative startups whose principal asset is their own technology, act as magnets for Japanese capital. In return for funding these technology-intensive ventures, Japanese companies want licensing, marketing, and coproduction agreements and in many cases exclusive rights to the technology that is developed. Alternatively, a Japanese company will back a venture ostensibly to build a product, hire local technicians with knowledge of the sought after technology, transfer that technology to Japan, and close down the operation after the transfer has been completed. This technique, whose forms range from minority investments in foreign companies to complete buyouts, was Japan's major route for transferring technology in the 1980s.

Some statistics will demonstrate its importance. According to Dreyfuss (1987:88), Japanese firms were putting $2 to 3 million annually into high-tech U.S. venture companies up to 1982, when Japan could still engage freely in simpler forms of technology transfer such as licensing and direct imitation of one type or another. By 1986, however, when overt transfers had become more difficult, equity investments in high-tech American firms had risen to $200 million per year. Herbig's research shows Japanese minority investments in U.S. companies growing "from forty deals in 1988 worth $166 million to sixty deals in 1989 worth $435 million" (1995:221). Levine, Gross, and Carey (1989:117) cite similar figures: $650 million in 120 U.S. companies between 1987 and 1989. They argue that equity investments helped Japan dominate the market for semiconductors, household electronics, and machine tools, and were a principal device for transferring emerging technologies in computers, bioengineering, and new materials. By the end of the 1980s most Japanese computer and chip manufacturers—Canon, Fujitsu, Hitachi, Kubota, Kyocera, TDK—had investments in American high-tech companies, often several.[32]

Around the same time, Japan began supplementing its foreign high-tech investment program with acquisitions of technology-intensive companies. In a study sponsored by the Economic Strategy Institute of Washington, D.C., Spencer listed 412 U.S. companies dealing in advanced materials, aerospace, biotechnology, chemicals, computers, electronics, robotics, semiconductor equipment, semiconductors, and telecommunications that were acquired outright by foreign interests or through a controlling investment between October 1988 and April 1991. Some 295 or 72 percent of the firms were bought by East Asian companies, 274 by Japan alone. Reid and Schriesheim (1966:80) provide figures for the period 1988–93 showing Japan as responsible for 437 of 722 U.S. high-tech companies acquired by foreign firms (England was second with 82 and France third with 49). The impact of these buyouts extends beyond the raw numbers shown, since Japanese companies use their control over upstream suppliers to wrest technology and other concessions from foreign high-tech manufacturers. In one famous case, Cray Computers, a leading U.S. supercomputer manufacturer that rebuffed Japanese offers for acquisition, was nearly forced out of business by its inability to obtain critical components from Japanese suppliers.

Some examples from the machine tool industry will illustrate the process. On September 11, 1995, the Tokyo newspaper *Nikkei Sangyo Shimbun* reported that Sumitomo Heavy Industries would hold a "technical exchange seminar" with its Canadian subsidiary Lumonics, a leader in the field of excimer lasers. Sumitomo bought the firm in 1989 and uses its technology in a variety of metal-processing equipment products. In the newspaper's September 22 issue, Seiko Seiki, another machine tool manufacturer, was reported to have bought the French firm S2M to acquire the firm's technology for magnetically suspended bearings used in vacuum pumps for semiconductor manufacturing equipment. On the same day, another Japanese newspaper, the *Shizuoka Shimbun*, reported that Star Micronics, a Japanese manufacturer of printed circuit boards that was trying to move into the field of numerically controlled lathes, would "use European and North American technology" made possible through buyouts of US and Swiss manufacturers.

Joint "research" and coproduction agreements with small U.S. companies are used by Japanese firms after particular technologies as an alternative to investing in the company. Peters observes that Japanese companies will establish R&D labs directly on the premises of a U.S. company "to tap into their pioneering research" (1993:223). Or the joint involvement can occur in Japan, as when U.S. companies are invited to participate in high-tech initiatives sponsored by the Japanese government. Such was the case with research conducted in Japan on micromachine technology, atomic manipulation, and fuzzy logic with Motorola, Texas Instruments, and IBM respectively—areas where the American companies had substantial leads (Reid and Schriesheim 1996:126). Japan has also been able to obtain critical aviation technologies through coproduction of U.S.-designed military aircraft, including the F-15/FSX (Prestowitz 1988:139), much of which found its way into commercial projects.

Technology Purchases

The variety of indirect programs Japan uses to identify and appropriate useful foreign technologies, and the zeal with which it pursues them, give ample testimony to the resourcefulness a country can muster to achieve its developmental goals without changing its social institutions. However, we should not lose sight of the fact that most of these technologies were simply paid for in cash, in the form of royalties and licensing fees. The numbers involved here are staggering.

According to Peters (1987:34), the Japanese government acknowledged 47,779 technology import agreements with foreign companies between 1951 and 1985. Herbig estimates Japan's bill for the thirty years up to 1980, when Japan obtained "the whole stock of Western technology," at $25 to 30 billion in constant 1980 dollars (1995:72). By 1985 Japan was paying $3 billion *annually* in technology licensing fees (25). Dalton and Genther provide similar figures, showing an increase from $853 million in 1982 to $2.6 billion in 1989 for licenses on American technology alone, despite the declining dollar exchange rate (1991:11). As Fialka pointed out, much of this technology was licensed at artificially low rates:

US firms, many faced with the alternative of running Japan's expensive patent gauntlet, sold some 32,000 technology licenses between 1950 and 1978. While Japanese firms paid $9 billion for the licenses, the technology they received was worth $1 trillion. (1997:58)[33]

Richard Samuels, author of a book on Japan's technological transformation, noted similarly that "By 1960 there was not a single substantial enterprise in any advanced manufacturing sector not a party to a [foreign technology transfer] agreement; in 1970 nearly 2,000 technology purchases were approved by the Japanese government, and in 1990 Japan remained a net importer of technology and more than 8,000 such purchases were approved" (1994:45). Samuels cited the "contemporary catch phrase" of Japanese industry: *ichigō yunyū, nigō kokusan* ("the first one is imported, the second one is made domestically") to describe what happens to foreign technology after it is procured by Japan. He further argued that Japan's notion of technological progress is "successful indigenization" (71).

Entire industries were created in Japan on the basis of U.S. technology imports; industries that went on to compete successfully against the American companies that developed the technology. Some famous examples are Japan's modern textile industry, which began with Toray's licensing of nylon from Dupont; Sony's licensing of the transistor from Bell Laboratories; the purchase of color television and VCR technology from RCA and Ampex; Kawasaki's licensing of robotics technology from Unimation. Thanks to American laws requiring Bell Labs to license its patents nationally *and* internationally, Japan was able to use Bell's research to boost its information industry to world standards (Okimoto 1989:74).

Where has this borrowing gotten Japan? Clearly straight to the top in terms of manufacturing expertise, balance of payments, and per capita income. However, it would seem that Japan has run into a law of diminishing returns, where investments in foreign technology—or in its acquisition—no longer guarantee competitiveness in a world market where product cycles are measured in months and an innovative idea can lead to a fortune overnight. As noted in the Introduction to this book, Japan is aware of the need to shake off its dependence on Western technology and to engage in its own creative research. But it will not achieve this goal soon, despite the money being thrown at it and amid signs that Japan recognizes the social and intellectual basis of Western creativity (and is trying to emulate *that*).

The problem is much like the impasse Japan faces in its linguistic development and, as I shall show later, is related to it causally on several levels. Just as the Japanese language has become dependent on a character-based writing system that, for all its awkwardness, does allow users to communicate after a fashion, so too has Japan become locked into an obsolete developmental paradigm that worked in the past but cannot be shed easily because of the institutions that have grown up around it. In both areas—language and society—it is hard to change these dysfunctional practices because neither can be isolated from the broader contexts within which they operate. Reforming written Japanese is frustrated by the structure of the language that evolved under the writing system's constraints. Similarly, "learning" scientific creativity becomes plausible only if Japanese are willing to make institutional changes that allow creativity to blossom.

Ironically, one such change needed for a creative society, I shall argue, involves replacing the language's character writing system with one based more firmly on phonetic principles. There are three good reasons why Japan may wish to consider doing so: first, the present writing system is too complex to be applied efficiently to science; its use entails perpetual economic costs that are not requited in an absolute sense. Second, Japanese writing is linked with a conservative ethic that impedes originality in science and thought. If character-based writing is an integral part of the culture, as both defenders of the orthography and those seeking its replacement insist, then any restructuring to promote creativity cannot neglect one of the culture's main components. Finally, psychological processes inherent in learning the character-writing system predispose its users to cognitive habits inimical to analytic and creative thought. This phenomenon, as we shall see, applies to individuals and to society as a whole. It is the most compelling reason for Japan to seek orthographic change.

But I am jumping too far ahead. The purpose of this chapter has been to demonstrate that Japan's economic miracle has depended more on that country's ability to appropriate Western technology than on anything creative in the culture itself. Far from validating the orthography, as Suzuki (1987), Taylor and Taylor (1995), and other champions of East Asian writing systems maintain, our data point to some serious anomalies in Japan's industrial development that weaken any prima facie claim about the utility of the country's institutions, including its nonalphabetic orthography. But before passing judgment on this issue we must look closely at industrial development in China and Korea, two countries that share many of Japan's cultural characteristics.

Chapter Two
Sources of Chinese Innovation

> With rich intellectual and material resources at home, China is com-
> pletely capable of boosting its high tech industry through its own efforts.
> —*Xinhua*, March 14, 1999

The Problem with the Cox Commission Report

One of the benefits of getting older is the perspective it gives you on
things. When growing up in the 1950s, I was told that China is a "sleeping
giant," temporarily down on its luck, but bound to recover its former glory
and rightful place at the center of the world stage. In the late 1960s, the
popular wisdom was that China had thrown off the shackles of bourgeois
economics and was undergoing a Great Socialist Transformation that
would restore the country's former glory and rightful place at the center of
the world stage. Success was just around the corner. A decade or so later
China had figured out what was standing between its present misfortune
and usual condition of prosperity: a gang of four scoundrels. After they
had been liquidated and their influence on Chinese society rooted out,
China would regain its former glory, and so on.

A lot can happen in fifty years, and, indeed, much has happened not
only within China but also in its relationship with the rest of the world. But
given the rhetoric over the past half century that has led to so many false
hopes about China's impending progress, one can be forgiven for being
skeptical about any officially sponsored panacea succeeding. I refer here to
the country's current infatuation with science, or more accurately, to the
government's attempt to apply its constrained view of science to further
state-defined development goals. Although the notion of China taking a ra-

tional approach to development is praiseworthy, particularly in light of the irrationality that has characterized much of China's recent history, there are signs that this newest program will bear as little fruit as the other top-down efforts China has made to achieve competitiveness in the modern world.

To begin with, the idea of using science to rebuild China isn't new. It was bandied about on a grander scale nearly a *full* century ago under the rubric of "science and democracy" by China's early twentieth-century modernizers, who sought to establish a foundation for economic growth based on what they identified as the twin pillars of Western progress. In retrospect, the movement never had a chance. Not only was it impossible to import these foreign institutions into traditional society without disrupting the sociopolitical fabric. China's late start guaranteed that it would fall victim to other countries that had begun to modernize earlier, notably Japan.

Now, some ninety years later, the Chinese government and its controlled media once again are making pronouncements about how science will turn things around—without the democratic complications the earlier activists were willing to put up with. I find the chance of this current effort succeeding to be slim for several reasons.

First, part of the present movement in China is simply hype to counter the embarrassment caused by the U.S. government's Cox Commission Report on China's illicit technology transfers and the political threat raised by Falungong. Coincident with the release in May 1999 of the unclassified version of the *Report of the Select Committee on U.S. National Security and Military/Commercial Concerns with the People's Republic of China*,[1] about which I shall say more, China launched a propaganda campaign to portray itself as the indigenous developer of "nuclear weapons, ballistic missiles, and satellites" (*liǎng dàn yì xīng*) in response to allegations in the report that the technology for these weapons was pilfered from the United States. The campaign was meant to restore China's international reputation in the face of evidence that the development of these and other systems owed more to foreign models than to anything China did on its own. It was also intended to bolster the confidence of China's own researchers who were engaged in efforts to upgrade weapons as a result of "lessons" learned from the Gulf War.

Shortly after this campaign had begun, China's leaders were taken aback by the appearance of demonstrators in the capital demanding an end to state persecution of their religious beliefs. Outflanked by the organizational skills of this popular, Buddhist-inspired sect called Falungong, whose membership included some party cadres and military officers, Beijing responded to their nonviolent appeal with a nationwide program of arrests and intimidation. An ideological drive was also launched against the group's "antiscientific" beliefs that conflicted with the "scientific" basis on which Marxism and the new China were founded. Science began to be extolled in the press as a substitute for the spiritual guidance Falungong offered. The regime's newly found enthusiasm for science should be understood in this context.

The second reason I am pessimistic about China's ability to excel in creative science is the government's narrow view of the intellectual foundation on which science is based. Creativity, as we shall see in later chapters, is bound up intimately with a style of thinking that moves beyond boundaries. *Radical* innovation of the sort the PRC government claims to be promoting depends in particular on access to models outside one's normal intellectual domain. Nothing could be more inimical to creativity than limiting the scope within which free inquiry is allowed to proceed. Yet that is exactly what the state does by declaring which topics may and may not be considered. Although incremental improvements to technology can be done under such a system, creative science requires more.[2]

China's political leadership thus is confounded by a dilemma. On the one hand, the country's international competitiveness depends on its ability to innovate, which is furthered by promoting an atmosphere of intellectual freedom. On the other hand, the regime's survival is based on its ability to constrain the enthusiasm for change to a limited area. There are clear indications that the government is aware of this trade-off and is trying to balance the conflicting demands, for example, by shifting the locus of national R&D from the state to the private sector while retaining overall control of research priorities.

However, even these modest attempts at reform are frustrated by bureaucratic inertia and the reluctance of state enterprises—including those affiliated with the State Council, the Chinese Academy of Sciences (CAS), universities, and military facilities—to cede control of their present equities. There is also some doubt about the government's willingness to back its grandiose plans with cash. A recent study of China's science and technology (S&T) policies published in an authoritative Beijing journal observed in conjunction with the country's *declining* rate of R&D investment:

when it comes to the actual allotment of appropriations, since S&T is an intangible item and it is not possible to see instant results, it is often overlooked when funds are scarce, even to the point where there may be a large decrease in the percentage of the GNP dedicated to S&T investment. (Li Xuefan 1999)

The study went on to note, "Of the eight main indices of China's competitiveness in various international arenas, only the index for China's competitiveness in S&T is steadily falling."

Finally, China's approach to science is and has been geared more toward technology transfer than indigenous development. Although denied by the regime, there is ample—indeed, overwhelming—evidence that China engages as a matter of policy in informal and illicit transfers of foreign technology on a scale that exceeds Japan's own prodigious efforts. The process, in fact, is so out of hand there is reason to doubt that China even distinguishes between innovations done domestically and those that are acquired through surreptitious transfers. On this score, the Cox Report, for all the attention it drew to China's covert efforts to procure foreign technology, barely scratched the surface.[3]

As we shall see, China, like Japan, has devised a wide range of techniques to relieve foreign countries of their advanced technology. Some of these methods are legal and ethical, others are of questionable propriety, while still others are prosecutable under the espionage statutes of the target countries. They include open purchases, cooperation and exchange agreements, sending students overseas for study, participating in international science projects, doing joint R&D with foreign firms, dispatching fact-finding missions abroad, inviting specialists to China for lectures and collaborative research, acquiring foreign high-tech firms, demanding technology for market access, mining open data sources, scanning technology through overseas affiliates, patent research and IPR infringements, exploiting foreign and expatriate scientists, building informal transfer networks in overseas Chinese communities, maintaining collection posts abroad under diplomatic cover, reverse engineering, technical penetration of foreign computers, and using cutouts and front companies to transfer restricted technology, to mention just the more common methods.

Against this variety of collection venues, covert acquisition of the sort dwelled on in the Western press pales in significance, accounting for only 20 percent of the S&T "take," according to Chinese intelligence officers

(Huo and Wang 1991). Most collection is done through open or gray methods. But let us focus for now on this one aspect of Chinese technology transfer, because it remains a significant means of acquiring foreign technology in absolute terms and relative to its use by other Asian nations.[4]

According to Nicholas Eftimiades, counterintelligence expert and author of the standard work on PRC espionage, China's intelligence operations against the U.S. industrial sector "have become so intrusive that senior U.S. law enforcement officials have publicly identified China as 'the most active foreign power engaged in the illegal acquisition of American technology' " (Eftimiades 1994). More recently John Fialka, author of a book on economic espionage and advisor to Congress on such matters, noted similarly that China "has flooded the United States with spies, sending in far more agents" than any other foreign country (1997:12). Responsibility for these operations is shared by China's Ministry of State Security (MSS), the country's civilian intelligence organization, and the Seventh Bureau of the Military Intelligence Department (MID), which is subordinate to the army's General Staff.

Unlike the intelligence assets of other major powers, which focus heavily or exclusively on political and military issues, the MSS since its reorganization in 1983 has had as its primary mission collecting foreign S&T data to support China's modernization (Faligot 1996). As the Hong Kong-based journal *Cheng Ming* reported in 1997:

In the past, the former Central Investigation Department [predecessor to the MSS] was mainly involved in gathering political intelligence, while the Second Department [MID] of the General Staff was responsible for military intelligence. In recent years, the MSS has shifted the focus of its work from political intelligence to economic, scientific, and technological intelligence. The Second Department of the General Staff is also beginning to focus on S&T intelligence in the military field. (Tan Po 1997)

Some idea of the scale of this S&T collection is provided by Eftimiades, who reports that "In recent years the PRC's clandestine collection operations in the United States have expanded to the point where approximately 50 percent of the nine hundred technology transfer cases investigated annually on the West Coast involve the Chinese" (1994:27). Some of these cases have resulted in sentencing or deportation for theft of high-tech devices such as radar and communications equipment, numerically controlled machinery,

torpedo and jet engine designs, imaging equipment, and laser fusion technology used to simulate nuclear explosions.[5] These counterintelligence
successes aside, most of the PRC's covert collection is never investigated by
law enforcement officials owing to China's policy of concentrating on midlevel technology, which is easier to acquire and draws less attention (Eftimiades 1994:28).

Hence the media focus on China's covert acquisition of high-tech weapons technology tends, in my view, to distract attention from the major challenge the United States and other advanced countries face, namely, China's
persistent and highly successful efforts to acquire all types of foreign technology through a *variety* of quasi-legal methods. Nowhere is this dichotomy
between perceived and actual threat more apparent than in the ongoing
debate about the PRC's nuclear force modernization. To summarize this
dispute, the Cox Commission argued on the basis of an extensive investigation that China over the past two decades stole:

classified information on seven US thermonuclear warheads, including every currently deployed thermonuclear warhead in the US ballistic missile arsenal. The
stolen information also includes classified design information for an enhanced ra-
diation weapon (commonly known as the "neutron bomb"), which neither the
United States, nor any other nation, has yet deployed. (1999:iii)

Chinese officials responded to U.S. press coverage of these findings by
characterizing them as "irresponsible and unfounded," "sheer fabrica-
tion," and "utterly groundless."[6] By March, when it was apparent the U.S.
government would not disclose the classified sources on which these findings were based, Chinese Premier Zhu Rongji was able to go on record
accusing the United States of "slandering" China for "underestimating
China's ability to develop military technology."[7]

Then a curious thing happened. At a press conference on May 31, 1999,
a Chinese government spokesperson claimed that the Cox Report had
missed the mark for the simple reason that there were no secrets to steal:
all the information needed to benchmark nuclear warhead design and performance was available through openly published sources. The spokesperson supported his claim by publicly logging onto Internet sites that
contained this type of information (Kynge 1999). A year later, the Beijing
based Chinese Nuclear Information Center, an ad hoc organization set up to
counter U.S. allegations of nuclear theft, took the unusual (and in retrospect

short-sighted) step of releasing a seventy-seven-page directory of foreign nuclear websites to demonstrate how information on constructing advanced warheads could be gleaned overtly (Platt 2000). In other words, China was claiming it did not steal the technology, but got it from foreign countries nonetheless.

This incredible admission, which does little to support China's other claim that its technology is based on indigenous research, tracks well with other assessments of PRC intelligence gathering. According to a foreign military expert stationed in Beijing, "There are hardly any real spies left. 95 percent of the information comes off the Internet or legally from laboratories and research centers, especially American ones."[8] Paul Moore, a former FBI analyst with twenty years experience in Chinese counterintelligence, argues in the same vein that China's approach to high-tech acquisition is piecemeal, done "a little bit at a time." Moore (1999) states:

As far as I can see, we are mishandling this threat to our national security because we are focused on the wrong questions, looking at who stole what information, in the expectation that our search will uncover one or more major spies. While it's possible there are major spies out there, it's not very likely.

Loeb and Pincus (1999) of the *Washington Post* put their fingers on the real problem, which is less dramatic than recent headlines suggest but at the same time more serious in its implications for America's security. The two cite experts' belief that "China methodically sifts information from open sources and combines it with many small leaks of secret information, typically culled one at a time from American scientists visiting China, a strategy very different from the Cold War model of moles and master spies."

I could not agree more. China's contribution, as it were, to the "science" of intelligence work lies in its demonstration of the usefulness of a low-key, systematic approach—the "vacuum cleaner" model used by Japan but, as the PRC is fond of saying, "with Chinese characteristics." We shall explore these characteristics in the remaining sections of the chapter. But the point I would make now is this: lost in the debate about *how* China transfers weapons technology is the stunning fact that China now admits to its dependence on foreign sources for what its leaders regard as core military technology. And for the purpose of the present exercise that is all that matters. For all the hype about Chinese self-sufficiency in innovation, the truth is that China suffers an intractable creativity deficit that is managed only by assiduous efforts to copy foreign models.

Open Source Collection

Nowhere is China's dependence on foreign ideas more evident than in its collection of open source information. If these efforts were limited to the routine diligence exercised by scientists the world over to keep up with developments in their field, there would be no cause for complaint. But such a characterization would understate the depth of China's efforts by several orders of magnitude. In fact, China has engaged since the 1950s in a massive, coordinated, and, for all intents, desperate struggle to absorb the fruits of Western creativity by scrutinizing the myriad technical journals, scientific reports, and other materials published abroad in printed and electronic form. Moreover, the collection is centrally directed by state institutes, which ensure not only that the relevant information is gathered but also that it is *put to use* to compete with countries where the technology originated. The process has evolved to the point where China's technology collection managers regard their task as a "science," exercised with rigor and subject to strict methods of evaluation (Huo and Wang 1991).

It is ironic that China, which demonstrates such a limited capacity to innovate in other areas, should have succeeded so well in the discipline of intelligence collection.[9] However, there is a precedent for this phenomenon in Chinese history dating back to the latter part of the nineteenth century, when China was also heavily focused on importing foreign scientific knowhow. Although aware of the scientific method behind this knowhow, late Qing intellectuals applied the tool not to discover new truths about nature but to textual exegesis, the scientific study of ancient texts, in which absolute truths were believed to reside. In both cases—the study of texts and the present concern with "intelligence science"—China has used science to elucidate existing ideas rather than as an adjunct to the process of creating new ones.

China's current round of efforts to bolster its economic and military standing by exploiting the technical materials of foreign countries began with the founding of the Chinese Academy of Sciences Institute of Scientific and Technical Information of China (ISTIC) in 1956.[10] Two years later, ISTIC became part of the State Science and Technology Commission (now the Ministry of Science and Technology), where it coordinated open source intelligence collection throughout the government.[11] Tong B. Tang, author of a book on China's science and technology development, noted that thanks to ISTIC's

professional advice, soon every ministry, most commissions, all the 21 provinces and the 5 autonomous regions created similar institutes. Furthermore, national and provincial exchange networks began to span the country. There are now about 300 and 3,000 of these networks, respectively. . . . In addition centers of scientific and technical information can be found in the seven big cities belonging to the original seven Administrative Regions. . . . The number of qualified personnel in all these organizations amounts to over 50,000. (1984:20)

Miao Qihao, who is affiliated with ISTIC's Shanghai institute, gives slightly higher numbers: "33 state ministerial and 35 provincial/municipal *qíngbào* institutes as well as thousands of basic cells, the information stations, in grassroots units. In [1985] the full-time workers of the system totaled about 60,000" (1993:49). Huo and Wang's figure for S&T collection networks, though startling, is consistent with these data. The two officers observed, "China's S&T intelligence cause has already been developing for more than 30 years. As of now, we have assembled a contingent of collection workers of considerable scale in about *4,000* intelligence organizations throughout all of China" (1991:23, my emphasis).

According to Tang, ISTIC is tasked by the PRC government "to compile, translate and report selectively but systematically current scientific and technical literature of all kinds from developed countries, including technical publications, dissertations, conference proceedings, video material, patent specifications, standards, catalogs, and samples" (1984:20). It is also heavily involved in English-to-Chinese machine translation and other types of data processing and delivery as part of China's effort to distribute foreign know-how to the military, state-run enterprises, and quasi-independent research institutions. It is probably not coincidental that computerized natural language processing is one of the few areas where China shows a real aptitude for state-of-the-art research, given its need to translate, catalog, and disseminate this high volume of foreign material.

Any doubt Westerners had about China's need to rely on foreign science to supplement its own lack of creative enterprise should have been laid to rest in 1991 with the publication of *Sources and Methods of Obtaining Na-*

tional Defense Science and Technology Intelligence by Huo Zhongwen and Wang Zongxiao. Irreverently dubbed "China's Spy Guide" by Bruce Gilley in his 1999 review,[12] the book provides a rare glimpse into the labyrinth of China's open source intelligence collection, confirming in detail what counter-intelligence experts have long thought to be true of that country's high-tech development.[13]

The authors, intelligence officers with thirty years experience in information collection, wrote early chapters of the book while instructors at the army's National Defense Science and Technology Intelligence Center (CDSTC) to help train collection specialists. Its final version is a synthesis of practical tips on information gathering and esoteric theory on the nature of intelligence and collection meant to serve as a guide for their colleagues. In it the authors describe an "all-China S&T intelligence system" that functions on multiple levels, including comprehensive foreign science collection centers in provinces, cities, and autonomous regions. This system, they note, was built out of recognition that the normal means used by scientists worldwide to keep up with international developments in their fields are inadequate for China's "special needs." China requires nothing less than a "transformation in collection work carried out with an eye toward assembling the intellectual wealth of humanity" (5).

Collection—as opposed to collaboration or creation—is seen by China's S&T managers as a necessary and cost-effective way to acquire competitive strategies. This decision to invest in "collection science" has borne fruit. As Huo and Wang point out,

Although China's information collection has experienced many ups and downs during these 30-odd years, it has nevertheless made outstanding contributions to the rejuvenation of the S&T intelligence cause, the invigoration of science and technology, the construction of the national economy, and the buildup of national defense. (23)

Huo and Wang describe in detail methods for collecting, evaluating, storing, and retrieving foreign S&T information and—lest anyone imagine this a mere formal exercise—for getting this information to the right people in a timely fashion. One section of the book considers ways to determine "consumer" needs, while another section proposes metrics to evaluate how well these needs are met. A "concise introduction" to selected intelligence sources is also provided, which despite its diminutive title qualifies easily as a world-class model of source analysis. Listed here are U.S. Congressional publications, AD reports (funded by the U.S. Department of Defense),[14] NASA studies, American Institute of Aeronautics and Astronautics publications, Department of Energy reports, and publications covering U.S. military technical specifications. Huo and Wang are sufficiently acquainted with the cataloging systems of these reports to give advice on dealing with inconsistencies in their numbering sequences.

The authors of *Sources and Methods* acknowledge that Western scientific journals "are the first choice of rank-and-file S&T personnel as well as intelligence researchers" (242). They then provide the results of a "core periodical survey" that lists the 56 most popular defense technology journals, including 33 from the United States and 12 from England. Another list of 80 journals includes 43 titles published in the United States, the most popular ones dealing with aerospace. More revealing than the lists of sources themselves is the comprehensiveness, mathematical rigor, and determination with which "collection science" is approached. For someone resigned to finding little novelty in China's S&T work, it is almost refreshing to discover research of this caliber and originality.

The collection done by the CDSTC where Huo and Wang worked is only a piece of a much larger picture. According to Xu Hongying, a librarian at the Academy of Sciences, China imported as many as 30,000 *different* foreign S&T journals per year between 1954 and 1990 through ISTIC, CDSTC, and a host of government ministries charged with overseeing China's technical development.[15] So vast is China's open source collection network that the main problem, according to Xu, lies in rationalizing the purchasing and distribution of these foreign journals. Echoing Huo and Wang's concern with scientific collection procedures, Xu states:

Neither macrocontrol nor microcoordination can be carried out without investigation, research, and data. To acquire reliable data involving different institutes, strict statistical methods and unified units are needed, especially in the research of journals.

Xu refers to the State Council's approval in 1957 of a "National Books Coordination Plan" to promote the "scientific collection of foreign S&T journals." It was supplemented thirty years later by a "Book and Information Service Coordination Committee" whose members include the primary open source collectors (ISTIC, CDSTC, the technical ministries, and various bureaus). Similar coordination groups were set up in the provinces, where in disregard of international copyright conventions the journals are copied and shared for the widest possible distribution. Xu, like Huo and Wang, minces no words about the goal of these collection activities, noting that to "accelerate the development of science and technology, the most economical and rapid means is to import, collect, and use foreign sci-tech journals and other documents in an organized way. It will help the technical staff access global information quickly, and surpass advanced international levels."

As an ironic footnote to these collection activities, Beijing's *Keji Ribao*, a daily newspaper of domestic and foreign science and technology, on May 21, 1998, reported on a symposium of S&T translators convened at Jiangsu Province's Engineering Translation Institute, whose participants reportedly lamented the shortage of qualified S&T translating talent. According to the newspaper, "The nearly 200 staff members at the institute, who translate materials at a rate of over 4,000 pages a week, still cannot keep up with demand."[16] The article noted that the "S&T translating trade has heated up considerably," which suggests China's foreign S&T collection is still expanding.

China's Thirty-Third Province

Next to open source collection, China's primary means of obtaining foreign S&T information is through the overseas Chinese community. There can be no question that China intensively targets ethnic Chinese abroad, including non-returning students, émigrés, and their descendants, to provide S&T support for what it euphemistically calls the "motherland" (*zŭguó* or "ancestral country"). These appeals are backed by dedicated outreach institutions, financial incentives, and a low-key but comprehensive style of recruitment that is consistent with China's approach to collection in general. Although Beijing assumes a lot in claiming the loyalty of all or even most Chinese-Americans (the main targets of its worldwide recruitment), its shotgun approach to collection has paid dividends here as well.

The rationale for seeking support from ethnic Chinese overseas stems in part from the size of this "brain pool." According to a study published in the August 1999 issue of *Zhongguo Rencai*, a monthly journal on employment policy and personnel issues, titled "An Analysis of Overseas Chinese S&T Talent," there are 600,000 overseas Chinese scientists and technicians, 450,000 of whom are concentrated in the United States. Most of these professionals are advanced students, or scientists who began their lives abroad as students and remained overseas to teach, do research in universities, or work in the laboratories of high-tech companies, most recently those in California's Silicon Valley (45–48).

The practice of sending students abroad, which resulted in this large population of expatriate scientists, began in the latter part of the Qing dynasty. According to Jia and Rubin, authors of a study on China's overseas "brain trust," some 90,000 Chinese studied abroad between 1850 and 1949, when the Communist government was established, including 19,000 in the United States and about 50,000 in Japan.[17] The number of PRC students who went abroad—mostly to former bloc countries—slowed to a trickle between 1949 and the start of China's "reform era" in 1978. During those three decades, Chinese students in the United States and Europe came mostly from Hong Kong and Taiwan.[18] From 1978 to 1996, however, the number of students who left China under the government's new education policy soared to 270,000. A year later it reached 293,000.[19] Most studies conclude that one-third of that number returned to China. Students returning from the United States are even fewer—about one in five.[20]

These students represent the cream of China's intellectual crop. John Fialka notes they "tend to be super-bright, an elite skimmed from a nation of over 1.2 billion people." Their high caliber is evidenced by a consistent ability to win research and training assistantships (1997:152). Jia and Rubin (1997) observe similarly that "Chinese students as a group received the largest portion of Ph.D.s awarded in the United States in 1995—about ten percent of the total. Taiwan was second." Other data from the August 1999 *Zhongguo Rencai* confirm what Americans know intuitively about the performance of Chinese scientists in the United States:

One-third of the department heads at the well-known US universities are Chinese (particularly in physics and mathematics departments). As many as one-half of the chairpersons of the respective 12 regions of the American Society of Mechanical Engineers are Chinese. One-third of the high-level engineers in the Apollo moon landing project were Chinese, and a total of more than 1,400 Chinese S&T personnel are participating in the American space cause.

Now a 33 percent return rate for 293,000 students sent abroad may seem harsh for a country trying to narrow the gap between its own scientific infrastructure and that of the West, given that these students are accomplishing so much for their host countries. But while China continues, publicly at least, to grieve the loss of its best and brightest to competing countries, other factors suggest that this situation is acceptable to Beijing's leaders as it stands. Whatever one might say about the "brain drain," 100,000 returning students trained in state-of-the-art Western science is a substantial talent base from which China's state-run and semi-private institutes can draw, and probably approaches the maximum number of high-level scientists who can be effectively employed at China's present stage of development.

Moreover, there is solid evidence that these returning students are responsible for the scientific progress China has made. Guo Dongpo, director of the State Council's Overseas Chinese Affairs Office, credits the first wave of returned students in the 1960s with laying the groundwork for China's modernization drive. By 1997, more than half the members of the prestigious Chinese Academy of Engineering were returned overseas Chinese.[21] O. Schnepp, who studied the effect of returned students on China's S&T structure, reported that most officials credit the program with "a significant impact on all aspects of Chinese science. . . . The exposure of a large number of Chinese scientists to world-level research, modern equipment, and up-to-date methods was considered a major contribution to Chinese scientific research and graduate education."[22]

Finally, China regards this "overseas talent pool" as a significant asset in its own right. Whereas returning students bring with them the skills they learned up to the time they left their host country, nonreturning students are a continuing source of up-to-date information on foreign technologies. The practice of encouraging students while still overseas to contribute to China's development has become especially viable in the past decade with the growth of the Internet and other types of high-speed communication.

An early example of the move to use overseas students for S&T collection, described in a PRC journal of S&T policy, is a program adopted by the State Natural Sciences Foundation in August 1992 "to subsidize the return of overseas students for short periods to work and give lectures." The journal viewed the program as highly effective and credited it with drawing 1,300 expatriate researchers back to China temporarily to share their knowledge and provide "services of various kinds." Participants, many of whom had graduated and taken up positions in their host countries, were asked to "continue serving the motherland while overseas in various ways according to their individual circumstances and capabilities."[23]

The policy of using students to transfer foreign technology on a real-time basis goes beyond the verbal support given by top figures in the party and government to include financial incentives as well. According to the same journal, students who contribute valuable S&T information are awarded subsidies "to carry out cooperative research and exchanges on a deeper level with greater continuity." Those selected for intense involvement return to China once or several times a year to coordinate with parallel research groups set up there. When not in China, they stay in frequent contact with their sponsoring organization via email, fax, and telephone. Recipients of long-term subsidies usually have finished their studies and moved on to teach or work in their host country. To remain eligible for support, they must work in projects that are technically more advanced than in China and maintain "good cooperative connections" with their handlers.

The use of overseas students for technology transfer is evidenced in a host of other statements that have appeared in the PRC media. On July 11, 1998, *Keji Ribao* proposed that China "take full advantage of the help provided by Chinese individuals studying abroad and by overseas Chinese." *Zhongguo Jingji Shibao*, a leading economic newspaper, argued on January 20, 1999, that if China cannot repatriate the people it sends abroad, it should use other paths to transfer their knowledge. A month later, Chinese nuclear weapons designer He Zuoxiu was quoted as saying, "The brain drain has its positive side. You use it to promote the exchange and transmission of scientific knowledge and technology."[24]

The October 10, 1999 *Beijing Qingnian Bao*, a newspaper affiliated with the Youth League of the Beijing Municipal Party Committee, offered further evidence of China's success in tapping the overseas talent pool. The paper described a visit to a high-tech trade fair in Shenzhen by 140 overseas students who had remained in the United States and Canada after completing their studies. The students reportedly brought with them important information on biomedicine, electronic communications, environmental technology, and electrical machinery. The magazine quoted the leader of one of the overseas groups as saying:

Although we are living abroad, our roots are in China. We have always thought to bring back to the motherland the fruits of what we have obtained abroad and repay our native country. We are grateful for the opportunity the high-tech fair has given us.

The following passage taken from the November 30, 1999 issue of *Zhongguo Rencai* argues, "a certain level of brain drain very possibly is an effective path for China to keep up with the world tide of technology and develop its own strength." The journal unabashedly states:

Finally, and most important, is that even though technical personnel studying over-seas remain there, they are also able to make their contribution to China's con-struction and development every bit as well as those who return to China. In the present age, a revolution has occurred in the transfer and dissemination of infor-mation. Technical personnel certainly do not need to return to China in person to be able to serve China. Rather, they may be able to utilize their superior circum-stances to make achievements in information exchange and teaching that they would not be able to do if they returned to China.

More recently, the May 9, 2000 *Zhongguo Shichang Jingji Bao* (an economic newspaper published by the Central Party Committee) defined what it called the new policy of "flexible circulation" as "when an individual is physically somewhere else, his or her talent may for all intents be regarded as being here" in China. Under this policy, students educated and working overseas will be able to move "between China and points outside China, al-lowing domestic enterprises to instantly master the latest S&T develop-ments and information." By working in high-tech facilities abroad and "returning to China for short periods," the modus operandi of technology transfer "moves from one-shot exchanges to sustainable long-term coop-eration," the newspaper explained.

China targets not just students but the entire expatriate scientific com-munity. The previously cited *Zhongguo Rencai* article "Analysis of Overseas Chinese S&T Talent" states, "In addition to students who left the mainland, Taiwan, or Hong Kong to study abroad and remained there, another im-portant constituent part of overseas Chinese S&T talent is to be found in second- and third-generation descendants of foreign citizens of Chinese origin." The decision to utilize this talent in the service of China's modern-ization is backed at the highest levels of government.

For example, in August 1999 the Chinese Communist Party Central Committee and State Council issued orders to intensify foreign coopera-tion in technology innovation. Calling for greater efforts to attract foreign expertise, the instructions read in part:

We shall further take practical measures and use various ways to attract outstanding overseas talent. Besides carrying out the existing preferential policy of the state, we shall make it convenient for such talent to obtain household registrations, housing, and schooling for children. All relevant departments shall make it convenient for Chinese and foreign personnel who undertake international cooperation and exchanges in high and new technologies to make contacts.[25]

A month later Vice-Premier Li Lanqing at a welcoming ceremony for one hundred expatriate Chinese scientists made the following comment on the need to tap the overseas Chinese community: "Bringing overseas Chinese scientists' talents into full play will be of significant importance to promoting China's exchanges with foreign countries in the field of science and technology and realizing science and technology modernization in China as soon as possible."[26] The vice-premier reiterated his call to rely on foreign scientists at a meeting of the "China Youth Science and Technology Innovation Campaign" held that October, where he asked expatriate scientists to continue bringing "back" their research results and "to be of service to China in various ways."[27] In November of that year China's official news agency reported NPC Standing Committee member Li Peng's congratulations to participants of the "Fourth Sino-American Technology and Engineering Conference" for their effectiveness in attracting overseas talent. The conference was attended by seventy overseas Chinese scholars who provided nearly one hundred "suggestions" for technological innovation.[28]

Similarly, the August 1999 issue of *Qianxian*, a monthly journal sponsored by the Beijing Municipal CPC Committee, reported what it called a "significant bridge effect" between China and emigrants who have succeeded abroad as scientists. According to the journal, overseas Chinese "are concerned with the progress and development of the motherland," are mindful of a "debt of gratitude" they owe to China, and "are happy to link up with their home of origin, invest there, exchange their science and technology and work for their home country's interest." Granting that much of this rhetoric represents wishful thinking, it is nonetheless true that Beijing regards overseas Chinese scientists as targets of opportunity to further China's goals.

S&T Outreach Organizations

At the forefront of these efforts to exploit expatriate talent is the CAS, an umbrella organization for 120 state-run research institutes, and its sister organization the Chinese Academy of Engineering. The CAS enlists support from foreign scientists—largely ethnic Chinese—in several ways. It elects overseas academicians as distinguished members of the body in recognition of their "outstanding contributions to China's international scientific exchanges and cooperation." Elections made in June 2000 raised the number of foreign scientists permanently affiliated with the CAS to thirty-six (four of the seven new members were ethnic Chinese employed at US institutions).[29] It also conducts annual drives to hire younger scientists who "have made contributions recognized worldwide or own patents for major scientific inventions and innovations," *Xinhua* reported. The news agency explained that those hired in the 2000 campaign, characterized as "the most extensive government-funded personnel introduction program in history," would individually receive on average $240,000 in research funds over three years, besides salary and housing benefits.[30]

Many of these scientists, mostly ethnic Chinese from America and Europe, are recruited to "consultant" positions in affiliated institutes.[31] Others are required to spend three months to two years in China working in such fields as mathematics, physics, chemistry, life sciences, and new high technologies (computer science, energy, new materials, and aerospace).[32] These blanket recruitment efforts are supplemented by programs that target scientists in particular countries. For example, in June 1999 CAS president Lu Yongxiang announced that his academy would establish a subsidy fund to draw outstanding scientists in Germany to affiliated research labs in China.[33] A year earlier, the China-Japan Center for Science and Technology Exchange—a CAS-affiliated group—signed an agreement with the Association of Chinese Scientists and Engineers in Japan to promote exchanges. The two organizations reportedly built a database of expatriate Chinese scientists in Japan to facilitate liaison.[34]

The CAS also sponsors visits by foreign scientists to "exchange" S&T information and establish a foundation for long-term contacts. Examples are easily found. A biologist from the University of California addressing a CAS conference in 1998 enjoined colleagues to "carry forward the national tradition and shoulder the historic task" of rebuilding China. Another academician of Chinese descent, also from a U.S. institution, reportedly told fellow attendees, "As early as my childhood, mother taught me to contribute to the country and the society," adding that more than half the research projects he chairs in the United States involve PRC scientists.[35] Earlier that year a Chinese-American Nobel Prize winner from Columbia University, in China on a CAS-sponsored visit, was reportedly thanked by Vice-Premier Li Lanqing for his "consistent concern and support for China's development" in science and technology.[36]

The number of people participating in these CAS "cooperative visits" is staggering. During China's seventh five-year plan (1986–90) 29,530 individuals were involved. In the eighth five-year plan the figure was 33,881 (Lian Yanhua 2000). More recently, the academy has been strengthening its system for evaluating overseas experts, presumably as targets for recruitment, and building communication networks among overseas scholars to augment its ability to access foreign scientific talent.[37]

Even more focused than CAS on recruiting foreign scientists is the Overseas Chinese Affairs Office of China's State Council. Identified by its director as "a Chinese government institution specialized in the work of overseas Chinese and foreigners of Chinese origin," the office has as its basic mission introducing to China advanced technology through the help of ethnic Chinese residing overseas, on an individual or group basis, or through corporations. Its activities range from sponsoring visits by foreign scientists to facilitating foreign investment in China's high-tech zones and buying shares in overseas Chinese companies—whatever leads to scientific progress and modernization of the motherland.[38]

Sub-national PRC entities also recruit foreign scientists and technical personnel. For example, in early 2000 Guangdong Province hosted a "talent fair" that 800 people attended, including Chinese working or studying in top American universities, research institutes, and Silicon Valley companies.[39] Beijing's municipal government, co-sponsor of Zhongguancun Technology Park, offers multiple incentives (including some that violate WTO guidelines) to attract foreign S&T personnel. The city went so far as to put a recruiting office in Silicon Valley to take advantage of the area's high ethnic Chinese population.[40]

Supplementing these official recruitment venues are those run by China's alleged NGOs, such as the All-China Federation of Returned Overseas Chinese (*Zhōngguó Quánquó Guēiguó Huáqiáo Liánhéhuì*, *Qiáolián* for short) and the China Overseas Exchange Association (*Zhōngguó Hǎiwài Jiāoliú Xuéhuì*, or COEA). Founded in 1956, *Qiáolián* describes itself as "a national nongovernmental organization under the leadership of the Chinese Communist Party." Its recruitment and information-gathering operations are overseen by a "Liaison Office" tasked with "developing exchanges and friendly activities between overseas Chinese compatriots inside and outside the country." *Qiáolián* openly acknowledges that it has "assisted the [PRC] government in attracting funds, technology, and talented persons" from the overseas Chinese community for the past twenty years, that it maintains a database on such exchanges, and that the organization actively promotes S&T transfers between overseas Chinese and their "ancestral land."[41]

The Chinese Overseas Exchange Association (COEA), founded in 1990 and headquartered in Beijing, identifies itself in generic ideological terms as "a nationwide nongovernmental organization made up of persons from various circles and all nationalities of China." COEA's "Economic and S&T Department" and a subordinate "S&T Office" facilitate exchanges with overseas Chinese scientists and technical experts. Curiously, its website also identifies another, unnamed office that, it says without elaboration, "examines the work situation of overseas Chinese and their dependents" and provides this information to the PRC government. Like *Qiáolián*, the COEA maintains databases on individuals and organizations that have made contributions to China, many of an S&T nature.[42]

Finally, expatriate scientists have organizations of their own founded on regional or disciplinary lines, such as the Chinese Association of Science and Technology and the General Committee to Promote China-U.S. Trade and S&T, both in New York, a dozen or more professional organizations scattered throughout Silicon Valley,[43] and the Chinese Institute of Engineers (CIE) with chapters in several U.S. cities. According to Jia and Rubin, most such alliances

have formed for social and networking purposes, but the more ambitious associations aim to contribute to China's modernization and increase its communication with the outside world. They promote US-China exchanges in science, technology, and trade by sending members to lecture in China, hosting Chinese delegations in the United States, and sponsoring joint seminars. (1997)

The CIE has been particularly aggressive in this respect. Made up of some 10,000 members, the organization co-sponsors biannual technology exchange forums in Beijing with China's State Bureau of Foreign Experts and other technology transfer groups. For the October 2001 event, CIE reportedly addressed more than one hundred high-tech issues *proposed by its*

PRC hosts in advance and engaged in "on-the-spot exchanges" with engineers and Chinese companies.[44]

Just as China overlooks little in its efforts to mine Western S&T publications, few opportunities are lost in exploiting the shortcut that expatriate scientists potentially provide to accessing the fruits of Western scientific innovation.

International Cooperation

Technology "exchanges" between Chinese and foreign institutions, such as cooperative agreements between governments, scientific information obtained at international conferences, and transfers that take place through companies, constitute another pillar of support for China's S&T modernization. Unlike the other techniques described—espionage, open source collection, and coopting expatriate scientists—transfers of this type are contractual or conducted within some kind of recognized bilateral framework.

Just as the U.S. government in the late 1950s and early 1960s ceded technology to Japan at little or no cost to shore up an ally against Communist expansion, so did Russia in the early and mid-1950s provide China with what RAND Corporation analyst Hans Heymann called "undoubtedly the most comprehensive technology transfer in modern industrial history." Russia's contribution to China's technological development "ran the gamut from scientific and technical education to project design, and from production engineering to creating a modern industrial organization" (Heymann 1975:6). Wendy Frieman's (1989) study on Chinese military R&D observed in the same vein:

Soviet assistance to China in the 1950s was the most massive international transfer of technology in modern history. Between 1950 and 1960, over 11,000 Soviet specialists were on site in Chinese facilities, where they were involved in every phase of military industry from basic research to prototype testing and serial production. (1989:262)

Frieman noted that after Russia withdrew in the early 1960s, "China could not hold on to the state of the art and fell considerably behind world levels in the years that followed." Although Russia has since resumed transfers of military technology on a scale that some in Russia's own defense ministry find alarming, China now has state-to-state S&T cooperative agreements with 89 other countries and "cooperative links" with 60 more.[45] These bilateral agreements, Simon and Goldman observed, "provide a means for cooperative research activities, joint projects, and the reciprocal movement of scientific data and literature between China and other nations" (1989:11).

China's most significant S&T agreements are those with the United States. In 1979, China and the United States signed a broad agreement on S&T cooperation and twenty-five protocols implementing that agreement in specific areas.[46] By 1997 the number of formal bilateral science agreements and memoranda of understanding between the United States and China had increased to thirty-two.[47] In an interview with Vice-Minister of Science and Technology Hui Yongzheng in the June 26, 1998, Hong Kong *Wen Wei Po* (a PRC-owned daily newspaper), Hui celebrated "the achievements made in Sino-U.S. scientific and technological exchanges over the last twenty years in 33 different fields," including aviation, telecommunications, and several nuclear-related disciplines.

These agreements led to "several thousand S&T cooperation projects," Hui explained. He was especially pleased with the results of the "8th China-U.S. Joint Committee Meeting on S&T Cooperation" held in Beijing in November 1997 (the forum runs every two years), noting that

At the end of the meeting, State Councilor Song Jian, on behalf of the Chinese side, submitted to the U.S. a list of 78 projects in 13 fields in which the Chinese hoped to carry out further cooperation with the U.S. The U.S. said they would give earnest consideration to the list.

No mention was made by Vice-Minister Hui of any corresponding requests from the United States. He did note a significant trickle-down effect of agreements signed on the national level on the readiness of local governments, research labs, and institutes of higher learning to pursue joint projects of their own. The impact of these derivative agreements on China's ability to introduce key technologies is enormous, surpassing the advantages gained by the national-level agreements themselves, inasmuch as they legitimize projects undertaken by American groups that depend at some level on government support. China's wider stake in international S&T agreements was summarized by the Beijing *Keyan Guanli* as follows:

Not only can effective international cooperation allow us to make progress in a number of specific research areas, it also facilitates the transfer of advanced foreign technologies and methods to Chinese laboratories and serves to build up our own laboratories and research area task forces. When we can obtain international cooperation funding from foreign channels, exploit international cooperation channels, and win the support of the other side, it is especially conducive to the building up of our own laboratories. (Lian Yanhua 2000)

Participation in international academic conferences, described by the authors of "China's Spy Guide" as a prime venue for transferring technology, is also boosted by the legitimacy national agreements confer on Chinese researchers. The value of these conferences for S&T collection can be gauged by the resources the State Natural Science Foundation (part of the State Council and the largest source of research funding in China) spends on them: 48 percent of the projects funded between 1991 and 1996 were for attending conferences abroad or sponsoring them domestically (Lian Yanhua 2000).

Recognition of China's eligibility to benefit from international scientific "exchanges" has also cleared the way for transfers through private companies. Denis Simon, coeditor of *Science and Technology in Post-Mao China*, observed that during its sixth five-year plan (1981–85) "China signed over 1,300 technology import contracts with foreign firms worth a total of US $9.7 billion." The seventh five-year plan targeted 3,000 key technologies, including core items used across wide areas (Simon 1989).

Significant as these technology sales are, they represent only a fraction of the transfers made to China by foreign companies, many of which are forced into "joint research" agreements as part of the cost of doing business in China. As S&T Minister Zhu Lilan said in March 1998:

The ministry will expand cooperation with other countries, but will shift the focus from technology and equipment introduction to joint research and development. Such efforts will coincide with economic and trade exchanges.[48]

In the same month, a science ministry journal laid out Beijing's trade-for-technology strategy in an article critical of foreign firms' monopolizing of key technologies. The journal argued, "using market access in exchange for technology is the only path China can go on at present to develop new high-tech industries."[49] A month later a newspaper published by the China Council for the Promotion of International Trade hinted similarly that tech transfer would be expected of foreign firms hoping to penetrate the China market.[50]

How have foreign firms responded to this pressure? According to a *Xinhua* report based on science ministry sources, more than seventy "Sino-foreign cooperative research groups" were operating in China by the end of 1998.[51] The report cited leading U.S. manufacturers of computer software and processing chips as examples of companies that set up "research institutes" in China reportedly "to extend the service life of their products and improve customer confidence." As was the case with market entry in Japan, no American manufacturer looking to sell goods in China can escape divulging proprietary technology. Sometimes the technology is not even related, as when China's National Aero-Technology Import and Export Corporation (CATIC) demanded and got five-axis metal working machines and other sophisticated equipment from a major U.S. aircraft manufacturer in return for an order for airliners.[52] Such is the mystique of the China market.

Nor has Beijing ignored the potential of Chinese multinational companies abroad as technology collectors. By the late 1990s, China had several thousand overseas firms operating in some 120 countries. Inasmuch as the technology levels of these companies are low compared to that of their host countries, Chinese firms seek to transfer foreign technology, as one PRC journal put it, by "taking full advantage of opportunities in these other companies' industrial and technological adjustments to acquire key technologies, driver technologies, and leading technologies through annexes, buyouts, and cooperation."[53]

China's Approach to Intellectual Property Rights

China's willingness to acquire technology through informal means is consistent with its lax attitude toward intellectual property rights (IPR) in general. This is a well-known problem that I need spend little time documenting. As Weidenbaum and Hughes have noted, "Many American firms have been hit hard by the lack of intellectual property protection in China. Only one out of 12 companies surveyed by the General Accounting Office in 1994 reported a satisfactory experience when trying to secure the enforcement of their property rights" (1996:140).

Although Chinese officials sometimes pay lip service to foreign requests that China take IPR violations seriously, there are clear signs that many Chinese do not regard patented discoveries as private property. For example, in a 1996 article titled "International S&T Cooperation and the Sharing of

Intellectual Property," *Keji Ribao*, the science ministry's official newspaper, complained that developed countries and their corporate groups, working from a position of strength, force an "inequitable distribution of the benefits of science and technology" on less-developed nations. Countries with the best research equipment end up with the rights to all new technology "depriving the other side of its legal rights. This is unacceptable."[54]

That same year the chargé d'affaires at China's embassy in Tokyo went on record acknowledging the difficulty Chinese have accepting IPR, given, as he put it, that China receives no patent fees for gunpowder, paper, and the compass.[55] Nicholas Eftimiades, who knows more about China's abuse of intellectual property than most people, observed in his study of Chinese espionage that

after reviewing these cases one is left with the distinct impression that Chinese businessmen see the illegal transfer of high technology not as a criminal act but as a simple business transaction. (1994:31)

Press reports suggest that some in China not only ignore IPR abuse; they elevate it to a moral imperative. An article titled "The International Economic Intelligence War," which appeared in a reputable PRC business-oriented newspaper,[56] argued that developing countries and China in particular need not consider "economic espionage" wrong, since doing so "is clearly inconsistent with the need for development in the present age." Instead it should be regarded as a legitimate means of obtaining technology from foreign sources and "a special activity that contributes to the development of a nation's economy and technology." Claiming a direct relationship between economic prosperity and a nation's willingness to steal, the article stated:

If a nation's economic spies can steal core technology or business secrets from their economic competitors in another country, they can help their own firms achieve victory in international economic competition at minimal cost.

The article went on to endorse wiretapping and more sophisticated techniques to intercept foreign corporations' microwave, satellite, and facsimile transmissions.

A report in the technology policy journal *Keji Jinbu yu Duice* titled "On the North-South Technology Balance" argued similarly that China cannot obtain the latest technology from advanced countries by the usual means, because monopolists are loath to share their inventions. "Under the strict control of the developed countries, the newest revolutionary results of science and technology can almost never be transferred to a developing country by technology trade," it asserted. China must therefore adjust its policies toward technology transfer to include strengthening information networks, building up cooperation with transnational firms to facilitate acquisition of their technology, and "making full use of personnel studying overseas to transfer and disseminate technology across countries." The journal was optimistic about using overseas Chinese who play key roles in the technological communities of advanced nations to redress China's "technology imbalance."[57]

There are indications that China will intensify efforts to transfer foreign technology through indirect means. An article in the July 2001 issue of *Keyan Guanli*—a bimonthly journal of the CAS Institute of S&T Policy and Management Studies—presented a fourteen-point plan to "more effectively utilize" overseas Chinese scientists and "persuade them to make contributions in various ways to China's science and technology development." The institute proposed what it called a "dual-basis model" whereby ethnic Chinese scientists working abroad are given "a sense of direction for serving China in a deep, sustainable and efficient manner." Parties to the process would be asked to contribute to "sensitive research topics of national importance" from their vantage points overseas. The article went as far as to endorse assigning overseas Chinese specific research tasks, noting that

When conditions permit, urgent domestic research topics can be selected, R&D organizations can be set up in foreign countries, and first-rate overseas Chinese experts can be invited to participate in them as financially sponsored projects. The final research results will go back to China.

The institute recommended forming an "Overseas Chinese Experts Data Center" under the Science Ministry to store information gleaned through science attachés on overseas Chinese scientists. To manage liaison with foreign S&T groups, the institute further proposed forming "China S&T Development Overseas Advisory Committees" in all major industrialized nations, with a mission to "build extensive contacts, congregate overseas Chinese experts, and solicit their contributions for China's science and technology."

A final recommendation concerned the need to maintain secrecy through the use of intermediaries, given that "recruitment of overseas Chinese experts is strongly related to the policies and sensitivities" of the targeted nations. Those involved in "delicate areas" of technology transfer, it warned, must "avoid broadcasting their recruitment and cooperation accomplishments in foreign and domestic news media, giving away leads, and creating an awkward situation" for the coopted participants.

This concludes my review of China's technology transfer practices. My purpose in bringing this information together is not to denigrate China's efforts to raise its industrial level and the living standards of a quarter of humanity. Indeed, I suspect that the reluctance of many scholars to discuss China's excesses in this area stems from their desire to see China overcome more than a century of poverty and become a developed nation. I share that sentiment completely.

But whereas Japan—with less incentive than China—has come to recognize that the cause of its incessant borrowing of Western ideas is a creativity deficit, I find few such acknowledgments in published Chinese sources.[58] On the contrary, hardly a day goes by when a PRC official does not publicly extol the "boundless creativity of the Chinese people," as if repeating the mantra will lend it substance. The argument that I pursue in subsequent chapters is that a *lack* of creativity, not necessarily among Chinese individually but within the culture, provokes the illegal and unethical practices documented here. Ignoring these facts serves no one's interests, least of all China's.

But before taking up the cognitive aspects of the problem, I need to round off this survey by the examining transfer practices used in Korea.

Chapter Three
Korean Technology Transfer

The 21st century may well belong to the East Asians, who value education and hard work.

—Insup Taylor

Copying the Copycat

Compared to those of China and Japan, very little has been published
on South Korea's efforts to transfer foreign technology. Recognizing this, I
began several years ago a systematic review of Korean newspapers, magazines, journals, government press releases, and Internet postings looking for
evidence that South Korea, like East Asia's other two major players, was engaged in programs to transfer core technology that it was unable to develop
indigenously. Literature distributed by Republic of Korea government entities and their quasi-official support organizations overseas were also examined, as were the speeches of South Korean science and technology officials
and published texts of corporate and official exchange agreements.

I was interested in learning whether my projections of Korean behavior
in science and technology as surmised from my understanding of the linguistic problem would be borne out. If the thesis that nonalphabetic East
Asian writing systems have a negative impact on their users' propensity to
engage in creative science is valid, then evidence of contemporary problems in this area in Korea should also be apparent. Alternatively, an absence
of such corroborating evidence could mean that the relationship I hoped to
establish between writing systems and scientific creativity is wrong, that my
analysis of the Korean writing system as a functional syllabary is misguided,
or that neither proposition is valid.

I need not have wondered. What began as a trickle of evidence soon became a flood. As it turned out, I was able to accumulate so much information on South Korean technology transfer, especially its informal aspects, that my chief concern now is to avoid giving the impression that Korea is any more active in this respect than the East Asian countries for which a body of scholarship already existed and which I did not have to research in such detail. In fact, as South Koreans themselves acknowledge, most of their technology transfer methods are modeled on Japan's successful efforts. Since many of these mechanisms are familiar, we will examine them only briefly in the next few sections before taking up techniques that are more uniquely Korean.

Until the last decade or so, South Korea supported its industrialization with technology imported through direct purchases and licensing, or through imitation of one type or another. Although both venues remain important, the cumulative cost of direct technology imports soon began to cut deeply into corporate profitability. According to the October 27, 1995, *Hanguk Kyongje Sinmun*,[1] South Korean companies licensed fewer than 7,000 foreign technologies between 1962 and 1990, for which they paid $3.4 billion in royalties. But as Korean products moved upscale and the technology needed to build them grew sophisticated, royalties paid to foreign companies climbed precipitously. In 1994, South Korea handed $1.28 billion to foreign firms for just 430 technologies.[2] By 1995, the figure had risen to $1.65 billion for American and Japanese technology alone. In the same year, South Korea's semiconductor industry—the country's leading exporter and main source of foreign exchange—paid royalties averaging 6.5 percent of sales.[3]

Something had to give. Complaints in the news media about "technological protectionism" that kept advanced technology in the hands of advanced nations were symptomatic of the pressure South Koreans were beginning to feel about the high cost of competing in world markets with technology they did not create. Moreover, direct purchases of foreign technology were not solving even the country's *short*-term problems. As *Hanguk Kyongje Sinmun* noted, not only were technology imports expensive, "they have been shown to be mostly ineffective in raising the technological level of South Korean companies" because the technology was obsolete by the time they obtained it.[4]

The same complaint was registered by Yi Sang-tae, former head of the

Ministry of Science and Technology's (MOST) Technology Promotion Division. Writing for the October 20, 1994 issue of *Sanhagyon 21*,[5] Yi argued that Korea needed to transcend the early stage of technology acquisition characterized by "bringing technological resources into the country through licensing and hiring foreign specialists" and advance to a mature stage wherein the technology is obtained through buyouts, overseas research facilities, and other cooperative ventures. According to Yi, in the latter part of the 1980s a few companies had begun overseas research activities, but by 1994 there were still only twenty such institutes abroad supporting work their parent firms were already doing. What Korea needs, Yi asserted, is a "positive" transfer strategy for acquiring wellspring technology through other means.

Others pointed to the same conundrum. In early 1994, the director of the Korea Institute of Science and Technology (KIST) stated that South Korea can "no longer survive without more fundamental measures to access outside sources of technology." Buying the technology would not suffice.[6] Similarly, MOST's Technology Cooperation Division chief argued that same year for a "bold strategy to internationalize our research and development in order to effectively utilize overseas R&D sources." South Korea's industrial think tanks reached the same conclusion about the need to obtain foreign technology systematically and on a more basic level. A March 1994 report from the Korea Institute for Economic Policy claimed that unless government and industry cooperated to "run the whole technology transfer process," it would be hard to continue selling products in advanced countries.[7] A few months later, a researcher at the Korea Institute for Industrial Economics and Trade proposed a "technology specialization system through which domestic industries can better absorb the technology of advanced countries."[8]

In response to these demands, South Korean corporate and government entities began a serious effort around 1993–94 to tap indirectly into the sources of foreign scientific and technological creativity. Faced with crushing royalty payments, shorter product cycles, and disappointment with its own attempts to create competitive technologies, South Korea took the same shortcut Japan did two decades earlier, aided—like China—by an expatriate community sympathetic to the fatherland's goals. Yet despite the availability of these models, or perhaps because of them, one cannot help but feel that these copycat efforts came too late. Korea's attempts to obtain leading technology from Japan, the country that pioneered indirect transfer, are notoriously ineffective because of Japan's awareness of and protection against the danger.[9] Similar ploys directed at the United States achieve less than they might because Japan and China have sensitized Americans to the issue. Nonetheless, a close look at these techniques will be instructive.

Borrowed Paths to New Technology

Overseas training, a well-established transfer venue used by Japan and China, is used by Korea to obtain technology at a fraction of its market value. To cite a few examples from the aerospace industry, in early 1993 Korean Air, South Korea's national carrier and manufacturer of aircraft assemblies, sent engineers to work on Boeing's 777 project. Samsung Aerospace, for its part, had sixty specialists at other U.S. aviation facilities for technical training.[10] Both Korean companies later joined a national consortium to build a mid-range passenger jet designed to compete with U.S. entries in the Asian market. More recently, *Maeil Kyongje Sinmun* reported an agreement between a ROK satellite consortium and the U.S. firm TRW to have forty-five South Korean personnel trained at their facilities. The newspaper quoted a Daewoo director as saying, "For a minimum investment, ROK companies involved in the project can acquire key satellite manufacturing technology" that will let Korea compete in an area where the United States has traditionally enjoyed an advantage.[11]

South Korean companies sign deals with foreign firms not just for their economic value but to obtain targeted technology. Known as "strategic cooperation," the process involves identifying gaps in indigenous technology, finding a foreign company that has the technology, and engaging the firm in some kind of cooperative relationship that results in its transfer. Korea's side of the relationship may involve funding commercialization, providing plant and equipment, contributing technology of its own, or facilitating market access. The South Korean government often participates at different levels of the transfer process to identify weaknesses in the indigenous S&T structure, find technology donors, and to subsidize the actual transfer. It is not always clear to the foreign partner that tech transfer is part of the agreement.

Media reports are replete with examples of South Korean government involvement in "strategic cooperation." On January 24, 1994 *Maeil Kyongje*

Sinmun described a Ministry of Trade and Industry (MOTIE)[12] "Plan to Strengthen Strategic Cooperation with Technologically Advanced Foreign Countries" that specified which technologies were to be obtained from which countries worldwide through cooperative systems. *Hanguk Kyongje Sinmun* on April 2, 1994, reported how the government's Small and Medium Business Promotion Corporation was helping transfer advanced U.S. electronics and computer technologies to ROK firms by acting as an intermediary for Silicon Valley-based American companies seeking financing. Other types of state aid to facilitate technological "cooperation" can be inferred from a report of MOTIE allotting $750,000 to support research with Japanese companies and another $250,000 for "structural activities for basic industrial technology cooperation" with Japan, a euphemism understood by all parties.[13] Prominent areas where ROK companies have used strategic cooperation to wrest technology from U.S. manufacturers are aerospace, high-definition television, multimedia equipment and software, and, more recently, microprocessors and application-specific integrated circuits.[14]

Just as Japan has discovered the advantages overseas subsidiaries offer in transferring host country technology, so has South Korea learned to use its overseas outposts and manufacturing facilities as a conduit for other countries' innovations. For example, in April 1993 Samsung Electronics set up Image Quest Technology in Silicon Valley and promptly hired a large number of local specialists in thin film transistor technology, used in liquid crystal displays, an important sector of the electronics market that ROK companies now dominate.[15] Hyundai Electronics meanwhile acquired a central processing unit for workstations, auxiliary memory, and laser disk drive technology from its U.S. subsidiaries by hiring local talent and cooperating with nearby American firms.[16]

Minority investments and buyouts of foreign companies are also used by South Korean firms to obtain patented technology. For example, in mid-1993, Samsung Electronics acquired Harris Microwave Semiconductor, a San Jose company that built products for the U.S. defense industry. Eight months later the renamed facility was producing gallium arsenide chips for use in commercial-grade mobile phones and high-speed computers—two areas for which Samsung's own silicon-based designs were not as well suited. In early 1995, Samsung Electronics bought 40 percent of the U.S. computer firm AST Research, gaining control over its 190 computer-related patents.[17] Between 1993 and 1995, Hyundai Electronics bought the U.S. disk drive manufacturer Maxtor with "accumulated technology and various patents"; NCR's Microelectronic Products Division (the nonmemory semiconductor division of AT&T's Global Information Systems) acquiring 690 patents;[18] then the remaining 60 percent of Maxtor, giving Hyundai Korea's first fully owned HDD manufacturing capability. Not to be outdone, Samsung put $10 million into the American disk drive company Integral, expanded the disk development resources of its U.S. subsidiary SISA, and started hiring more local experts.[19]

I have highlighted these acquisitions by the electronics subsidiaries of Korea's two largest conglomerates, Samsung and Hyundai, because of the industry's importance to South Korea's economy and because these two groups are considered to be the ROK's top developers of *indigenous* technology. Examples of technology-driven takeovers in other industries are easily found, such as aerospace, alternative fuels, iron and steel, medical equipment, nuclear power, numerically controlled machinery, optical devices, pharmaceuticals, telecommunications, and even high-tech musical instruments. Buyouts of technology-rich foreign corporations are often supported by soft government loans, tax incentives, and other state subsidies.[20]

ROK companies and national labs also obtain technology by hiring "talented" foreigners with expertise in areas targeted for development. Historically those persons were ethnic Koreans who had emigrated or were studying overseas, but in recent years the eligibility pool has grown to what ROK newspapers call "pure foreigners." Examples from the aerospace industry were reported in *Chugan Choson*, a weekly news magazine, which described how technicians in U.S. factories are hired to "brighten the prospects of our aviation industry."[21] The magazine noted that Samsung planned to recruit 140 foreign aeronautical specialists, forty from the United States and the rest from Russia, for its new aerospace division.[22]

Recruiting is also done openly at job fairs held in the United States and Europe, sponsored jointly by Korean conglomerates and state-affiliated foundations. According to the September 30, 1997, *Chonja Sinmun*, each of South Korea's four main electronics companies—Samsung, Hyundai, LG, and Daewoo—have separate overseas hiring programs with annual recruitment targets in the hundreds. Even smaller companies have discovered they can "overcome the technological gap with competitors in advanced countries" by hiring that country's nationals, *Maeil Kyongje Sinmun* noted on February 8, 1994. The newspaper, Seoul's equivalent of the U.S. *Wall Street*

Journal, likened the strategy of hiring foreign experts to "using barbarians to control the barbarians."

ROK government involvement in foreign hiring is well documented and includes in addition to programs aimed at expatriate Koreans (discussed below) sundry employment incentives for top scientists regardless of their ethnicity. On May 11, 1995, *Maeil Kyongje Sinmun* reported that the South Korean government would recruit some three thousand "top overseas personnel" with a knowledge of advanced technology. The newspaper quoted a high-level government source as saying it was impossible to produce enough scientists from Korean universities to sustain Korea's economic growth, and that "for now there is no alternative to recruiting high-level brains from overseas." Government inducements to attract foreign scientists include dual nationality, exemptions from property holding restrictions, and matching funds to companies hiring top foreign "brains."[23]

Overseas Research Institutes

Borrowing another cue from Japan, by late 1994 South Korea had begun looking at overseas "research" as an inexpensive way to obtain foreign technology. The goal was to staff overseas facilities with host country scientists who would transfer expertise to their Korean employers, or buy out foreign research institutes for the same purpose. In early 1995 *Hanguk Kyongje Sinmun* named the following electronics laboratories as examples of South Korea's decision to push globalization of R&D by employing local research personnel: Samsung Electronics San Jose Research Institute (85 employees), LG Electronics Goldstar San Jose Center (10), Goldstar NAL in Chicago (15), Hyundai Electronics SEMR Research Institute in San Jose (29), and LG Semicon GSEA in San Diego (60 employees doing "semiconductor technology surveys").[24] Later that year LG Data Communications and LG Semicon established a lab in San Diego staffed with thirty U.S. research personnel.[25] Daewoo Electronics began building a worldwide network of twelve electronics R&D centers in eight foreign countries, including two in the United States.[26]

Besides these private ventures, the science ministry in early 1995 drafted plans to build eight R&D centers abroad: two each in Australia, China, England, and Russia (in addition to the three centers it was already operating in Russia). These centers, in the ministry's view, represented an "expansion of South Korea's S&T diplomacy" to "penetrate" foreign countries and "develop economically useful technology through strategic cooperative research."[27] Later, MOST issued another report stating that seventeen such state-funded institutes were in the works in England, France, Germany, and Russia for aerospace, advanced materials, energy, satellites, thin film technology, sensors, marine science, and factory automation.[28]

A 1995 survey by the ministry's Science and Technology Policy Institute (STEPI) of 124 large and 184 smaller South Korean corporations showed that 51 of the firms had established "overseas research labs or local subsidiaries for technological development."[29] In addition, CEOs of half the larger and a third of the smaller firms responded affirmatively about plans to pursue overseas research through local facilities or by "acquiring technology through local plants overseas" (which apparently qualified as research). The United States and Japan were the countries of choice. The institute concluded, "Korean companies are getting away from simply buying foreign technology and are strengthening their overseas research activities by establishing centers aimed at getting key technologies directly on site."

Later in 1995, South Korea's automakers got into the act. In June, Kia opened a $70 million R&D complex outside Tokyo staffed with 150 technicians hired away from Toyota, Nissan, and other Japanese companies. Kia planned two more centers for Detroit and Los Angeles and another for Frankfurt, Germany.[30] Hyundai Motors announced its intention to build automotive research centers in the same four cities and a fifth one in Yokohama as part of its "global R&D system."[31] Daewoo Motors was building or planning research centers in the United States, Japan, and Germany staffed with local personnel.[32] Samsung Motors, Korea's newest (and now defunct) entrant in the automotive field, planned to invest $258 million in four overseas R&D institutes by 1998 to serve as "bridgeheads" to advanced technology.[33]

By 1996, the move toward overseas research as a preferred transfer venue was well underway. In one thirty-day period, the ROK media reported five new major R&D facilities abroad, including LG Semicon's Düsseldorf center, described as the "hub" of a Europe-wide information gathering network. LG reportedly uses this "strategic outpost to get an early jump on developing world-class commercial products" and to ensure that "good, strategic use was being made of Europe's R&D resources and infrastructure."[34] Samsung Aerospace began expanding its overseas research installations from fourteen labs in nine countries to twenty-four facilities spanning twelve countries,[35] while Korean Air planned a research lab in San Francisco "to secure foreign experts in aircraft research."[36] In July, *Hanguk Kyongje Sinman* reported Daewoo Electronics' plan to invest $1.6 billion in twenty advanced research centers worldwide.[37] It noted that Daewoo would have a "global technology development network" of *seventy* such overseas centers by 2000.[38]

These "bridgeheads into the technological source land of advanced countries" continued to grow in number. By mid-1996 the Korea Industrial Technology Association (KITA) counted sixty-two such units operating, of which thirty-three were in the United States.[39] This figure referred only to corporate labs overseas. In August 1996, the Ministry of Science and Technology described two separate categories of government-managed overseas research facilities.[40] The first type is affiliated with ROK national laboratories, state-funded universities, and ad hoc cooperative organizations, and is aimed at specific technologies or at foreign technology in general. Although billed by MOST as non-profit entities, *Hanguk Kyongje Sinmun* reported that ROK manufacturers send their own technicians to these centers under government "auspices" to channel technology back to their firms directly.[41]

The other type of government-sponsored overseas research facility is an extension of the so-called "distinguished research centers" set up at South Korean universities by the Korea Science Foundation (KOSEF), a subsidiary of MOST. Korean universities famous in certain fields are designated for special funding as Science Research Institutes or Engineering Research Institutes. They are then encouraged by KOSEF to establish laboratories abroad to "globalize basic scientific research." KOSEF began the program in 1995 and was funding eighteen overseas labs by mid-1996. One ROK newspaper noted that these centers are "reaping the results of research done overseas in all types of advanced technological fields," and that thirty-eight such facilities would be built to "penetrate the scientifically and technologically advanced countries" by 2000.[42]

Statements by South Korean officials suggest that they view these overseas R&D centers less as forums for scientific cooperation and more as vehicles for early access to the research results of foreign countries. Writing in the June 30, 1996, issue of *Sanhagyon 21*, S&T minister Chong Kun-mo qualified his appeal for more indigenous R&D with the statement:

Of course, creatively oriented science and technology does not mean we have to put all of our efforts and intellect right away into scientific investigation and basic research. Choosing an "intermediate advance strategy" that involves grafting our own original technology onto the basic and wellspring technology of advanced countries established up to a competitive level, and being able to commercialize it before they do, can be a very useful approach.

Chong's views were consistent with those of KOSEF, to which *Chonja Sinmun* attributed the following statement:[43]

KOSEF figures the reason for the boom in establishing overseas labs by top ROK research centers is because by setting up local laboratories in the advanced research institutes of relatively developed overseas countries the centers can make free use of the high-tech research equipment and materials of advanced countries and acquire information on research and technology at the pre-competitive stage.

KITA, for its part, named the functions of overseas R&D centers as "meeting local customer needs, monitoring technological developments, acquiring new technology, and employing high caliber research professionals of the host country."[44] A Daewoo official conceded: "In Korea we work mainly on developing commercial technology, while our American labs develop future-oriented strategic products."[45] I have not observed KITA or other South Korean institutions commenting on the benefits the host country receives through this type of cooperation.

Academic Connections

As one who has spent much of his professional life working with Asian students in the U.S. and benefiting from the hospitality of academic colleagues in Korea, Japan, and Taiwan, I view the Asian presence on American campuses as a blessing. Still it is hard to ignore the fact that the large number of East Asian students who matriculate at U.S. colleges every year represent one of the richest venues for technology transfer of the many such venues East Asian countries operate. This is as true of South Korea as it is of China and Japan.

The figures tell part of the story. In September 1996, there were over 150,000 East Asian students studying in the United States at the undergraduate level or above, including 39,613 Chinese students from the PRC and and 32,272 from Taiwan, 45,531 Japanese, and 36,231 students from South Korea, according to the New York-based Institute of International

Education.[46] Some 42 percent of the Korean students were enrolled in graduate courses—mostly science, technology, and business management. The knowledge these students acquire at American universities is so important to South Korea's industrial competitiveness that ROK corporations seek to recruit them, along with American citizens of Korean ancestry, directly from U.S. campuses.

For example, on September 5, 1995, *Hanguk Kyongje Sinmun* observed that South Korea's industrial groups were greatly increasing their hiring of overseas graduate students and devising new strategies to attract them. Citing industry sources, the paper said that the ROK's four big technical conglomerates—Samsung, Hyundai, LG, and Daewoo—were expected to hire fifteen hundred foreign degree holders, more than double the figure of the previous year. Reporting the same development, *Maeil Kyongje Sinmun* on October 3, 1995, stated that South Korea's major manufacturing groups would each hire from thirty to three hundred advanced degree holders from U.S. colleges in the latter part of the year. Recruitment would be aimed at "ethnic Korean-Americans and Koreans studying abroad."

Two years later, *Hanguk Kyongje Sinmun* reported: "While job opportunities for college grads at home are getting narrower, Korean businesses' employment doors are wide open to students currently studying abroad and regarded as promising employees, as the conglomerates step up their recruitment efforts in the United States." LG reportedly sent a thirty-person recruiting team to MIT, Harvard, UCLA, Stanford, and other prestigious universities to hire five hundred "Korean students." Samsung had *sixty personnel officers* scouting American campuses in 1997.[47]

Academic recruiting usually begins through local briefings, arranged in some cases by Korean graduates of American colleges sent back to their alma maters by their South Korean employers. It is also done over the Internet, or at job fairs run by professional employment firms, such as one hosted in Los Angeles in September 1995 by a dozen ROK companies to interview some 2,000 "ethnic Koreans and Koreans studying overseas who had come from all over the United States to seek jobs in South Korea or with its US subsidiaries."[48] Campus fliers are also used. A while ago someone put a brochure in my mailbox titled "Job Opportunities for Doosan Group." Science and business "candidates of Korean nationality"—a term meaning all ethnic Koreans regardless of citizenship—were invited to send photographs and resumes to addresses in Korea or the United States.

Many South Korean "students" in the United States are already employed.

The January 14, 1995, *Korea Herald* reported a plan by the Ministry of Science and Technology to expand the number of Korean technicians sent overseas by the government to obtain Ph.D.s from 182 in 1994 to 250 in 1995. In addition, the government planned to "dispatch" 460 researchers to foreign institutes that year. *Hanguk Kyongje Sinmun* had editorialized earlier for an increase in the number of Koreans given support to study abroad "so advanced foreign technology can be obtained."[49]

In another technique modeled after Japan, Korean companies invite U.S. universities to form "international industrial-academic cooperative associations" for joint study of advanced technology. Samsung Electronics in 1995 was doing research in memory semiconductors with Stanford, the University of Texas, and the University of Arizona; in nonmemory semiconductors with the University of Illinois; and in LCD units with Kent State. LG Electronics had assembled a "joint research cooperative structure" of thirty-two foreign universities, including MIT, Stanford, and Purdue, with an investment of $10 million.[50] Kolon Data Communications spent $400,000 for a laboratory in an industrial complex run by MIT, staffed with MIT engineers, expatriate Koreans, and Koreans studying abroad.[51]

Academic cooperation can also take the form of joint research contracts between South Korean government labratories and American universities, such as deals signed by MOST's Electronics and Telecommunications Research Institute (ETRI) in 1994 for computer software and high-speed communications technology. In both cases ETRI had immediate plans to pass the technology on to ROK manufacturers.[52]

Finally, Korea also funds academic "centers of excellence" in an effort to attract international scientists to Seoul to share their knowledge. In mid-1994, the Korea Institute of Science and Technology (part of the science ministry) reportedly hired a famous U.S. scientist from Berkeley to help build a world-class research center in South Korea.[53] A few months later, the Korea Advanced Institute of Science and Technology (a state-run graduate school) announced plans to host another center of excellence featuring a number of Nobel Prize winners invited to teach and conduct research.[54]

Academic connections also facilitate Seoul's participation in joint international research. Since the initial research is noncommercial, countries are more willing to share technology than they would through conventional channels. As KIST's director himself put it, "Since the advanced countries allow us access to technology in such public domain areas as environment and energy, having government-funded institutes participate in international technology development activities can be a golden opportunity to acquire the latest technology for a small fee."[55]

Using Technology to Obtain Technology

Paralleling the growth in the use of academic links as a transfer venue, the Internet and online databases are also proving to be of immense value in helping South Korea obtain foreign technology. In March 1994, the Korea Institute of Industrial Technology Information (another MOST affiliate) spent $7.5 million upgrading its KINITI-IR (information retrieval) system, a nationwide network that provides online access to advanced industrial technology in foreign and domestic databases. The network reportedly "makes available in a systematic fashion industrial, scientific, and technological data needed by Korean industry for R&D and technical development."[56] Subscribers can access eight foreign databases holding some 18 million items from foreign sources.[57]

In mid-1994, MOST's Systems Engineering Research Institute (SERI) linked its Korea Research Online Network (KREONet) with a data network operated by the European R&D information center DANTE, providing South Koreans with "easy access to the most up-to-date S&T information available in Europe."[58] One SERI official called the system a "magic box" for South Korean S&T development. Then in September 1995 SERI reported that it had linked KREONet with Japan's IMNET through underwater fiber optic cable. Billed as a "high-speed information highway between South Korea and Japan," the connection allows ROK researchers to access computer networks belonging to Japanese universities and research labs directly, without going through the Internet.[59]

Meanwhile the Korea Research and Development Information Center (KORDIC, part of KIST) announced in 1994 an automated machine translation system that gave Korean researchers access to the JOIS database of the Japan Information Center of Science and Technology using *hangul*-based queries.[60] KORDIC was already operating an online database service called KRISTAL (Korea Research Information of Science and Technology Access Line) that provides domestic and foreign S&T data to ROK companies, universities, and national labs, according to a *Brief Users' Guide* published by

KIST in September 1994. It also connects to a database of scientists in the former Soviet Union (called CISSTMAN) and to computers with information on 4,319 scientists in the United States and 1,436 in Japan.[61] In 1996, the system was upgraded (KRISTAL-II) to store some 1 million foreign S&T items to support more detailed searches.[62]

Besides these government-run databases and search engines (including others I shall discuss later in the chapter), private and semi-private South Korean companies also purvey electronic access to foreign S&T data. In August 1995, Korea PC Communications working jointly with patents lawyers announced it would provide online information on foreign technology, products, and projects in semiconductors, computers, and software, along with detailed information on persons and points of contact for transferring this technology.[63] In 1997, the Korea-U.S. Foundation for Industry and Technology Cooperation (KUFIT) opened an Internet site called "Korea-U.S. Technet" to provide ROK companies with "up-to-date information necessary for technological cooperation with U.S.-based firms," including a directory of sources that facilitate high-tech transfers.[64]

Korean corporations also use the Internet for foreign recruitment. In 1995, Korea Telecom advertised (in English) on the news group <soc.culture. korean> for specialists in switching, mobile and satellite communications, microwave technology, and network management. The ROK government-invested company used a recruiting service run by Samsung's Information Systems Business, which posts ads from various Korean companies to the Internet. Daewoo Electronics went online in early 1995 to "recruit high-quality research personnel in next generation state-of-the-art research fields." Daewoo reportedly expects "to easily secure outstanding research persons from the advanced countries through free exchanges with prestigious universities and research institutes throughout the world."[65]

Some Korean companies go a step further in their electronic recruitment efforts. According to the May 11, 1996 *Maeil Kyongje Sinmun*, Cheil Food and Chemicals in an effort "to secure the services of top-notch people in a timely manner" compiled a database of foreign students and technical experts, including ethnic Korean scientists in the United States and foreign job seekers who had applied for positions over the Internet. Cheil also sought "to obtain data on foreign officers resident in South Korea, on the sons and daughters of diplomats, and on high-level internationally oriented people from developing countries, and vigorously expedite their recruitment."

Institutional Collectors

As noted in the foregoing discussion, the South Korean government is intimately involved in transferring foreign technology, at little or no cost, from
what it calls the "advanced countries." The number of government institutions engaged in these efforts runs up quickly—more than two dozen by
my count—if research institutes affiliated with ministries, councils that
cross ministerial boundaries, and various ad hoc organizations receiving
government support are included. The profusion of collectors is perplex-
ing not only to outsiders trying to understand South Korea's S&T transfer
structure but also to the ROK government itself, which periodically attempts to consolidate foreign technology collection and rationalize its
distribution.

By and large, three state institutions play the major, formal roles in the
government's foreign technology collection: the Ministry of Science and
Technology (MOST), the Ministry of Trade and Industry (MOTIE), and
the National Intelligence Service (NIS, formerly the Agency for National
Security Planning or NSP). MOST and MOTIE have direct analogues
in Japan's Science and Technology Agency (now MEXT) and Ministry of
International Trade and Industry (now METI) and, like the two Japanese
organizations, are bureaucratic rivals. NIS, as we shall see later, is tasked
with covert collection of foreign technology in addition to its regular
intelligence-related activities; it functions in this sense like China's Ministry
of State Security.

MOST and MOTIE conduct technology transfer operations directly or
through their affiliated offices. Their activities range from benign to hostile. An example of the former is MOST's ROK-U.S. Science and Technology
Forum held annually in Washington, D.C., which serves as a corridor between South Korea's S&T establishment and U.S. high-tech companies.
The forum's goals were reported as "advancing national R&D proposals,
promoting joint research in basic sciences, and developing a plan for ROK-
U.S. cooperation in advanced industrial technology."[66] At the other end of
the spectrum are reports of MOST using its twenty consolidated offices
overseas to step up the flow of foreign S&T information gathered at "strategic sites" throughout the world,[67] and that the same ministry (through
KINITI) has been running "workshops" to train specialists in technology
transfer.[68]

A second category of institutional collectors is, of course, South Korea's corporations, which rival MOST and MOTIE in the resources they direct at acquiring and indigenizing foreign technology. Samsung's intelligence network is reputed to be "massive, pervasive, highly effective," and, in some estimates, even more important to the conglomerate's success than its management. Samsung expects every employee to act as an intelligence collector. Besides the information employees gather on their own, the conglomerate also runs an "acquaintance survey system" through which employees above a certain rank are queried about friends and relatives in politics, business, finance, and the media.[69]

Information obtained by Samsung personnel who have been sent abroad is stored in the group's Overseas Areas Research Institute. Third-year employees returning from a year abroad rotate for one week through the institute, while those stationed overseas four to five years spend *three months* being debriefed. Their information is passed to Samsung's subsidiaries, where special teams evaluate, classify, and enter it in databases.[70] In addition, Samsung opened an Industrial Business Research Institute in 1994 to act as a clearinghouse for business intelligence on foreign countries. The institute was staffed with some one hundred full-time area specialists, including former diplomats, Koreans with foreign citizenship, Korea Trade and Investment Promotion Agency officials, and Samsung employees with experience abroad.[71]

Samsung's technology collection efforts can be quite proactive. In July 1993 the chief of its production technology team used a fake ID to enter an LG refrigerator plant to spy on its rival.[72] The next year another Samsung subsidiary, Samsung Heavy Industries, was implicated when four of its employees were arrested inside another company's crane factory photographing parts and equipment.[73] These cases, which the Seoul media called the tip of the iceberg,[74] apply to industrial espionage done domestically, although there are indications that the practice extends overseas. For example, one news magazine described the case of "a South Korean company 'S,'" which sought Russian electronics technology. According to the magazine, company S "took shortcuts and was able to get a whole blueprint on microfilm of the technology it wanted." It then "used other means," presumably a bribe, to enlist a Russian technician's help in explaining the blueprint.[75]

Closer to home was Iljin Corporation's theft of industrial diamond technology from General Electric. The incident, described by Schweizer (1993:

176–85), was widely reported in the ROK press because of GE's initial decision to sue the company in court instead of seeking an outside settlement, which is the usual practice.[76] General Electric's suit was based on evidence that Iljin had paid a former GE employee more than $1 million for stolen materials related to its diamond technology. Although GE won the lawsuit, it opted to settle privately because of the likelihood the U.S. court's ruling would not be enforced in South Korea.[77] Reacting to the suit, *Chugan Maegyong* claimed the contract with the ex-GE worker "followed a general principle of civil society which regards technical consultations with retired technicians in a given industry a universal practice carried out by all companies in modern industrial society."[78] Another major business publication, *Hanguk Kyongje Sinmun*, warned, incredibly, that the U.S. move "clashes directly with the ROK government's policy of indigenizing foreign technology."[79]

While intensely competitive in their marketing practices, South Korean corporations are able at times to cooperate in the one area where their interests coincide: obtaining technology from foreign companies. In 1994 a group of specialists from industry and academia founded a private organization called the Advanced Industrial Technology Institute in order "to support research, analysis, and cooperative projects that relate to technology innovation and transfer between countries." According to *Maeil Kyongje Sinmun*, which covered the story, the group's purpose was "to meet the challenges of international technological competition" by providing input to national technology policies and through consultation with ROK companies on their technology development plans. The institute reportedly focuses "on finding and carrying out projects related to technology cooperation, joint research, and information exchange."[80]

Between these two categories of collectors—government ministries and private corporations—is a third category of ROK organizations best characterized as "quasi-official." Operated ostensibly as private non-profit foundations or associations, these groups carry out the same role in the area of technology transfer that South Korea's industrial organizations (e.g., the Federation of Korean Industries, the Korea Iron and Steel Association, etc.) do for the economy at large, namely, helping implement state policy and providing feedback to policy makers, while bridging gaps in Korea's S&T collection structure. Among scores of such institutions, the most prominent are the Korea Trade and Investment Promotion Agency (KOTRA), the Korea Science and Engineering Foundation (KOSEF), the Korea-U.S. Foundation for Industry and Technology Cooperation (KUFIT), and the General Federation of Korean Science and Technology Organizations.[81]

Modeled on Japan's JETRO (see Chapter 1), KOTRA historically has served a dual role as promoter of foreign trade and collector of business intelligence, including technology of value to Korean companies. This last function has assumed great importance in recent years in recognition of the need to support ROK competitiveness with technologically sound and innovative products.

KOTRA's ability to provide technological information to South Korean corporations is enormous. According to *Maeil Kyongje Sinmun*, the organization in 1993 invested $375 million into a "global information network" with hubs in Los Angeles, Brussels, and Singapore to collect reports on trade issues and perform various "surveys" for the government and South Korean corporations.[82] The same newspaper noted that KOTRA was embarking on a plan to provide concentrated support to smaller Korean businesses as well, particularly those that are technology intensive.[83] Then in 1996 KOTRA announced a reorganization that would put 82 bureaus and 111 "spokes" in 64 countries by 1999. These spokes are not offices per se, but individual field agents working out of overseas residences, who are responsible for "continuously providing information on the locale" to which they are assigned.[84] The plan was striking enough to earn a comment from the editor, who worried about how a lack of supervision over these "one-person intelligence agents" might lead to incidents.[85]

Besides its collection efforts, KOTRA actively promotes high-tech collaboration between ROK and foreign companies by arranging technology exchange fora. In 1994, KOTRA with backing from MOTIE held its "First ROK-U.S. Technology Plaza" in San Jose to "promote the transfer of advanced technology held by US firms for South Korea's technological development," according to *Maeil Kyongje Sinmun*. The newspaper observed that ROK companies attending the event were less interested in buying U.S. technology than in "more genuine forms of cooperation, such as establishing joint investment companies and joint research projects."[86] In 1995 another Technoplaza was run in Chicago, again with MOTIE's support. A 1996 event was held in New Jersey; KOTRA officials were especially pleased by the participation of U.S. university-affiliated research labs, which they considered a "turning point in the efforts of technology-hungry Korean companies to uncover providers of new technology."[87]

KOTRA also organizes "Technomarts" several times a year in South Korea or other countries "to build an information distribution system for technology transfers between companies and related institutions" (*Maeil Kyongje Sinmun*, March 2, 1995). Unlike its U.S. Technoplazas, they are semi-permanent and can include several countries as participants. One such technomart that opened in 1996 in Seoul under the theme "U.S. Advanced Technology Meets Korean Production Technology" was backed by both KINITI (a MOST affiliate) and KUFIT (a MOTIE client), demonstrating that the rival bureaucracies can make common cause on issues that count.[88]

Two more quasi-official institutions, one old and one new, round out our sketch of this aspect of Korea's technology transfer structure. The Korea Science and Engineering Foundation (KOSEF) was established in 1977 to launder the distribution of science ministry funds to favored colleges and programs and promote international cooperation in basic science. I have already described KOSEF's role in establishing overseas laboratories through its Science and Engineering Research Centers on ROK campuses.[89] KOSEF also sponsors postdoctoral research abroad (2,600 students since 1982, two-thirds of whom went to the United States), invites foreign scientists to South Korea for collaborative research, and brokers exchange agreements with foreign S&T agencies, including the U.S. National Science Foundation. It also acts as the nominal patron of the Korea-U.S. Science Cooperation Center in northern Virginia (see below). The other half of KOSEF's charter is serving the needs of Korean industry through cooperative seminars and its "Research Results Utilization System"—a network of databases with information on patents, research personnel, and technical reports.[90]

The Korea-U.S. Foundation for Industry and Technology Cooperation was established in 1994 with MOTIE funds to "transfer U.S. technology to South Korean small and medium-sized businesses."[91] *Maeil Kyongje Sinmun* called it an "appendage" of the Federation of Korean Industries and noted that it was authorized to lend individual ROK businesses importing certain U.S. technologies up to $500,000 with interest deferred.[92] A KUFIT press release dated October 8, 1997, described the foundation's main role as "a catalyst in facilitating the establishment of practical joint technology development projects," as distinct from MOST/KOSEF's more abstract orientation. KUFIT is also chartered to organize collaborative fora (such as the technomarts and technoplazas) with U.S. high-tech institutions, and to "dispatch personnel to U.S. corporations and technology research institutes to update themselves with the current status of development and to acquire production technologies." The press release revealed the essence of KUFIT's mission in the third paragraph as "the acquisition of top-notch technologies" from the United States, which "is never easy now that technologies are ever-changing and while technological protectionism is widespread."

Exploiting Expatriate Koreans

There is overwhelming evidence that Seoul manipulates expatriate scientists to transfer host country technology. For example, in May 1995 *Maeil Kyongje Sinmun* reported a high-level government source acknowledging "the technical personnel who really got the ROK semiconductor industry off to a start were ethnic Koreans in America."[93] The official went on to describe how South Korea would continue using Korean scientists abroad to compensate for a shortage of technical experts. In September of that year the science ministry announced its intent to "strengthen the recruitment of ethnic Korean scientists and technical personnel overseas to collect foreign scientific data."[94] That same month the Seoul press reported the completion of a "Korean Hall of Science and Technology" built to facilitate exchanges between visiting and domestic Korean scientists.[95]

South Korea's efforts to recruit Korean scientists living abroad were endorsed by former ROK president Kim Yong-sam in a 1996 Seoul speech before overseas Korean scientists, whom Kim asked to serve as a "bridgehead" for developing their "home country."[96] Acknowledging their contribution to Korea's technical progress, Kim said his government would streamline policies to facilitate more participation by overseas Koreans in the ROK's S&T programs. Two days before, the head of the American chapter of the Seoul-based "General Federation of Korean Science and Technology Organizations" had announced the establishment of a new Science and Technology Information Institute to "collect the latest US technology for transfer to Korea."[97]

This General Federation is an umbrella organization for more than 10,000 expatriate scientists divided into fourteen national chapters with a permanent headquarters in Seoul. According to *Chonja Sinmun*, the group has been holding "academic conferences" in South Korea since 1974 designed to give overseas Korean scientists an opportunity to "contribute to the fatherland's scientific and technological development and raise its competitiveness by exchanging with one another future state-of-the-art technology and S&T information."[98] The 1996 conference attracted 286 overseas "scientist-compatriots," 119 of them from the United States. Attendees were expected "to introduce the latest trends in foreign science and technology to Korea," and make a "major contribution" toward improving Korea's industrial technology and international competitiveness.[99]

Exchanges between Korean-American scientists and ROK technical personnel are not limited to the information that changes hands at conventions. Nor are they confined to esoteric scientific problems. At a press conference held for the heads of the fourteen overseas chapters, the president of the General Federation said there must be a "close cooperative relationship between the overseas Korean S&T associations on the one hand and South Korean companies overseas and their employees on the other hand."[100] Driving home the commercial goals of the exchange, the federation leader reportedly stressed the need for "close cooperative relationships between overseas scientists and technicians and South Korean companies here and abroad," adding that "starting this year, we will build up our capability to keep track of overseas S&T associations' activities and the information they provide."

The General Federation, as one might expect, is allied closely with the ROK's science ministry, as evidenced by their joint sponsorship of fellowships and other cooperative programs designed to promote early links between Korean scientists overseas and the ROK's private and state-run S&T facilities. The most egregious example I ran across is a joint project instituted in 1993 to "attract and make use of" expatriate Korean scientists and engineers working overseas in S&T fields. Subsequently known as the "Brainpool Project," its purpose was described as inducing "overseas Koreans and other foreign scientists to help South Korea acquire at an early date the newest science, technology, and know-how in the R&D stages in advanced countries."[101] The program offers foreign scientists with postdoctoral experience various rewards in exchange for six months of service at a South Korean sci-tech facility. Some fifty-seven foreign specialists were recruited in the first year, most of whom had Korean surnames and lived in the United States.[102]

The Federation is also connected with MOST through a joint center run by its largest and most important chapter—the Korean-American Scientists and Engineers Association (KSEA, formerly in Rockville, Maryland and now based in Vienna, Virginia) and KOSEF, which acts as a MOST subsidiary. This "Korea-U.S. Science Cooperation Center" began operating in 1997 with a mandate to "revitalize scientific and technological cooperation and information exchange between Korea and the U.S."[103] Portrayed in its English language literature as a cooperative research facility, it was described more frankly in the ROK media as an apparatus for coordinating technology transfers between Korean-American scientists and their South Korean counterparts. According to a science ministry press release dated February 13, 1997:

The center will be used as a place for mutual exchanges and cooperation between the 30,000-plus Korean scientists and engineers in America and scientists and engineers from the two countries. At first it will carry out academic interchanges and exchanges of information to raise mutual understanding and trust between the two countries' science and engineering communities. Over the long term, it will develop into a center for S&T cooperation between the two countries, finding and arranging joint research projects, and brokering industrial technology cooperative projects.

Maeil Kyongje Sinmun reported a day later that:

The main projects include expanding S&T cooperation and cultural exchanges, training second-generation [expatriate Korean] science students, and supporting KSEA. In addition, it will actively support Korean scientists and engineers in the United States and explain plans for applying advanced technology to South Korea.[104]

There can be no doubt that the center is controlled by the ROK government to channel American technology to South Korean S&T facilities and ultimately to the ROK companies against which U.S. firms compete. A MOST memorandum to KOSEF dated January 5, 1996, stipulated that KOSEF establish the center with MOST's financial support (article 1), that MOST cover the cost of the building (article 3), and that KOSEF make quarterly reports to the ministry on project results and planning (article 6).[105] The official connection was brought out again in MOST's February 13, 1997, press release, which affirmed that "MOST/KOSEF signed a project trust agreement" with the corporation running the center. It is also apparent in the membership of its board, whose four standing directors include the secretary general of

KOSEF, the science ministry's Science and Technology Cooperation Division chief, and the science counselor to the ROK embassy.

KSEA, with one to four branches in each of thirty-four states, is the largest but not the only expatriate S&T organization providing support to the "fatherland." Twenty more were listed in a directory of web servers hyperlinked to the online Korean-American Science and Technology Newsletter,[106] such as the Association of Korean Physicists in America (AKPA), the Korean Computer Scientists and Engineers Association, the Korean-American Aerospace Specialists Association, and several others. The newsletter posts a "Calendar of Scientific Meetings in Korea," announcements for positions at South Korean laboratories, and information on the ROK-U.S. "Technomarts." In view of the goal of these expatriate organizations to facilitate technological exchanges with South Korea, a sovereign foreign state, it is disturbing to note that many key members appear to hold sensitive posts at US government facilities. Among AKPA's membership, for example, are seventy employees of nuclear and other high-tech weapons-related U.S. research laboratories.[107]

Korean companies also position themselves to exploit expatriate sensitivity to their country of origin, although the relevance here to technology transfer is less transparent. For example, *Maeil Kyongje Sinmun* reported a comprehensive move by Dacom, a telecommunications firm, to catalog 103,000 shops and the 11,000-plus businesses and public organizations owned by ethnic Koreans in America. The newspaper said the information would be made available to companies in South Korea and to the "overseas Korean community" at large to "support their economic activities and the flow of information."[108]

Any doubts I had about how the South Korean government views the role of expatriate scientists were dispelled by a thirteen-page document entitled "A Plan to Make Use of Foreign Scientists and Engineers," drafted by the science ministry in August 1996.[109] The program, meant to address inadequacies in South Korea's S&T efforts, called for bolstering the country's scientific base and circumventing "technological protectionism" by identifying and recruiting scientists overseas who are willing to transfer new technology to the Republic of Korea. While acknowledging the success of past recruitment efforts, the report argued that "to build the foundation of a strategic global system to procure top personnel,"[110] Korea must "get more intelligence on top foreign scientists and engineers through cooperation with overseas Korean scientists and engineers associations."

Besides the science ministry, the report also named the Ministries of Finance and Economy, Justice, and Education as responsible for aspects of the program and stipulated that concrete plans to implement its measures be worked out by each government ministry.

Seoul's Response to the "IMF Crisis"

In 1997 South Korea faced a catastrophic liquidity crisis caused by corrupt lending practices and business over expansion. Soon after the International Monetary Fund (IMF) bailed the country out of its immediate financial difficulty, the Korean press and government began referring to the problem as the "IMF crisis," the implication being that foreigners were to blame. Inevitably, the "IMF crisis" became a rallying point for intensified foreign technology collection.

A few weeks after the magnitude of the economic problem had sunk in, the ROK government asked its national labs to help overcome the crisis by rendering "practical" support for product development and by "internationalizing" their research activities. KIST responded with a program to "conduct personnel swaps, information exchanges, and joint research with 57 institutions in 19 countries"; the Korea Institute of Machinery and Metals (a MOST affiliate) went ahead with plans for joint R&D centers at Stanford and MIT; and ROK officers stationed overseas at state-funded research centers stepped up their "systematic gathering of information on [host-country] research institutes, technologies, and personnel.[111] South Korean companies launched "more aggressive 'head hunting' operations" to recruit foreign technical experts.[112]

Coordinating S&T collection efforts with the needs of ROK manufacturers—long a bottleneck in South Korea's transfer programs—was also to enter a new dimension as a result of programs drafted by MOST's Science and Technology Policy Institute. According to a report released on December 9, 1997, separate collection programs run by the Ministries of Foreign Affairs, Trade and Industry, Science, and Defense were to be brought under a single "Science and Technology Foreign Cooperation Committee" to systematize collection strategy, integrate local operations, and avoid duplication of effort.[113] The committee was to be divided into groups of specialists by geographical region, who would interact with organizations such as KOTRA and STEPI on the one hand and the national labs, universities, and ROK companies on the other.

Designed to counter the "reluctance of advanced countries to transfer science and technology," the formula also called for local "Korea Centers" to collect S&T information and to create new overseas branches of government offices, national laboratories, and private companies to expedite transfers. In addition, STEPI offered to form an "Overseas Science and Technology Information Center" to integrate data collected by "overseas Korean scientists and engineers associations, Korean diplomatic and consular offices in foreign countries, large ROK trading companies, and the overseas offices of national labs."[114]

The program's final design surpassed even STEPI's ambitious proposals. The following article from the July 14, 1998, *Chonja Sinmun* describes what some might consider a blueprint for economic warfare, but which in the present study we prefer to treat as a tragic admission of the country's failure to keep pace with the world in science.

Foreign S&T Information Collection to Be Strengthened

South Korea's system for collecting foreign science and technology information is being greatly strengthened by the creation and execution of an annual foreign S&T information collection plan.

The Ministry of Science and Technology [MOST], having recently enacted "Regulations on Collecting and Making Use of Foreign Science and Technology Information," decided to go on and strengthen its existing foreign intelligence collection system with diversified collection venues, such as science attaches stationed abroad, intelligence councils, South Koreans dispatched to international organizations, business persons traveling overseas, and overseas research centers.

To accomplish this, MOST will redesignate its R&D information centers as "integrated foreign science and technology information management centers" and conduct annual surveys of ROK companies, universities, and national laboratories to find out what foreign science and technology information they need in order to expand foreign intelligence collection and its domestic utilization. MOST will form and run a Foreign S&T Information Council [to head the operation] composed of fifteen or fewer members chaired by the chief of its Science and Technology Cooperation Division.

MOST will also organize and operate ten intelligence councils through overseas science attaches, to be composed of expatriate Korean scientists and engineers, overseas science organizations, overseas research centers affiliated with South Korea's national labs, and people connected with local South Korean companies and research institutes, forming a broad-scale overseas human network for in-depth intelligence collection.

MOST in addition will engage full-scale in collecting and distributing foreign science and technology information through cyberspace, strengthening the links between providers of information and its customers. Moreover, it will require Korean businessmen traveling seven days or more overseas to turn in data when they return to South Korea on the information they collected overseas.

A system of rewards will be put into effect for cases where the scientific and technological information and materials that individuals and organizations provide are judged to be of great importance for domestic scientific and technological development.[115]

Chonja Sinmun followed up with an editorial endorsing the program.[116] The government's decision to move in this direction, the editor said, was based on its belief that the country cannot "overcome IMF strictures" or boost its technology base without augmenting its ability to collect against foreign scientific and industrial targets. He also noted that the science ministry's move to strengthen foreign technology collection coincided with a realignment in the intelligence service's function toward "collecting foreign economic, industrial, and scientific intelligence."

South Korea's intelligence agency has a history of gathering information on foreign technology. Schweizer wrote in 1993 that the "NSP is active widely overseas and has a close relationship with the enormous conglomerates that dominate the Korean economy," adding that it "has run scores of bag operations against U.S. businesses" (17). He also said that in 1980 the NSP was given a new mandate to conduct "espionage to aid South Korea's economic development." Predating by more than a decade the PRC government's own shift in attitude toward expatriate scientists, the committee charged with the NSP's reorganization, according to Schweizer, "called for a new approach to relations between the intelligence service and Koreans living overseas. Rather than viewing overseas residents as potential threats, they were to be viewed as possible recruits and allies" (206).

Schweizer's assessment is consistent with my own findings on the intelligence agency's role based on ROK media reports over the past few years. On May 6, 1993, *Chungang Ilbo* noted that the NSP had put more emphasis on collecting foreign technology and was hiring "specialists in industrial intelligence." The following year *Tonga Ilbo* said the agency had made economic information gathering its "top priority" for 1994. The newspaper cited an address by the NSP chief to South Korean President Kim Yong-sam promising to "emphasize the collection of economic, industrial, and environmental data" to help South Korean industries prepare for the "coming era of borderless competition."[117] *Yonhap* in late 1997 stated that President-

Elect Kim Dae-jung was drafting measures for the NSP that entailed an "intensive build-up of economic information-collecting capabilities" against overseas targets.[118] Media reports in early 1998 suggested that the agency was contemplating *selling* foreign S&T intelligence to South Korean corporations.[119] A "master plan" issued in 1999 listed "collecting intelligence on industrial technology" as the most important foreign agenda item.[120]

These chapters have shown that East Asian "ingenuity" today is a myth. The region clearly suffers from a shortage of innovative talent, as evidenced by these desperate attempts to assimilate the creations of others. It remains for me to show where the origin of this problem lies.

Chapter Four
Asia's Creativity Problem

A student accustomed to elaborate reasoning and detailed argument would be at a loss to understand what these Chinese philosophers were saying.

—Feng Yu-lan

Four Measures of Dependency

The first part of this book was meant to drive home a truth which Asian policy makers appreciate but which escapes many Westerners, namely, that East Asia's modernization has depended almost entirely on innovations brought in from the West. This fact is apparent on four levels. To begin with, it is inherent in the concept of modernization, at least as that concept is understood in the East. As evidenced in the phrase "advanced countries of Europe and America," which is invoked by East Asians as a common standard of comparison, progress in East Asia is measured by an ability to match or digest the scientific advances made in the West. This observation has been the focus of scholarly attention for several decades and there is no point belaboring it here.[1]

Explicit recognition of this dependency by East Asian government officials and S&T managers constitutes another level of confirmation. As noted in the Introduction to this book, over the past decade or so science administrators in all three countries—Japan, China, and South Korea—have mapped out plans to reproduce what they believe to be the infrastructure responsible for Western scientific creativity, oblivious to the fact that these foreign research institutions are, in Marxist terms, only the superstructure of underlying social relationships, which the East Asian reforms don't begin to touch. Putting aside the deeper question whether creativity can be copied at all, this current effort to emulate Western creativity is simply an extension of a formula devised in China more than a century ago called *tǐyòng*: using Western techniques while keeping the essence of Eastern culture.

Aware of the limits of their own technology, nineteenth-century East Asian modernizers imported Western-style factories and (selectively) administrative and educational institutions as means of shielding traditional patterns of behavior that made up the core elements of Asian culture. The idea was to adopt only what was needed for survival and to preserve the legacy of indigenous culture as defined by its privileged strata. The formula did not work then and will not work now, because resisting change in some areas interferes with a society's ability to institute changes overall. This is doubly true when the culture one is trying to protect is strongly inimical to change. One can go on *grafting* innovations made by other societies onto one's own, but it is futile to plan for a society of thinkers willing to innovate in prescribed directions only.

A third measure of East Asia's dependence on Western science is the massive borrowing documented in the preceding chapters. Technology transfer—from purchase to theft—is not unique to East Asia. Most countries practice it, some more zealously than others. France, Israel, and the former Soviet Union are notorious Western examples. But there are differences between the universal practice and what we have seen to be true of the technology transfer practiced by the East, differences that involve more than the variety and scale with which these operations are carried out.

In the West, technology transfers supplement the basic research conducted by corporations and national laboratories. Western companies typically seek outside technologies that add to the marketability of products or ideas already within their grasp. When a European company sets up a research lab in the United States, it is aiming not to skim off new ideas about future products but to adapt technology it already owns to a new market. In East Asia's case, technology transfer is a *substitute* for basic research. Although incremental improvements to existing technologies are achieved by Asians in quick succession, fundamental changes of the sort that characterize the Western approach to development are rare.

A fourth measure of Asia's reliance on Western innovation is found in the foreign terms that make up its scientific vocabulary. Since a word's origin reflects the source of the concept it represents, the thousands of Western technical terms in East Asian languages, in contrast to the handful of words brought into European languages from Asia, demonstrate clearly the one-sided nature of the East-West science relationship. We met this theme earlier in connection with Japan's recurring cycle of foreign adaptations, but mention it again because it aptly illustrates the depth of Asia's dependence on Western science and because it brings us closer to our goal of identifying the root cause of this dependence, which I believe to be fundamentally linguistic in nature.

There are three ways Asian languages import Western vocabulary: by adapting a word and its phonology, by calques or "loan translations," or by borrowing the Western word as it is. Adaptation is facilitated in Japanese and Korean by indigenous phonetic scripts that allow users to represent foreign terms by imitating the original sounds. Due to phonological differences between the source and borrowing languages, these adaptations often end up being caricatures of the original sound, although they are generally recognizable for what they are. To promote identification with the source concept, Japanese and Korean scientific dictionaries often provide the original Western term after the *kana* or *hangul* entry. Glossaries for newer fields such as microelectronics, computers, and bioengineering depend so heavily on Western vocabulary that they are often indistinguishable from bilingual Japanese-English or Korean-English dictionaries.

Chinese, which has no approved phonetic script, uses its characters as a syllabary to represent foreign terms when the words are still new. This purely phonetic use of the characters is becoming popular in Chinese-speaking areas despite the penalties incurred from excess redundancy.[2] Alternatively, Chinese replaces the morphemes in the foreign term with indigenous equivalents and renders the term as a loan translation, for example, (Mandarin) *húizhuǎn pán* ("rotation" + "plate") = "rotary disk" and *màichōng fēnxi qì* ("pulse" + "analyze" + "device") = "pulse analyzer." Japanese and Korean also use this format to introduce foreign terms. Although all three Asian languages often share a common character-based equivalent of a borrowed Western term, the universality is compromised by different character shapes,[3] varying degrees of character literacy, and the option Koreans have of writing the term in *hangul.*

Closely related to loan translations are Western-inspired terms coined in East Asia through Sinitic morphemes that model the foreign concept but not the structure of the word. For example, Japanese *shūha* ("periodic" + "wave") = "frequency" and *kembikyō* ("reveal" + "tiny" + "mirror") = "microscope." In this case, the connection with Western vocabulary is less obvious, although the stimulus for the coinages is known to historians. Lacking terms to render new Western concepts, Asian scholars search for Sinitic morphemes whose meanings approximate the Western concept. Since these morphemes are expressed in Chinese characters, little attention is paid to the viability of the sound. The result is a large number of homonyms, which lead to ambiguity in speech and, I suspect, in scientific thought as well.

The third major class of linguistic borrowings is foreign (generally English) words, in their original alphabetic representation. While still uncommon in nontechnical discourse, the scientific writing done in China, South Korea, and Japan introduces Western vocabulary directly into the text, often without elucidating comments. Readers are expected to know enough about the subject and the foreign language to understand it. Excused by Asians as "international" practice, it is English and other Western terms that inundate the languages of the East, not vice versa, constituting yet another indication of Asia's reliance on Western innovation.

Outsourcing Creativity

I have given examples of East Asia's dependence on Western science and technology but have not sufficiently emphasized that this borrowing involves not process or even product technology, but what Asians refer to as "wellspring" technology. No one denies the extraordinary ability of East Asian manufacturers to upgrade existing products, streamline and improve (Japanese: *kaizen*) production processes, and commercialize products from technology that exists in laboratories. By the same token, few people, least of all East Asians, would dispute that the region's ability to generate wholly new technologies has not kept pace with its accomplishments in manufacturing, nor with the West's capacity for scientific innovation.

This assessment is widely shared by scholars of East Asia's postwar development. Herbig, after giving due credit to the Japanese for process innovation, notes that "Japanese have rarely made a spectacular discovery or product breakthrough that has led to an entirely new industry." He further states that most of the country's technological innovations came from theories and ideas developed in the West (1995:16). Herbig cites a MITI study covering 1960–80 that credits Japan with 26 technological innovations, only two of which were considered radical, compared to 237 innovations in the United States, 65 of which were radical. Private surveys show the same disparity. In 1995, Herbig was still able to write, "Few examples exist to date of Japanese originality in technological development" (64).

Others, including scholars disposed to see Japan's accomplishments in a more favorable light, have come to the same conclusion. Peters concedes the "Japanese culture and approach to research is particularly well suited to manufacturing process R&D and is not suited to R&D leading to product innovation. Indeed in most industries, Japanese importation of technology and Japanese R&D has not led to radical new product introductions" (1987:184). Okimoto, while acknowledging the Japanese government's efforts to bolster basic R&D, argues in the same vein "None of the national research projects has yet achieved momentous breakthroughs in state-of-the-art technology. Some have failed to reach even modest objectives" (1989:67).

The "step-by-step" (Japanese: *ippo ippo*) approach to technological change, with a corresponding disdain for radical innovation, also describes the attitudes of Chinese and Koreans. Fischer's observation that China has "a continued preference for process innovation rather than product innovation" (1989:129) can be (and has been) applied to the other Asian countries. Frieman's thesis (1989:277) that Chinese have done well at making "incremental improvements" to technology imported from abroad, but have not made revolutionary changes to technology is applicable to the region generally. South Korea's failure to generate substantive technological innovations was evident at the 1993 Taejon Science Exposition, a showcase meant to highlight the nation's scientific accomplishments, which lacked any sign of progress in the basic sciences.

It is important not to confuse rhetoric with results. The Chinese press from about 1997 began extolling "new, creative technology" (*xīn chuàngzàoxìng jìshù*) as the key to the country's future competitiveness. The impression one gets is that China is poised to become a hotbed of scientific progress. In South Korea, too, it has been impossible for several years to read anything on technology development that does not hammer at the same theme of replacing adaptation and improvement with basic scientific research. The hidden message in both cases is that neither country has made much headway in this endeavor and each is desperately doing what it can to refocus the efforts of its technological community.

Complementing these calls for more emphasis on basic research is a shift in technology transfer patterns away from buying and licensing technology and toward acquiring foreign technology in its early stages. Forced by heavy royalty payments and shorter product cycles on the one hand, and by frustration in their own attempts at basic science on the other, East Asians have developed various ways of "outsourcing creativity." One such device is the overseas research center, operated by Japan and South Korea as "bridgeheads into the technology source land" of advanced countries. Functioning at first as technology scanning facilities, the institutes evolved into venues to transfer advanced technology from foreigners willing to market their knowledge of new techniques, and ultimately became full-fledged laboratories for sponsoring creative research by host country scientists.

The same ersatz creativity is also evidenced in the links East Asian countries foster with foreign universities, which in the West are at the cutting edge of basic science. According to Herbig, "Every major U.S. research university has at least one Japanese corporate research facility nearby" (1995:219). Reid and Schriescheim report that Japan spends more on U.S. university-based research than any other foreign country (1996:97). In Chapter 3 I noted many instances of similar efforts by South Korea to harness the creativity of foreign universities. Although China's efforts still lag in this regard, the country cannot be accused of neglecting opportunities presented by the open atmosphere of Western institutions to further its S&T agenda. China, like Japan and South Korea, has sent large numbers of students and researchers overseas as much to learn *how* research is done as to transfer knowledge of specific products.

This last point is illustrated by China's recent policy shift toward its overseas students, noted in Chapter 2. While lamenting the loss to China of students who stay overseas after completing their formal studies, China's science managers now recognize that these unreturned students represent a huge asset in terms of their ability to contribute not just to existing Chinese research programs but to future paths for basic research. This forward-looking approach to the use of expatriate scientists stems from a realization that China's future depends on its ability to generate entirely new technologies or, failing that, to access new technologies abroad while they are still ideas, long before they hit the marketplace or battlefield.

Whether China will succeed in its attempt to do creative work in a wide spectrum of sciences, or achieve the more modest goal of excellence in selected areas, remains to be seen. Discussions in the PRC media about the need to promote creativity suggest that the issue involves more than a decision to invest capital and remove the more blatant political obstacles to scientific inquiry. Certainly there are few indications that China has been able to translate its rhetoric about creative research into tangible world-class achievements. To the contrary, China's government-sponsored programs to foster innovation are the antithesis of the laissez faire approach needed for creativity to emerge. Shrill warnings about the need for more basic research and endless reminders about China's creative past tell us more about the dilemma China faces than about the country's prospects for scientific renewal.

Meanwhile, in Japan and Korea the verdict is already in: efforts to supplant foreign borrowing with indigenous research in basic science have floundered, not for lack of funding or interest, though they admittedly are factors, but for the simple, compelling reason that Japanese and Korean scientists are not very creative. Although many reasons are given for this lack of creativity, the existence of the problem is hardly disputed. Van Wolferen, for example, notes:

For three post-war decades the creativity problem did not worry anyone much, since many basic inventions were in the public domain and technology could be bought cheaply. But as Japanese industry begins to reach into areas in which no one else is ahead, and as foreign patents become less simple to obtain than in the past, the need for Japanese inventions increases. (1989:89)

Herbig concludes that "no solid evidence exists that basic research has been fruitful in Japan," adding that this "basic shortcoming in research stems from its weakness in creativity."[4] Dreyfuss observes similarly, "The underlying reason that the Japanese need to tap American brain power is to make up for the great weakness of their industrial juggernaut: the lack of basic research and creativity" (1987:84). Evidence of Korea's failure to achieve prominence in science is available in indices of scientific papers that show South Korea ranking last or nearly last among developed countries year after year in the number of technical articles published. Internet newsgroups are also rife with speculation on topics such as "What Ails Korean Creativity,"[5] and its implications for the country's international competitiveness.

Science and Technology

If East Asia lacks scientific creativity, how does one account for the wealth of technological achievements made there today and throughout history? Do not science and technology occupy a continuum in terms of the creativity they require? If so, then is East Asia's creativity "problem" simply the result of a social preference that accords priority to practical achievements over theoretical speculation, and that can, therefore, be addressed by directing resources at a higher end of a sliding scale?

The answer is both yes and no. East Asians, now and through most of their history, have been more prone than Westerners to apply their talents to projects that promise practical returns. Problems are solved and improvements are made not by rebuilding structures from the ground up but gradually, through "adjustments" (Japanese: *chōsei*[6]) to existing paradigms. Westerners are apt to neglect incremental change for new approaches that may end in a quantum leap forward but often just fizzle out. In Rosenberg and Steinmueller's view,

American thinking about the innovation process has focused excessively upon the earliest stages—the kinds of new products or technologies that occasionally emerge out of basic research, the creative leaps that sometimes establish entirely new product lines, the activities of the "upstream" inventor or scientist rather than the "downstream" engineer. . . . [Japanese] have a much deeper appreciation of the economic significance of these vital development activities than their American counterparts. (1988:230)

These "vital development activities" certainly qualify as creative, and the fact that they may also lead to improvement in a company's bottom line hardly makes them less so. By the same token, it makes no sense to call "creative" the useless flights of fancy that characterize much of what passes as original work in the West. For this reason, serious definitions of creativity include peer recognition as a qualifying measure. It should also be noted that creative advances occur both in science (knowledge formatted with reference to general truths) and technology (the application of knowledge to practical purposes). Neither field holds a monopoly on creative insight, nor is insight per se the normal path of progress. Science, like technology, mostly proceeds step by step, with every legitimate inspiration preceded by multiple frustrations and followed by endless verification and adjustments.

These caveats aside, there does seem to be a *qualitative* gap between the

creativity usually associated with technological innovation and that underlying the paradigm shifts that give rise to entirely new products and knowledge. Moreover, this distinction is a function not just of the magnitude of
the difference in end states but of the nature of the mental and social
processes that lead to the new state. Additive changes are useful to a point.
They may, indeed, be a necessary part of the process leading to radical innovation. But beyond that point, a different mindset is required, characterized by an ability to balance knowledge with spontaneity. Moving from
incremental change to radical innovation, in other words, is not simply a
matter of a significant number of people "deciding" to emphasize less of
one and more of the other. The two types of creativity are tied to deep-
seated differences in psychology and social norms.

This gap between types of creativity—one radical, the other incremental; one associated with knowledge breakthroughs, the other with routine
development—has been noted by scholars concerned with the general case
and with Asia in particular. Copp and Zanella in their study *Discovery, Innovation, and Risk*, draw an early distinction between the two kinds of thinking
needed for progress in the two areas, noting that "Scientific discovery and
reasoning does not always foster technological development [and] a great
deal of technical innovation can proceed without a full understanding of
the underlying science" (1993:ix). Herbig observes similarly that

Creativity and innovation may be intimately related but are distinct concepts. Innovation is almost always a collaborative enterprise, requiring the cooperation of numerous individuals. In contrast, creativity is viewed as a flash of insight, an "ahha"
experience in which two bodies or matrices of thought, considered remote from
one another, are suddenly joined. (1995:10)

Herbig identifies the latter process with the stereotype Western model of
creativity that "reflects frontier thinking and is based on the concept of individual freedom, which favors the discovery of new ideas and product
breakthroughs. . . . it cannot be forced but must be allowed to develop
spontaneously in its own way after the proper conditions have been provided" (10). Japanese creativity, on the other hand, is "responsive, eclectic,
focused, and practical. [Its goal] is not just to create new products and
ideas but also to build teamwork and a sense of harmony . . . Japanese creativity is like fusion: Ideas from many people are gathered, assimilated, and
squeezed into a new product" (11).

Although Japan's approach to creativity has served the country well materially, it is also responsible for its poor showing in basic science. While manageable in earlier times when change happened more slowly, we have seen how the stepped up pace of product innovation during the last few decades has forced Japan to rely increasingly on foreign support for new ideas. This neglect of abstract, creative science in favor of what Herbig calls "idea refinement" and "idea recycling" (1995:8) seems, moreover, to have existed through most of Japan's history. Yukawa observes that it was not until the Meiji Restoration (1868) when Japan, influenced by Western thought, began developing an intellectual foundation for abstract science. There was nothing comparable in Japan's intellectual tradition to the "thoroughgoing rationalism" needed for modern science to emerge (1973:55–66).

Nakamura offers a similar assessment of Japan's past, noting that it was largely "as a result of Western influence [that] the Japanese people attained any degree of scientific self-consciousness and objective perception" (1964:574). Intuitive perception of concrete reality made the Japanese consummate technicians but was inadequate as a tool for exploiting and understanding science. This characterization of Japan's past remains applicable today.

Science in the Middle Kingdom

The above comments pertain to Japan, a country that until recently made no claim to creative accomplishment in the basic sciences, and that is widely perceived as the world's foremost practitioner of borrowing and adaptation. What about China? Here the perception is different, although the details vary depending on one's point of view.

Chinese themselves are convinced that their present condition vis-à-vis the advanced Western countries is an aberration from the historical norm, when China led the world in the variety and sophistication of its technology. This "temporary" condition may seem long from a Western perspective but is thought to be brief in the Asian scheme of things. Westerners, for their part, largely accept the notion of a long and fruitful Golden Age of Chinese Science, exemplified by its Four Great Inventions of paper, printing, gunpowder, and the compass (the fact that they can be counted on the fingers of one hand seems to trouble no one.) Finally, there is Joseph Needham's multivolume *Science and Civilization in China*, which

Western Sinologists believe debunked the misguided notion that China cannot do science.

I might be more charitable and ignore this false image of Chinese science were I not convinced that this and innumerable other myths, which run the gamut from language to politics, play a principal role in perpetuating problems inimical to China's own self-interest and to the world's greater happiness. To get right to the point, few of China's scientific accomplishments had anything to do with the kind of creativity we are discussing here. What is at issue is the ability of a people to deliberately confront objectified problems, reduce them to their core conceptual elements, and reorganize these elements to provide an abstract, unified explanation for phenomena that could not be understood in terms of the old paradigm. Whether this new paradigm leads to practical uses depends on a different set of skills, as does the refinement of particular applications and so on. While China's ability to find concrete applications for existing ideas is legendary, its record of novelty in basic science is less stellar.

One must bear in mind that complexity is no measure of creativity. To the contrary, creative solutions *reduce* complexity and are considered valid to the degree that they are parsimonious. Given its size, population, long history, and continuous contacts with non-Chinese people, the fact that China has evolved into a complex civilization supported by many technological innovations is no more a function of scientific creativity than a biological organism's complexity, generated through successive mutations and environmental interaction, is a measure of *its* creativity. In both cases the innovations owe little or nothing to deliberate reflection, and cannot be construed as creative in the same sense as used to describe the outcome of abstract, concept-driven science.

But what of Needham's long history of Chinese science? Surely it counts for something? There are two ways to handle this objection. One can impugn the work as the product of a Marxist, a Sinophile, and a person who "so identifies himself with his material that he overestimates the achievements of Chinese science" (Nakayama, 1973:25–33). By this logic, my own book could be dismissed as the work of a Libertarian, a Sinophobe, and a person so convinced of the disutility of character-based writing that he would deny China's scientific accomplishments just to make a point. A *far* better tactic would be to examine what Needham himself had to say about Chinese science.

Although known for his praise of Chinese science, Needham carefully distinguishes between China's "practical" science and the "modern" science that emerged in the West. The latter skills, which Needham concedes never developed in China, include "the application of mathematical hypotheses to nature, the full understanding and use of the experimental method, the distinction between primary and secondary qualities, the geometrisation of space, and the acceptance of the mechanical model of reality" (1969:15). China's method was to observe, classify, and record the perceived facts of the concrete universe, "and if they failed . . . to apply hypotheses of modern type, they experimented century after century obtaining results which they could repeat at will" (46).[7] Although this approach worked up to a point, the "continuing general and scientific progress manifested" in China "was violently overtaken by the exponential growth of modern science after the Renaissance in Europe" that proceeded on a theoretical foundation (213).

Needham, for all his love of Chinese science, was puzzled by "the lack of theoretical science in China [despite] the high level of technological progress achieved there" (1956:11), believing the cause to be an absence of political democracy, which he attributed to "environmental conditions" (1969:152). It seems to me that this is a classic case of the cart going before the horse, but we will defer judgment on the sequence of causation until later.[8] On the other hand, his conclusion that China failed to develop modern science is disputed neither by those critical of Needham's approach nor by those sympathetic to it.

Qian Wen-yuan, a physicist who refutes Needham's overdrawn conclusions about China's role in the history of science, states, "China's incapability of developing modern science has been so conspicuous that, even with conscious and official importation, the state of non-development nevertheless dragged on and on" (1985:50). Qian argues that although China had science in the sense of "a systematic knowledge of natural phenomena," it had no "axiomatic and quantitative comprehension" of phenomena needed to pull these facts together (102).

Nakamura concedes that "In ancient times China was ahead of many other countries in the field of natural sciences" but adds that "Chinese science was finally surpassed by modern ones of the West" due to China's failure to shift from practical to theory-based science (1964:189–90). Nakayama notes in the same vein that with no systematic and abstract view of nature, "Chinese science and technology remained an unorganized mass of fragmentary empirical knowledge lacking a nucleus up to the beginning of Westernization" (1973:34).

The emphasis on concrete knowledge and corresponding disinterest in abstract, theoretical pursuits that we saw to be true of Japan also characterizes China's attitude toward science. Sivin states "In China there was no single structure of rational knowledge that incorporated all the sciences. Knowing was an activity in which the rational operations of the intellect were not sharply disconnected from what we would call intuition, imagination, illumination, ecstasy, esthetic perception, ethical commitment, or sensuous experience" (1980:6).

Baum argues similarly that "China's major achievements were in the areas of observation rather than conceptualization, concrete thinking rather than theoretical speculation, induction rather than deduction, arranging ideas in patterns rather than developing theories to explain patterns" (1982:1170). These descriptions of traditional China are similar to the one offered by Suttmeir of *present* Chinese scientific practice:

It is frequently said that Chinese science has a capacity for theoretical understanding, but an incapacity for linking theory to practice. Yet, in technological practice . . . there is a tendency to be oblivious to the underlying theoretical principles from which the preferred, and often "right" technological practice is deduced. Instead, simple empiricism and inductivism characterized by ad hoc trial-and-error approaches are used. (1989:379)

Simon and Goldman's description of Chinese creativity hints at the linguistic explanation I will offer in subsequent chapters. They begin by noting, "The creators of China's most significant scientific and technological achievements were not literati; they were primarily artisans and craftsmen who had a master-apprentice relationship, which meant that few of their discoveries were written down" (1989:4). The literati who, if you'll pardon my saying it, *were* literate and

whose educational attainments might have made possible more substantial forms of theoretical conceptualization, did not build models, establish hypotheses, or conduct experiments in a systematic fashion. They did not develop the mental ethos associated with scientific investigation—such as skepticism, innovation, and inquiry into the unknown, processes associated with scientific and technological development. (5)

In the authors' view, the two groups of semiliterate artisans and character-literate scholars used different "mental processes."

Robert Logan, in spite of his flawed understanding of the Sinitic writing system, does manage a reasonably accurate linguistic account of the different ways orthography affected thought in East Asia and the West. We will take up Logan's theories in detail later. My immediate interest in his work is the dichotomy he sets up between Chinese and Western thought, which is remarkably similar to Herbig's description of the differences between Japanese and Western approaches to science (1995:8–13) and is consistent with the findings of the China scholars cited above. Logan credits Western thought as being linear, logical, deductive, abstract, causal, and rational while Chinese thought is seen as nonlinear, analogical, inductive, concrete, mystical, and intuitive. As a result of these differences, Logan writes, Chinese practice "concrete science" and Westerners practice "abstract science" (1986:49). In his view, modern science

really means abstract theoretical science, which began in Europe during the Renaissance. [It is] thus a peculiar outgrowth of Western culture and is little more than three hundred years old. [China, for its part] created what was probably the most sophisticated form of nonabstract science the world has known. But technological sophistication by itself does not guarantee the development of abstract science.(51)

Nor does the accumulation of concrete facts guarantee that the facts will be reinterpreted creatively. Unlike the case for many physical phenomena, there seems to be no threshold in the creative process where accretions in quantity transform spontaneously into discontinuous structures. Although creativity theorists are agreed on the need for detailed foreknowledge of the relevant intellectual domain for creativity to emerge, the aggregation of facts by itself is insufficient. Other considerations, such as an individual's ability to analyze these facts, relate them causally to one another, hypothesize new relationships between them on the basis of abstract models borrowed from different domains, critically evaluate emergent configurations, persuade one's peers of the creation's validity, and so on all play indispensable roles that are not addressed by a concrete-bound, perceptual mindset. All the skills East Asians bring to acquiring and improving technology do not equate to success at basic science.

Concrete and Abstract Thinking

I need to say more about the differences between East Asian and Western patterns of thinking, because they help explain the technology transfer practices discussed in the first part of this book, and because they figure prominently in my description of the role orthography plays in shaping innovation styles. I would also like to add a few words about classification in general.

Many of us are uncomfortable making generalizations about people and I feel that discomfort acutely. There is something innately troubling about broad characterizations of people's behavior—not to mention that of whole peoples—based on traits expressed unevenly throughout a population. We have learned to give fellow humans the benefit of doubt because experience has taught us that lumping people into groups and making generalizations about individuals on that basis tends to reward the generalizer with embarrassment or worse.

Meanwhile disciplines from sociology to linguistics are founded on the expectation that human behavior *can* be categorized, and that many such categories coincide with the natural boundaries of people who share a culture. Such people, almost by definition, show a tendency to think and act in ways not shared by other cultures. The different cultures compete, compare, and exchange information. Risk gets spread out as humans experiment with different approaches to their common condition and adapt their lifestyles to particular ecological niches. Group-specific behavior—diversity on the worldwide scale—is thus a prerequisite for human survival.

Unfortunately, it is easy to misinterpret group preferences as imperatives binding on all members all of the time. This leads to comprehensive value judgments: "Westerners are *too* rational." "Asians are *too* interested in practical matters." Science begins to serve ethics, and ethics begins to serve bigotry. This is an old problem, one which I would like to avoid here. On the one hand, I am arguing that the use of two distinct types of writing in the East and West has made people more or less apt to engage in creative science. Since these two types of orthography help define cultures that are geographically and ethnically discontinuous,[9] there is no hiding the fact that my comments on thought apply to two distinct groups, which become more distinct as we elucidate these differences. This much is inescapable.

On the other hand, there is nothing in the literature on creativity that implies an *absolute* connection between the creative behavior of all individuals and the groups that they compose. Societies can make creativity more or less difficult for their members depending on how their institutions are structured. But talented persons frustrated by a society hostile to new ideas often find ways to emigrate to parts of the world where the requirements for creativity are better understood and appreciated. Alternatively, they can do their part to remove the obstacles to creativity in their own society. This may involve taking a fresh look at traditional group practices, including those associated with language and writing.

By and large, intelligent and sensitive observers of good will have noted that Westerners, schooled in the alphabetic tradition, tend as a group to be more inclined toward abstract analysis and generalization than East Asians. Conversely, members of the "Chinese character cultural sphere" have shown less aptitude as a group for abstract pursuits while exhibiting proportionately greater skill at collecting and applying concrete facts. These traits are apparent in the technology transfer practices described above: both in East Asia's reliance on abstract Western ideas, and by the sheer volume of information East Asians collect at the concrete level as part of their approach to innovation. The likelihood that these two traits are causally related occurred both to Kahaner (1996:183) and to Hansen (1996:33), who argue independently that Japanese are obliged to gather a lot of information because they are not good at analyzing it.

This preference for what Herbig calls "holistic right brain thinking as opposed to rational left brain analysis" (1995:12) underlies the differences we noted above in connection with Japanese and Western accomplishments in science. As Herbig states, "The Japanese emphasis is on empirical rather than theoretical knowledge. The Japanese believe that the experimental result is primary and the theory and data are secondary" (99). The concrete tendency of Japanese thought is apparent not just in science but also in the whole spectrum of life activities. Van Wolferen observes similarly that there is "no widely persuasive approach to life based on a set of consistent ideas" (1989:239). With no "logically ordered hierarchy of abstractions . . . individual things and ideas coexist in a feast of incongruity" (237–38).

Nakamura believes these characteristics existed through most of Japan's history. Noting that "logical consciousness begins with consciousness of the relation between the particular and universal" (1964:535), he goes on to state "the neglect of logic is one of the salient features of traditional Japanese ways of thinking. Concrete intuitions are favored much more than abstract concepts devoid of any tangible connection with the humanly perceived world" (543). As a result of this propensity to shun abstract universals, "the imaginative power of the Japanese people, ever since ancient times, has been limited to, and has rarely gone beyond the concrete and intuitive world of nature" (558).

Besides Japanese thought, Nakamura also examined the thought of China, India, and Tibet. The four peoples share significant cultures and traditions through many centuries of contact. Despite these congruities, Nakamura's description of Indian and Tibetan thought (neither people use the Sinitic orthography) as rational, logical, systematic, and speculative seems closer to the Western pattern than to anything in East Asia. Conversely, he finds "more points of similarity than points of difference" between Japanese and Chinese thinking (347). Chinese "reluctantly dwell on that which is beyond the immediately perceived" (180). They are "concerned with particular instances, little interested in universals which comprehend or transcend individual or particular instances. They thus seldom created a universal out of particulars" (185–86). Strong in "formal conformity," Chinese remain "oblivious to errors in the underlying logic" (230).

Chinese preference for concrete facts led them to seek authority in precedent, which abetted a static worldview. Neither trait supports creative innovation, not in science, which is our concern here, and not in the arts, where the same disinclination toward abstract expression plus the reverent repetition of classical models (e.g., poetry and painting) is evident.[10] The difficulty East Asians have doing original science hence is just one dimension of a mindset that accords high value to concrete facts and scant attention to their abstract validity or the relationships between them. If this also sounds like a description of language use in East Asia, where words are ill defined and the connections between them are loosely specified, the similarity is not coincidental. I shall discuss this relationship presently, but first we need to expand our framework.

Philosophical Traditions

Chinese philosophy is not concerned with abstract disquisition into the nature of the universe. It does not seek general explanations for phenomena, nor does it try to order events behind a prime mover. Logic—depersonalized rules to express thought—is outside its tradition. Instead, Chinese philosophers' primary interest has always been human relations. Practical from the start, China's thinkers have focused on rules for governing society, regularizing personal interaction, and bringing order to political chaos. If Western philosophy's achievements were metaphysical, the genius of Chinese philosophy is profoundly moral.

These standard comments on the difference between Chinese and Western philosophy should seem familiar. I culled them from my notes to an introductory course on Chinese thought, and offer them here, in the context of my earlier statements about concrete and abstract thinking, to demonstrate that East Asia's preference for practical thought is not just part of its approach to industrial development. *It is part of East Asia's intellectual tradition.* As such, one cannot dismiss the phenomenon as recent or as event-specific. Concrete, holistic, intuitive thought is a basic element of the culture and antecedent to much of it.

There is another reason why I brought this classroom description of Eastern versus Western philosophy into the present discussion. I could never understand why the traditions are treated as exclusive. Chinese philosophy is said to eschew rationalism *in favor of* a moral inquiry into the nature of human relations. East Asian philosophers *look beyond* the egocentric habits of Western thinkers to the role of individuals in the social order. Asian thought is at one with nature *in contrast to* Western philosophy, which is antagonistic to it. And so on.[11] This is how Chinese philosophy is taught and understood. I can't say I have ever been satisfied with it.

Portraying East Asia's disinterest in logic and analysis as the flip side of an ethical focus devalued in the West, instead of explaining the absence of the former tradition in terms that make sense, is entirely too facile. It is time to acknowledge that the failure of East Asia to distinguish itself in analytical pursuits has little to do with any *choice* its thinkers made and everything to do with the fact that abstract thinking and analysis did not come easily to its intellectual elite. I am not sure that couching this problem in conciliatory language performs any service to those peoples. One could even construe it as a form of condescension. Here is an example of what I mean, written by an eminent Sinologist:

Western technology, with its high efficiency but narrow specialization and rigidity of function, is the product of a rupture: in order to conquer Nature, Western man chose to cut himself off from it. Chinese civilization, on the contrary, endeavored to maintain the primordial unity; but the price of its uninterrupted communion with the world was a reduced capacity to control it. (Leys 1996:30)

My point here is that Chinese civilization "endeavored" to do nothing of the sort. Rather, China from its earliest efforts to irrigate the northern loess region to the present Three Gorges dam and hydroelectric project has been engaged in an ongoing war with nature, limited only by China's ability to devise or import ways to defeat it.[12] *Choosing* to live "in harmony with nature" never entered into it. China did what it could with what it had and the fact that it did not do more tells us more about Chinese creativity and the mindset behind it than about any conscious choice.

If we remove the face-saving platitudes, Leys's dichotomy does ring true. Technological progress is a rupture with nature in the same sense that all analysis is a rupture. Elements are torn from an existing whole, examined, and rearranged in new configurations. The operation presupposes the ability to identify a whole's component features, which in turn depends on recognizing abstract elements shared across categorical boundaries and the relationships between them. The objectified pattern is added to one's inventory of abstractions, often as an image, where it is compared and completed or fused with schema from other domains, immediately or over a period of time, in a way that is still only dimly understood.

What we do know is that the creation of novel constructs depends in the first instance on reducing nature to its core features. Thus, an ability to savor natural complexity has little to do with controlling nature.[13] It may, as Leys suggests, be inimical to it. By the same token, if a people after showing every sign of willingness to confront nature still fails, relatively speaking, to cut through its "primordial unity," this may indicate a diminished interest in analysis, or to put it in positive terms, a stronger preference for holistic thinking. One would expect this preference, where it exists, to show up in the philosophical tradition. In East Asia that is exactly what we find.

Here is Nakamura's description of the Confucian classics, which formed the basis for orthodox Chinese thought:

The tendency to value and devote attention to the particular rather than the universal is observable in many different aspects of Chinese culture. The Five Classics, which are the works of the highest authority regarded as providing the norms for human life, contain, for the most part, descriptions of particular incidents and statements of particular facts. They do not state general principles of human behavior. Even the Analects of Confucius records mostly the actions of individuals and the dicta of Confucius on separate incidents. (1964:196)

These comments apply to the philosophy of the Chinese state, the system of thought in which literate Chinese were schooled from childhood. Not only is there nothing in the makeup of Chinese character-based writing to serve—as we shall see later—as a primer or model for analytical thinking. The writings expressed in this orthography, particularly the exemplars of received orthodoxy, were similarly devoid of abstract and universal content. The philosophical tradition was thus both a symptom and a cause of China's fixation on concrete phenomena and corresponding neglect of analysis.

What of Buddhism, the other great intellectual tradition shared, like Confucianism, by China and the other countries of the Chinese Character Cultural Sphere? Here the parallels between concrete philosophy and mindset are even more striking, because of changes that were made to Buddhism in the process of its migration to East Asia. To quote again from Nakamura:

Buddhism, which had set forth, in the Indian manner, general and universal principles, was often presented to the Chinese through concrete examples and individual instances. Zen [Chan] explanations were of this sort. The true nature of the Buddha [in the Chinese view] comes not in words but only in concrete experience. Ethics is grasped on the basis of particular experiences. Universal truth is in the human being and not in universal propositions. (1964:196)

Nakamura contrasts this Chinese concern for particular events with Indian thought, which "paid attention chiefly to universals" (1964:200). Needham similarly observes, "From the second century A.D. onwards atomistic theories were introduced to China time after time, especially by means of the Buddhist contacts with India, but they never took any root in Chinese scientific culture" (1969:22).

China's treatment of Buddhist logic was one of neglect. Nakamura points out, "the non-logical character of Chinese thought is particularly conspicuous in Zen Buddhism, which is the most sinicized of Chinese Buddhist sects. Early Zen was not non-logical . . . However, a non-logical tendency soon manifested itself and eventually prevailed" (193). Nakamura compares Chinese ignorance of logic with "the importance and vitality of logical studies in Tibet" (193), which inherited its Buddhism from both India and China but whose orthography, unlike that of China, is quasi-alphabetic.

Sivin also noted the absence of logic in Chinese scientific thought: "A severely logical and axiomatic corpus of proofs like that of Euclid never emerged to provide a unifying standard of rigor in the quantitative sciences" (1980:8). Qian views the neglect of logic as a central cause of China's failure to develop modern science:

the great deficiency in old Chinese mathematical thought was the absence of rigorous proof, in particular, the absence of a system of deductive geometry. This configuration correlates with the lack of formal logic and the dominance of associative (organicist) thought. . . . In other fields of science, the Chinese way of thinking generally lacked accuracy in defining, exactness in formulating, rigor in proving, and logic in explaining. (1985:67)

Much the same is true of the Japanese attitude toward logic. Herbig's description is typical:

Japanese logic, as influenced predominantly by Buddhism, is fuzzy, circuitous and cyclical. . . . Zen Buddhist philosophy does not place great value on rational thought alone but more on spiritual enlightenment and intuitive understanding. This emphasis on intuitive understanding explains in part Japan's traditional weakness in basic scientific research, in which logical reasoning plays a central role. (1995:11–12)

One should not confuse intuitive understanding—a cardinal tenet of Zen Buddhism—with the "ah ha" experience found in some forms of creativity. The latter experience is believed to be a sympathetic response to the sudden pairing of two previously unrelated "matrices" of thought, each being an abstract characterization of a separate problem, situation, or event (Koestler 1964). An analysis of a problem's parts must be done for the experience to happen at all. The *satori* or "sudden enlightenment" achieved through Zen meditation is purely contextual. A whole is understood, or thought to be understood, in its context without regard to the parts. There is no analysis (it is actively discouraged) and nothing new is created. As Herbig puts it, "Intuition is self-knowledge of the whole in contrast to reason, which busies itself with parts" (1995:12). Logic has no role here.

Karel van Wolferen, a long-time observer of Japanese society, notes, "in Japan, one meets intelligent people who claim that 'logic' is something invented in the West to allow Westerners to win discussions" (1989:236). Given Japan's insistence in trade negotiations on the differences, for example, between Western and Japanese stomachs, it is not surprising to find the same type of argument advanced in philosophy. In both cases, the reluctance to acknowledge universals is noteworthy. Van Wolferen explains that "Neither the three major Japanese spiritual systems (Shintoism, Buddhism, Confucianism) nor [Western] scientific thought has given the Japanese tools of leverage over their environment" (1989:236). My own review of East Asia's philosophical traditions finds little evidence of the analytical mindset needed for scientific creativity. This pattern as we shall see is also expressed in East Asians' use of language.

Thought and Linguistic Style

Given my emphasis on the relationship between writing systems and creativity, it will be useful to end this chapter by addressing language issues, in particular the notion of linguistic abstraction.

One belief held strongly by American linguists is that there are no primitive languages. Nor is any language supposed to be better than any other. All languages evolved to suit the needs of their users. And while different languages vary in the way they represent the world, all have adequate resources to express its phenomena. Blessed with this infinitely adaptive tool, each speech community finds its own way to symbolize its relationship to the world and support communication among members. The particular mechanism is irrelevant.

This argument troubles me because I resent the way it was forced on me in school, along with other mantras like universal grammar, language acquisition devices, and the characterization of writing as an imperfect representation of speech (more on this later). I would have preferred to become convinced of these truths myself or to have been led to them more gently. I also have a problem with the leap from relative adequacy (the needs of the group) to absolute parity (all groups have equally useful tools), but am willing to lay these doubts aside and treat linguistic variation from a less controversial perspective, namely, that of how languages are *used*. I recognize that sociolinguists will not be happy with the distinction between structure and use either, but I ask that you bear with me through this exercise.

For the record, I give no credence to claims about Chinese grammar's inability to express counterfactuals. Nor do I attribute much significance to other Indo-European-centric complaints about Asian languages' failure to specify this or that syntactic marker. I concede that these differences *may* relate in some fashion to distinctions in the way reality and thought are parsed. But it would be better to withhold judgment on the matter until specialists offer more compelling arguments one way or the other. As I said early on, there is little support for a strong theory of linguistic determinism and a fair amount of evidence against it.

But what of the way available structures are used? It is one thing to reify language, but quite another thing to describe the pragmatics of choice. If users prefer to write or speak in a certain way, it may not be because the language dictates that choice, but because the community has also developed metalinguistic norms for *how* a language is to be used. I am referring to linguistic styles, those of individuals and of whole communities. Linguistic style may or may not affect thought, but it almost certainly *reflects* thought. Accordingly we should find the same preferences in the way a speech group views and uses its language that we find in philosophy and other more explicit representations of a community's psychology.

And indeed, examples of East Asia's preference for concrete elements and distaste for analysis are evident at each linguistic level. Syllables are not split into abstract phonemes, sentences are not segmented into words, and discourse until recently was not divided into sentences. Although China has a tradition of phonological study, it focused on rhymes[14] and never was able to break decisively through the syllable barrier to identify abstract phones or features of phones.[15] It is difficult for Westerners soaked in an alphabetic tradition to appreciate that speech does not reduce automatically to phonemes or features, but comes across perceptually to those outside this tradition as concrete syllable sounds that are indivisible on the surface level. It is only after someone, as a result of prior analysis, has pointed out that the /t/ and /p/ in "top" are, on some abstract level, the same as the /t/ and /p/ in "pot" that the sounds begin to appear the same.

I am not claiming a difference in the principles of East Asian and Western language phonology (anymore than I would assert a difference between "Asian" and "Western" logic). Phonology is universally depicted by protocols that derive their utility from being language independent. I *am* claiming a difference in the way East Asian and Western language users *perceive* phonological structure, the one concretely and the other abstractly, in a way that parallels the psychological differences noted above. We will take up this critical problem in detail later.

Moving to the next level, we note that a word in any language is no more naturally perceived than a phoneme. While all languages have them, the *concept* of a word is a written language artifact. There is little in the unanalyzed speech stream to identify word boundaries, and nothing in preliterate speech communities to enhance one's awareness of them. Linguists, despite their commitment to a speech-oriented discipline, acknowledge that words are abstractions that depend on orthography—specifically alphabets that use word division—for their formal identity. Westerners have a good grasp of words because they have learned to recognize them through print.

East Asians, whose orthographies do not distinguish words, had no concept of a word. Evidence for this comes from two sources. First, there is no indigenous word for "word" in the major East Asian languages. The terms that do exist were used freely to mean anything from "morpheme" to "expression." When pressed for a translation of "word," East Asians even today commonly choose a term that means "written Chinese character" (Chin. *zì*), which cannot be analyzed easily, either in terms of the phonology it represents (a syllable) or in terms of its own graphic structure. Moreover, the semantic referents of these *zì* turn out to be morphemes—basic, unanalyzed units of linguistic meaning. What we have here is not a symbolic relationship at all but an indexing of three concrete units. The link between sign and meaning in Sinitic, whether phonological by syllables or orthographic by characters, is always between one type of concrete unit and another.

My second reason for claiming that Asian languages lack clearly defined words comes from usage. Having no provision in the orthography for word division,[16] Asian writers can and do invent words on the fly. Character-morphemes are juxtaposed (not truly linked) on the basis of their individual meanings and what the writer thinks the combined meanings collectively represent. Usually these combinations correspond to terms in dictionaries or popular use. Often, however, the morphemes are combined as freely as words are in English, the difference being they are not, like words, intended as separate concepts but are supposed to convey a unitary concept, albeit one not in anyone else's lexicon.

As a result both of this practice (many consider it a perversion) and of the morpheme-bound psychology that the orthography reinforces, East

Asians tend to lose sight of the meaning of a word and focus on the meanings of its constituents (Nakamura 1964:223; Yamada 1987:98). Morpheme combinations, meant to be grasped as synthetic wholes, are not perceived as such because their concrete roots are always evident as a reminder. The lesson to be drawn, which will figure importantly in our discussion of creativity, is that there is no real synthesis without prior analysis.[17]

Nor can there be syntax without words. I will not argue that Chinese or other Asian languages have no grammar or words. I have spent too many years at the blackboard explaining Chinese and Korean vocabulary and grammar to buy into either notion. I *am* saying that, due to a weak concept of word and a diminished concern with the abstract way words fit together, East Asians feel less need to use the syntactic tools they do have to present their ideas in what literate Westerners would consider a clear and precise manner. I have commented on this problem before (Hannas 1997:285–87), as have many others of both East Asian and Western nationality, and so will not belabor it here. Asian languages are difficult to understand and to translate not because of their structure or even the orthography, bad as that is. They are difficult because of the way Asians use them.[18]

My main point, and the thought I want to leave with you as we close this chapter, is that East Asians can present their ideas clearly and logically when they want to, but usually they do not want to. Asian writers, operating within a certain tradition, generally feel no obligation to write in a way that allows their readers to deduce meaning directly from a discourse. Instead readers must *impute* meaning to a text whose units are poorly specified and whose structure is often ambiguous. Induction, not deduction; natural syllables, not abstract phonemes; morphemes, not objectified words, are the hallmarks of language use in East Asia. The same neglect of logic, abstraction, and analysis seen in philosophy and other areas of East Asian culture is manifested here in the common elements of communication and thought. How these characteristics play specifically in the creative process is the subject of the remainder of this book.

Chapter Five
The Anatomy of Creativity

> To ask a Japanese to think in English terms amounts to asking an Impressionistic landscape painter to adopt the methods of a land surveyor.
>
> —Arthur Koestler

Overview of the Creative Process

It is time to sum up what has been noted about innovation in East Asia and move to more technical areas that will provide the tools needed to explain these observations. In the previous chapters I documented the present dependency of Japan, China, and South Korea on Western ideas and showed that this dependency is most acute in basic science, where theory and abstraction play a paramount role. We glanced at some distinctions between concrete and abstract thinking, saw how these differences are exhibited in East Asian and Western innovation patterns, and buttressed these observations with data from social psychology and intellectual history. I also gave examples of how language and orthography interact with thought, described some parallels between linguistic and social development as a prelude to the case I shall make for linking creativity with orthographic types, and hinted about the dynamics of creativity.

The argument that we shall pursue hereafter has two parts. I will show that the Chinese character-based writing used in East Asia has inhibited creativity on several "macro" levels that derive from the writing system's complexity and its poorly defined links with the sounds of spoken language. This task will occupy the last few chapters of the book. Our immediate goal will be to identify some basic psycholinguistic and neurolinguistic traits associated with writing, both alphabetic and character-based, that relate on a "micro" level to creative thinking. To achieve this goal, I must be more specific about the creative process, as both a personal and social event. I must also describe its cognitive aspects and, where possible, its neurological correlates to demonstrate how writing systems influence a people's disposition to create.

Creativity studies, like other areas of psychology, have both popular and scientific dimensions. Originally a minor field of psychological research, creativity burst into the public eye in the mid-1960s with the publication of Arthur Koestler's *The Act of Creation* (1964), the first rigorous attempt to explain creativity in a format accessible to laypersons. The release of this 750-page treatise was timed perfectly, capturing the anti-authoritarianism of the era and helping to shape it by the nature of the subject and the spirit in which it was delivered. Koestler, a lifelong critic of the behaviorist paradigm that dominated what would later be called cognitive science, set out to humiliate this school of thought and the mechanistic worldview it supported by focusing on human creativity, the one trait behaviorism was least equipped to handle.

Koestler's blend of science and romanticism made the book pivotal in another sense by serving both as a springboard for the pop psychology that found "creativity" in trivial endeavors and for serious inquiry into the matter by empirical scientists seeking verifiable antecedents for such concepts as "bisociation" and "matrices of thought." The former trend culminated in a number of alleged practical guides for increasing personal creativity through meditation, out-of-the-box thinking, and so on. This approach mostly ignores the findings of creativity science on the roles of preparation and verification. Unfortunately, it captured the public's fancy like much of the left- and right-brain theorizing of the 1970s did, preempting widespread appreciation for genuine scientific research into the nature of creativity.

As we shall see, there is no shortcut to creativity. Nor is there much anyone can do to enhance creative ability beyond investing the time and effort to master a knowledge domain, caring enough to think about it, and, perhaps, situating oneself in an environment where new ideas are rewarded. The notion that creativity could be linked with self-actualization and psychological fulfillment for the many is belied by the observation that society's most creative individuals are often oddballs plagued by frustration or obsessive types immersed wholly in their discipline—in modern terms, self-absorbed personalities with limited social skills. Successful societies tolerate these individuals (and the structures that support them) at great expense to short-term efficiency and at some risk to their own survival. To romanticize this process is to misunderstand it.

On the positive side, careful research has produced many solid (if quieter) studies on creativity over the past three decades. Our focus throughout this chapter will be on the findings of this latter group of specialists, who are interested in describing creativity as it happens, not in prescribing steps for its magical attainment. Significant progress has been made in this area by scholars from several disciplines, including psychology, neuroscience, information science, and sociology. Despite their different approaches—and without minimizing the disagreement on certain issues—there does seem to be a consensus on what constitutes the main parameters of creativity. Enough is understood now about creativity to allow us to examine its links with other psychological and sociological phenomena, including language and writing.

Contrary to what one would expect, specialists have found that human creativity depends on manipulating knowledge that already exists. The same maxim that one cannot create something from nothing in the physical universe also applies in the notional realm. Although creative insights seem to occur "out of the blue," most of what is needed to produce the insight is already there, in the prepared mind, in one form or another. The key to creativity lies in juggling these existing forms to produce new (and useful) configurations.

That creativity proceeds from known patterns has long been appreciated. Philosopher Brand Blanshard sixty years ago defined invention as the problem of "how an end, already partially realized in the mind, gets the material to extend or complete itself." Invention begins with "a collision between a system or order already present in the mind and some fragment that ought to be included in this and yet remains outside it" (1939:129–30). Churchland's definition of scientific creativity as "the capacity to see or interpret a problematic phenomenon as an unexpected or unusual instance of a prototypical pattern already in one's conceptual repertoire" (1995:278) likewise recognizes the role of existing knowledge in the creative process.[1] I emphasize the importance of prior knowledge as an antidote to the popular notion of creativity as cost-free and spontaneous. While creativity often involves breaking through mental "barriers" (reorganizing knowledge networks), there is no creativity without a network of structures to build on.

These structures, technically speaking, are mental models of natural phenomena, realized as recurrent patterns of neuronal activation. They range from general patterns of wide applicability (highly abstract configurations distilled from multiple inputs) to specific rules for particular circumstances. To deal effectively with one's habitat, people learn to perceive environmental features and events as instances of stereotypes, that is, generalized representations of phenomena probably based on relational attributes. Synaptic firing patterns invoked in the brain in response to recurring external stimuli become fixed (the relative weights of their neuronal configurations are strengthened), enabling individuals to recognize and respond appropriately to most situations they encounter.

The challenge—the opportunity for creativity—comes when perception of an event fails to elicit a useful match from one's store of mental representations. As Holland et al. put it, "To represent environments fraught with novelty, mental models cannot rely exclusively on precompiled structures. Flexibility can come only through the use of *combinations* of existing knowledge structures" (1986:16). Deductive logic—applying fixed rules within an existing framework—cannot interpret a novel situation whose features lie outside that framework. New structures must be generated through induction, either by refining existing patterns or creating new ones.

One type of inductive change involves evaluating "the system's rules as instruments for goal attainment, improving them where possible and favoring the better ones in application" (68). A goal-directed search is made of existing mental models that correspond approximately to the surface features of a problem (more accurately, to one's analysis of those features). A solution is achieved when a match or near match is located. This lesser form of creativity corresponds to Brick's (1997:8) "intrarepresentational" rule changes, which "do not depend on similarity judgments. They constitute a way to reorganize a given context." In terms of the material presented in previous chapters, this process equates to the incremental improvements in technology that constitute the bulk of real-world innovation. While "creative" in a broad sense, they do not constitute "breakthroughs" as the term is usually understood.

Holland et al. concur that these "procedures for refining existing rules, though important, are inherently limited to rules already in place. If these rules are inadequate in important ways . . . no amount of refinement will make up the deficit" (1986:78). There is, however, a second, more thoroughgoing type of inductive change used to "generate plausibly useful new rules that are capable of extracting and exploiting regularities in experience" (68). In this case, abstract patterns that have already been defined *for other domains,* or exist at a deeper, more general level, act as models for remapping or completing the elements of a problem by analogy.

This second form of induction is employed only after deliberate attempts have been made to understand problems in more or less familiar terms.[2] It differs from the template matching that characterizes the first type of induction by requiring a fusion (or "bisociation") of two separate configurations—an existing "source" pattern and one's mental representation of the problem, called a "target" pattern. Combining the two patterns yields insight into problems that resisted solution in their original form. Brick calls this more radical process "interrepresentational," which unlike the first variety "involves more than one representation. . . . What is transferred to the target is either structural traits or contents of the source, and the change pertains to the target" (1997:8). The process works not logically but *analogically.* It is responsible for the sort of breakthroughs that characterize scientific progress as it is stereotyped in the West.

Stages of Creativity

Lay notions of a distinction between innovative and creative thinking correlate with these two hypothesized mental processes. Using an existing representation to understand a situation or solve a problem is not truly "creative" if the representation is normally invoked in that domain. Creativity in the deeper sense involves reaching outside the domain to identify a data set as an instance of a scheme that is usually applied to different *kinds* of data. A subset of this process occurs when a partial source analog is recovered that is similar enough to the target to attract the problem solver's attention. The partial scheme is amalgamated with the target representation to produce a new structure more basic than either the target or the source.

The two inductive processes used in innovation versus creativity differ as much with respect to how the target data are handled as they do in the type of mapping strategies employed. In the lesser variety, target elements—perceived units and their relationships—are treated more or less as a given. By given I mean they are recognized as familiar elements in one's repertoire of domain-specific components. These elements can be shifted about or replaced within the limits of what the overall conception requires. But a major remapping of the problem set (target) is precluded by the "chunkiness" of these elements, that is, by their status as indivisible units, and by what this chunkiness implies for their relationships with one another. This is a critical point that requires elaboration.

The matrices available to structure the elements of a problem depend, ultimately, on how one defines its elements. If the integrity of what are regarded as indivisible parts remains absolute, the potential for reordering is correspondingly limited, meaning that the matrices available for a problem's representation are likely to be those already within the domain. Conversely, when the chunkiness of a representation is reduced by an analysis that penetrates its predefined units, the material becomes susceptible to representation *by structures outside the domain*. Analogies with hidden structures thus are facilitated by the randomness of the initial "workspace" (Hofstadter and FARG 1995:228).

Gick and Lockhart (1995) argue, in the same vein, that formulating a problem is as important as finding a source to complete it. In their words:

Two important processes exist. The first is the generation of a representation of the problem, or the problem solver's understanding of problem elements and operations that can be used to solve the problem. The second is a search for a solution within the constraints of the representation. If the implementation of a solution succeeds, then the problem solving stops; if it fails, then the problem solver might go back and try to formulate a new representation for the problem that may be more effective, might keep searching within the same representation for a different solution to implement, or might get stuck and give up. (199)

Success in solving novel problems depends on the availability of source analogs, and also on one's ability to couch a representation in terms general enough to facilitate deep matches but specific enough to preserve the problem's essence. The importance of problem representation is captured anecdotally in phrases like "You have to ask the right questions to get the right answer." Regressing to deeper (more abstract) sources on which to base an analogy—the other half of the road to insight—is expressed by the phrase "reculer pour mieux sauter" or "move one step back to jump two steps ahead."

The creative process encompasses more than the two core aspects that I just described. Most specialists distinguish four independent phases of creativity, including preparation, incubation, inspiration, and verification

(Abra 1988:16; see also Jaynes 1976:44; Poincaré 1982:389; Martindale 1995:251). Csikszentmihalyi and Sawyer's (1995:333) four-stage characterization substitutes "insight" for "inspiration" and "evaluation" for "verification" but is otherwise identical. As they describe it:

Although there are subtle variations in the definitions of these stages of creative insight among different researchers, we propose the following unifying framework: The first stage, *preparation*, which is stimulated by external pressures or by intrinsic motivation, involves focused conscious work, such as studying or analyzing data. These rational thought processes provide the raw material on which the subconscious can begin working.

A period of *incubation* ensues, followed by *insight*, and a lengthy period of *evaluation*. The authors note "Insight is part of an extended mental process. It is based on a previous period of conscious preparation, requires a period of incubation during which information is processed in parallel at a subconscious level, and is followed by a period of conscious evaluation and elaboration." I shall discuss these stages in more detail in the next few sections.

Some researchers add a fifth stage—communication of results (Abra 1988:16)—in deference to the role of peer recognition. As we shall see later, there are intimate links between what appear to be individual creative acts and the culture within which these acts occur. Having one's creation examined by peers not only satisfies the usefulness criterion that keeps the enterprise grounded in reality. The attitude of society toward the creativity of its members determines whether someone is disposed to create in the first place. Adding this fifth phase to the creative process closes the cycle of events by offering an explanation for creativity's nebulous beginning (the disposition of individual thinkers to create) in terms of the process's end result (degree of social acceptance).

Breaking Down the Whole

Creativity is difficult because it conflicts with a human requirement to perceive phenomena in terms of existing categories. As Brick (1997:12–13) states, "The ability to categorize is of fundamental value for the simplest train of thought. If a subject cannot identify and reidentify the object he reasons about, then he cannot entertain any continuous, coherent thoughts." Turner (1988:3) noted similarly that people categorize to avoid being swamped by the world's complexity. These categories "cut our worlds into clusters [and] the fitness of our cognition will depend upon the fitness of these conceptual cuts." Mental models in the form of concepts and relationships between concepts are built to interpret raw sensory data, so that the phenomena they are associated with become identifiable and predictable. Such categories persist to the extent that they model events "accurately," in a way consistent with the needs of survival.

Creativity on the one hand relies on these models. For analogies to work, a large repertoire of source patterns or "prototypes" must be available in one's mind to guide the reconfiguration of a problem's data. We learn these prototypes, according to Churchland (1995:279), "solely within the domain of observable things . . . in response to one's ongoing sensory experience." Concrete events are modeled on the basis of what we regard from past experience as stable units (collections of properties that can be manipulated as wholes) and plausible ways of linking these units. The modeling is a two-way street: sensory experience is ordered, and prior assumptions about order are validated or adjusted (alternative neural mappings are selected and strengthened).

Along with this "horizontal" formation of category structures, the mind also seeks to integrate commonalties from different category domains into what Koestler (1964:621) referred to as a "vertical abstractive hierarchy." Just as sensory data "filtered" or categorized by perceptual mechanisms are used to shape categorical associations, so do these activated patterns serve as the data on which a more abstract set of assumptions is based. This "vertical progress in abstraction" (recognizing a particular pattern as an instance of a more general one) is the key to creative discovery.[3] Although mastery of a categorical domain requires intelligence (recall and logic), it does not equate to competence in drawing inferences *between* levels, where a different set of skills (analysis and pattern recognition) are needed.

Turner (1988:4) also distinguishes categorical (Koestler's horizontal) and analogical (vertical) connections, but views the distinction in more fluid terms. As he puts it: "Deeply entrenched analogical conventions we no longer find inventive. We regard them as straightforward category connections."[4] Like Koestler, Turner views category structures as "dynamic and subject to transformation under the pressure of analogy." If categories structure the world as we know it, analogies "can inventively induce us to build new connections, and recast or tune others. A powerful analogy can re-structure, disturb, influence, and change our category structures, and successful analogical connections can ultimately become part of our category structures" (5).

Unfortunately for creativity, the same category structures on which analogy operates also serve as a brake on innovation. In Turner's words, "category structures highlight certain connections between concepts, and mask possible alternative connections" (3). Ward et al. (1995:128) note similarly that "bringing to mind specific objects can inhibit creativity: the central properties of those objects set up roadblocks on the routes to innovation." For the analogical mechanism to work, the target structure must be *analyzed*, that is, stripped of its concrete trappings, and reduced to a form to which abstract source patterns can relate.

There is unanimous agreement among creativity specialists, and cognitive scientists in general, on the need to *dis*integrate problems—dissolve the relationships between their units and what pass as "units" themselves—for analogical mapping to occur.[5] We noted earlier Hofstadter et al.'s argument that analogy is facilitated by randomness in the problem space. This hypothesis, which accords with the commonsense view that smaller pieces can be reordered more easily than large chunks, was verified empirically by Hofstadter's group through computer simulations. One aspect of these trials, which Hofstadter calls "an accurate description of the underpinnings of a typical paradigm shift in the human mind" (1995:257), involved "breaker codelets" that went into operation when snags were hit. Their "purpose is to arbitrarily break structures that they find in the work space, thus reducing the system's attachment to a viewpoint already established as being problematic" (258). The analog of these codelets in human cognitive operations is the conscious exercise of analytical skills on a problem set.

Calvin, like Hofstadter, uses a competitive model to explain the evolution of "a more intelligent solution to a problem" (1996:104). In Calvin's scheme, "The brain activity patterns associated with thinking a thought" get copied, occasionally with changes, and the variant patterns compete. The process is accelerated by

fragmentation and the isolation that follows: the darwinian process operates more quickly on islands than on continents. For some fancy darwinian processes requiring speed (and the timescale of thought and action certainly does), that might make fragmentation processes essential. (105–6)

The better one is able to isolate the core universal elements of a problem through fine-grained thinking, the better one's chances are of finding these elements in existing "source" patterns. To Calvin, who views intelligence as the ability to discover "some new underlying order," creativity is predicated on breaking a "pattern into meaningful parts and recombining" them (14–15).

Findlay and Lumsden (1988), on whose work we shall draw extensively here and in subsequent chapters, describe the cognitive processes leading to creativity as follows:

A α-node is an informational unit at higher levels of semantic organization, obtained from the distillation of information from subordinate nodes at lower levels of organization. . . . The creative process involves the production of a novel schema (a discovery) indexed by a new α-node. (22)

Findlay and Lumsden's nodes essentially are concepts representing "pertinent information from personal experiences." A schema is defined as "a network of nodes and links." Concrete-bound nodes serve as the basis for high-level patterns (α-nodes). Creativity occurs when two or more of these α-nodes, constituting the target data and source pattern(s), have been activated and are represented in working memory. The authors add:

With regard to discovery, it is more likely that the production of new α-nodes is based on the establishment of connections among these primitive elements rather than among the α-nodes themselves, simply because the overwhelming advantage of vertical chunking as a means of cognitive economy implies that when α-nodes are activated, they have a more or less unitary representation in working memory. At least initially, conscious attention may be required to *partition this representation into discrete elements of lower cognitive order*, thereby creating the opportunity for new linkages. (22, my emphasis)

In contrast to the automatic and, for all intents, subconscious search for appropriate source patterns to map problem data, the up-front analysis needed to prepare data for reorganization (not to mention the subsequent labor to verify any new construct that emerges) entails a deliberate, conscious effort to isolate units, or the features of what are believed to be "units," from their original context. There is nothing easy or natural about this analytical process. As Seifert et al. put it,

Obviously, if ultimate insight is to occur in resolving a difficult problematic situation, the problem first has to be taken seriously and confronted head-on. The would-be problem solver needs sufficient motivation to spend significant amounts of time on an initial careful analysis of the problem situation, pushing ahead as far as possible with it, forming a coherent memory representation of the problem, and using all the available information in a solution attempt. (1995:110)

The need for preparatory analysis is especially great when the source and target domains share few surface characteristics, as is often the case in breakthrough science. Similarities between distant domains become evident only when the elements of the target representation have been abstracted to a level that coincides with potential source patterns. According to Vosniadou and Ortony (1989a:8), "Empirical work in analogical problem solving show that both adults and children have great difficulty retrieving a remote analog that can satisfy the target problems goals. . . . The problem often lies in the fact that neither children nor adults represent the problems at a level abstract (context-free) enough."

Ward's (1995) description of the need for abstract analysis at the early stage is uncompromising. It deserves to be quoted at length: "There are intuitive, empirical, and theoretical reasons for believing that people will be more innovative, as judged by deviations from characteristic category attributes, if they begin the task of imagining a new entity by considering a highly abstract categorization of what properties the entity ought to possess rather than if they begin retrieving and modifying a specific entity" (170). Modifying specific entities is precisely what is involved in run-of-the-mill innovation. Moving beyond these incremental changes requires thinkers to cast lower level representations in an abstract light. Ward explains why:

The heightened accessibility of an initially retrieved or presented example (or its component attributes) makes alternative examples or attributes less accessible or retrievable. By moving to a more abstract representation, one may be able to lessen the dominance of any one instance and better equate the accessibility of other items. One may then be able to retrieve an alternative item, perhaps a less typical one, or synthesize a novel item from the abstract principles. (172)

Radical restructuring demands that the thinker think on an abstract level. Abstract thought, in turn, requires separating elements from their concrete context through analysis. Popular belief notwithstanding, creativity turns out to depend at least as much on disintegrative and analytical skills as it does on integrative or synthetic talents.[6] Analysis is needed both at the beginning and, as we shall see, the ending phases of creativity. It underlies the process to that extent.

Advancing Backward

How fragmented must representations be for creativity to happen? We need to talk again about language, both to remind ourselves of this study's focus and because of the role language has and does *not* have in the creative process, particularly in its middle or "unconscious" phase.

There is reason to believe that human consciousness is founded on language or on the symbolic manipulations that make up the heart of language. Jaynes argued in *The Origin of Consciousness in the Breakdown of the Bicameral Mind* that subjective consciousness "is built up with a vocabulary on a lexical field whose terms are all metaphors or analogs of behavior in the physical world" (1976:55). Jaynes viewed the bulk of language as based on metaphor and conscious mind as "a metaphor-generated model of the world . . . the invention of an analog world on the basis of language." The "self" is also an artifact of conscious thought, inseparable from the metaphors we create. As he put it, "consciousness is an operation rather than a thing, a repository, or a function. It operates by way of analogy, by way of constructing an analog space with an analog 'I' that can observe that space, and move metaphorically in it" (65–66).

The link between language and self-awareness has also been articulated by Illich and Sanders (1989), and by a number of other scholars who draw parallels between the externalizing of ideas through writing and the concept of a detachable self. We will discuss this line of thought in the following chapter in the context of alphabetic writing. Meanwhile, note the similarity between Jaynes's view of consciousness as language-based and Deacon's thoroughly modern notion of human consciousness as symbol-driven. Deacon argues, "No matter what else various theorists might claim about the nature of consciousness, most begin by recognizing that to be conscious of something is to experience a representation of it" (1997:448). From this follows the likelihood that changes in the form of representation—from iconic through indexical to symbolic—entail changes in the type of consciousness represented, the last type being peculiar to humans—the only "symbolic species." Although we share primitive consciousness with lower animals, the specific consciousness humans experience is a function of symbol use and is, accordingly, linguistic in nature (449).[7]

Our ability to create and use symbols is supported by what Deacon terms a "nested hierarchy, where certain conditions in the lower levels of consciousness are prerequisite to the emergence of consciousness at each higher level" (449). They include, most basically, the brain's ability to model iconic relationships (signs that signify by virtue of sharing a property with what they represent) and, one step higher, indexical relationships (signs whose specific character is causally dependent on the objects to which they refer). Just as indices are relationships among icons, so are symbols (conventional signs that depend on an interpretant for their meaning) relationships among indices (78). Symbols are formed by recognizing relationships between the objects to which a group of indices refer. Once a symbol is formed, however, the direction of dependency reverses (in Deacon's terms: the "mnemonic strategy" shifts), and the objects themselves become identified indirectly in terms of their relationships within the higher scheme (87).

There are some interesting features in this semiotic-cognitive hierarchy that bear directly on creativity. Recall Findlay and Lumsden's α-nodes, described as "informational units at higher levels of semantic organization" obtained by distilling information from lower structural levels. Creativity, in their system, involves reconfiguring elements lower on the cognitive scale so that they are "indexed" by a new α-node (1988:22). It involves *regressing* from a higher cognitive state, where symbol manipulations prevail, to a relatively lower state, where information is represented iconically (by stimulus generalization) or indexically by what Deacon calls "spatial-temporal correlation or part-whole contiguity" (1997:79). Language and the symbols on which it is based have no role in this part of the creative process *and actually impede it*. This fact, well attested in the creativity literature, will be treated at length in Chapter 9.

Viewed within this cognitive assembly, Jaynes's identification of language with metaphor and his distinction between thought and consciousness make perfect sense. If metaphor is the use of analogy on the symbolic level to extend—and in that sense create—language, what we regard as "genuine" creativity is the use of analogy on the *indexical* level to form new associations among the nonverbal tokens that refer to real world elements. Logic, which Jaynes describes as "the justification of conclusions we have reached by natural reasoning," accounts for just a small part of our thinking (1976:41) and, unlike the preparation and validation stages of creativity, does not figure into the incubation and insight stages at all.[8] As Jaynes put it, "Our minds work much faster than consciousness can keep up with. . . .

The picture of a scientist sitting down with his problems and using conscious induction and deduction is as mythical as a unicorn" (42–43).

Koestler's verdict on the role of conscious, symbolic thought in creativity's middle phase is identical: "not only verbal thinking but conscious thinking in general plays only a subordinate part in the brief, decisive phase of the creative act itself," he stated. The "role of strictly rational and verbal processes in scientific discovery has been vastly overrated" (1981:13–14). Hesse concluded similarly that "standard forms of logic and linguistics" are irrelevant at this stage. She summarized the view of creativity scientists on this issue as follows:

It has long been obvious that the human problem solver does not generally think deductively or by exhaustive search of logical space. Propositional logic relies upon enumeration of premises, univocal symbolisation, and exclusively deductive connections, and these cannot be either a good simulation of human thought or an efficient use of computers. In real human thinking the meanings of concepts are constantly modified and extended by parallels, models, and metaphors, and the rational steps from premises to conclusion are generally non-demonstrative, being carried out by inductive, hypothetical, and analogical reasoning. (1988:318)

There is little to suggest that mental models are stored *primarily* as linguistic constructs. Indeed, much of linguistics is concerned with how deeper, preverbal thought is translated into a verbal format. Language, in its idealized written mode especially, is logical, serial, and symbolic. It is an affirmation of the conscious, focused self. What creativity needs in its insightful stage (as the metaphor suggests) is a categorically different mindset, one that is spatial and visual, not serial and verbal.[9]

Visual metaphors abound in scientific and popular accounts of creativity. We "dream up" a solution, use our "imagination," "see" how a problem "comes together." The primacy of visual over verbal thought in creativity's decisive phase has long been recognized and is undisputed.[10] Johnson, paraphrasing Kant, described "a level of imaginative activity at which we organize our representations into unified wholes." It is not a concrete mental image as such, or "an abstract conceptual or propositional entity." What appears is "an abstract structure of an image . . . the recurring structure or pattern of our imaginative process of forming an image." These schemata "represent a level of cognitive activity where form and structure emerge in our understanding *prior* to propositional judgment" (1988:29, my emphasis).

This imagery finds its ultimate expression in dreams. Dreams are novel constructs built on prior experiences through free association. Although inadequate as a model of creativity (where the "free" association is guided), dreams mirror creativity's incubation phase by being independent of what we view in conscious states as "the imperatives and continuity of the real world" (Mandler 1995:13). People sometimes do dream real solutions to vexing problems, but the experience is uncommon. When it does occur, it is only after a period of time has passed, which is also true of insights that emerge from wakeful (but preconscious) states. As Langley and Jones explain it,

There is no inherent reason why the retrieval cues must be *external*; they might also be internally generated during periods of free association, and this is exactly what dreams provide. But because the chains occurring in dreams are semirandom, they provide little more direction than chance external cues. Thus, dream-based illuminations may be delayed as long as those based on interactions with the environment. (1988:198)

The search for source analogues, while "unconscious" and language-independent, is not completely random but depends crucially on feedback from the parts of the brain that are coding the target. The trick seems to be keeping the problem's elements "in mind" while letting the rest of one's thoughts stay loose enough for candidate sources to emerge. Blandshard (1939:164–65) called this connection between the one type of process and the other "the guidance of the immanent end of thought," noting that "So far as the analogies are random and heterogeneous, thought is adrift on the tide of association." Simonton (1995) and Martindale (1995) both explain the process in terms of location and level of neuronal activation. Here is Martindale's account:

During the preparation stage of the creative process, attention must be focused. That is, a few nodes are highly activated and dominate consciousness. These nodes encode ideas thought to be relevant to the problem at hand. Of course, the creative solution lies in ideas thought to be irrelevant. During incubation, the nodes coding the problem remain primed or partially activated in the creative mind. In the uncreative person, the nodes coding the problem are deactivated. Rather than remaining in the back of the mind, the problem is forgotten. As the creator goes about his or her business, many nodes will be activated. If one of these happens to be related to the nodes coding the problem, the latter become fully activated and leap into attention. (256)

Martindale calls this state in which many nodes are weakly activated "primary process thinking." It corresponds to the preconscious, nonverbal thinking identified by other cognitive scientists as characteristic of the incubation phase. His term recognizes the evolutionary, structural, and operational primacy of nonsymbolic thinking, the opposite of "secondary process thinking" that is characterized by "a state of focused attention, where a few nodes are strongly activated," as required for logical and other types of serial operations, including most language use (1995:259). Although Martindale does not say so, another way to describe these two distinct categories of thought are, respectively, "right track" and "left track" in recognition of the categorical split in thinking styles generally associated with the brain's two hemispheres (Taylor 1988).

Bisociation and the Bisected Brain

Summarizing what I have written up to this point, there appear to be three distinct cognitive requirements associated with creativity that bear on what I shall have to say later about the relationship between creativity and orthographic types. First, people need so-called "left track" analytical skills to isolate the elements of a problem from their concrete setting, and to express these elements abstractly enough to facilitate matches with stored models. Second, one needs to be able to visualize these segments of the problem out of their linguistic and symbolic contexts, as elements in an (evolutionary) lower part of the cognitive hierarchy where thinking is done by the "right track" processes of analogy and association. Third, people must be able to carry out the two processes in a complementary fashion, so that abstract target patterns elicit appropriate sources, near matches suggest better target representations, and proposed solutions are critically evaluated. In other words, data from the two processes must be exchanged.

There is strong evidence that these three cognitive requirements correlate with the brain's hemispheric activities. Analytical and abstracting tasks invoked during creativity's preparatory phase are characteristic of the logical operations carried out in the left hemisphere of most (but not all) people's brains, hence the term "left track."[11] The spatial (multidimensional) thinking that supports the *ana*logical associations needed during incubation is probably conducted in the right hemisphere. Insight, the sudden matching of the target representation with an abstract, nonverbal source pattern, depends on communication between the two halves. In the validation stage, the left hemisphere takes over again to scrutinize the right brain's analogical proposals by logical analysis. Both hemispheres are involved separately and together in creativity.

Scholarly acceptance of distinct hemispheric roles in the creative process, while widespread today, was delayed by an early oversimplification that cast the notion in a bad light. Just as popular psychology had confused the middle phase of creativity with its whole, ignoring the analytical and sweaty parts of the operation, so did the original view of creativity as a "right-brained" activity err by omitting the critical left hemisphere contributions and the requirement that the two hemispheres operate in tandem. Creativity scientists working on the fringe of mainstream psychology were not eager to add another link to their misbegotten identification with the counterculture.[12]

I considered leaving the hemispheric discussion out of the present study for the same reason. Although it is unlikely this book will be linked to the counterculture, some of the points raised here about Asian orthography and technology transfer will be seen by some as challenging or controversial. Since it is quite possible to argue my points about orthography's influence on cognitive processes without referring to the physical seat of those processes, why add to the exposure? But the evidence tying hemispheric activities to creativity is so overwhelming that I concluded the association could not be ignored even in a summary presentation.

Let's look first at the neurological evidence. Rauch's 1977 study of brain-damaged patients showed that people with portions of their left hemisphere removed re-presented the same problem over and over, unable to settle on an answer even when appropriate solutions had been achieved. Conversely, patients with right hemisphere lobotomies would perseverate with the same hypothesis, failing to produce alternative solutions after the inadequacy of the original formulation became apparent. Later studies replicated these findings (Fiore and Schooler 1998:355). Generating analogical solutions to logical problems, often through nonverbal images, is associated with the incubation phase of creativity. The inability of people with right brain damage to perform this task suggests that the function is localized to the right hemisphere. By the same token, evaluating analogical solutions through logic defines creativity's validation stage, and the failure of left-brain-impaired subjects at this task likewise points to a localized activity.

These hemispheric biases apply not only to phases of creativity. They are global in nature and manifest some well-known dichotomies. For example,

Jaynes noted, on the basis of clinical tests of normal and commissuro-tomized patients and patients with left or right brain lesions, "that the right hemisphere is more involved in synthetic and spatial constructive tasks while the left hemisphere is more analytic and verbal." The right brain "sees parts as having a meaning only within a context" that is, as wholes; the left "looks at parts themselves" (1976:119). Springer and Deutsch found that patients with right hemisphere damage do worse on "non-verbal tests involving the manipulation of geometrical figures, puzzle assembly, *completion of missing parts of patterns and figures,* and other tasks involving form, distance, and space relationships" (1998:16, my emphasis).

Although they were not *designed* to support creativity, these innate differences in hemispheric processing styles are what make creativity possible. Fiore and Schooler list four typical right hemisphere traits that are consistent with creativity's incubation phase, including: "reliance on non-verbal processes, avoiding perseveration, access to nondominant interpretations, and perceptual restructuring" (1998:350). Schooler and Melcher, citing their own research and that of others, on the other hand found significant overlap between analytical problems and logical arguments—associated with creativity's early and late stages—in terms of competition for left hemisphere processing space. Their use of the same cognitive resource derives from the fact that they are serial operations and depend on verbal memory "to maintain and manipulate information" (1995:125).

Language itself has long been known to be a left hemisphere activity, which coincides with our observations about symbolic activity and "secondary process thinking." Its left lateralization goes beyond phonology to core linguistic structures, as evidenced by sign language's dependence on the left hemisphere, not the right as one might expect from its spatial orientation. According to Calvin and Ojemann, "Deaf patients using sign language are just as impaired with left brain strokes as the rest of us, and their sign language is just as unimpaired by right brain strokes as ours is" (1994:65). The symbolic activity behind all forms of language—spoken, written, and signed—has its locus on the left, which has important implications for the mind's ability to learn and apply analytical techniques, as we shall see.[13]

Recently a number of studies have argued for right hemisphere involvement in language (Beeman and Chiarello 1998). A closer look at these arguments confirms, however, that language, as understood by most linguists, is very much a left brain activity. Although the right hemisphere is involved in language comprehension, it is concerned chiefly with the figurative meanings of words and relating words to context (146). As Deacon puts it, the right hemisphere is involved in the large-scale processing used to fit words and sentences into larger units such as "complex ideas, descriptions, narratives, and arguments" (1997:311–12).[14] Its methods are holistic, as opposed to those of the left hemisphere, which focuses on manipulating language's components. The identification of a part of language with the right hemisphere suggests, however, that what resides in the left is not language per se but the neurological connectivity that governs language's analytical and logical features.

This observation is supported in part by the finding that neural activation is more constrained in the left hemisphere than in the right, giving the left hemisphere the ability to "modulate and restrict the scope of available meanings to those that are closely related to the current context" as required for the solution of logical problems (Chiarello 1998:145). The right hemisphere "maintains a broader range of related meanings, including those which may have been eliminated by more selective LH processes," allowing it to participate in the analogical routines needed for creativity's middle phase. With the ability to access distant (nondominant) interpretations "more concepts are likely to be accessed [by the right side] and more divergence from the current approach is likely to occur" (Fiore and Schooler 1998:360).

The physical basis for these hemispheric differences seems to be greater functional connectivity in the brain's right half, as indicated by denser interneurons in the language areas and more dendritic branching, a higher ratio of white to gray matter, a greater diffusion of deficits caused by lesions, and more diffuse evoked potentials in the right (Beeman 1998:257). The two halves function differently because they are built differently.

Creativity exploits these differences. Problems are analyzed by the left brain, whose sparse architecture facilitates focusing on parts. The right, meanwhile, with its enhanced connectivity seeks divergent analogues for left brain encodings. Its proposals are scrutinized by the left. On this matter— the cofunctioning of the two hemispheres—there is broad agreement. As Fiore and Schooler note, "most problems involve long and extensive logical reasoning, punctuated every now and then by an insight regarding an alternative way to proceed. Such hybrid problem solving processes highlight the close integration that insight and noninsight processes may often entail" (368). The right and the left work together to create solutions (I wish our political process worked this well). The organization is described eloquently by Bruce West and Jonas Salk in an essay where they wrote:

The mind may also be seen as a unit made up of two interactive distributed functions which may be referred to as intuition and reason. The brain, with its right and left hemispheres, may be seen as the binary structure for the functioning mind with its cofunctioning of intuition and reason. (1988:160)

We have accounted for the separate phases of creativity in hemispheric terms, but what of our earlier point about the need to coordinate these processes? Creativity depends not only on the capacity to formulate problems and evaluate solutions (left hemisphere) or on the ability to generate multiple hypotheses (right hemisphere). It also requires that these activities be linked. In an intriguing article, Bogan and Bogan argue that creativity depends in part on what they call "transcallosal interhemisphere exchange" used to enable the "integrated use of verbal and visuo-spatial thought" (1976:257–59). The authors point out "There is an inbuilt antagonism between analysis and intuition requiring subtle mediation to obtain a common ground." This is done by the callosal fibers joining the two halves, which host both excitatory and inhibitory activity (260).

These fibers share the same global qualities of other neurons in their susceptibility to selection and strengthening through use, so that their ability to mediate data exchanges between the two hemispheres is enhanced and shaped by their exercise of cognitive demands. As we shall see later, alphabetic writing's requirement for ongoing mediation between fractional and integrative thought processes plays the same role here in preparing the brain for creative thinking that the alphabet's analytical demands play in acclimating the brain to fine-grained, abstract thought. In both cases the brain adapts to the tasks it is called on to execute. The end purpose of these demands—reading and writing or working through a creative process—is irrelevant. All that matters is that the processes be congruent.

Living on the Edge

Creativity above all is a balancing act. One shuttles between a world shaped by rules and predictability and a different realm where freedom and randomness govern.[15] Creativity demands that the complementary operations captured in such dichotomies as serial-parallel, logical-analogical, rational-intuitive, verbal-visual, and fractional-holistic be optimized to support one another without jeopardizing the integrity of either operation. Coordination is as important to creativity as the separate operations are themselves.

Students of creativity have consistently pointed out the need to coordinate these two distinct types of processes. Blandshard spoke of creativity as the "result of two influences, on the one side the psychological and mechanical, which would drive it along the trail of association, and on the other the logical, whose attraction if sufficiently powerful, keeps it in the groove of necessity" (1939:127). Mitchell wrote of the need to explore "many plausible angles of possible interpretations while avoiding a search through a combinatorial explosion of implausible possibilities" (1993:22). More recently, McGraw (1997) described the need for "top down control with bottom up processing." Too much freedom produces nothing useful or meaningful, while too much control takes out the "sparkle."

The difficulty of achieving this balance is evidenced both by creativity's scarcity and by the distribution of cognitive traits throughout populations. Our world is littered with intelligent left brain types skilled in the verbal arts or particular disciplines who pass through their lives without generating an original idea. The phenomenon has been described well by Thomas Kuhn (1962) and requires no elaboration here. On the other side are the inveterate visionaries and dreamers able to associate everything but unable to follow a single line of thought. What both lack is balance, or the ability to navigate what is commonly referred to as the "creative tension" set up by conflicting demands for freedom and order.

We learn to resolve this tension in the creative sphere when the environment provides us opportunities to grapple with analogous conflicts elsewhere. Language, which requires that we shift between unstructured thoughts and an ordered system, is one such venue. This is especially true for people whose written language approximates (but does not coincide exactly with) speech, where the interplay between formal writing and spontaneous speech acclimates users to the task of mediating opposing demands in exercising what is probably a unified process (Hannas 1997:245–47). Political society, of course, constitutes another venue where individuals reconcile the impulse to freedom with the need for order, to the extent that societies delegate that responsibility to individuals.

What then is needed for individual creativity? Amabile and Check list three elements: "*domain-relevant skills,* including everything that the individual knows and can do in the target domain; *creativity-relevant skills*, including cognitive styles, personality styles, and work styles that are conducive to the generation of novel ideas, and *intrinsic task motivation*" (1985:59). The authors consider the last item, motivation, "just as important as the role of intelligence, memory, and learning." We shall see later how society plays an important role here by affecting one's disposition to create. Their first two elements, however, relate directly to our argument about the need for both left and right track expertise (and the ability to mediate the two).

I emphasize that left track skills in this context refer almost entirely to analytical talent and domain mastery, *not* to intelligence per se. Specialists concur on the need for substantive expertise in a specific area. According to Gardner, "Individuals are not creative (or noncreative) in general; they are creative in particular domains of accomplishment, and require the achievement of expertise in these domains before they can execute significant creative work" (1994:145). Johnson-Laird expressed the same requirement in reverse, in terms of knowledge about what *cannot* be done. He noted, "The exceptional thinker has mastered more constraints—to be used generatively as opposed to merely critically—and thus has a greater chance of making the required mapping" (1989:328). Churchland pointed out the need for people to be

sufficiently learned to have a large repertoire of powerful prototypes whose novel redeployments are worth exploring in the first place . . . and who are sufficiently critical to be able to distinguish between a merely strained metaphor on the one hand, and a genuinely systematic and enabling insight on the other. (1995:279)

The creative individual must be knowledgeable about the field in which he or she creates. This requirement supposes sufficient intelligence, as measured by IQ tests, to master a knowledge domain. That said, there is widespread agreement among creativity specialists that intelligence is a "necessary but insufficient" condition (Eysenck 1994:200). Past a certain point, IQ does not seem to matter. Findlay and Lumsden state:

The correlation between IQ and creative ability is relatively modest, up to about IQ 120, beyond which it appears to weaken even further. . . . Hence, despite the interest in IQ studies, their value for understanding creativity, discovery and innovation may ultimately prove quite limited. (1988:36)

Finke, Ward, and Smith report various studies, which found that "people with low IQs tend to be uncreative, whereas people with high IQs can be either creative or uncreative" (1996:28). The minimum IQ requirement relates to what I said earlier about domain mastery, whereas the irrelevance of a high IQ suggests that more than (left track) intelligence is involved. Martindale's remarks on this subject are worth quoting:

The more intelligent one is, the more one can learn. There should, then, be a correlation between intelligence and creativity, and there is—but only up to an IQ around 120 or so, and then the correlation essentially vanishes. One finds extremely intelligent people who are not in the slightest bit creative and extremely creative people who are not wildly intelligent. (1995:253)

Left-track intelligence of the sort reflected in IQ tests is superfluous beyond what is needed to assimilate existing knowledge within a domain. One uses this knowledge to represent problems and evaluate solutions. Between these two phases of preparation and verification, associative (right-track) skills are needed, the exercise of which has even less to do with IQ than the left track skills that precede and follow it. Herein lies the province of what James (1890:360) and Simonton called the "intuitive genius." For highly creative people, Simonton noted, "Fewer connections are habitual or even properly symbolized." Unlike the analytical genius, knowledge used by the intuitive genius is distributed more evenly. "Because mental elements are more richly interconnected, appreciably more ways exist of passing from one element to another" (1988a:402).

If high IQ has little to do with creativity, extreme fluency in associative thinking by itself cannot lead to creativity either. The right track analogue of the high IQ type is the schizophrenic, who has lost touch with "reality," that is, the logical relations between ideas. The creative thinker and the schizophrenic differ in their ability to weigh and balance. As Eysenck described it, for both creative and psychotic personalities the concept of relevance "is broadened, and ideas and associations become relevant that would not appear to be so for the ordinary person. Creative thinking is distinguished from schizophrenic thinking by a more critical assessment of the products of such thinking" (1994:231).

Abnormally good left track or right track skills are less important for creativity than the ability to mediate both types of functions, exercised in adequate measure. No one in his or her right (or left) mind would question the intellectual abilities of East Asians. If creativity and high intellect did correlate, there would be no grounds for the present thesis. On the other hand, neither Westerners nor Asians claim a monopoly on schizophrenia. Both sides of the world have their share of overly active right-brained personalities able to find associations where there are none.[16] What matters for creativity is that these bicameral skills be integrated. It makes sense, accordingly, to view external factors that facilitate coordination between the two types of skills as part of what makes certain people and groups more creative than others.

Later I shall describe in detail the effects of writing as a facilitator (or inhibitor) of creativity-related skills. We will also look at the link between cultures steeped in particular orthographic traditions and their adaptation to creativity tasks. Finally, we will consider some derivative or associative properties of writing that relate indirectly to creative behavior.

Here I shall merely register the specialists' view that social structures and norms have an important impact on individual creativity. Brick pointed out that "a society that promotes and encourages creativity and strives for novelty and unexpected solutions to problems will probably foster more people that behave in a way that we would call creative than a society that is indifferent or negative" (1997:6). Mandler noted, "Both the creative artist and scientist are part of a cultural tradition that values the novel construction and seeks out novelty. On the other hand, there are social and cultural conditions in which the novel is avoided and considered inappropriate (e.g., in authoritarian societies)." Societies that value harmony above all else will view creativity "as destructive of existing values and standards" (1995:21–22). Hennessey and Amabile concluded, "There is no doubt that salient factors of extrinsic constraint in the social environment can have a consistently negative impact on the intrinsic motivation and creativity of most people most of the time" (1988:34).

Social constraints that frustrate one's motivation to create are also expressed by the absence of diversity. Dunbar, who studied the cultures, work processes, and creative results of different scientific laboratories, found that the one lab in his sample whose staff did not use analogical reasoning made no progress in understanding their research task. He further noted, "All the staff in this laboratory came from highly similar backgrounds and consequently drew from a similar knowledge base" (1995:384–85). Findlay and Lumsden noted in the same vein that background knowledge needed to generate analogies "depends not only on the individual's capacity to learn and store information, but also on such macroscopic factors as the accessibility of diverse sociocultural environments" (1988:17). Homogeneous, politically centralized societies thwart creative impulses—and eventually the disposition of its members to create—by depriving individuals of opportunities to enrich their store of potential source analogs.

Simonton cited three more social factors related to creativity that will be seen as particularly relevant in the present context. One is the effect of conformist education. As Simonton put it, "the iconoclastic facet of creativity—the capacity to produce genuinely original chance configurations—quite obviously requires that the young creator not be excessively socialized into a single, narrow-minded way of associating ideas" (1988a:413). Another factor is privacy. Simonton offers the following technical explanation for its need:

Social interaction may elicit a social-interference effect. . . . The mere presence of others tends to raise arousal, which in turn increases the likelihood that highly probable responses will be emitted at the expense of responses less probable. Because the chance-permutation process demands access to low-probability associations, such socially induced arousal would necessarily inhibit creativity. To the extent that the presence of others implies the possibility of evaluation, this interference effect would be heightened all the more. (404)

Finally, Simonton points to the need for societies to tread a narrow path between political pluralism ("creativity increases whenever a civilization is fragmented into a large number of sovereign nations") and the violent events that sometimes accompany fragmentation. He writes, "Wars between states, for instance, tend to produce an ideological zeitgeist that may not welcome innovation, and creativity is definitely unlikely to come forth after a political system crumbles into total anarchy, as registered by military revolts, dynastic conflicts, political assassinations, coups d'état, and other exemplars of chaos among the power elite" (415).

As in the personal sphere, creativity demands that societies live on the edge between stasis (left hemisphere perseveration) and chaos (right hemisphere randomness).[17] Stability is needed as a baseline for survival and for individuals to build up a store of domain-specific knowledge. On the other hand, society must be able to tolerate enough pot stirring, skepticism, and "creative dissent" to make innovation safe and respectable for a

critical minority of individuals. The challenge is to keep the two requirements in balance—a goal that meshes fairly well with the Western ideals of
federalism, minimal government, and linear progress. East Asian society
historically has been less adept at achieving this balance, as evidenced in its
view of "progress" as a cyclical movement from stability through chaos and
back to stability. China in particular, with its highly centralized authoritarian governments, cannot seem to stay on the cutting edge, and is either
falling off the one side or the other into rigidity or chaos.

The Western and Eastern traditions seem to offer, respectively, exactly
what is needed to foster and to frustrate scientific creativity. Among the
many factors that have influenced members of the two cultures to think
and act in creative and noncreative ways, orthography perhaps stands out
as the most important because it touches on processes that underlie a basic
difference in the two culture's cognitive styles. Its effects on creativity began with the origins of both civilizations.

Chapter Six
Creativity and the Alphabet

First, there was the emergence of consciousness in the higher animals and secondly the much more remarkable transcendence when hominids experienced self-consciousness.

—John C. Eccles

The Role of Writing in Language

In the preceding chapter I remarked on psychologists' belief that language acts as a barrier to creativity. Creative thinking requires that the thinker retreat from symbolic thought to a more basic mode of cognition that is more nearly visual than verbal. Symbolic thought by its nature predisposes one to consider problems in existing categories. We benefit enormously in our day-to-day lives from this ability to cast reality in familiar terms and manipulate knowledge structures through a directory of pointers. At the same time, these structures inhibit us from "visualizing" data in new ways. Recurrent neural activation patterns, literally models of our past successes, do not yield easily to reformation. Designating these constructs with verbal markers validates their status as units, strengthening their resistance to change.

We shall consider this problem in detail in a later chapter. Our task now is to demonstrate how writing—a representation of language—facilitates creativity by helping people overcome their conceptual biases as speakers of a symbolic language. More to the point, how can writing, which is believed to have a conservative influence on language, act as a catalyst for radical thought? To answer these questions we must be more specific about how language, writing, and speech interact and about how these mechanisms relate to the way we think.

In essence there are two conflicting interpretations of how writing maps onto language. One theory, associated with the views of American linguist Leonard Bloomfield (1933) and the early behaviorist school of psychology, holds that language literally *is* speech and that no legitimate distinction can be made between the abstract knowledge that generates a linguistic expression and the concrete speech act itself. In this view, writing acts as a secondary system—its units are symbols of symbols. As Scinto (1986:1) put it, "Traditional accounts of the nature of language have viewed written language as a derivative symbol system, one that enjoys only a parasitic status with respect to oral language." Scholars who support this older view cite the ontogenetic and phylogenetic priority of speech as their basis for identifying speech with language, and the fact that all writing is to a greater or lesser degree based on phonology.

A newer interpretation is that writing and speech each *manifest* structures generated through the body of rules that make up a language. Instead of "representing" speech, writing and speech are both viewed as parallel expressions of language—in Scinto's words, "as equipollent systems that equally manifest man's linguistic capacity" (2). Transformational rules produce a string of elements from a deep, abstract representation of the thoughts one wishes to convey. These elements are then realized orally through speech or visually through writing. Although the units of writing ideally bear a relationship with those of speech, it is less important that one be specified in terms of the other than that the units of both media be adapted to the practical tasks with which they are associated.

This modern view of writing and speech as alternative expressions of language arose more or less independently among scholars on different continents engaged in a variety of disciplines. In Europe, the debate had never been whether writing represents speech or language but whether writing and speech represent even the same language (Amirova 1977:5, 35; 1985:4). Eastern European scholars in particular were under no compulsion to tailor their research to American intellectual paradigms and as a consequence produced many innovative ideas on the relationship between language, writing, and human psychology, some of which we shall touch on below.[1]

In the United States, Bloomfield's structuralism was eclipsed in the early 1960s by generative grammar, which rejected the behaviorist tenets on which this older view of language was based. Unlike the structuralists, who excluded higher cognitive functions from the study of language, the newer school of linguists embraced them, regarding abstract, objectified language—language that more closely resembles polished texts than speech—as the foundation of linguistic science. Instead of looking at language from the bottom up, the younger linguists studied language, if not from the top down, then at least in terms of models that seek to explain mental processes. Even phonology, the most concrete part of the linguistic hierarchy, was shown to depend on abstract manipulations and on "units" that have no direct analogue in speech. With the focus on generative forms, it was immaterial whether the content of these forms was sounds or written symbols.

Adherents to Bloomfield's views on writing, fixated on the apparent fact that speech preceded writing in the evolution of human societies, also failed to take into account some clues about the nature of writing that were evident in the evolution of their own discipline. As I shall note presently, awareness of language—the whole of it and its particular structures—became possible only with the appearance of writing. Prior to that, language and speech *were* indistinguishable, and remain so today in preliterate minds, because no alternative way to express language existed. What was true of language in general was also true of its components, including those at the lower end of the scale where the structuralists felt most at home. Although not a fact that they were prone to dwell on, the concept of phonemes, which is where the structuralists did some of their best work, was derived from alphabetic orthography, not the other way around.

Setting aside the issue of primacy, which has less to do with the relationship between writing and speech than with the philosophical choices of individual scholars, and looking at the relationship from a functional perspective, it has long been apparent that writing and speech use separate neurological channels. For example, the notion that reading involves translating written symbols into sound and then listening to one's own inner speech—a legacy of the structuralist paradigm—has been discredited in a dozen different ways (Hannas 1997:153–58). Although phonological recoding *can* be used by readers to access lexical items, it is neither the only nor even the preferred route.[2] The functional independence of speech and writing is further demonstrated in neurolinguistic studies showing that *either* speech *or* reading can be selectively impaired, and that disorders in the one area do not correlate with disorders in the other (Paradis et al. 1985).

Given the overwhelming evidence that language is not a synonym for speech, and that writing, like speech, has a semiautonomous relationship with the structures that make up language, the important questions to ask pertain not to the relationship between the two media, which has largely been decided, but to the psychology of those holding such negative views about writing. Why was writing neglected by American linguists? And why do a few academics insist even today that writing is a secondary phenomenon whose significance is overstated absolutely and relative to speech?

These are not trivial questions. As we shall see, sensitivity over the status of writing reflects deep-seated differences in attitudes toward scholarship and society. Moreover, the failure to recognize writing's full role in human cognitive development has unnecessarily delayed the integration of promising lines of research in multiple disciplines. It has, for example, inhibited the exploration of links between writing systems and culture and frustrated the articulation of conclusions "intuitively and tentatively reached by many scientists" about the effect of writing on the historical development of thought (de Kerckhove 1988:417).

At first I thought the problem stemmed from the conditions surrounding the rise of linguistics in the United States. On the one hand, the early linguists' studies of Native American languages, which were mostly unwritten, prejudiced them against writing. Although this may have been one reason for their neglect, it could not have been decisive, since similar conditions in the Soviet Union failed to generate the same antipathy. On the other hand, linguists' eagerness to found their discipline on a scientific basis more or less guaranteed that they would try to explain their data in terms of the era's leading paradigm: hard core reductionism. Following the lead of psychologists, linguists sought to reduce language to its most concrete observable elements—the sounds of speech—and were less interested in higher structures not amenable to a mechanistic approach, such as those typically reflected in writing.

This latter explanation rings true, given that the direct hostility toward writing mostly vanished when linguists replaced their reductionist model with one able to accommodate what the structuralists had disparaged as mental phenomena. The paradigm shift that began with the demise of billiard ball mechanics in physics wound its way through the social sciences and humanities, where it should never have been applied, resulting in a new willingness by linguists to investigate data whose cognitive antecedents were not directly apparent. The inability of a few language scholars to make this transition has had no consequence for linguistics overall, although their nuisance effect is still felt in the less commonly taught languages, which are more shielded from academic scrutiny.

Recently I have come to believe that other factors contributed to this tendency to marginalize writing. Linguists were forced to acknowledge writing's role as a direct expression of language by the logic of their own theory of grammar. Nonetheless, complaints can still be heard among some linguists, including generative grammarians responsible for the new view of language, about the unnaturalness of reading and writing. People learn to speak almost effortlessly, it is argued, whereas literacy is acquired only through a deliberate effort, and often not at all. If writing is a part of language, why is it so hard to learn?

Another sign of lingering resentment toward writing is the humanities' current fondness of so-called "oral societies." This term seemed ludicrous to me at first because it suggests that preliterate societies have found their own path to communication equal in value to that of literate societies, and indeed this is often the message intended. So if oral societies do not read and write, then literate societies cannot hear and speak? And what can "equal" possibly mean when survival itself depends nowadays on leveraging the artifacts of literate culture? It is not hard to poke holes in the logic of these assumptions, as Goody and Watt were already doing three decades ago with their complaint about the "sentimental egalitarianism" that compares oral societies favorably with those that read and write (1968:67).

While I have little sympathy for this approach to "solving" literacy problems by denying its value, my research on creativity has convinced me that the categorical notion of an oral society is valid, inasmuch as it conveys much more than the absence of a particular skill. It reflects a unique mindset, as different from the literate mindset as orality is from the absence of language altogether. Moreover, I will go as far as to endorse the term "semi-oral society," for reasons that I shall get into later, to describe societies not necessarily with low literacy rates but whose particular type of literacy inhibits its members from acquiring the full range of cognitive benefits potentially available through literacy. This view no doubt will be criticized as "elitist," as are the views of most scholars who have explored the implications of writing, but I think the issue is important enough to risk censure from some quarters.

And if, despite my first impression, oral society does mean more than a lack of literacy, I will also concede the one good argument the language-as-speech group has been able to make, namely, the unnaturalness of writing. Writing *is* unnatural, not because of its mechanics,[3] nor even because it has existed too briefly to have spawned a heritable acquisition device such as that supposedly available for speech. Learning to read and write is difficult because it involves exercising the unnatural skills of analysis and abstraction. Literacy presupposes an ability to recognize, on some level, that language is *not* speech. This major feat of abstraction, that even literate people sometimes are unable consciously to achieve, opens one's mind to the power of abstraction generally, laying the basis for introspection, creativity, and self-consciousness.

This latter point has been made by other scholars with respect both to writing as a whole and to its individual components (the notion of the phoneme). I mention it here to demonstrate that if language were speech, and writing were a representation of speech, none of this unnaturalness would be felt. People would simply map the one system of signs onto the other, without the conceptual frustration typically experienced in becoming literate. Nor would the cognitive differences between oral and literate societies be as great as researchers have found them to be.

Writing and Abstract Thought

Linguists' reluctance to treat writing as a part of language had ramifications in other areas. As Wrolstad pointed out, their neglect made it easier for sociologists and cultural anthropologists to downplay writing's cognitive role and to minimize the differences between literate and illiterate societies (1976:35). Instead of focusing on the psycholinguistic distinctions between the two types of cultures, scholars spent far too much time extolling the "complexity" of oral languages, that is, those without writing, as if complexity itself were the core issue. This spirit pervades linguistics even today, evidenced by its dictum that "there are no primitive languages," and continues to deflect scholarship from the main problem, as I see it, of why people in oral societies *think* differently.

What are these differences between oral and literate thought? We noted that writing is difficult to learn because it serves as an early exemplar of the difference between an abstract entity and its concrete representation. Writing objectifies language, distancing what is said from the person who said it and the particular circumstances that accompany an utterance. It causes one to focus on the meaning of a discourse regardless of what it seemed to mean when it was first presented. For a written text to be understood, the reader must provide a context metaphorically distant from what the reader qua hearer would recognize through an oral exchange. Learning how to do this is a wrenching experience, but at the same time one that frees the mind from its dependence on the here and now, not just in language but in the exercise of thought generally.

Oral societies spare their members this trauma at the expense of miring their thinking in concrete events. As Ong noted, "A sound-dominated verbal economy is consonant with aggregative (harmonizing) tendencies rather than with analytic, dissecting tendencies." It fosters situational thinking "rather than abstract thinking" and a mindset that is "more communal and externalized, and less introspective than [that] common among literates. Oral communication unites people in groups. Writing and reading are solitary activities that throw the psyche back on itself" (1982:69, 73). Ong attributes these differences in thinking to the technology of writing, without which "the literate mind would not and could not think as it does" (78).

Donald in his classic study *Origins of the Modern Mind* observes similarly "the major products of analytic thought . . . are generally absent from purely mythic cultures. A partial list of features that are absent include formal arguments, systematic taxonomies, induction, deduction, verification, differentiation, quantification, idealization, and formal methods of measurement" (1991:273). Donald attributes "the switch from a predominantly narrative mode of thought to a predominantly theoretic mode" to what he calls "a shift in the relative importance of the two major distal-perceptual modalities, from auditory to visual representation." Summarizing the differences between the two types of cultures, he states:

There are two broadly different modes of thinking evident in modern humans. One is sometimes called narrative thought, and the other is variously called analytic, paradigmatic, or logico-scientific. In modern culture, narrative thought is dominant in the literary arts, while analytic thought predominates in science, law and government. The narrative or mythic dimension of modern culture has been expressed in print, but it is well to keep in mind that in its inception, mythic thought did not depend upon print or visual symbolism; it was an extension, in its basic form, of the oral narrative. (273)

Scholes and Willis (1991), whose work on phoneme perception I discuss later, observed the same cognitive differences between nonliterate and literate people that Donald and others claim exist between oral and literate societies. According to the two scholars, nonliterates have difficulty with analogies and "appear unable to classify things on the basis of geometrical categories or other abstract properties. Nonliterate adults employ, we would suggest, the same concrete operational processing as preliterate children." In their view, "the handicap of illiteracy is far more profound than is suggested by the inability to read. Illiteracy is more accurately seen as a complex of linguistic and cognitive competencies qualitatively unlike those of literates" (228–30).

David Olson, who has thought about the cognitive impact of writing on traditional oral societies more than anyone, believes that writing "split the comprehensive process into two parts, that part preserved by the text, the given, and that part, the interpretation, provided by the reader" (1986:318). Writing forces a distinction between what one thinks a text means and what is actually in the text, the former being subjective and concrete bound, the latter being objective and abstract. This distinction carries over into thought generally, providing what Olson calls "the model, more than that, the precise cognitive categories or concepts needed for the description and the interpretation of nature; that is, for the building of modern science" (304).

Derrick de Kerckhove has also written extensively about the relationship between writing and cognition. In his view, "Oral languages are always, of necessity, 'contextualized.' Their usage is both field- and context-dependent. Even at their metaphorical best, they remain grounded in biological needs. Under such conditions, discoveries and innovations made possible by direct, oral communication can never stray too far away from the need to respond to established environmental (or situational) conditioning" (1988:107). Abstract thought, which we identified earlier as the sine qua non of scientific creativity, is a function of the literate mind.

The transition from context-bound situational thinking to abstract, analytical thinking that occurs when individuals become literate represents the achievement on a personal level of what some cognitive scientists now recognize as the most recent stage in the development of thought. We noted above Donald's description of "mythic" (essentially oral) and "theoretic" (literate) cultures, characterized respectively by concrete and abstract modes of thinking. The cultures are the last two of four evolutionary stages Donald identifies, each based on changes in the representational structure of thought (1991:274). The first stage of "episodic" thinking is the most basic form of cognition, which focuses on discrete events of limited duration; there is no modeling of relations between events. "Mimetic" thought, which succeeds it, depends on the representation of features that transcend specific events. Sophisticated modeling of environmental inputs enables mimetic cultures to achieve skill levels adequate for tool making and many types of advanced communal activities despite the absence of language. Symbolic thought, a function of oral language, underlies Donald's third stage of "mythic" thinking, characterized by the advent of conceptual knowledge and pragmatic technologies. Abstract thought is the basis for the final stage, which Donald calls "theoretic" or scientific culture (334–35).

These stages are cumulative. That is, earlier forms of representation provide the foundation for more advanced forms. Successive cultures continue to use the earlier modes of cognition where appropriate. What changes, beyond physical accretions to the brain's structure, is the way the brain models the world. As Donald notes, "The key word here is *representation*. Humans did not simply evolve a larger brain, an expanded memory, a lexicon, or a special speech apparatus; we evolved new systems for representing reality" (3).

Donald's emphasis on representation as the main factor in cognitive evolution is consistent with Terrence Deacon's views on the progress of thought discussed in the preceding chapter. Deacon identifies three categories of semiotic relationships—iconic, indexical, and symbolic—that the brain learned to model in the course of its development. Iconic relationships, in which a part of a stimulus is used to represent an object or event, correlate with Donald's episodic thought. These icons form the basis for indices that model relationships between events, corresponding to the mimetic thinking that makes up Donald's second stage. Symbolic representation is the third stage of cognitive evolution in both of their systems.

Donald, however, goes on to make a qualitative distinction between the two major classes of symbols, verbal and written, based on the distinctive modes of consciousness associated with them. Interestingly, many of the stereotypes he identifies with oral and literate cognitive styles parallel the dichotomies between right- and left-brain thinking that we described earlier. This suggests that writing may be at least partly responsible for the lateralization of language's more analytic functions to the left hemisphere.[4] Jaynes also identified two distinct types of human consciousness, one concrete and reactive, the other abstract and introspective. He linked the shift from the former to the latter type with a change in the physical locus of symbolic thought, which he believed was shared equally between the brain's two halves (bicamerality) but which later came to be directed primarily by the left hemisphere. Writing, in his view, served as a catalyst to promote this shift (1976:208, 302).

Walter Ong argued that writing did not just promote the changes Jaynes described; rather, it *embodied* them. Ong states, "the early and late stages of consciousness which Julian Jaynes (1976) describes and relates to neurophysical changes in the bicameral mind would also appear to lend themselves largely to much simpler and more verifiable description in terms of a shift from orality to literacy" (1982:29). The shift from the diffuse consciousness characteristic of Jaynes's bicameral and Donald's mythic culture to the focused, egocentric self-consciousness of modern theoretic culture was, to use a contemporary analogy, embedded in the software of writing. As Ong put it:

Whatever one makes of Jaynes's theories one cannot but be struck by the resemblance between the characteristics of the early "bicameral" psyche as Jaynes describes it—lack of introspectivity, of analytical prowess, of concern with the will as such, of a sense of difference between past and future—and the characteristics of the psyche in oral cultures not only in the past but even today. The effects of oral states of consciousness are bizarre to the literate mind, and they can invite elaborate explanations which may turn out to be needless. Bicamerality may simply mean orality. (30)

Russian psychologists were among the first to describe the parallel between the acquisition of literacy and a change in the dominant mode of thinking from concrete to abstract. Experiments conducted by A. R. Luria (1976) with preliterate and literate farmers showed gross differences in the way objects were viewed (holistically or analytically), and in the ability to identify abstract relationships. Luria also found nonliterates focusing on the pragmatic aspects of problems (the how) while literate people were more interested in their theoretical aspects (the why). Luria concluded, "cognitive processes change qualitatively, as a result of literacy, and in changing they radically alter our perceptions of reality."[5]

Lev S. Vygotsky's work with schoolchildren led him to the same conclusions. Observing the time lag between the onset of speech and a child's acquisition of writing, Vygotsky rejected the notion that the delay had anything to do with the need to relearn language. Writing takes more time to learn, he argued, because it is associated with a "high level of abstraction" for which speech provides no antecedent (1962:98–99). He further maintained, "when an individual comes to master writing, the basic system underlying the nature of his mental processes is changed fundamentally as the external symbol system comes to mediate the organization of all his basic intellectual operations."[6] Instruction in a given area "influences the development of the higher functions far beyond the confines of that particular subject," making writing and abstract thought inseparable (102).

Western scholars who investigated writing and culture have also argued for a direct relationship between literacy and abstract thought. H. Innis wrote in 1950 that writing caused people to apply "their minds to symbols rather than things. . . . Writing enormously enhanced a capacity for abstract thinking which had been evident in the growth of language in the oral tradition."[7] Goody and Watt (1968:44) believed writing established "a different kind of relationship between the word and its referent, a relationship that is more general and more abstract, and less closely connected with the particularities of person, place and time that obtains in oral communication."

George Miller summarized the results of a famous conference held in 1972 on the relationship between speech, learning, and reading by noting, "the written proposition is a tangible representation of an act of thought. It is a physical thing, an object, and it can be reacted to as any other object can. Thus writing made it possible to react to one's own thoughts as if they were objects, so the act of thought became itself a subject for further thought. Thus extended abstraction became possible" (374).

Merald Wrolstad in his 1976 article "A Manifesto for Visible Language" captured what writing experts felt about linguists' neglect of writing and the effect of this neglect on the understanding of cognitive development. He also added an interesting argument to the data linking writing to abstract thought by noting that "symbolization involves first a process of abstraction; the starting point is something to abstract from. The advantage visible symbols have from the start is that their roots lie in representation. . . . Audible signs are almost totally arbitrary from the beginning" (32).

The link between writing and abstract thought was taken up by Ong in 1982, who argued "All thought, including that in primary oral cultures, is to some degree analytic: it breaks its materials into various components. But abstractly sequential, classificatory, explanatory examination of phenomena or of stated truths is impossible without writing and reading" (8). All conceptual thinking is abstract, but "oral cultures tend to use concepts in situational, operational frames of reference that are minimally abstract" (49). David Olson expanded his earlier theory[8] that writing forces a distinction between concrete form and abstract content in his 1994 book *The World on Paper*, where he attributed the awareness of ideas and scientific development to the abstract mindset caused by writing.

Brian Stock, who studied literacy's impact on medieval thought, reached the same conclusion about writing and abstract thinking. "A distinction likewise arose between the content of what was perceived and the status in reality assigned to it by the process of sifting, classifying, and encoding. . . . Sets of rules, that is, codes generated from written discourse, were employed not only to produce new behavioral patterns but to restructure existing ones." Stock believed that "literacy, as it actually penetrated medieval life and thought, brought about a transformation of the basic skills of reading and writing into instruments of analysis and interpretation" (1983:11).

Such are the effects of writing. Abstraction. Analytic thinking. The birth of formal knowledge and founding of science. Pretty fair achievements for "mere symbols of symbols."

Alphabetic Literacy and Modern Science

Literacy promotes abstract thinking by making one aware of a hidden structure conceptually distinct from the concrete elements that embody it. Absent writing, people cannot formally distinguish language from the sounds through which it operates. By providing an alternative to speech, writing draws attention to its abstract antecedent in several ways.

First, since written language shares some but not all the mechanisms used in speech, a contrast is set up between the part of language that disappears—concrete sounds—and the remainder of language that writing utilizes. An unitary process is found to be composed of separable parts. Second, each of the two media, sharing a common focus, is perceived to be *standing for* the same thing. The discovery that an entity can be used to represent something else introduces one to the availability of abstraction as a cognitive tool. Third, since the units of speech and writing cannot, for historical and pragmatic reasons, be derived from each other, linking the two must be done on an abstract level that is beyond direct observation. Mediating the relationship between the two types of units acclimates one to dealing with abstract associations.

These arguments concern the language mechanism itself. Other scholars have applied the same type of argument to the content of language. As noted in the preceding section, writing enables us to separate what is said from the concrete trappings of oral communication. It externalizes a message, exposing its information to objective analysis. The effect operates on literate persons as readers, and also in their capacity as writers by reminding them of the difference between what they thought they wrote and how the text actually appears a day or two later.

It is difficult for literate people to appreciate the effect literacy has on thought because we take for granted the cognitive style associated with literacy. I personally had a hard time accepting the arguments made by Olson, Ong, and others not because of any flaw in the logic or lack of empirical evidence, but simply because I could not duplicate in my head the preliterate state of mind they described. Most of us (except physicists and all software developers) try to ground theory and long chains of logic in familiar terms to guard against flights of fancy. Although the argument for a cognitive gap between literate and preliterate thought is persuasive, *feeling* the difference is another matter entirely. Apparently it takes an act of abstraction to appreciate life without abstraction. Explaining this issue has also been a bit of a chore and I suspect the reason is the difficulty one has finding metaphors to describe a cognitive transformation so basic that it seems to preempt their use.

If writing encourages abstract thought, then it stands to reason that the more abstract a writing system is, the more strongly it influences the development of abstract thinking. This thesis has been entertained by scholars with backgrounds as different as Arthur Koestler and Ovid Tzeng. In Koestler's view, conceptual thought emerged with the development of abstract symbolization from an earlier stage where thinking was done in images. This process was supported by the evolution of writing as it developed from pictographs to higher levels of abstraction (1964:173). Tzeng and Hung (1988:275) note that the evolution of writing seems to have taken a single direction: at every advance, the number of symbols in the script decreases, and as a direct consequence the abstractness of the relation between script and meaning increases and the link between graphemes and phonemes becomes clearer. This pattern of development seems to parallel the general trend of cognitive development in children and thus may have important implications for beginning readers of different orthographies.

Writing in both China and the West began by depicting the physical characteristics of certain objects. The written symbols used by the Sumerians in the fourth millennium B.C., and by the ancestors of the Chinese a thousand years later, originally had no connection with the sounds of language, or with natural language at all. They were icons of particular phenomena, which later came to represent *classes* of objects. This shift from concrete objects to referents of greater abstraction was accompanied by stylization of the symbols themselves. As the particular nature of the symbols disappeared, they began to be associated with words.

With the primary association between written symbol and object replaced by a direct link between the symbol and a word, writers were able to represent words for which no written symbols existed by using symbols for other words that had the same sound. Instead of inventing a new form that mimicked the physical characteristics of its referent—a task complicated by the abstract nature of many referents—existing graphs were used for their phonetic value alone. This practice eliminated any *necessary* connection between the symbols and the phenomena they represented, raising the level of abstraction a notch higher.

Writing thus came to identify sound (and morphemes to the extent that different graphs were used for the same sound). However, the sounds represented were syllables. No attempt was made, either in China or initially in the West, to identify subsyllabic segments. The connection between symbol and sound was holistic, not analytic. What abstraction did occur was of the sort described above that applies to literacy in general. The major analytical step of identifying and symbolizing phonemes, as depicted in the alphabet, remained to be taken.

Ancient Greece is popularly regarded as the first civilization to use phonemic writing, but this notion is misleading. The alphabet evolved incrementally, its development having begun many centuries before the Greeks made their contribution. By 1400 B.C., Semitic people in the Middle East were using a default alphabet based on twenty-four symbols distilled earlier by the Egyptians from hieroglyphs to represent the language's most common syllables. Over time the Semites learned to ignore the vocalic aspect of the syllables and treat the graphs *as if* they represented only the initial consonant phonemes. As Lafont (1988:93) noted, "The true significance of the Canaanite invention was not the leap from syllabic to phonemic representation, but from a fully syllabic system to one in which the vocalic part was not differentiated within the syllable." Since the roots of Semitic languages depend more critically on consonants than vowels, it was sufficient to depict only the consonants and let the reader supply the vowels from context.

The consonantal alphabet, derivatives of which are in use today, differed from all previous systems by its de facto representation of phonemes. According to Goody, the traditional view, held by the Greeks themselves, is that the Greek alphabet is an adaptation of Phoenician (another Semitic group) consonantal writing and dates from the eighth century B.C. Another view holds that it originated in the eleventh century B.C. and was descended, like Old Phoenician, from Canaanite writing (1987:46–47). In any case, what the Greeks apparently did was reassign four symbols used for Semitic consonants that the Greek language lacked to represent Greek vowels.

Even here it seems likely that the Greeks backed into their "invention." Vowels were depicted occasionally by the Phoenicians with supplementary signs added to the consonant orthography. As Bolinger described it, the Greeks simply did "consistently what the Phoenicians had done sporadically: to add the interpretative vowel signs to all their syllables. What they themselves must have regarded still as a syllabary thus became an alphabet by accident" (1968:170). The phonemic alphabet was not founded deliberately through a creative cognitive process. Rather it resulted from a series of adaptations, each leading to a higher level of abstraction. The Greeks did not invent an alphabet because they were good at abstract thought; they became good at abstract thought because they were the first to use a full alphabet.[9]

The Greeks were also first to develop abstract modern science, perhaps the only civilization to do so indigenously.[10] As Robert Logan, author of *The Alphabet Effect*, has noted, the science practiced in China was "phenomenological, not abstract, and concerned with practical questions. It was based exclusively on observation and not on some theoretical foundation" (1986:22). It remained for the Greeks to give science logical and analytical characteristics, a feat that Logan attributes to the cognitive effects on Greek thought of a fully phonemic alphabet. China failed to develop abstract science because it had no fully phonetic system of writing. Without this tool, China lacked the cognitive model to transform practical science into an abstract discipline.

Logan's thesis as it applies to China has been criticized by DeFrancis and others for its mistaken claim that Chinese writing is "ideographic." As DeFrancis (1984:133–48) and I (1997:104–9) both noted, there is no writing system—in China or anywhere in the world—that directly encodes thought. All writing encodes language, and thought only through language. Chinese characters are no exception. Like every other orthography, it is based largely on phonetic principles.

That said, it seems unfair to blame Logan, who is not an Asia specialist, for accepting the notion that Chinese writing is idea-based, since this misconception was caused by Sinologists (it is still perpetuated by many of that same group, although mercifully not by those trained in linguistics). Moreover, Logan's *instincts* about Chinese writing and the ill effect it has on science were right on track. As we shall see, Chinese writing, though based on sound, fails critically to extend its analysis of sound beyond naturally occurring syllables. It functions, phonetically at least, as a large syllabary, so that in linguistic terms its development stopped at a level reached in the West more than 3,000 years ago, before the fractionalization of syllables into phonemes had begun.

Although Logan's argument for a connection between Asian writing and concrete thought requires some adjustment, his thesis about a link between the alphabet and abstract science has widespread support. Goody and Watt argued that the Greeks developed unique skills in logic and scientific classification through their use of the alphabet. They noted that Plato himself in *Theaetetus* "compares the process of reasoning to the combination of irreducible elements or letters of the alphabet into syllables which, unlike their constituent letters, have meaning" (1968:52–54). Goody later wrote "there are clearly some links between the general growth of science and the growth in the development of more abstract writing systems" (1987:65).

Eric Havelock in *The Literate Revolution in Greece and Its Cultural Consequences* called the alphabet "a piece of explosive technology, revolutionary in its effects on human culture, in a way not precisely shared by any other invention. . . . [It] furnished a necessary conceptual foundation on which to build the structure of the modern sciences and philosophies" (1982:6). Havelock reiterated his argument in an essay titled "The Oral-Literate Equation: A Formula for the Modern Mind," where he argued for a direct, causal connection between the Greek alphabet and modern scientific thought (1991:24).

Others such as Donald credit ancient Greece as being "the birthplace of theoretic civilization" where "all the essential symbolic inventions were in place for the first time." However, Donald backs off from Logan's view that the alphabet caused this transformation because, as he put it, "phonetic scripts, in the form of various syllabaries, had been in existence for almost 2000 years" (1991:340–41). The psycholinguist M. Martin Taylor concedes, "the development of the Greek alphabet coincided with the development of logical modes of philosophical thought" but adds that this "temporal coincidence could have been causally related; but it is hard to imagine how such a relation could ever be proved" (1988:356). Findlay and Lumsden state "a correlation between rates of innovation and degree of alphabetization is not of itself sufficient to demonstrate a causal link or 'adaptive' connection between the two" (1988:168).

This skepticism is reasonable and needs to be addressed. I shall try to show in the remainder of this chapter that there is indeed a causal relationship between use of a fully phonemic alphabet and the development of modern scientific thought. I will also describe how this relationship figures into the creative process.

The Alphabet as a Cognitive Facilitator

In the preceding chapter I identified four (possibly five) stages of scientific creativity, namely, preparation, incubation, inspiration, verification (and communicating results). The *preparation* stage involves subjecting to critical analysis a problem that defies conventional solutions until the problem is reduced to its constituents. Unlike innovation, where changes are additive, creativity requires that existing structures be reconfigured to accommodate data inconsistent with the received paradigm. Deconstructing these concepts into their abstract antecedents is the necessary first step.

Incubation—creativity's second stage—differs radically from the first stage in being beyond one's conscious control. Abstract elements generated by logical processes seek models from one's store of source representations to guide their reconstruction. In contrast to the focused approach needed during preparation, incubation requires a relaxation of top-down constraints so that opportunities to access novel source models are maximized. The process is identified with the brain's right hemisphere, with its denser connectivity and parallel style of information processing.

A third stage of *insight* occurs when a new synthesis is achieved between the target data and a source model. The subjective feeling of something coming together is a function of this pairing of data from two disparate realms. The new structure is subjected to a critical analysis by left hemispheric processes meant to *validate* the synthesis. Both of these latter stages—insight and verification—depend on one's ability to lateralize data from one hemisphere to the other and to coordinate discrete and diffuse modes of processing. Finally, *communicating* the discovery to an audience of peers is facilitated or inhibited by the willingness of the culture to accept novelty.

Each of these stages, I submit, presupposes cognitive skills that are developed or reinforced by alphabetic literacy. In fact, the two sets of skills correspond so well that it is tempting to regard the alphabet as more than a facilitator of creativity. Rather, it is a model of the act itself. Let's look first at the alphabet's contributions to creativity's preparatory stage.

There can be no question that the alphabet plays a leading role in the development of analytic thought. Historically writing begins with the iconic representation of physical phenomena and proceeds through various stages where the link with language intensifies, until its units become identified with syllables, at which point development usually halts. This pattern is observed in cultures that founded writing indigenously (Sumerian, Mayan, and presumably Chinese) or assimilated the concept and early prototypes from other civilizations (Japanese *kana*, the pre-*hangul* Korean syllabaries, Vietnamese *chū nôm*, and some West African and Native American systems). The evolution typically stops when a language's syllables each have holistic representations.

Moving beyond syllables to subsyllabic segments is difficult both for individuals learning an alphabet and for nonalphabetic cultures in general. The difficulty is exemplified by the historical tendency of writing to end its development at the syllable stage, and in the cognitive problems young readers have learning phonemic abstractions that correspond to nothing in the concrete world. Alphabetic literacy requires that one learn to dissect whole units into their intangible constituents, manipulate these abstract entities, and identify specific instances of sound (allophones) as members of abstract classes (phonemes) on the basis of shared features.

These skills bear directly on operations used in creativity's analytic or preparatory stage. James (1890:507) in describing this stage identified a phenomenon that most of us in the alphabetic tradition take for granted, but that is central to the ability to perform analysis. In James's words, "Why the repetition of the character in combination with different wholes will cause it thus to break up its adhesion with any one of them, and roll out, as it were, alone upon the table of consciousness, is a little of a mystery." The act of isolating a common element from the concrete environments where it resides, however, is exactly what is required of alphabet users when they learn to identify abstract phonemes within the syllables that embody them. As Scholes and Willis note,

Phonemes are intensional. Dividing the continuum of speech into discreet, sublexical, subsyllabic units involves using mental constructs that have no reality in the physical world. The reference of any phoneme is its function in the phonemic system in which it obtains; a phoneme is, by definition, not a sound but a set of contrasts, it has an intensional interpretation. Any system of graphic symbols by means of which phonemes are represented is, then, likewise intensional. (1991:226)

The abstractness of phonemes is apparent both in the trouble people have learning them and in sound spectrographs that show consonant phonemes subsumed by the vocalism that carries these sounds. Their identities are further obscured by changes they undergo in different phonetic environments. The physical substance associated with a given phoneme is often so flimsy that identification comes down to which competing analysis linguists ultimately (and sometimes arbitrarily) decide on. In other words, phonemes are conventional. But this fact has no bearing on the psychological impact of the exercise on children learning these conventions, which for most people in an alphabetic tradition represents their first and most significant foray into the world of analysis.[11]

How this process of identifying phonemes leads to the acquisition of analytical skills, which in turn facilitate the early stage of scientific creativity, has been described by several scholars. As Logan put it, "It is our claim that the constant repetition of phoneme analysis, every time it is written in an alphabetic form, subliminally promotes the skills of analysis and matching that are critical for the development of scientific and logical thinking" (1986:109). Fragmentation of concrete cognitive structures, the first step in the journey toward a new synthesis, is modeled largely on skills acquired and reinforced through use of an alphabet.

De Kerckhove argues in the same vein that the literate bias in the West "has been to break down information into parts and to order such parts in a proper sequence" (1986:290). Doing so clears the ground for the emergence of novel structures. As de Kerckhove explains,

Regarding discovery, there is an inversely proportional ratio between the extent to which data is contextualized and the ability to recombine it, that is, to discover and create. . . . Western cultures . . . accustomed as they are by their coding system to break down information into its smallest components, and to recombine and re-order raw data into properly aligned and classified arrays, have a permanent access to the possibility of recombining individual units. (1988:108)

More recently, Leonard Shlain, author of *The Alphabet Versus the Goddess*, has argued that alphabetic literacy played the major role in effecting a general shift from right- to left-brained thinking, with profound implications for human society. Shlain notes that in contrast to images, whose parts are perceived simultaneously by the brain as wholes, alphabets force people to scan in a "linear sequence" and use analysis to break "each word down into its component letters" (1999:5). He further states:

An alphabet by definition consists of fewer than thirty meaningless symbols that do not represent the images of anything in particular; a feature that makes them *abstract*. . . . To perceive things such as trees and buildings through images delivered to the eye, the brain uses wholeness, simultaneity, and synthesis. To ferret out the meaning of alphabetic writing, the brain relies instead on sequence, analysis, and abstraction. (5)

Alphabetic writing provides a model for the analysis that creativity requires. We shall return to this theme in Chapters 8 and 9, where I explain the implications for creativity of nonalphabetic writing, which puts no such analytic demand on its users. Meanwhile, we must examine the relationship between the alphabet and other stages of creativity. Although the connections between alphabetic writing and creativity's incubation, insight, and verification stages have received less attention from scholars, they are no less significant.

As I noted earlier, there is an emerging view among creativity specialists that the brain's left and right hemispheres act semi-independently in the creative process. Each hemisphere carries out tasks to which it is structurally suited. The discrete cognitive style of the left hemisphere allows it to perform the analytic functions needed to reduce a problem to its abstract elements. These reduced patterns serve as input to the right hemisphere, where parallel searches are conducted for analogous representations that act as a model for the data's reconfiguration.

This *synthetic* operation exactly mirrors what occurs in the LH-dominated analytic stage. And just as the decomposition of syllables into phonemes offers a model for analysis, so does the recombination of phonemes into syllables, syllables into morphemes, morphemes into words and so on facilitate the exercise of synthetic operations, including those needed for creativity.

Although synthesis is a part of all languages, including those with non-alphabetic writing (or no writing), alphabetic writing nurtures this skill by defining the targets. Preliterate cultures are notoriously inept at identifying words, sentences, and higher discourse units. Users of syllabic or Chinese character-based scripts likewise have a weaker grasp of linguistic units beyond the syllable level, as evidenced in their writing practices, simply because the orthography levies no such requirement. Alphabets, by contrast, usually have rules for word division and punctuation that depict higher linguistic structures. In East Asia neither word division nor punctuation is part of the indigenous tradition. There is no explicit model for synthesis in Asian orthography, just as there is none for analysis.

Analysis and synthesis are complementary functions, both in the orthographic sphere and in the cognitive realm for which orthography serves as a model. Synthetic operations benefit by the granularity of the data. By parsing wholes into abstract parts, the likelihood of novel constructs emerging is multiplied. But synthesis is more than a random combination of elements. It is governed by rules that specify what potentially can go with what for the structure to retain its usefulness in the context of which it is part. Although the LH in creativity's validation stage rejects many if not most such "legal" insights, the structures presented for validation would not get that far if they did not manifest an inherent plausibility imparted by systemic constraints.

An exact analogue—model in our terms—for rule-governed synthesis is found in the way alphabet users combine phonemes to produce phonologically valid sequences that may not correspond to actual syllables and words (e.g., *slape). Similarly, there are morphological constraints on words, and syntactic constraints on sentences, that alphabet users are forced to live with because the orthography makes them transparent. When words and sentences are clearly identified, the basic rules associated with each linguistic level are guaranteed a space within which to operate. The addition of these constraints would seem at first blush to contradict the primary requirement for randomness, which is certainly true of creativity's first stage. But we are dealing here with a combined process, whose requirements vary by stage. If analysis requires the destruction of conventional order, synthesis demands that the decomposed elements be reordered according to rules (i.e., more abstract patterns), which is precisely what happens both in the generation of language and in the production of novel concepts.[12]

There are other ways alphabetic literacy promotes right hemisphere synthesis. I referred earlier to the phenomenon, well known to creativity scientists, of language inhibiting creativity—despite everything I have written about the alphabet's utility as a creativity model. Concepts must be named to be manipulated. But by naming them, the structures take on legitimacy and immunity from dissociation. Solutions to problems are sought outside these protected boundaries, even when the key to a solution may lie in disbanding a flawed (or outdated) concept. According to de Kerckhove (1988:106),

the authors [Findlay and Lumsden] seem to assume that linking is predicated on conceptual cognitive operations, independently of linguistic operations, when in reality, even at the level of the selective stabilization of synaptic connections, every semantic "node" may itself be dependent on the boundaries created by linguistic categories *and* structured by the kind of access we have to such categories.

I will take up this critical problem in detail in Chapter 9. It will suffice here simply to note that the affinity between lexical markers and the concepts they identify varies in strength according to the type of marker used. Spoken words bind to a concept most strongly for the same reason preliterate people find it difficult to separate their thoughts from concrete matters, namely, a lack of contrast between speech and an alternative representation that would lead to the isolation of their common antecedent. Similarly, when a morpheme is identified by a single marker ("address"), there is nothing to distinguish the address from the concept.[13] Syllabic writing changes things only minimally, since the relationship between the spoken and written address is holistic. By using an address that is fractional and abstract, alphabetic writing distances the address from the concept, weakening the external bond that holds it together.

Alphabetic writing also contributes to the brain's creative assets by identifying vowel phonemes, and hence restoring a balance between the two hemispheres. Recall that vowel symbols were the last to be added to the alphabet's inventory of phonemes, postdating by centuries the emergence of consonantal alphabets. Traditional Chinese phonological study was also able to identify consonants in syllable-initial position as evidenced by the "spellings" used in the *fǎnqiè* ("reverse cut") system to describe characters' sounds by analogy, and by the separate status consonants had in rhyming dictionaries. Vowels, however, were lumped together gratuitously in a character's "final" sound, which included medials, nuclear vowels, phonemic tone, descending diphthongs and triphthongs, and final consonants (treated as a class of tones). Neither the Western nor East Asian tradition considered vowels to be of comparable importance to consonants.

This neglect of vowels by traditional orthography and lexicography seems to have been caused, at least in part, by the left-lateralization of language's basic functions. Although consonants, and syllables with consonants, lend themselves to processing in the brain's left hemisphere, autonomous vowels, which resonate at lower frequencies than consonants and do not have meaning in themselves (Jurdant 1988:395), are more naturally processed on the right. Infants for a time do perceive vowels in their right hemispheres, until suppressed by the left-hemispheric dominance of speech. With no orthographic cues to separate vowels from the syllables in which they occur, vowels get processed on the left as part of the syllable, with a consequent attenuation of right hemisphere function and sensitivity. This hypothesis has been confirmed by laboratory tests on preliterate Westerners and on Japanese subjects, who show a clear left hemisphere advantage for almost all sounds including vowels, which neither *kana* nor *kanji* orthographies separately distinguishes. Literate Westerners, however, show an opposite tendency to perceive vowels in the right hemisphere, which Jurdant attributes to the *reactivation* of "a specific cortical sensitivity of the right hemisphere" induced by the "graphic autonomy accorded to the vowel by the alphabetic system" (1988:388–89).

How this phenomenon relates to creativity is evident in the following passage:

The "vision" of vowels, to which the right hemisphere has access because of the alphabet, would translate into an incomprehensible and *diffuse* request, carrying an *infinite* number of possible sensory and behavioral interpretations. The alphabetic system is thus at the origin of a very peculiar cortical effect: the vowel has become the foundation of an *indetermination* on both the cognitive and cultural levels, which affects the left hemisphere all the more since it is the graphic breakup of the syllable unit that produces the effect. . . . The left hemisphere is *forcibly required* to comment on the sensorimotor effect triggered by the vocalic data perceived by the right hemisphere. (395, my emphasis)

Thus not only does the breakup of the syllable, induced by alphabetic orthography, support the analytic (left hemisphere) function needed for creativity's first stage. The syllabic fragmentation produces the same tutorial effect on the brain's right hemisphere by restoring to it the nondiscrete functionality used in creativity's second stage, which was coopted by the left brain's "ownership" of language.

But this is only part of the story. Note Jurdant's statement about the left hemisphere being "required to comment" on right hemispheric data. Jurdant expands this observation a few lines later by pointing out that the restoration of equilibrium between the two hemispheres facilitated self-consciousness, "as produced by a quasi-permanent commentary by the left hemisphere on our sensorimotor reactions to vocalic graphic data." My interest in this passage relates to its applicability to the latter stages of creativity, which depend on sharing data between the brain's two halves. Editing the right hemisphere's tentative proposals exactly describes the validation stage of creativity.[14] To the extent that alphabetic literacy models this process, we have what appears to be another case of cognitive facilitation. Not only does use of an alphabet facilitate the analytic and synthetic stages of creativity, it also enhances hemispheric exchange, which I noted earlier is more important to creativity than abnormally good left or right hemisphere skills.

Coordination of creative cognitive processes is facilitated by the alphabet on yet another plane. Alphabet users spend their lives shifting back and forth between concrete and abstract units. Spellings are *abstracted* from sounds, and pronunciations are *synthesized* from spellings, in an ongoing exercise of these two critical skills. For users of syllabic scripts, however, it all happens on the same level. There is no comparable exercise of analytic and synthetic skills. Alphabetic literacy also entails moving continuously between letters and words, which is analogous to what Koestler called movement within the "vertical abstractive hierarchy," that is, abstracting a pattern on one level and applying it to another. The process mirrors the essence of the bisociative act.

Finally, alphabetic writing facilitates the communication of novel ideas, corresponding to what some researchers call a fifth stage of creativity. According to Havelock (1982:72), if a script is inherently ambiguous, material written in that script, to be understood, must have a limited range of content and rely on formulaic patterns. "Expected and recognizable discourse becomes highly traditional both in form and content" (75). Syllabaries in particular "encourage a selectivity practiced at the expense of the oral originals, a selectivity which concentrated upon central facts and sentiments, at the expense of the more unique, eccentric, and we might say, the more personal element in the oral repertoire" (96). Ong noted in the same vein that "Traditional expressions in oral cultures must not be dismantled: it has been hard work getting them together over the generations, and there is nowhere outside the mind to store them" (1982:39).

Alphabets have no such limitations. Like all writing systems, an alphabet frees "the mind of conservative tasks, that is, of its memory work, and thus enables the mind to turn itself to new speculation" (41). Unlike syllabaries and character-based scripts especially, the discrete and meaningless elements on which an alphabet is based convey no inherent bias toward past conventions.

The Nonspecific Nature of Cognitive Functions

In the previous section I gave examples of how alphabetic literacy promotes scientific creativity in each of its stages. These examples ultimately are hypotheses. We assume that the analytic, synthetic, and coordination skills required of alphabet users actually end in changes to the brain's cognitive structure, and that these changes apply universally, not just to the specific "module" through which they are introduced. For these assumptions to be credible, we must show (1) that cultural artifacts, such as an alphabet, induce changes to the brain, and (2) that such changes can apply to a broad spectrum of cognitive activities.

I will defer to later the question whether generations of exposure to an alphabet creates a heritable tendency toward creativity. Such a product of gene-culture coevolution would probably take the form of a genetic disposition to respond adaptively to cues in the environment—the use of an alphabet, a creative ethic—rather than a mature, fully elaborated structure, such as the language acquisition device claimed by some linguists for language. Although the cumulative effect of this "weak" tendency could be decisive, I am claiming more than a general disposition. My argument is that learning an alphabet, particularly in one's early years, has an immediate re-ordering effect on the brain, which uses these structures for functionally similar tasks, including those involved in creativity.

The claim, in other words, is that culture shapes the brain, not in some metaphorical sense—but literally. There is widespread agreement among neuroscientists that a significant part of the brain's design depends on stimuli produced by interaction with the features of an environment. This conclusion does not erase the nature-nurture controversy over the causes of behavior, since there is much room for disagreement over what part of behavior is genetically defined and what part is owed to learning.[15] Moreover, attributing the brain's final design to culture seems in one sense to be no less deterministic than a comprehensive genetic theory. Instead of concentrating all developmental instructions within the genome, evolution has found it expedient to attenuate risk and promote ecological fitness by externalizing many of these instructions and allowing them to vary from one culture to another. Individual development is still constrained, though the illusion of choice helps make things bearable.

The physical process by which these external cues are reflected in the brain's architecture is by now fairly well understood. According to Pasco Rakic, many of the brain's neurons and their projections and synapses are initially overproduced, resulting in an early structure of diffuse but ill-defined connectivity. Later, as we interact with the environment, neurons or their processes compete for some resource such as electrical stimulation or surface contact with an adjacent cell as provided "by a variety of environmental factors, including functional activity" (1989:443). Connections that compete successfully for stimulation are stabilized and survive as a model of the environmental activity that provided the stimulation. Although the brain's basic structure is genetically determined, its fine detail is left to competitive interaction. As Rakic describes it,

In the central nervous system initial developmental events such as cell proliferation, neuronal migration, and the outgrowth of axons may orderly proceed in the absence of activity-dependent cues. In contrast, the latter phases of development that includes the elimination of neurons, axons, and synapses and the shaping of the final circuits or topographical maps may be regulated by the state of electrical

activity within the system . . . the precise pattern of synaptic activity cannot be predicted even with full knowledge of the instruction contained in the cell genome.
The responsiveness of the developing brain to environmental influences, including
experience, may be the anatomical basis of diversity in human behavior, talent, and
creativity. (1989:453–54)

The brain's final design is environmentally determined. What we do,
and what we are exposed to, affect its actual structure. Donald agrees that
environmental factors, including culture, impact significantly on the shape
of the brain. In his words, "Cultures restructure the mind, not only in
terms of its specific contents, which are obviously culture-bound, but also
in terms of its fundamental neurological organization. . . . Culture can literally reconfigure the use patterns of the brain" (1991:14). He includes
among the cultural influences "styles of reading and writing" (11). Deacon
is unequivocal in his view of the importance of culture, and linguistic culture in particular, on the brain's design. Addressing the issue of epigenetic
influences, he notes that "the brain's wiring is determined by virtue of the
interaction of information conveyed by its connections, so the way that information is analyzed ultimately becomes reflected in the way the brain regions are 'designed' by this activity" (1997:221).[16]

The link between written language and the brain's physical development
was brought out in the General Introduction to de Kerckhove and Lumsden's collection of essays on *The Alphabet and the Brain,* where the two argue
that "a specific writing system requires a specific set of neurological responses and decipherment strategies. The precision evidenced by a given
writing system is thus a reflection of selective precision required from the
brain" (1988:6). Luria, the psychologist, also pointed out the importance
of culture, and written language in particular, on early cognitive development. As he described it,

The tools that human beings in society use to manipulate that environment, as well
as the products of previous generations which help shape the mind of the growing
child, also affect these mental forms. In his development, the child's first social
relations and his first exposure to a linguistic system (of special significance) determine the forms of his mental activity. (1976:9)

These arguments support the hypothesis that interacting with a particular writing system, as a salient feature of the environment, leads to changes
in the brain's structure, which once established set the stage for analogous
behavior in other areas. Writing typically is acquired well before the brain's

cortical topography has been stabilized. Gazzaniga noted, "the developing child is gradually establishing a set of brain circuits that, once in place, can be selected by an environmental event—an assumption that studies of the developing human brain have shown to be true. Up into the teens, new cortical networks are being generated" (1992:60). Galaburda's description of cortical structure at the time language is acquired reflects the brain's receptivity to cultural artifacts in this stage of its development:

By the time the human infant is fully exposed to its linguistic environment, local and far reaching neural connections are mostly established, *though synaptic and connectional architectures are not.* It would appear, therefore, that established synaptic architectures are not required for the initial stages of learning a language. Rather, they may emerge as a result of initial learning. (1989:461, my emphasis)

The thesis that the cognitive skills associated with an alphabet reinforce skills needed for scientific creativity assumes that structures imported for a specific task are available for other tasks with similar requirements. Psychology and neuroscience support this generalist view. Vygotsky argued decades ago that "instruction in certain subjects develops the mental faculties in general, besides imparting the knowledge of the subject and specific skills," referring to this as the "transfer of training" (1962:96). More recently, Calvin noted "Many organs are actually multipurpose and change their relative mix of functions over time. . . . it's far easier for the brain to be multipurpose than it is for any other organ system" (1996:93–94).

Calvin's views are representative of the "distributive" school of neuroscience, which regards all or most cognitive activity as a product of calculations done throughout large parts of the cortex. There can be no conflict between this school of thought and the thesis that analogous behaviors share a common neurological substrate. Calvin goes on to argue, however, that even a modular view of the brain's structure need not be interpreted too narrowly, since "any 'expert' modules are also generalists."[17] This rule also applies to those cortical areas that support linguistic functions. As Calvin put it, "One of the hazards of naming things in the brain is that we expect something called the language cortex to be devoted to language. But . . . cortical specialization is far more generalized" (101).

Taylor shares Calvin's belief that the brain's language areas support more generalized behavior. In his view, "Any mechanisms used for language are available also for nonlinguistic perception or behavior, though they may have been refined and extended for use with language" (1988:324). Deacon rejects "language modules" entirely, arguing that language uses neural substrates that support multiple functions. Galaburda, commenting on a paper on hemispheric expressions of dyslexia,[18] noted, "Findings of non-linguistic as well as linguistic deficiencies in dyslexics would show either that language-related genes are shared among several cognitive capacities or that the factors interfering with their expression also interfere with genes related to other cognitive capacities." (1989:170). Either way, the research demonstrates a link between writing and other cognitive tasks.

To sum up, neuroscience and psychology support the thesis that cognitive structure acquired through one type of behavior can facilitate other, similar behaviors. We have seen that the functional requirements for creativity and for using an alphabet are isomorphic, if not identical. Linking the two skills is justified not only by data that show alphabetic cultures at the forefront of scientific innovation. It is also consistent with the findings of cognitive science.

By demonstrating a link between the alphabet and creativity, I have fulfilled half my agenda. It is now necessary to show why other types of orthography *fail* to produce the same cognitive effect. To do this, we must take a closer look at the structure of East Asian writing.

Chapter Seven
Asia's Orthographic Tradition

> The inability of Chinese characters to meet modern needs has been apparent to many Chinese for almost a hundred years.
>
> —John DeFrancis

Chinese Writing

Understanding the issues raised in this book presents two types of linguistic challenges. On the one hand, many of us steeped in the conventions of alphabetic writing tend to overlook the impact the alphabet has had on Western culture. Literate Westerners especially, who regard alphabetic writing as though it were a part of nature, are unlikely to ponder its cognitive and social dimensions and may fail to appreciate the full import of this technology. To understand the alphabet's significance we must rethink assumptions held about writing since childhood.

On the other hand, applying to the East Asian situation what linguists in the alphabetic tradition have learned about writing's role in creativity requires some knowledge of Chinese character-based systems. In this case, the challenge arises not just from naive assumptions about the nature of orthography but also from inadequate or misleading information about Asian languages and writing. Much of what we know, or think we know, about East Asian writing has been shaped by nonspecialists, who are often confused about the nature of these scripts, or by writers with a political agenda eager to manipulate the public's perception of this "unique" form of writing.

This is not to deny the existence of sober-minded scholarship on East Asian orthography.[1] It is just that Gresham's Law applies here as in other areas: bad information (or disinformation) has tended to drive out good in forming the lay view of Chinese character-based writing. Accordingly, the present chapter's goal is to provide the reader with enough accurate information about East Asian orthography to grasp the arguments made later in this book about its impact on creativity. The effect, I hope, will not be unlike the relationship between science and fiction, where truth has stranger and more profound implications than myth.

This chapter also provides a context for the case I am making on cognitive grounds against Chinese characters and the syllabic scripts derived from them. It is important to understand that the negative effects of character-based writing are not balanced by any linguistic benefits that accrue to their users. In fact, the argument that Asian orthography inhibits creativity is just one of many reasons why those who use these systems may wish to consider taking the final step toward modernization and replace them with an alphabet of letters.

We begin this chapter by considering Chinese, the first East Asian language to be written and the one with which the greatest variety of myths are associated. One such myth is that Chinese writing is well suited to the language using it. This statement is true only in a trivial sense: there is a mutual dependency between the language and writing, but it is self-generated. Let me be more specific.

As evidence of the appropriateness of this writing to the language, linguists point to the close fit between the monosyllabic structure of most Sinitic morphemes (basic units of linguistic meaning) and the fact that characters each "have" meaning; to Chinese characters' ability to discriminate the language's many homonyms; and to the seven or more mutually unintelligible "dialects" in China that supposedly are unified by the character script. The theoretical basis for this belief is the American structuralists' dictum that writing plays a secondary and comparatively unimportant role in language. The notion that writing, being "mere symbols of symbols," could shape the evolution of a language was incomprehensible.

Were it not for this tendency to downplay the significance of writing, students of East Asian languages might have asked *why* Chinese morphology, in the standard language at least, is largely monosyllabic. Or why Mandarin and the Sinitic parts of Korean and Japanese tolerate so many homonyms. Or why China finds it hard to unify the "dialects" under one standard, despite the political incentive to do so. If these and other linguistic anomalies were traced to effects the writing system has on the language, then the close "fit" between the two would lose its positive import and be viewed instead in terms of one system (writing) influencing the other (speech). Admitting a dynamic interplay between East Asian writing and speech would also lay the groundwork for accepting alternative orthographies, whose present "unsuitability" would disappear with use.

Chinese characters were not designed to represent Chinese (or any other language) but as icons of physical phenomena. That is, they were *pictographic* in origin. The early symbol for "tree" looked like a tree, the symbol for "mountain" resembled a mountain, and so on. Given the limits to this approach and, presumably, the inefficiency of trying to create a semiotic system anew when a system of signs—language—already existed, Chinese began using written symbols to represent things based on their phonetic contiguity. If the sound of the word for an object represented pictorially by a character was similar to the sound of another object with no written symbol, the character was borrowed to represent it. In time, the character lost its connection with the *object* it resembled and was perceived as a symbol for that object's word and sound.

In this respect, Chinese writing paralleled the development of writing in the West. The transition from symbol-as-icon to symbol-as-sound was also promoted by the stylization that occurred as "writers" sought to eliminate unnecessary strokes, reducing the visual similarity between symbol and referent. Chinese continued to create new characters by combining two forms to represent a concept that in some sense incorporated both meanings, for example, by linking the symbols for "sun" and "moon" to represent "bright." However, this ideographic technique was overshadowed by the phonetic borrowing described above, which took on a new twist. As the number of referents associated with a symbol increased, Chinese added semantic signs (the so-called radicals or *bùshǒu*) to indicate which of several meanings was intended. Thus the form 其 pronounced *qí* (in Mandarin) means "chess" with the wood radical 棋 written to its side, "period of time" with the moon radical 期 appended, and "his, hers, its" with no radical. These semantic-phonetic compounds now make up 85–90 percent of the character inventory.

The earliest known character inscriptions, on shells and bones, date from around 1200 B.C., by which time the conventions for creating characters had been established. Although pictographic and ideographic principles were used in the early stages of the system's development, Chinese by this time had mostly abandoned those techniques in favor of the phonetic approach, which remains the primary means of forming new characters to this day. By doing so, the system acquired an indissoluble link with the spoken language, albeit one that is not evident to casual observers accustomed to alphabetic writing.

The link Chinese characters have with Chinese language is two-fold. On the one hand, most of these block-shaped symbols represent morphemes in Chinese. Morphemes are a language's smallest units of meaningful sound. They may or may not be words. For example, "hunter" in English is a word composed of two morphemes "hunt" and "-er." The first morpheme is also a word but the second is not, since it cannot stand by itself. Similarly, the word *lièrén* (hunter) in Chinese consists of two morphemes; *liè* with the basic meaning of "hunt" and *rén* with the basic meaning of "person." Whereas *rén* is also a word able to stand alone, *liè* is not, since it is always joined with other morphemes (a "bound" form). Morphemes have more diffuse meanings than words, as seen in both the English and Chinese examples.[2]

Since each morpheme is associated with a sound, characters representing morphemes ipso facto acquire a sound. Hence not only are the characters linked to a specific language by virtue of representing that language's morphemes, they are also in a direct sense representing the language's sounds. The key difference between the way characters represent sounds in Chinese and the way letters represent sounds in English is that Chinese does it holistically. Each character as a whole, or in compound characters through its "phonetic" part (which is or was a whole character itself), portrays a morpheme's sound by convention. There is no discrete modeling of sound in the design of the written symbol. None of the strokes or groups of strokes that make up a character or its phonetic element has a defined relationship to the sound (normally a syllable) or any part of the sound.

Because Chinese characters represent both morphemes and syllables, linguists use the term "morphosyllabic" to identify the system within the taxonomy of world orthographies. Does this mean all Chinese morphemes are made up of one syllable? Not at all. Although this is *largely* the case in modern standard Mandarin, particularly as it is written, it was not true of the archaic language, nor does it apply to the spoken language in its many varieties. Rather, the monosyllabism of Chinese morphology is an artifact of character-based writing, which imposes a one-to-one relationship on the language's sound, script, and meaningful units. Given the holistic relationship between characters, their meanings, and their sounds, characters as the most conspicuous *units* in that triad define all legs of the relationship, including the link between sound and meaning—a link that is reinterpreted in terms of the writing system's requirements.

Studies by Boodberg (1937), Kennedy (1964), and Mair (2001) show that earlier stages of Chinese had many multisyllable morphemes, a fact that was apparent even in the written record. Modern varieties of Chinese such as Shanghainese and Min (Taiwanese), which lack a written standard, retained this feature and may even have expanded it. This is typical of languages the world over. Chinese Mandarin—written Mandarin especially—with its monosyllabic morphology is an anomaly even within the Chinese family of languages. There are two ways the character writing system brought this about.

First, there is significant pressure on users to impute meaning to *each* character of a multi-syllable morpheme, even when the morpheme's one meaning is expressed over all of the syllables. The fact that Chinese feel obliged to assign as many characters to a term as there are syllables in the term is a function of the shift that occurred in the typology of Chinese writing to a phonetic-based system. This change did not, however, nullify the practice of associating a meaning with each character. If two characters in a single term share the same meaning, one character tends to take on the meaning of the whole term. That character is then used alone or in new compound terms with different morphemes, in a de facto validation of the reduction process.

The other way characters impose a monosyllabic morphology on the language is through their high degree of graphic redundancy. Whether one regards syllables or morphemes as the primary targets of representation, we are dealing, in earlier stages of the language at least, with several *thousand* items, each with a unique symbol. The large number of different symbols entails a commensurate degree of complexity in their forms, more than the complexity that is associated with their sounds. With so much visual information available, there is no need to use all characters of a polysyllabic morpheme if any one character is distinct enough to convey the meaning of the whole term.

Both practices reinforced the expectation that each graph would have a meaning of its own, besides its monosyllabic pronunciation. It was not so much a case of literate users going back and reanalyzing existing morphemes (although this did and does occur) as it was an ongoing, coevolutionary process. New accretions to the literary language, introduced through writing, were adjusted to conform to the emerging one character = one morpheme paradigm. The process continues today, when single-morpheme polysyllabic foreign expressions, represented at first in Chinese with as many characters as there are syllables in the word, are stripped of all but one syllable-character. New indigenous terms, and even calques based on foreign models, meanwhile are built up deliberately from monosyllabic morphemes, which given their sparse phonetic properties cannot maintain their identity as morphemes without the characters' support. The result is a standard language made up of thousands of single-syllable morphemes.[3] Were it not for the written characters, this situation would not exist.

Another effect characters have had on Chinese and the Sinitic parts of other Asian languages is a high incidence of homophony. Since Chinese characters convey a great deal of visual information compared to the phonetic information associated with them, there is no incentive for writers to take a word's sound into account when introducing new vocabulary. Thus a term that is clear when written may make no sense at all when spoken. While this gap between visual and auditory redundancy is less noticeable for everyday terms, the literate lexicon, which accounts for most words in Chinese and *all* vocabulary shared between East Asian languages, was built with the expectation that terms would be identified visually, not aurally. Accordingly, words are formed from combinations of monosyllabic morphemes that have few distinguishing phonetic characteristics.

The problem is not just with exact homonyms, which number in the thousands, but with near homonyms or paronyms—words that differ only minimally, by one phonetic feature. Although context and other paralinguistic devices help speakers sort out the differences, readers of texts have fewer extrinsic cues. They depend almost entirely on the graphical information before them. As long as the text is in Chinese characters, phonetic ambiguity is not an issue. But the conflict between the amount of information needed to make a discourse intelligible in speech and the type of information Chinese characters provide tends to create a wider gap between the spoken and written norms than one finds in alphabetic cultures, with cognitive implications that I will discuss in later chapters.

Chinese characters, far from resolving the Sinitic homonym problem, in fact created it. Another area where the characters are perversely credited for solving problems they cause is China's so-called "dialect" issue. Although few Chinese would agree with me, the term "Chinese" does not refer to a language but to a *group* or *branch* of related languages that have less in common than the Romance languages have with each other. Besides Mandarin spoken in the north, Chinese includes six or seven other major languages used in the remainder of the country and abroad, among which Cantonese, Shanghainese, and Min (which includes Taiwanese) are the most prominent. These "southern" varieties are primary languages for tens of millions of Chinese speakers. For Shanghainese it is closer to 100 million.[4] Each has significant differences in phonology, vocabulary, and syntax and all are mutually unintelligible.

In any other context these nonstandard varieties would be regarded as different languages. But in China they are treated as "dialects" (*fāngyán*)[5] for political expediency and because, with the marginal exception of Cantonese, they lack writing.[6] Orthography, besides its tangible effect on the development of a language and on the psychology of its speakers, confers legitimacy on a language and political status on its users. Since the non-Mandarin varieties of Chinese are mostly unwritten, they are portrayed as less than full-fledged languages, even though they qualify as languages by any linguistic measure.

The other factor supporting the lay notion that these languages are dialects is the belief that the writing system transcends their differences. Literate Chinese supposedly are able to read texts based on different varieties of speech when they are written in characters. In a sense this is true. Since characters depict sounds holistically, it matters little whether one reads a character or a series of characters in Mandarin or with the sounds of some other Chinese "dialect." But does this unify China linguistically or does it perpetuate the divisions? Let's look closer at this transdialectal phenomenon.

Since Cantonese, Shanghainese, and other nonstandard varieties differ from Mandarin not just in sound but also in vocabulary and grammar, the characters cannot bridge this gap by themselves, even with their relative neutrality toward sound.[7] Much of the core vocabulary of non-Mandarin Chinese has no counterpart in Mandarin and no recognized character representation. Conversely, many Mandarin terms for which characters do exist are foreign to non-Mandarin speakers. The fact that nonstandard speakers can read a text in the standard language simply means that these speakers are bilingual. They have learned written Mandarin *as a second language.* They know enough vocabulary and grammar to make sense of Mandarin texts, much as I know enough French words and grammar to read that language (without being able to pronounce it convincingly, much less to speak it fluently). If Chinese characters have unified the Chinese languages, then the alphabet has unified French and English.

The characters do allow nonstandard speakers to use their own pronunciations to read Mandarin texts. So instead of acclimating to the national standard, nonstandard speakers reinforce their own speech habits and add to the vitality of their "dialect" by introducing new vocabulary from Mandarin, which they pronounce their own way by analogy. Whether alphabetic scripts *should* be used to provide China's non-Mandarin speakers with the means to become literate in their own language is a political question outside the scope of the present inquiry. But one thing is certain: since non-Mandarin speakers are forced anyway to learn a second language, it would make more sense from the viewpoint of those promoting unity if this bilingualism were achieved through Mandarin written in the *pinyin* alphabet.[8] The incentive to learn the national standard, including its pronunciation, would be higher than it is today if one's ability to read depended on it. As it is now, nonstandard speakers work their way through standard texts using whatever pronunciation comes naturally, not fully learning Mandarin and not reading their own languages either.

So much for the unity provided by Chinese characters. One can argue that the characters unite China culturally. But the linguistic argument for unity is nonsense. There are—to put it bluntly—no absolute advantages to using a character script, not anywhere in the world, and not in China. The only utility characters offer is relief from the distortions their own use created.

On the other hand, their complexity saddled Chinese speakers with a significant handicap. This handicap extends beyond the impediments that are usually cited to encompass serious obstacles to creative thinking. While this thesis, given its import, will remain controversial for some, virtually no one disputes that the number of Chinese characters and their complexity represent heavy burdens on their users.

Estimates of the number of characters vary widely depending on the criteria. The largest dictionaries have upward of 50,000 entries, many of which are variants or have dropped out of use. Calculations based on modern sources yield a figure of about 6,900 characters, 4,500 of which are enough to read most types of materials (Hannas 1997:130–33). Each character, which has on average ten to twelve strokes, is unique and must be learned by itself. Although they can for purposes of pedagogy be broken into recurring components, the components themselves number over 1,000 (850 phonetics and another 200 or so radicals). It is not enough to remember what components a character has, since they are positioned differently with respect to each other depending on the character. And not all characters can be broken down into radical plus phonetic.

The time needed to learn and write Chinese characters is justified by those who favor them by appeals to culture and aesthetics. Linguistically, however, the argument that the characters are *intrinsically* better suited to the language than an alphabet is empty. This applies not only to their use in China but also to the claim that they "unite" East Asians by allowing them to read one another's languages. If Chinese characters cannot bridge the gap between "dialects" in China, they are even less able to overcome the typological distinctions between Chinese, Korean, and Japanese. Not only are the languages themselves different. Independent changes made to character shapes in China and Japan have eliminated much of the continuity the system used to have, rendering even the shared Sinitic vocabulary obscure. The transitivity ascribed to characters is just one more myth in the rich inventory of fables associated with Chinese writing.

Japan's Mixed Script

Chinese characters suit Chinese because they generated this "suitability" themselves. What of Japanese, the other major East Asian language where characters still play an obligatory role? As I pointed out earlier in this book, *kanji* (the Japanese word for "Chinese characters") helped Japan absorb thousands of Sinitic loanwords during the fifth through eighth centuries, when Japanese was first written. Since the two elements—writing and Sinitic vocabulary—were introduced simultaneously, the same dependency between phonetically vague morphemes and characters that exists in Chinese found its way into Japanese. Borrowed Chinese morphemes, which are as common in Japanese as Latin and French are in English, have fewer phonetic distinctions relative to speech than they have visual distinctions relative

前言

說文解字三十卷，後漢許愼撰。愼字叔重，汝南召陵（今河南郾城縣東）人。由郡功曹舉孝廉，再遷，除洨長，入爲太尉南閣祭酒。嘗從賈逵受古學，博通經籍，時人爲之語曰「五經無雙許叔重」。所著除說文解字外，尚有五經異義、淮南鴻烈解詁等書，今皆散逸。

許愼作說文解字，創稿於和帝永元十二年（公元一〇〇），至安帝建光元年（公元一二一）九月病中，始遣其子沖進上。從創稿至最後寫定歷時二十二年，爲生平最經心用意之作。成書之後，經過數百年之展轉傳寫，又經唐朝李陽冰之竄改，以致錯誤遺脫，違失本眞。宋太宗雍熙三年（公元九八六）命徐鉉等校定付國子監雕板，始得流傳於世。徐鉉弟鍇亦攻說文之學，作說文繫傳。故世稱鉉所校定者爲大徐本，繫傳

Traditional Chinese character text (Yin Yun-chu, *Introduction to Shuowen Jiezi*, 1972).

科技界举行钱学森科学贡献暨学术思想研讨会

在我国著名科学家钱学森９０华诞前夕，中国科学技术协会、中国科学院、中国工程院、国防科学技术工业委员会今天(12月10日)在北京共同主办"钱学森科学贡献暨学术思想研讨会"。

全国政协副主席、中国工程院院长宋健出席会议并作了题为《科学技术的巨擘，中国人民的骄傲》的专题报告。

宋健说，钱学森９０年所走过的充满艰辛、奋斗和辉煌成就的历程，是中国现代科学技术从无到有、从弱到强发展过程的缩影。他是２０世纪中国先进知识分子的卓越代表和发展中国科技事业的坚定旗手。

宋健说，钱学森具有高度的民族自尊心、民族自信心和民族自豪感，在他身上充分体现着中国知识分子的优秀品德。在几十年的科学研究和工程实践中，他一直以具有多领域的科学造诣、丰富的科学想象力、敏锐的科学直觉和勇于实践、勇于创新的精神而著称，在很多科学技术领域中做出了开创性的贡献。

PRC news item in simplified characters (www.cast.org.cn, December 11, 2001).

富士通、セキュリティー対策ソリューションを体系化

掲載日：2002/07/31 媒体：日刊工業新聞　ページ：6 文字数：456

富士通は３０日、ウイルスによる業務停止や取引情報の機密漏えいなどのリスクから企業活動を守るためのセキュリティー対策ソリューションを体系化し、これに基づく１１種のソリューションの提供を発表した。

同社が培ってきたセキュリティー構築ノウハウをまとめ、ソリューションごとに「規準ポリシー」や「運用手順書」を用意し、具体的なセキュリティー対策を導入支援する。こうした試みは業界では初めて。

新体系は、（１）セキュリティー対策を支える組織の管理体制の改善や向上を推進する「組織規定レイヤ」（２）組織の情報資産をＩＴで守る「インフラレイヤ」（３）業務で要求されるセキュリティー機能を実現する「アプリケーションレイヤ」―の３階層で構成。

自社製品に加え、各社の業界標準製品を含めたトータルなソリューションを提供する。主なソリューションは組織ポリシー策定（価格５００万円から）、不正アクセスを防ぐセキュリティー監視サービス（同１８０万円から）、不正アクセスのタックテスト（１８万円から）など。

今後３年間で１５００億円の販売を見込む。

Japanese news item in mixed *kanji-kana* script (*Nikkan Kogyo Shimgbun*, July 31, 2002).

第一章　한글專用成就의 推理的 豫想

　　한글專用主張으로는 한글專用이 우리 國民의 必須的인 課業이라고 생각하는것 같다. 그리고 모든 知識人들은 그 可否의 理論을 다 짐작하여서 다시 더 들을 必要가 없다고 생각할것이고 또 그 可否의 兩者中의 하나를 先入主見으로 確固하게 判斷이 되어 있을 것이므로 여기서는 그 可否의 理論들을 一旦 제쳐놓고 한글專用이 다 成就되었다는 狀態를 생각해 보기로 한다. 即 國家的으로 國語의 狀況이 어떻게 되기를 期待하는 것이냐를 따져 보기 위해서 「한글專用이 다 成就되었다」라는 假想을 하고서 그때의 國語狀況을 推理해보자는 말이다. 그런데 萬一 筆者의 推理에 偏見이나 歪曲이 있다고 생각 나거던 讀者의 맘에 맞도록 고쳐서 推理해 보기를 바란다. 筆者는 自己豫想을 固執할 아무 理由도 없고, 다만 豫想을 해 본다는 그 自體에 重要한 意義가 있다고 생각할 마름이다. 眞짜 한글專用을 想像해 보기 위해서 年代는 한 70年後라고 하자. 現代의 國民들은 有識, 無識間에 漢字的 精神이 뿌리가 깊어서 眞짜 한글이라도 假짜로 되어 버린다. 아주 깨끗한 한글國語의 狀況을 推理해 보려면

South Korean character-*hangul* text (Pak Chong-so, *Kuk'o ui changnae wa hanja ui chaeinsik*, 1972).

해킹·정보유출 원천봉쇄 정보보호시스템 만든다

해킹이나 정보유출을 원천 차단할 수 있는 세계 최고 수준의
능동형 정보보호시스템이 국내 기술로 2006년까지 개발된다.

정보통신부는 정보통신망 자체를 사이버 공격으로부터
보호하기 위한 '차세대 능동형 네트워크 정보보호시스템'
개발계획을 확정·발표했다.

이번 계획은 지난해 4월부터 한국전자통신연구원(ETRI)을
중심으로 산·학·연 전문가의 기획과정을 거쳐 최종 확정된
것으로 시큐어(secure) OS기술, 능동보안센서, 보안관리
프로토콜 등으로 구성된 시큐어 엔진을 개발한다는 내용이
들어 있다.

개발될 시큐어 엔진은 라우터 등 통신망 접속노드에 탑재해
통신망 침입을 탐지, 역추적, 복구해주게 된다.

South Korean news item in all-*hangul* (Chonja Sinmun, February 2, 2002).

Chương trình update của Windows XP bị chặn

Hôm qua, phát ngôn viên của Microsoft cho biết, các kỹ sư đang sửa một lỗi kỹ thuật trong máy chủ web. Lỗi này ngăn cản người sử dụng Windows XP tải các bản phần mềm update. Hãng cũng sẽ cho ra miếng vá lỗ hổng an ninh mới.

Sự cố này xảy ra khi các kỹ sư cố gắng update phần mềm trên máy chủ. Microsoft chưa khẳng định có bao nhiêu người bị ảnh hưởng, nhưng cho biết có khoảng 8 triệu người download chương trình update phần mềm của Windows XP mỗi tuần.

Tin này quả là không dễ chịu đối với những người sử dụng Windows XP bởi họ đang có nguy cơ bị ảnh hưởng bởi hai lỗi an ninh nghiêm trọng được thông báo tháng trước. Những lỗ hổng này có thể để cửa ngõ cho máy tính bị hacker xâm nhập và chịu những cuộc tấn công từ chối dịch vụ.

Vietnamese news item (VNExpress, January 15, 2002).

ཕན་བདེའི་འབྱུང་གནས་རྫོགས་པའི་སངས་རྒྱས་རྣམས། །

དམ་ཆོས་བསྒྲུབས་ལས་བྱུང་སྟེ་དེ་ཡང་ནི། །

དེ་ཡི་ལག་ལེན་ཤེས་ལ་རག་ལས་པས། །

རྒྱལ་སྲས་རྣམས་ཀྱི་ལག་ལེན་བཤད་པར་བྱ། །ཁ །

Tibetan orthography (from "Homage to Avalokiteshvara," *Thirty-Seven Bodhisattva Practices*).

to writing, creating a wider gap between the two media than what is normal for alphabetically written languages.

In fact, phonetic ambiguity is more of a problem in Japanese than in Chinese because of changes the Sinitic loans underwent. Ancient Chinese, the name given to the language used in northern China around A.D. 600 when Chinese writing and vocabulary were introduced to Japan, had some 3,800 syllables supported by several final consonants and tones.[9] Japanese, however, has fewer than 300 distinct syllables, which meant that the borrowed Sinitic sounds had to be reduced to match Japanese pronunciation. Tones, phonemic in Chinese, were leveled out entirely. Since Japanese also lacks syllable-final consonants (-*n* is a syllabic nasal sound), Chinese words with consonant endings were rendered in Japanese by merger (-*m*, -*n*, -*ng* > -*n*) and by adding a second syllable to the morpheme (-*ki*, -*ku*, -*ti*, -*tu*) whose first consonant captured the original word's consonant final. Even with this device, Japanese ended up with only 319 different sounds for its entire corpus of Sinitic morphemes.

The result is a language whose literary lexicon has few phonetic contrasts. It is noted that a Chinese syllable can be associated in Chinese with two dozen or more characters depending on its meaning. This ambiguity is managed by linking monosyllabic morphemes into polysyllabic compound words. For example, *kē* ("category") and *xué* ("study") become *kēxué* ("science"). In Japanese the number of characters associated with a Sino-Japanese sound (the *onyomi* or "Sinitic reading" of a character) exceeds the number in Chinese by an order of magnitude. Considering just the 4,775 characters in Andrew Nelson's popular *Japanese-English Character Dictionary*, we find 105 characters pronounced *sō*, 160 characters read *shō*, and so on. The numbers grow in large dictionaries that have 10,000 or more characters.

Japanese speakers combine these morphemes into multisyllable words. But the number of homonyms and paronyms is still overwhelming. The Russian linguist Korchagina found two dozen words in a modern Japanese-Russian dictionary pronounced *kōkō*, another twenty-three pronounced *kōshō*, and so on (1977:43). Some of these words cannot be properly identified even in context. Using the Chinese *kēxué* example given, the equivalent Japanese sound *kagaku* means either "science" or "chemistry." Although *kanji* erase this ambiguity in writing, their availability deprives speakers of the incentive to generate phonetically viable words that can be understood independently in speech. Some Japanese linguists have tried to excuse this state of affairs by calling Japanese a "visual" language, as if readers of other languages are somehow less able to get information off a written page. Other linguists, such as Mantaro Hashimoto (1987), have conceded that the Sinitic word-building mechanism in Japanese is no longer viable.

If *kanji* provided any linguistic benefit to compensate users for the distortions they cause in speech, then perhaps their use could be justified. But their effect on Japanese writing has been just as devastating as it was on Chinese, yielding by all accounts an orthography so complex that it makes Chinese seem simple by comparison. The problem begins with the fact that Japanese and Chinese are typologically different. Chinese is an isolating language whose syntactic relations are determined by word order and grammatical particles. Hence, writing that language in characters is less convoluted than it could be because there is no need to represent inflection. Words are written with as many characters as there are syllable-morphemes. There are no morphological changes for the writing system to capture.

Japanese is an agglutinative language whose words are inflected to show grammatical relations. Unlike Chinese, Japanese verbs and adjectives are divided into stationary roots and endings that change to reflect a word's syntactic role. These changes must be shown in the orthography. To do this, Japanese write inflected words in two parts. The fixed or content part is depicted by one or more *kanji*. The inflected part is rendered phonetically in a syllabary called *kana,* in this case *hiragana.* This co-use of multiple scripts adds a layer of complexity to a system already made complex by the *kanji.* Moreover, the boundary between where *kanji* stop in a word and *kana* begin is variable and confusing. Since the same Japanese *kanji* is read differently depending on the word it represents (see below) the *kana* at the end of a word is sometimes arbitrarily pushed forward into the word's semantic part to give readers a clue to which word is meant. The benefit is at the expense of the writer, who must memorize separate rules for how each inflected word is parsed by the orthography.

Inflection was one of two drivers behind the evolution of *kana.* The other was the need to write Japanese names, which have no equivalent in Chinese and no *kanji* with which to write them. The problem was solved by using *kanji* phonetically as a syllabary. Since each character had a monosyllabic or nearly monosyllabic *on* pronunciation[10] modified for Japanese speech, Japanese used some *kanji* for their sound alone, irrespective of their meanings, to "spell" the sounds of a Japanese word. Eventually this subset of *kanji* was reduced to the forty-eight symbols needed to represent the language's basic syllables (mora). The symbols were also stylized to the point where they lost any resemblance to their original shapes. Two *kana* sets were thus created: *hiragana*, which are cursive in form, and *katakana*, which are angular. Since they are mixed with *kanji* in the same text, the system is known as a "mixed script" (*kanji-kana majiribun*).

Besides being used for Sinitic vocabulary, *kanji* are also used to write indigenous Japanese words that have roughly the same meaning as the character has in Chinese. For example, the character 家 ("family, household") pronounced *jiā* in Mandarin and *ka* in Sino-Japanese represents a Japanese word with a similar meaning pronounced *ie*. Although they share the same character, the Japanese word is unrelated etymologically to the Chinese morpheme. These *kunyomi* or "native readings" of characters enable Japanese to perceive *kanji* as a part of their language, a perception not shared by Koreans for reasons I shall discuss. They also make a complicated system more difficult by requiring readers to determine whether a *kanji* represents a Sino-Japanese morpheme or a native Japanese word.

As if more complexity were needed, *kanji* tend to be linked not with one Japanese word but with several that have the same broad meaning. The character 生, which has the general meaning of "life," can be read a dozen ways depending on its particular meaning. Now the same character in Chinese also has a range of nuances, but that range is subsumed by the same spoken sound. By contrast, there can be as many *kunyomi*, that is, native Japanese words, assigned to a character as the character has nuances in Chinese. These *kun* readings, which vary from none to several depending on the character, are in addition to the borrowed *on* pronunciations, which also tend to stack up as a result of a word and its character being introduced from different parts of China at different times. Sometimes context provides the only clue to which reading is intended.

In principle, each subscript has its own semantic domain. *Kanji* are used primarily for content words, especially nouns and verbs. *Hiragana* portray elements of the language used for syntactic relations, such as inflection and grammatical particles. They also render indigenous words that have no *kanji* representation. *Katakana* are used chiefly to write onomatopoeia and Western loanwords, which in some types of materials are as common as the Sinitic vocabulary. They are sometimes used alongside individual *kanji* to show their pronunciation (*furigana*). This practice of using one set of symbols (*katakana*) to explain another set (*kanji*) is officially discouraged but refuses to disappear, which suggests that Japanese at times are confused about how to interpret the *kanji* that make up the backbone of their orthography.

Although these guidelines for use exist in principle, the division of labor between *kanji* and *kana* is not nearly so clear-cut, in part due to attempts to improve the system. The Japanese government in 1946 began a series of reforms that limited the number of *kanji*, simplified their shapes, and regularized the sounds with which they are associated. Like all attempts to streamline character-based systems, the chief effect of these reforms was to transfer the complexity from one arena to another. With fewer *kanji* and approved readings, users are forced to avoid words whose *kanji* fall outside the approved list or spell them out, syllable by syllable, in *kana*.

Now with the possible exception of John DeFrancis, I would be the last person to complain about a character-based orthography yielding to phonetic writing. But these halfway reforms, meant to breathe life into an ailing system, erased what little regularity the system did have by disrupting the natural semantic-based assignment of orthographic elements. Content words previously expressed in *kanji* now appear in *kana* if their original representation failed to make the approved list and *if* a writer is disposed to follow the new convention. Readers must pause to consider whether a string of *hiragana* represents a substantive element or part of the grammar. Moreover, compound words previously written with two or more *kanji* are now split into half-*kanji*, half-*kana* if one of the word's characters is proscribed, which disrupts the flow of thought as readers shift from one mode of processing to another.

The price this complex system exacts from Japanese users goes beyond the difficulties involved in learning it, formidable as that task is. Japanese industry, for all its technological sophistication, is pinched by this orthographic bottleneck that makes office work less efficient than in countries where writing is done alphabetically. Software development, another area where Japan's output is less than it could be, is also hampered by the need to deal with the vagaries of the mixed script. These problems are in addition to the cognitive drawbacks the script entails, on which we will focus in subsequent chapters.

Korea's "Alphabet"

Compared to Japanese, Korean writing is a model of simplicity. Although this is a source of great pride to Koreans, on an international scale the orthographic picture is not as enviable as it appears locally. Koreans still struggle with the legacy of Chinese characters: in the South, where *hanja* (Chinese characters) are part of the orthography; in the North, where the characters paradoxically are taught as an *aid* to understanding all-*hangul* texts; and in both countries, where the characters left their mark on the design of the *hangul* alphabet. Five hundred years after the invention of *hangul* and more than fifty years after it was rehabilitated after Korea's release from foreign occupation, the orthographic situation is in a state of flux.

Chinese characters were used in Korea as early as the first century B.C. to write the Chinese language. By the fifth century A.D. Koreans were borrowing them to record elements of their own language. Two techniques made this possible. *Hanja* could be used semantically to represent indigenous morphemes in a system called *idu*. Like the *kun* readings in Japanese, Korean words were associated with the characters "directly" on the basis of their meanings. Alternatively, a character could stand for a borrowed Chinese morpheme and its sound.

Korean, like Japanese, is an agglutinative language with inflected endings that must be captured in writing for a text to make sense. Chinese characters were sometimes used for this task when their meanings coincided with Korean grammatical morphemes. But as the identification between Chinese writing and the Korean language grew, Koreans began to interpret *hanja* in terms of their *sounds*, both the Sinitic sound associated with each *hanja* and the sound of any Korean word the character represented. A subset of characters was eventually used to spell out indigenous morphemes that were hard to depict semantically.[11]

This phoneticization of characters in Korean might have led, as it did in Japan, to a full-fledged *kana*-like syllabary had it not been for one significant fact. Unlike Japanese with just a few hundred syllables to distinguish, Korean speakers use some 1,100 different syllables. For historical periods, the inventory was closer to 1,700. Depicting each syllable with a unique graph would have required a syllabary that rivaled in size the number of commonly used Chinese characters. Evolution of the character script in

Korea had reached a dead end. Although *idu* was used until the nineteenth century in formal state documents, writing Korean in a style that approached the vernacular meant reaching outside the inherited tradition.

Hangul (literally, "Korean writing"[12]) was Korea's answer—a phonemic alphabet invented to fill the void where *idu* and other character-based systems left off. Although the idea for an alphabet was known to Koreans through Sanskrit and the central Asian scripts, *hangul* itself, including its shapes and mapping relationship to the language, owes little to foreign influence. It appears to have been the brainchild of the country's monarch, who was personally involved in its design and popularization. Promulgated in 1446 under the name *Hŭnmin Chŏng'ŭm* ("correct sounds to instruct the people"), the system was promoted initially as an aid to help people learn the sounds of Chinese characters, although some Korean scholars believe it was meant from the start as a substitute for character writing.

At present, *hangul* uses 40 letters to represent the language's 19 consonants and 21 vowels (13 of which are diphthongs). Of these letters, 16 are actually compounds made from basic letters to represent tense consonants, glides, and labialized vowels, so the real number of symbols is on a par with Western alphabets. Some letters are shaped to depict the position of the tongue and other speech organs used to form that particular sound. While its origin is lost on most readers, the care and sophistication that went into the system's design is noteworthy.

There is no reason why these *hangul* symbols could not be strung together serially, as letters are in the West, to spell out words. Korean linguists did experiment with this idea more than fifty years ago to facilitate the use of *hangul* with typewriters and printing equipment. Nonetheless *hangul* has always been written in small, character-like blocks, with two or more *hangul* letters squeezed into the matrix depending on the number of phonemes in the syllable. The letters vary in shape, size, and position, according to their phonological roles. This arrangement complicates printing. It also focuses Koreans' awareness on syllables instead of on the fractional parts that make up syllables. Whether this syllabic convention was adopted out of habit or to help disguise the radical nature of *hangul*, its connection with Chinese writing is apparent.

This important issue aside, *hangul* is in all other respects an excellent system potentially able to represent Korean without support from Chinese characters. However, historical and linguistic factors continue to give the characters a role in the orthographic practices of both Koreas. Sixty percent or more of Korean vocabulary is formed from Sinitic morphemes introduced through Chinese characters with the expectation that they would be written and read in the same manner. Accordingly, when written in *hangul,* Sino-Korean words lose some distinctiveness due to their relative lack of phonetic contrasts.

Linguists who favor using *hangul* as a stand-alone system, without Chinese characters, argue that the same potential for ambiguity exists in speech but Koreans suffer no impediments in this regard. Why should there be a problem *writing* phonetically? And in fact novels, newspapers for the most part, and other forms of popular literature get by without *hanja.* Technical literature or serious genres where Sinitic morphemes dominate the discourse is another story. For people who know *hanja,* the texts are clearer when these morphemes are in characters. South Koreans therefore sometimes mix the two systems together. *Hanja* are used for borrowed Chinese vocabulary when the word is perceived as problematic. Often this means writing the word's first use in characters and subsequent appearances in *hangul.* All other words, including common Sinitic terms whose use is well established, are written in *hangul.*

The chief difference between this and Japan's mixed script is Koreans do not write indigenous words with Chinese characters. The earlier *idu* practice was abandoned. *Hanja* today represent Sino-Korean vocabulary and nothing else. Restricting Chinese characters to Sinitic words has made Koreans less enamored of Chinese characters than the Chinese or even the Japanese, who link *kanji* to indigenous vocabulary. As a result, Koreans tend to use *hanja* only when needed to disambiguate vague Sinitic terms, whereas the Japanese use them wherever they can.

Another reason all-*hangul* writing works involves something called "false *hangul.*" Texts written in *hangul* are intelligible, some say, because a reader's latent knowledge of Chinese characters makes the Sinitic terms more comprehensible. Even though a word is written phonetically in *hangul,* one can sort out the possible meanings by guessing what the sounds *potentially* mean. The argument resembles what used to be claimed by American educators for Latin, which supposedly facilitates learning high-level English vocabulary.

Given that the Koreans who make this argument are character-literate scholars opposed to script reform for their own reasons, I was inclined at first to doubt its validity. Moreover, had not North Korea abandoned Chinese characters entirely for all-*hangul* writing? However, it turns out the North also had trouble with all-*hangul* writing and was forced to reinstate characters into the schools. Junior and senior high school students are now taught 2,000 Chinese characters, some 200 more than in the South and 55 more than in Japan.[13] DPRK college students are exposed to more than 3,000. Although North Korea for all intents stopped using *hanja,* the success of its all-*hangul* script depends on learning the characters as background.

Writing Reform in East Asia

At this point I would like to comment on writing reform, because it has played an important role in the development of East Asian orthography. Since the subject has been covered in a number of studies, I shall be brief.[14]

Writing reform in East Asia is not at all like proposals made in the West to revise English or some other language's spelling rules, which mostly go unnoticed by the public. In East Asia orthographic revision has attracted considerable attention from language experts and other interested persons, leading at times to major changes in writing practices. Interest seems to wax and wane with the health of the economy and the country's political fortunes.

Of the three East Asian countries that use Chinese characters, Japan was the first to consider ways to simplify the orthography or replace it. Contact with European missionaries and traders in the eighteenth century persuaded some Japanese of the need to switch to all-phonetic writing. By the beginning of the Meiji period (1868–1911) serious proposals had been laid out to limit the number of Chinese characters, abandon them entirely for all-*kana* or alphabetic writing, and in one extreme case abandon Japanese altogether.[15] Membership in reform groups at times numbered over 10,000. Although suppressed by nationalism during the war, these movements paved the way for a dozen lesser revisions carried out between 1946 and 1981, which addressed the mixed script's worst excesses.

Paradoxically, nationalism in China was associated until recently with efforts to *reform or replace* the character script, as part of a larger effort to modernize (DeFrancis 1950). Several different approaches to character simplification were considered in the 1920s and 1930s, which led to reforms that reduced the number of strokes in characters and the number of characters in use. An effort was also made to expand the role of phonology in characters, both to simplify the system and prepare the nation for fully phonetic writing. Economic growth after 1975, however, and disillusionment with radical reforms in general dampened the enthusiasm for positive change. Although the government disavows plans to replace characters with *pinyin*—China's alphabetic notation—*pinyin* is quietly becoming a de facto second script in a number of applications, including the critical area of computing.

In Korea, writing reform has focused on the use of all-*hangul*. Unlike China and Japan, where much attention has been paid to limiting character use, Korean reformers for the most part view the issue in terms of using some *hanja* or none at all. The availability of *hangul* as a phonemic orthography affords them that option. By the same token, *hangul*'s own success and its national character have diverted Korean attention from the use of an alphabet of Western letters. Although several romanization schemes were devised (and changed as many times) to represent Korean internationally, there is no serious movement to replace *hangul*.

Korea first adopted all-*hangul* writing in 1895 as an egalitarian measure introduced by a reform government. Although the program was short-lived, the possibility of writing without Chinese characters continued to intrigue Koreans through the Japanese era (1910–45), erupting into a full-fledged movement at the end of the occupation to oust *hanja* entirely. By 1949 the North was using *hangul* without characters for all publications, including technical materials. South Korea in 1948 legislated all-*hangul* for official documents, but was forced to rescind the measure under pressure from conservative elements. The struggle between those who favor all-*hangul* and those willing to use it with a limited number of Chinese characters continues to be played out today in government, the schools, and among publishers.

Vietnam's Unfinished Reform

China, Japan, and Korea—the three nations of the "Chinese character cultural sphere" at which most of the arguments in this book are directed—were not the only countries to have used Chinese characters. Vietnam through most of its history also used them to write both Chinese and its indigenous language. Accordingly, many of the issues connected with character use described here and in later chapters could apply to Vietnam, given the influence that Chinese characters had on the language, its system of writing, and the psychology of its users.

Nevertheless I am mostly leaving Vietnam out of this study for two reasons. First, I have not determined that technology transfer of the sort practiced by other East Asian countries is carried out by Vietnam except at the most rudimentary level. Vietnam's science publications and journals on S&T policy are devoted to agriculture, worldwide news, and sadly, exhortations about the need for science to rebuild the country. There is no mention of appropriating Western technology as discussed in the other East Asian countries' publications. Centuries of foreign domination, decades of warfare, and years of socialist reconstruction have left Vietnam in no position to compete for or to absorb the high-tech innovations that are central to the economies of the major regional players.

Another reason for omitting Vietnam is that the country no longer uses characters as part of its orthography. Although still employed decoratively, they have not been used to record the language for nearly one hundred years. Vietnamese is written today with a combination of Roman letters and diacritics that enables it to get by on its own without Chinese characters despite a heavy overlay of Sinitic terms. Unlike Korea, where a knowledge of *hanja* supports all-*hangul* writing, Chinese characters are not taught in Vietnamese schools. Vietnam's independence from written Chinese is nearly complete.

Like other countries on China's periphery, Vietnam was using characters to write Chinese and elements of Vietnamese by the eighth century, when China's Tang dynasty was at its peak. Adapting the characters to Vietnamese was facilitated by the structure of the language, which like Chinese is uninflected. There are no multi-syllable syntactic elements or morphological changes to complicate the representation. But with nearly 5,000 different syllables (including six tones in the north), a practical syllabary based on Chinese characters never emerged. Although characters were used for Vietnamese words of similar sound, the assignments were not generalized to *all* words of the same sound.

As in Japanese, a character in Vietnamese could have many pronunciations depending on which Sino-Vietnamese word it represented. The difference is that there are few or no cases of Chinese characters used *semantically* for *native* Vietnamese words. Multiple readings of characters were the result of importing them into different parts of the country where pronunciations varied. Also sound change and semantic drift in China caused the same character to be borrowed in Vietnam for different but etymologically related words. Given the long history of contact between the two languages, the number of Sino-Vietnamese words depicted by one character grew to the point where Vietnamese writers would often use diacritics to show whether a character represented an older or more recent borrowing.

Adaptation of the character script did not stop at existing characters. Writers invented entirely new characters specifically for indigenous Vietnamese words (or in some cases for Sinitic morphemes so well established that they were no longer perceived as borrowings). Two principles were used to create the new symbols. A pair of characters, whose combined sense equated to the meaning of the Vietnamese morpheme, could be written together as a unit. More commonly, Vietnamese followed the Chinese practice of making new characters out of semantic-phonetic compounds. One character chosen for its resemblance in meaning to the Vietnamese word and another for its resemblance in sound were squeezed into an imaginary block to form a new character that identified the Vietnamese morpheme. This practice, combined with the straightforward use of actual Chinese characters for borrowed and some indigenized words, was called *chū̃ nôm* or "southern writing."[16]

Since Chinese characters are already complex, merging two of them into one unit produced a system so intricate that it had no hope of becoming a tool for popular literacy. The void was filled by a romanized script designed by missionaries and systematized in the mid-seventeenth century. The alphabet's applications grew as its users expanded. There was no sudden transition to phonetic writing, such as that envisioned by early (and naive) advocates of writing reform in China, Korea, and Japan.

Vietnam's alphabet, which has the misleading name *quốc ngũ* ("national *language*"), was established before the thousands of Western-inspired Sinitic compounds of recent coinage had been absorbed. These terms were introduced gradually through the phonetic writing system, enabling Vietnamese to make whatever adjustments were needed to ensure their intelligibility. Users were not inundated from the start with a lexicon of ambiguous terms. Vietnamese orthography also benefits from the language's rich inventory of syllable types—four times as many as Mandarin. Words written phonetically thus are more distinct in Vietnamese, with fewer homonyms than in other East Asian languages.

Notwithstanding this achievement, Vietnamese continues to divide discourse at the syllable boundary despite the existence of polysyllabic terms, which in most other alphabetic systems appear as units. Although written with a phonemic alphabet, Vietnamese text is segmented at intervals of one to seven letters depending on the (orthographic) length of the syllable. The main vowel is marked with a diacritic for tone. There are historical and psychological reasons, which I shall address presently, why the Vietnamese, like other East Asians, still focus on syllables instead of words. These reasons involve universal constraints on perception and Vietnam's long cultural and linguistic ties with China. In this respect *quốc ngữ*, for all its sophistication, still follows the Sinitic paradigm.

Chapter Eight
The Concrete Nature of Asian Writing

> Cognitive science often carries on as though humans had no culture, no significant variability, and no history.
>
> —Merlin Donald

The Universal Asian Syllabary

East Asian orthography is enormously complex. As noted in the previous chapter, the number of units that make up the inventory of Chinese symbols and the complexity of their design is mind-boggling. Literacy in Chinese means being able to read and write—as a base line—some 4,000 to 6,000 different characters. Although many graphs share common elements, there is no efficient way to describe how these elements combine into characters, as evidenced by the many indexing methods used in dictionaries and by the hundreds of coding schemes that have been designed for inputting characters into computers.

Complicated as the characters are, their relationship to Chinese Mandarin is straightforward. Most characters are pronounced as a single syllable.[1] The combination of a distinct character and a syllable sound identifies a morpheme. This formula can be stretched pretty thin, for example, when foreign words taken into Chinese are analyzed as having as many morphemes as syllables, or when morphemes whose meanings have been lost are shielded by their unique representation. By and large, however, Chinese does hold to a one-syllable-per-character-and-morpheme format, which though debilitating in terms of its sensory effect,[2] does mitigate some of the complexity.

Japanese inherited the Sinitic complexity and added convolutions of its

own. Unlike Chinese, a character in Japanese normally has multiple pronunciations depending on the number of indigenous and Sinitic morphemes associated with it—usually two but sometimes a dozen or more.
Although other orthographic clues such as the use of *okurigana* (*kana* after
the character) and *furigana* (*kana* wedged between columns of characters)
help identify a word, the correct reading ultimately depends on one's
ability to interpret context. Moreover, Japanese uses not one but three
scripts mixed together according to etymology and other conventions.
Complex as the system appears to be, the real difficulty lies in its operation, which has provoked unflattering comments even from those who
have learned it well.[3]

Koreans also mix Chinese characters with a phonetic script, but there
are differences in the way the formula is applied. Japanese expect that
characters will be used wherever they can be used. Koreans tend to use
them only as needed to clarify a text. Of course, this need is self-fulfilling,
since the availability of Chinese characters discourages Koreans from developing real, phonetic solutions to ambiguity. Another difference between the two systems is that Korean uses characters only for Sinitic terms.
Indigenous words are not written with Chinese graphs, so the complex
mapping system used in Japanese is absent in Korean. That said, there is
still the problem of learning 1,800 or more characters and the added complexity (from an information processing standpoint) of adjusting the size,
shape, and position of *hangul* letters to fit in a square matrix.

Vietnamese, the fourth major East Asian language to have used Chinese
writing, replaced the characters entirely with a phonetic alphabet. Yet for
all its simplicity relative to other East Asian writing, Vietnamese orthography retains a degree of complexity uncommon in an alphabetic system.
Unlike English, which uses just 26 letters to represent the language's 40
phonemes, Vietnamese uses 29 letters for 30 phonemes *plus* five diacritics
placed over and below vowels to represent tone. Since some of these vowel
letters already bear special markings, the combination produces a text
which, in appearance at least, seems almost as cluttered as the Chinese-
based writing it replaced. This impression is strengthened by the Vietnamese practice of putting spaces between syllables, so that viewed at a
distance the units do superficially resemble character text.[4]

Why does Vietnamese orthography emphasize syllables instead of words?
One could argue, as indeed many have, that the syllable is the most natural

unit for representation. I have already discussed the abstract quality of sub-syllabic segments and pointed out that their recognition for most people depends on access to a prior analytical model, usually an alphabet. The same is true of the larger-than-syllable-sized units that comprise most of a language's words. What is or is not a word is no more apparent from natural speech than is a phoneme. Both are artifacts of alphabetic literacy, established by introspection and convention, although once established they become part of one's representation of reality.

The decidedly *unnatural* depiction of words in writing is a product of a long tradition of abstraction, comparable to the abstract thinking that underlies phonemic orthography. The two devices—letters and word division—are complementary features of a system that has gone beyond the representation of concrete elements into the abstract design of the language. Vietnamese orthography's lack of word division marks the script as a transitional artifact, one that imported the trappings of the Western orthographic tradition—a fully elaborated phonemic alphabet—but not the other major feature common to alphabets, because there was and still is no consensus on what are the language's words.

There is no reason why the word *Việt nam* could not be written in Vietnamese as a linked sequence, as it is in English and other alphabetically written languages.[5] Doing so would allow the script to shed its obligatory use of diacritics and perhaps other symbols as well, since the information given by word boundaries would make much of the detailed phonetic specification redundant. But with no agreement on what constitutes words, Vietnamese has no choice but to represent the only other linguistic units on which, by virtue of its concrete nature, agreement does exist, namely, syllables, and represent them in enough detail to compensate for what they lack in abstraction. In so doing, it betrays its cultural, if not etymological history as a descendent of the Sinitic family of syllable-based scripts.

This failure of East Asian writing to transcend concrete syllabic units is obscured by the variety of systems in use there, ranging from full use of characters (in China), through partial use (Japan, South Korea), to nonuse (North Korea, Vietnam). Yet a close look at these individual systems reveals that they all share this common characteristic. East Asian writing, in principle and practice, is and always has been syllabic.

As we have seen, Chinese in its modern *báihuà* (colloquial) and traditional *wényán* (classical) styles is written in what can best be described as a morphosyllabic writing system.[6] Graphemes correspond to morphemes and both correspond to syllables. There is some question about which of these connections is the primary link between the language and writing system. Since several dozen characters may have the same monosyllabic pronunciation, one can argue that characters map primarily onto the morphemes of the language, where the fit is nearly one-to-one; their identification with syllables would be a consequence of the fact that the morphemes are monosyllabic. On the other hand, it is easy to find exceptions to the one character = one morpheme formula, whereas almost no characters in Chinese are pronounced as more or less than a single syllable.

Nor does any *part* of a character correspond to a subsyllabic element. To the extent that Chinese characters can be usefully analyzed at all, one often finds graphic components that reappear in different characters with the same or similar sound, and hence are associated with a given sound or class of sounds. These so-called "phonetics," like the full characters in which they appear, equate to a syllable and nothing smaller. The only analysis that can be said to have occurred is the de facto willingness of Chinese to ignore inconsistencies in tone, initial consonant aspiration, and other types of homorganic variation that arose in the language's evolution (or were allowed for convenience's sake when the characters were being constructed) so these elements could be shared more widely throughout the corpus.

Conceivably, the development of phonetic variation between syllables written with the same sign, coupled with China's own tradition of phonological study, might have led to changes in the graphic representations to reflect, in a more or less principled fashion, the evolving sound changes *if the "phonetic" were the only part of the character* and if attention had been drawn exclusively to this feature. Users would have been forced by the growing mismatch between symbol and sound to create written distinctions which, lacking any other motivation, might have been keyed to changes in the pronunciation itself. It is not hard to imagine how such a trend could lead to a segment or even feature-based orthography. Had this occurred, history would have been different.

Instead, Chinese writers and lexicographers preferred to clarify the ambiguities that developed between written symbols and their referents by attaching components borrowed from other characters on the basis of their ascribed meanings. Intended to remove ambiguity in cases where a character had or developed multiple meanings, the more important effect of these semantic-plus-phonetic (*xíngshēng*) characters, I believe, was to direct attention from phonetic inconsistencies that, unmasked, would have been intolerable. With the introduction of this new type of symbol, which now comprises 85 percent of the corpus, vague or misleading cues about the pronunciation of a character could be accepted given the character's dual role as a *morphological* unit. Buoyed by its semantic association, the accuracy of its phonetic representation became less critical.

These semantic determinatives (known as "radicals") prevented Chinese writing from following the path toward full phoneticization (and ultimately alphabetization) taken by the world's other major orthographies. With less pressure on the system to develop phonetically, Chinese writing locked itself into an iconic relationship with the elements it represents, where all parts of the sign relate to each other as whole units without the benefit of abstraction. Graphemes lack a discrete correspondence with the elements of the sound they represent, and both graphemes and syllables equate to ill-defined "units" of meaning. The system from top to bottom is holistic and utterly concrete.

What masquerades in Chinese as complexity is simply the result of the writing system's failure to transcend the concrete world of perceived phenomena. The situation is only marginally different for the other East Asian languages that Chinese influenced. The thousands of Sinitic loans that inundated Japanese, Korean, and Vietnamese inculcated users with the same concrete linguistic habits that paralyzed Chinese and with the same unrelieved penchant for iconic representation. Units of meaning were lined up with natural syllable sounds. Abstraction and analysis were not part of the equation.

Orthographically the situation was no different. Japanese use of Chinese characters is entirely syllable-based. Sinitic readings (*onyomi*) of characters differ from the original Chinese sounds by the addition of an extra syllable to cover final consonants in some of the original syllables. Like Chinese, the representation is syllabic. Native readings (*kunyomi*) of Chinese characters also follow a strict syllabic format. Although many Japanese morphemes end with consonants, the practice is to render the consonants orthographically in *kana* as part of a consonant-vowel (CV) syllable. Now if the representational rules for *kanji* were based entirely on meaning, the whole root of an inflected morpheme, including its consonant final, would be subsumed by the character and its derivational inflection would be handled by one of the a-i-u-e-o *kana* signs instead. The phonetic mandate to depict CV syllables apparently was strong enough to override this morphological feature.

The above remarks apply to the *kanji* part of Japan's mixed script. *Kana*, for its part, is the archetypal syllabary. Derived from Chinese character shapes, the two *kana* systems are able through combinatorial formulas to render the language's spoken syllables with just 48 symbols, without compromising the syllable format. For example, the long syllable *kyō*, which has no single *kana* sign, is written with the three *kana* きょう corresponding to *ki* + *yo* + *u*. The English equivalent would be to write the word "today" as "tee" + "oh" + "dee" and so on using syllables for each phonemic segment. Geminate consonants, which also lend themselves to representation as segments, are handled in Japanese the same way by syllable signs. Far from reflecting the language's syllable-based phonology, *kana* helps create it by imposing syllables where none exists. To call Japanese writing syllabic is an understatement.

This brings us to Korean. Chinese characters are used in South Korea, if at all, to represent monosyllabic Sinitic morphemes. These morphemes and the words they make up constitute some 60 to 90 percent of the Korean lexicon, depending on the type of text and how the words are counted. Although Sino-Korean vocabulary is not always written in characters, it is taught with characters in school, the theory being that words can be understood better by learning their morphosyllabic roots. This philosophy also governs education in the North, where instruction in Chinese characters forms a significant part of the school curricula, despite their nonappearance in most types of text.

Hangul, the phonetic orthography that is used alone or in conjunction with Chinese characters, never escaped the most salient feature of Chinese writing, namely, its focus on syllables. For all the ingenuity that went into designing *hangul*, its inventors forewent many of the cognitive and mechanical advantages of an alphabet by arranging its letters not serially, in imitation of speech, but as small square blocks that emulate the shape of characters. While excused by some as an effort to highlight the syllabic aspects of speech (which indeed it does), historical evidence suggests that the convention was mostly a ploy to assuage the sensitivities of a China-dominated court.[7]

Instead of freeing Korea from China's linguistic straightjacket, the promoters of *hangul* went on to explain their creation as an instrument to help master the sounds of Chinese characters! From its inception, *hangul* was linked linguistically and socially with the dominant East Asian writing system. If this were not enough, *hangul*'s designers diluted whatever cognitive benefits might have been had from its analytic nature by requiring that a letter's size, shape, and relative position be defined by its location within the syllable block. This practice shifted attention away from segments and toward syllables, so much so that the syllable is regarded today by printers and educators alike as the basic unit on which *hangul* fonts and formal instruction are based. It is, in essence, treated as a syllabary, albeit one whose structure is well motivated.

Ch'oe Hyon-bae (1894–1970), linguist, educator, and Korea's most outspoken advocate of replacing Chinese characters with all-*hangul* writing, was aware of this problem with *hangul*'s syllabic orientation. He later designed a sequential system whose segments were modeled on a combination of *hangul*-like and other alphabetic letters (1946:145–87) to help overcome the limitations of what would later be called *hangul* word processing. I sometimes wonder if he was aware of this larger, cognitive issue as well.

The conclusion to be drawn is that *all* officially sanctioned writing in East Asia is syllabic in design or in practice, from the Chinese characters that began East Asia's literary tradition to the nominal alphabetic systems that might have become truly alphabetic under more congenial circumstances. The complexity these systems display on the surface merely compensates for their failure to achieve the level of abstraction attained by the two dozen-odd letters of a Western alphabet.

The Syllable in East Asian Speech

The prevalence of syllabic orthography in East Asia, and in the early development of writing everywhere, is a result of the syllable's concreteness.[8] Unlike segments and words, whose identities are based on abstraction, syllables can be distinguished directly from speech itself. They are perceptually prominent and recognizable within the context they appear. There is no need to enlist outside criteria. As such, they are natural units for representation.

The prominence of syllables in the history of writing is repeated in the ontogeny of linguistic awareness. Clinical observations and studies of preliterate children, adult illiterates, and people literate in nonalphabetic orthography point consistently to the ease with which speakers are able to isolate syllables, in contrast to the difficulty they have identifying segments.

Jacques Mehler in his study of early speech perception observed that infants discriminate syllables "from each other on the basis of a physical difference that is insufficient to allow babies to discriminate an identical difference in a nonsyllabic environment" (1989:197). Goswami and Bryant (1990) noted that preliterate children have no difficulty identifying the initial sounds and rhymes of syllables (the same level of distinction achieved in traditional Chinese phonology), but go on interpreting alphabetic letters as syllables for some time into their reading instruction. Liberman et al. (1974) found that half the American four-year-olds they tested could distinguish the syllables in English words, whereas none could distinguish phonemes.

Bertelson and De Gelden argued on the basis of their own experiments and a comprehensive review of the literature that adult illiterates in societies where illiteracy is the norm have trouble identifying phonetic segments *and* larger discourse units. By contrast, rhyming and other types of syllable identification tasks are carried out by illiterates reasonably well. The authors explain "rhyme decisions do not require analysis into segments proper and can be carried out at the level of syllables by appreciating some holistic sound identity or similarity" (1989:13–14).

If syllables are natural phonological units, some syllable types are more natural than others. Specifically, CV syllables are the first to be acquired in the normal course of speech development and the last to be lost in cases of pathology. David Ingram (1978), who studied children's acquisition of syllable types, found that CV syllables are learned earliest, followed by those of the CVC and VC pattern. Conversely, Blumstein observed from the distribution errors of aphasic speech that CCV syllables are reduced to CV, and if a single consonant is lost in a CVC syllable, "it tends to be lost in the final position" (1978:195).

This elemental CV canonical type is also the one most commonly encountered in the Sinitic and indigenous phonologies of East Asian languages, and the form to which East Asian phonology generally aspires. As far as I am aware, there are no syllables in the area's languages with initial consonant clusters of the CCV type. Unlike the phonology of many European languages where initial clusters are common and at times complex (try saying the Russian word ВЗГЛЯД [vzglyad] meaning "look"), no contemporary East Asian language, including Vietnamese or the so-called Chinese "dialects," has this feature.[9] Although present in earlier forms of Chinese, consonant clusters were lost entirely or submerged into other parts of the syllable.

Nor are there consonant clusters in syllable final position of the type VCC, despite their commonness in European languages (e.g., German *strumpfs* for "of a stocking"). Although Korean *hangul* displays syllable final clusters, this is a morphological convention and not part of the phonological syllable. Either these *hangul* clusters are pronounced as a single consonant (for example, [tak], not *[talk] for the *hangul* form 닭 "chicken") if in isolation, or the "second" consonant becomes the initial consonant of the following syllable: [tal] + [ki] meaning "chicken (nom.)."[10] Although syllable final single consonants of the type (C)VC do exist in most East Asian languages, they are perceptually less distinct than when they appear in the initial position and are severely restricted in number. Their presence in the orthography in many cases reflects distinctions that have been lost or that applied to the extended community of speakers when the writing convention was laid down and were never part of any one speaker's competence.

For example, *hangul* permits a wide range of syllable final consonants in the orthography to replicate a word's underlying morphophonemic structure. Phonologically, however, only seven such final consonants exist, including the most commonly encountered set of oral and nasal stop consonants -*p*, -*t*, -*k*, -*m*, -*n*, and -*ng*, that is, a maximally distinct set, and the consonant -*l*. According to Martin and Lee, "When the basic form of a word ends in something else, the 'something else' must be reduced to one of these consonants, unless the word is followed . . . with a vowel" (1969:xxiii). Similarly Vietnamese writing distinguishes only eight orthographic consonant finals, which reduce in speech to the standard six-consonant set.[11] Japanese phonology, the simplest of the lot, arguably has *no* syllable final consonants. As noted above, consonant finals inherited from early Sinitic borrowings were given a vocalic supplement [i] or [u] and treated as the second syllable of a two-syllable morpheme. Final -*n* in Japanese is not treated as a consonant at all but as a "syllabic nasal."

Chinese phonology from the earliest period for which reliable reconstructions exist (circa A.D. 601) to the present evidences the same progressive loss of syllable final consonants. Cantonese and Southern Min, which most nearly approximate Ancient Chinese phonology, are both limited to the oral and nasal consonant set -*p*, -*t*, -*k*, -*m*, -*n*, -*ng* (Taiwanese and some Cantonese dialects additionally have a final glottal stop). Since none of the oral stop finals are released, the sounds are more difficult to distinguish than in English and other Western languages, and in fact were treated in traditional Chinese phonological study not as consonants but as a class of tones. The obligatory nasalization of vowels preceding final sounds -*m*, -*n*, and -*ng* in Southern Min suggests the eventual erosion of this series in at least some of the Min dialects.

In other Chinese languages the loss of final consonant distinctions is further pronounced. Wú reduced the -*p*, -*t*, -*k* to a single glottal stop. The -*m* final has merged with the other nasals, as in Mandarin, and in one dialect (Ningbo) the -*n* and -*ng* endings merged into a single phoneme with its two phonetic values in complementary distribution. Mandarin, the national standard, has eliminated all vestiges of stop finals including the glottal stop. Although the -*n* and -*ng* remain, they merge for some speakers after the high front vowel.[12]

The prevalence of CV(C) syllables in East Asian languages to the exclusion of all other types contrasts with the full range of syllable forms present in Western languages. This fact is doubly striking given that three and possibly all four of these East Asian languages have no verifiable genetic connection with one another. Although extensive sharing of Sinitic vocabulary accounts for some of the phonological similarity, the same restriction on syllable types also applies to the indigenous part of non-Sinitic East Asian languages. The absence of consonant clusters and the tendency to eliminate all but the simplest syllables is characteristic of the area's phonology as a whole, an example of what linguists (for want of an explanation) label an "area tendency."

I am not going to insist there is a causal relationship between this fact and the parallel use of syllabic orthographies in East Asia. Verifying such a hypothesis would require taking into account detailed historical data that are beyond the scope of the present study. Still, one cannot help but be struck by the observation that the alphabetically written languages of the West all have complex syllabic structures, while those of East Asia, whose orthographies are syllabic, have syllables with relatively simple segmental phonologies. Causation, if it exists, could work in either or both directions: the reduced number of spoken syllable types in East Asia is one factor that makes the operation of syllabaries mechanically feasible. On the other hand, the enforcement of a syllabic paradigm by the orthography could motivate literate speakers—and the rest of the population by example—to focus more strongly on the languages' syllabic aspects. Reversion to the canonical prototype would be an outcome of that process. Since alphabetically written languages can reflect the phonology of complex syllables as easily as they can the simpler types, neither of these influences would occur.

Whether there is a direct relationship between the prominence of syllables in Asian orthography and phonology, an indirect link, or simply a psychological one (reinforcement), the important fact for the present study is this: East Asians when they are writing or speaking are focused on syllables. As such, their linguistic awareness is kept within circumscribed parameters. There is no need for them to project beyond the concrete level to analyze smaller units or to synthesize larger ones. Despite their fabled complexity, East Asian languages use the most simplistic configuration possible: basic units of meaning (morphemes) map onto syllables of the simplest type, and both are expressed by holistic, nonanalytic graphemes. Abstraction plays no part. Even Korean *hangul* and Vietnamese *quốc ngữ*, which are analytical by design, adopt the syllabic configuration in practice.

To put the matter in bald terms, what qualifies in one (restricted) sense as dyslexia in the West represents the East Asian psycholinguistic norm. Pinker defines dyslexia as "a difficulty in reading that is often related to a difficulty in mentally snipping syllables into their phonemes" (1994:322). In a famous article titled "Teaching Reading by Use of a Syllabary," Gleitman and Rozin suggested that this conceptual hurdle could be overcome by separating phonemic analysis from the basic reading process. Instead of requiring children to master two novel processes simultaneously, the authors proposed that the concept of reading be introduced through syllables, which are natural and present no new obstacles to the learner. The problem of segmenting the syllables into phonemes could be tackled later (1973).[13]

Gleitman et al. went on to note in another study that five-year-olds "have the greatest difficulty of all in segmenting words or syllables into phonemes. . . . this generalization holds for a variety of judgmental linguistic tasks (so-called metalinguistic tasks), of which reading acquisition is only one" (1989:93–94). This fundamental problem with literacy acquisition in the West has been noted by many linguists and psychologists. According to Bell and Hooper, "the structure of culturally based activities under the headings of language use, language play, and language art consistently show that segments are less accessible than the groups of segments that serve as prosodic domains and rhythmic units. The dominance of syllabaries in the development of writing systems is a celebrated instance" (1978:19). Morton called phoneme segmentation "the most important single aspect of learning to read" (1989:56). Scholes and Willis (1991:218) found that phoneme identifications could

be done easily by subjects who could read alphabetic orthographies. They could not be done, however, by prereading English-speaking children, nor by older children who read languages whose orthography is not alphabetic.

The low incidence of dyslexia in East Asia can be connected specifically to the absence of any phoneme segmentation requirement in the orthographies. The price East Asians pay for the lack of this impediment, however, is an inability to identify abstract units of language. In an article titled "The Ability to Manipulate Speech Sounds Depends on Knowing Alphabetic Reading," Read et al. (1986) tested two groups of Chinese—one literate in both the Chinese character script and alphabet *pinyin*, the other literate in the character script only—for their ability to add and delete consonant phonemes. The study found that those literate only in Chinese characters did no better than Western illiterates at identifying phonemes, while those who had learned the *pinyin* alphabet did as well as Western subjects who were literate in their own alphabetic script.

This striking affirmation of the irrelevance of phonemic analysis for most East Asians reminds me of a story told to me by the late A. Ron Walton, who taught me Chinese linguistics when I was a graduate student. Many readers of the present book will remember Dr. Walton for his contributions to Chinese language pedagogy, but his major theoretical work was done in Wú (Shanghainese) phonology. Walton claimed, and I have no reason to doubt him, that one of his former classmates at Cornell who was also working with Wú phonology had his dissertation held up for months by his refusal to include a phonemic analysis in the study. Now this was a pretty gutsy thing to do, especially at Cornell, but the student, who had acquired a deep appreciation of the psychology of Wú speakers, insisted that phonemes had no relevance to the community, and that the only linguistic unit that mattered was the syllable. The student ended up compromising with his mentor by *appending* a phonemic analysis to the dissertation.

The story is consistent with my own experience with nonstandard Chinese languages, which unlike Mandarin lack officially sanctioned alphabetic

notations. Most of the dozen or so native tutors I had the pleasure of working with had exposure to an alphabet through English, but were otherwise
linguistically naive. In most instances[14] my tutors could not understand
why I was so intent on cataloging segmental (and tonal) distinctions, and
were completely baffled by my search for phonemes. Although they had no
trouble recognizing distinctions in their own speech at the syllable level,
including some I could not hear myself, most were quite unable to tell me
why such-and-such a syllable sounded different, even with their latent
knowledge of the English alphabet.

Typically what happened was as the studies progressed and we were able
to record utterances in an alphabetic notation my tutors would start telling
me to what part of a syllable they thought a particular distinction pertained
and what the most appropriate letter would be to transcribe it. Finally (and
incredibly) I noticed them altering their own pronunciation depending on
the letters and tone marks I used to record what they had said! In the span
of a few months, an informant would replicate the history of alphabetic
awareness, moving from concrete syllables to segments and abstract phonemes, and ending at the point where orthography starts affecting pronunciation (confirming meanwhile what my professors had told me about
keeping my notes out of sight).

Since my interest was more in learning the languages than in doing accurate field studies, I was willing to overlook some of this sloppiness for the
sake of expediency. But here is the whole point: unlike the Mandarin
speakers in Read et al.'s study whose literacy in *pinyin* biased them toward
phonemic analysis, these informants initially were unable to analyze their
own languages into segments, and in fact resisted the exercise (or just
barely tolerated it). Despite their ability with the English alphabet, they
had never applied this understanding to their native speech, and hence be-
haved at first in the same way as those whose Mandarin literacy depended
wholly on Chinese characters.

East Asians literate only in the traditional orthography share with pre-
and illiterate populations in their society and the world over a fundamental inability to identify phonemic distinctions. We have seen in preceding
chapters that the ability to make these distinctions serves as an exemplar
for analysis and abstraction in general. Just as the presence of an orthographic model for analysis in the West has stimulated the development of
an analytic mindset, so has its absence in the East deprived East Asians

of comparable skills or, at least, of an early definitive opportunity to acquire them.

Significance of Tibetan and Vai Studies

Claims about the psychological effects of alphabetic literacy have been based largely on the impact of this orthography on Western society. Progressive changes in the dominant mode of orthographic representation in the West—from pictographs through logographs (word writing), syllabaries, consonant alphabets and, finally, to fully phonemic writing—led to changes in the way literate Westerners address reality. Abstraction and analytic thought, the sine qua non of Western philosophy, had their roots in the alphabet, which promotes these skills as a by-product of its operation. Habits of thought that began as linguistic functions were generalized to other areas, taking their place within the matrix of skills that form the basis for scientific creativity.

Others have noted the absence until recently of a creative ethic in East Asia coinciding with a neglect of analytic thought in the area's philosophical traditions. In the material arena as well, East Asia's technological achievements show little of the creative discontinuity associated with the "breakthrough" science performed in the West. Innovation has been incremental, and as we saw earlier highly derivative, owing to East Asians' disposition to concrete thought, reinforced by the orthography. Unlike Western alphabets, which force an analytic mindset on their users, East Asian syllabic writing makes no such demand. As a consequence, abstract and analytic skills are less diffused throughout the population.

These parallel arguments, one the mirror of the other, are supported by events that together strongly suggest some element of mutual dependency. Objectified science and speculative philosophy coincided with the appearance of a phonemic alphabet, and failed to appear where the dominant orthography lacked the alphabet's analytic characteristics. A connection between orthography and creativity is also supported by a review of the cognitive basis for creativity, which shows a close match between skills acquired through alphabetic literacy and those needed for creativity at each of its stages. The two types of data support the thesis that alphabetic writing has a reordering effect on thought and stimulates creativity.

The problem with this thesis is that I am attributing to one feature of a multifaceted culture, namely, its orthography, the wherewithal to induce effects that define the same culture. The argument would benefit significantly by examples of different orthographies in one culture producing effects associated with the other. It would be better still if the same cognitive effects claimed for one orthography were manifested in a culture that has no connection to either of the two under study. The creative skills displayed by first- and second-generation Asian scientists in the West who have learned an alphabetic script, read the literature, and exchange thoughts in an alphabetic milieu constitute one such example. But I want to reach outside the languages and cultures we have already looked at for fresh material to support my hypothesis.

The reader will recall from Chapter 4 how Tibetan thought is distinguished from Chinese and other East Asian philosophy by its emphasis on logic and metaphysical speculation. According to Nakamura (1964:339), Tibetans "main interest was in the strict definition of technical terms, establishment of scholastically detailed rules for their use, and the expression of all kinds of scientific thinking by means of syllogisms." These are the very features Logan and others claim exist in Western thought but are lacking in East Asia's cognitive tradition. Logic, the apotheosis of analytical reasoning, in fact formed the core curriculum in Tibetan monasteries and was taught to children at age ten (340).

A parallel difference is found between Tibetan and other East Asian orthographies. Tibetan writing, an adaptation of an Indian alphabet, is widely characterized as a conservative system whose spellings preserve historic distinctions lost in today's standard dialect. Such criticism seems rather lame when read in English, where the fit between sound and spelling is notoriously poor. In reading Tibetan one quickly learns to discount the surplus symbols and eventually to depend on them to show morphological distinctions not apparent in speech. The importance of Tibetan for this study, however, is not the quality of its alphabet, but the fact that it has one at all, in contrast to other languages under Chinese influence, which use some form of syllabary.

The 28 consonant symbols of the Tibetan alphabet[15] have as their default value a consonant plus the vocalic element [a]. Although the consonants are pronounced with the vowel when named (just as in English), in practice the default [a] is replaced by one of four other basic vowels as needed, each represented by its own unique symbol. *Ko* is written with the two symbols $k(a) + o$, ku is written with the symbols $k(a) + u$, and so on. *Ka* itself is written with just the one symbol. One thinks of them as symbols for pure consonants as one's skill in the language develops. This attitude is reinforced by the use of the symbols as simple consonants (without the implied vowel) when they appear in syllable final position. There is no question that the system is and functions largely as an alphabet.

Although some Tibetan sounds appear in the writing as composite blocks, composed like Korean *hangul* of one to four letters, this is not the only possible configuration. Root elements consisting of a consonant and a vowel written above or below the consonant with other super- or subscript letters, are often preceded and followed by one or two more letters, in the serial fashion common to alphabets the world over, which serve as phonetic affixes affecting the core pronunciation. To drive the point home, Tibetans add small marks at syllable boundaries (there is no word division), yielding a format one to four spaces long per syllable, unlike the one-to-one correspondence in other East Asian scripts. In Tibetan, there is a great deal of rigorous—not to say pedantic—phonological analysis forced on the user by the writing, a fact that coincides with the analytic nature of Tibetan thought.

The second example I want to bring up is the Vai, a Liberian people who invented a syllabary to record their language. Some Vai are literate in the syllabary, others in English, still others in Arabic, while a number remain illiterate. The Vai were the subject of a famous study conducted two decades ago by Sylvia Scribner and Michael Cole, who sought to test Goody, Havelock, and Vygotsky's hypothesis that literacy affects cognition (see Chapter 6). Scribner and Cole's finding that "there is no evidence in these data to support the construct of a general 'literacy' phenomenon" (1981:132) had a significant impact on the academic community. Even some scholars identified with what Olson (1994:41) calls the "Toronto school" were motivated to temper their claims.[16]

Now one man's goose is another man's gander. Scribner and Cole's study showed that literacy in the Vai syllabary was not enough to produce the cognitive effects claimed for writing in general. As they put it, "Our results furnish little support for speculations that literacy is a precondition or prime cause for an understanding of language as an object" (157). The two found no evidence of the cognitive effects that abstract reflection on language is supposed to produce, neither on individual patterns of thought, nor in the achievements of the group as a whole. In their words,

Although the Vai invented an original writing system and a social mechanism for transmitting it, Vai society has not gone beyond the kind of restricted literacy described for northern Ghana by Goody (1968) or "craft literacy" discussed by Havelock (1976). Vai script literacy does not fulfill the expectations of those social scientists who consider literacy a prime mover in social change. It has not set off a dramatic modernizing sequence; it has not been accompanied by rapid developments in technology, art, and science; it has not led to the growth of new intellectual disciplines. (1981:238)

What Scribner and Cole did show—and this needs to be shouted loudly—is the inability of *syllabic writing* to generate the same cognitive effects that the Toronto school, working within the alphabetic tradition, had claimed for literacy generally. Their negative finding, in other words, had nothing to do with alphabetic literacy and everything to do with the point I have been making here and throughout this book about the "semi-oral" nature of syllable-based literacy. To the extent that their study involved alphabetic literacy at all, the researchers found that literacy in English combined with formal schooling in the alphabetic tradition in fact *did* produce the effects that Goody, Vygotsky, and others had predicted (1981:132).

Not surprisingly, Scribner and Cole found that advanced Vai literates were better than other groups "in their ability to handle syllables as the unit of communication" (185). The script produced only those cognitive effects it was equipped to facilitate. By the same token, literacy in Vai, which has no word division, did not enhance its users' ability to identify larger abstract units. The authors reported, "We quickly discovered that there is no lexical item that can be unequivocally identified with the English word 'word.' . . . [A]ll of the evidence suggests that basic units for Vai writers are meaning-carrying phrases (which sometimes consist of only one word) rather than words in our sense" (143, 149).

Vai users do not distinguish what their orthography fails to discriminate.[17] As I stated earlier and will dwell on at some length in the following chapter, East Asians similarly have a vague concept of "word," and until recently had none at all, because their scripts made no provision for them. Neither the Sino-centric cultures of East Asia nor the Vai of West Africa evidence any substantive ability to handle abstract concepts at either end of the linguistic spectrum, not at the phonemic level, which their writing bypasses, and not at the level of words, which the writing does not identify either.

By the same token, both groups display a marked preference for concrete thought, as shown in the Vai case by the content of their writing. Scribner and Cole observed that "Consistent with Havelock's predictions for writing systems with many representational ambiguities, we found that the content of Vai letters largely concern topics that draw on the recipient's background knowledge of the writer's circumstances. We also found little in the way of original expository text" (240). Olson, in reviewing the study, also remarked on the concrete focus associated with Vai literacy, "While the non-schooled literate could distinguish things and names for things, the discourse about the relation was problematic" (1994:39).

Although Vai literacy failed to generate the level of cognitive facilitation connected with what Logan has termed the "alphabet effect," Scribner and Cole's conclusion that literacy in the Vai script does not lead to cognitive differences with nonliterates (1981:258) may be overdrawn. The authors themselves acknowledged "Vai script literates are better conversationalists about formal features of sentences than their nonliterate neighbors" (159). They also found enhanced skills in some linguistic tasks, such as semantic integration, to be a common effect of literacy that cuts across all script types (184). Finally, the two conceded their study may not have been able to measure the full effects of literacy for the simple reason that Vai literates do not use their written language for many functions.

If the uses of writing are few, the skills they require are likely to be limited when compared with literacy functions in modern, technologically sophisticated societies. They may be used to accomplish only a narrow range of tasks in a few content domains. Such a pattern can be expected to give rise to specialized or specific literacy-related skills—the pattern we found in our studies. (1981:258)[18]

Goody picked up on the same flaw, noting that the cognitive facilitation claimed by Vygotsky and others is "surely still possible if one does not assume immediacy of effect" (1987:225). Olson likewise argued that Scribner and Cole missed the point by assuming "that the cognitive implications of literacy can be determined by examining the direct impact on the individual who learns to read and write. Learning to read and write is at best an introduction to the world of literacy." Olson dismissed their argument that schooling—not literacy—produces the cognitive changes that distinguish literate from illiterate societies for not recognizing that schooling is a literate institution (1994:42).

Whether literacy has an immediate impact on cognitive structure or an indirect influence is of less concern to me than what Scribner and Cole did show, namely, that literacy in a syllabic orthography does not produce the cognitive changes that affect people in alphabetic cultures. Their work with this West African people, who owe nothing culturally or linguistically to East Asia, validates the hypothesis made here for syllabic writing generally, just as Tibetan demonstrates the ability of alphabetic writing to produce cognitive effects contrary to those of the wider civilization of which it is a part.

Hemispheric Processing of Chinese Characters

Alphabets differ from earlier forms of writing by the extent to which they encourage abstract thinking. By forcing one to analyze syllables into segments and phonemes, alphabets acclimate individuals and whole societies to the use of analysis as a cognitive tool. Concrete units are split into their abstract antecedents, which is the first step of the creative process. Synthesis, the other part of creativity, is facilitated by the practice one gets grouping linguistic elements into larger wholes. This constant shifting between analysis and synthesis, between the discrete and diffuse patterning associated with consonant and vowel phonemes, and between different levels of linguistic abstraction conditions alphabet users to making these cognitive transitions generally.

Creativity also requires that data be exchanged between the brain's left and right hemispheres. Left brain skills nurtured and refined by alphabetic literacy are used to break problems into their constituents as a precondition for creative reordering. These abstract "target" patterns become the input for associative processes conducted in the right hemisphere. Provisional solutions assembled in the right hemisphere are evaluated in turn by left brain analysis. It is the middle stage of creativity, where fragments are completed or recombined, for which the alphabet's contribution has been less well appreciated, although as we have seen its effects here are equally significant.

Neglect of the alphabet's associative function and its ability to facilitate analogous processes in the brain has been paralleled by an overappreciation of the right hemisphere's role in creativity and by the popular notion of the right hemisphere as the "seat" of creativity. This naive view, which differs from the integrated, bicameral model of creativity proposed now by specialists, marginalized creativity studies for many scientists because of the right hemisphere's identification with affective aspects of the mind. It seems that any cognitive process that is strange and poorly understood—such as creativity, but also intuition and psychic phenomena—is attributed reflexively to the right brain, where scientific accountability is held to be unnecessary or impossible.

Fascination with the right brain's associative powers coincided during the late 1960s and 1970s with a growth of interest in Eastern mysticism and in Asian civilizations, which were believed to represent an alternative to the rationalism of the West. In the humanities, this trend was expressed, among other ways, by larger enrollments in East Asian language courses and by an uncritical acceptance of the systems used to write these languages. Chinese orthography, despite everything DeFrancis and other responsible scholars had written about it, was perceived as a negation of the left-brained culture that the students of that era were struggling against.

This intuition appeared to be confirmed by early psycholinguistic experiments that seemed to show Chinese characters processed in the brain's right half, in contrast to alphabets, which are processed in the left. Tachistoscopic studies conducted by Tzeng et al. for Chinese (1978) and by Hatta for Japanese (1977, 1978) on single-character stimuli showed strong right hemisphere involvement in their processing. This finding contrasted with experiments showing primary left hemisphere support for alphabetic scripts and for Japanese written in *kana* (Hirata and Osaka 1969; Endo et al. 1978). Jones and Aoki (1988) also found greater involvement of the right hemisphere in *kanji* than in *kana* identification. These studies encouraged the notion that phonetic writing is processed one way, while Chinese characters, like images and other holistic stimuli, are processed in a unique manner.

Such differential processing, if it did occur, would force us to adjust our thesis that Chinese characters are comparable psycholinguistically to other East Asian syllabaries and amenable to treatment as a single typological group. Moreover, if one can argue that alphabets promote creativity by sharpening left brain analysis, it would seem that an orthography processed in the right brain would, by the same logic, enhance that hemisphere's own particular contributions. And indeed similar claims have been made.

Fritjof Capra, in *The Tao of Physics*, subtitled *An Exploration of the Parallels between Modern Physics and Eastern Mysticism*, wrote:

The classical Chinese word was very different from an abstract sign representing a clearly delineated concept. It was rather a sound symbol which had strong suggestive powers, bringing to mind an indeterminate complex of pictorial images and emotions. The intention of the speaker was not so much to express an intellectual idea, but rather to affect and influence the listener. Correspondingly, the written character was not just an abstract sign, but was an organic pattern—a 'gestalt'— which preserved the full complex of images and the suggestive power of the word. (1985:103–4)

Chinese characters are regarded here not as a vehicle to express language, but as a way to get *around* language, as symbols that offer readers a window into the whole essence of a thing by refraining from, well, *spelling it out*. Needham, who also spared no effort in drawing parallels between quantum physics and Eastern mysticism, likewise was fond of classical Chinese for this same reason, and of the *Tao Te Ching* in particular, which is undoubtedly the least precise and most widely interpretable text ever written. Both writers found truth in the basic Taoist premise that analysis robs an object of its essential unity, clouds one's understanding of reality, and that language is especially guilty in this respect. Chinese characters by bypassing language and left brain analysis present a truer *picture* of reality, in this interpretation.

The reader will recognize this claim—that Chinese writing escapes the confines of language by presenting ideas directly—as an instance of the ideographic myth, which we saw in the previous chapter to be untenable. The notion, moreover, is getting a bit old. As DeFrancis noted, "From the seventeenth century right down to the present scholars have debated just how to utilize the universal quality attributed to Chinese characters" (1984:161). But there is no more truth to the myth now than when Peter DuPonceau first criticized it in 1838. Chinese characters represent linguistic elements, namely, syllables and morphemes. Like writing everywhere, the system is inextricably tied to natural language. Although the relationship can be masked depending on how the mapping takes place, *all* writing depicts elements of a language and is subject to the same limits as language. Characters are no exception.

The argument for direct, intuitive access to thought through Chinese characters has also been disproved by subsequent studies showing that characters are processed—like all other writing systems—in the brain's *left* half. Ovid Tzeng, who helped pioneer hemispheric studies of character processing, eventually became curious about whether the tests with single-character stimuli had anything to do with what actually happens in reading. Taking account of the fact that "the perceptual unit in reading may be much larger than single characters," Tzeng redesigned his experiments using two-character stimuli and found a strong left-brain dominance (Tzeng et al. 1979). Tzeng and Hung later acknowledged "there is very little evidence, from either experimental or clinical studies, to suggest a stronger right hemisphere involvement in the linguistic analysis of Chinese logographs." Rather, the "data provide unequivocal evidence against any suggestion that Chinese logographs are processed in the right hemisphere" (1988:284–85).

Tzeng's finding of LH involvement in character processing based on tachistoscopic experiments with healthy subjects was replicated by studies of Chinese patients with right and left hemisphere lesions. As expected, his team found that patients with right brain lesions were unable to draw pictures properly. However, they "wrote the full and completely correct characters without any linguistic errors." Conversely, those with left brain lesions "produced good copies of geometric figures and well-configured (if simplified) drawings," but did terribly on the characters. Tzeng et al. concluded that Chinese characters are processed in the left hemisphere, like all other forms of writing, and that "they may be represented in the same way as words transcribed by alphabetic letters" (1986:148–49).

Meanwhile, Hatta working with Japanese substituted two-character units corresponding to words for the one-character stimuli he had used earlier and achieved a complete reversal of effects. The RH dominance manifested when the characters were viewed individually disappeared when they were presented in their linguistic context (1978). Summarizing these Japanese laterality studies, Paradis, et al. noted, "the only pattern that has consistently emerged across a variety of studies is that two-character word stimuli written with any type of script will produce a RVF [left hemisphere] advantage" (1985:32). They also found "no clinically documented pattern of greater impairment for *kanji* with right hemisphere lesions" (166).

It's time to put to rest the notion that Chinese characters offer any unique cognitive benefits to compensate for their failure to promote the creative behavior found among alphabet users. The belief that the characters, by not specifying phonetic detail, let readers access ideas without distortion is a myth with no basis in linguistic or psycholinguistic research. Chinese characters, like all other forms of writing, are processed in the brain's left hemisphere. As we shall see in the next chapter, not only do they add little to one's ability to think creatively, but by representing linguistic signs concretely, they obstruct creativity by making it harder to separate concepts from the signs that hold them together. Far from facilitating right brain association, the characters are instrumental in impeding it.

Syllabic Literacy and the Quasi-Oral Society

The belief that East Asians care more than Westerners for spiritual matters has less to do with "alternative" right-brain thinking than with the failure of the dominant orthography to impart cognitive skills associated with analytical thinking. Lacking an early and ubiquitous model of abstraction, such as that available to literate Westerners through the alphabet, Asians as a whole have acquired fewer characteristics of what Donald (1991:274) calls "theoretic" culture. As such, East Asian thought is heavily tinged with the mythic elements of preliterate society. Syllabic writing does not support a different view of reality, not in East Asia and not anywhere else. It simply fails to express reality to its fullest extent.

As Olson noted, "what the script-as-model does not represent is difficult, perhaps impossible, to bring into consciousness. What is represented tends to be seen as a complete model of what there is" (1994:260). Although syllabic literacy does provide—beyond the social and intellectual benefits of literacy itself—a measure of metalinguistic awareness as evidenced in the Vai studies, it stops short of the full complement of abstract skills that created the Western philosophical and scientific traditions. By representing language, syllabic orthography allows its users to think beyond the immediate context of events. That much is indisputable. But by failing to represent it abstractly, the orthography puts severe constraints on the scope of this awareness.

The marginal nature of Chinese character-based orthography is evident at each linguistic level. Speech sounds are represented concretely. They are not analyzed into segments or abstract phones. Morphemes—basic elements of meaning—are depicted instead of words that correspond to complete concepts. The lack of clearly defined words leads to ill-defined sentences, not only in classical texts, which are often nebulous and subject to varying interpretations, but even in modern scientific writing. Sentences run on interminably, much as in speech, with little thought given to segmenting ideas. The style is often vague, as if East Asian writers do not appreciate the need to present their work as an objectified, self-sustaining whole independent of personal context.[19]

Such is the legacy of syllabic writing. It supports literacy, but with few of the supplementary benefits that are associated with literacy in the West. East Asian orthography thus stands midway between pre- and fully developed writing, not only in an evolutionary sense but also in terms of its impact on the cognitive habits of its users. The strength of this link between orthographic type and culture can be appreciated by citing once again the features that Donald, writing within an alphabetic tradition, associates with "theoretic cultures," namely,

formal arguments, systematic taxonomies, induction, deduction, verification, differentiation, quantification, idealization, and formal methods of measurement. Arguments, discovery, proof, and theoretical synthesis are part of the legacy of this kind of thought. (1991:273–74)

How many of these characteristics describe the kind of thinking done in East Asia traditionally, or for that matter today? On the contrary, they represent precisely that set of cognitive features that both Needham and Logan agree are missing in China, and which Nakamura says are absent from East Asia entirely. Qian Wen-yuan, the physicist and intellectual historian, reached the same conclusion. Here is what Qian had to say about Chinese scientific thought:

we can seldom find the dimmest consciousness of scientific axiomatisation . . . the great deficiency in old Chinese mathematical thought was the absence of rigorous proof, in particular, the absence of a system of deductive geometry. This configuration correlates with the lack of formal logic and the dominance of associative (organicist) thought. From our Sino-European comparison, it is clear that the deficiency was not just in mathematics; it hindered the development of modern science as a whole. In other fields of science, the Chinese way of thinking generally lacked accuracy in defining, exactness in formulating, rigor in proving, and logic in explaining. (1985:66–67)

It is evident that we are looking at two distinct types of cultures, whose intellectual foundations are qualitatively different. If writing, as Donald and many have argued, was responsible for the changes in thinking that attended the shift from mythic to theoretic culture, then consideration must be given to the type of writing involved in the process, since the cognitive effects of this shift have not been uniform. Neither the mystical orientation of East Asian thought represented by Taoism and Zen (Chan) Buddhism, nor the concrete practical strain of East Asian philosophy expressed by Confucianism, have much in common with the theoretic culture created in the West by alphabetic literacy. On the other hand, both such tendencies—the mystical and the pragmatic—are characteristic of oral cultures and the preliterate society Donald describes.[20]

East Asia's syllabic writing could not lay the groundwork for a complete transition to the theoretic culture on which modern science depends. In particular, it has not supported the cognitive skills needed for scientific creativity, neither in its analytic nor its synthetic phases. I have described some of the technical reasons why this is so. In the next chapter we will consider another such dimension to the problem.

Chapter Nine
The Impact of Language on Creativity

> Sometimes I stare at a common printed word until it looks strange and unfamiliar. The letters pull apart in my mind and separate so far that the unity of the concept that they designate together disappears.
> —Robert Lucky

Language and Thought Revisited

In previous chapters we saw how alphabetic writing facilitates creativity by modeling its essential processes. Problems that resist solution in terms of existing paradigms are reduced to their basic components through analytical skills developed in the course of becoming literate. Reassembling these abstract components into new and coherent structures is aided in turn by habits built up through exercising the alphabet's synthetic functions.

In the former instance, the alphabet promotes analysis by forcing its users to consider details of phonology that are not apparent on the surface level. Concrete syllables are analyzed into basic segments and further reduced to abstract phonemes. The process is analogous to the conceptual deconstruction that occurs in the first phase of creativity. In the latter reconstructive phase the creative thinker is guided by the same type of constraints that ensure phonological and lexical constructs conform to legal patterns. In both the linguistic and the cognitive realm in general, reality is defined by abstract rules that must be followed for a creation to have validity.

In addition to these task specific features, alphabetic literacy promotes creativity by developing critical coordination skills. These skills entail the ability to shift between concrete and abstract thought, manipulate discrete and diffuse phonetic data, mediate analytic and synthetic operations, and coordinate the transfer of data between the brain's left and right hemispheres. The alphabet also paves the way for creative thinking by teaching the mind to deal with abstract representations. While all writing systems achieve this effect to some degree, alphabetic writing maximizes the effect by extending the process in both directions, through discrete modeling of speech sounds and through a representation of complete lexical items. It is this second area—the link between alphabetically written words and creativity—that will occupy us throughout this chapter.

I want to focus on a phenomenon alluded to earlier, one that is well known to creativity (and creative) scientists, namely, the complaint that language interferes with creativity. We are now at a point in this study where I can suggest an explanation for this phenomenon that builds on what we have learned about the dynamics of creativity and the role of orthography in the creative process. Exploring this aspect of creativity will also lead to a better understanding of how alphabets promote original thought and how nonalphabetic writing inhibits it.

It seems contradictory to assert that language stands in the way of creativity, given all I have said about how writing helps make scientific creativity possible. But the two facts conflict only if one accepts the Bloomfieldian notions that language is speech and writing is a representation of speech. Writing and speech, I have argued, serve as semi-independent mechanisms for translating abstract language into a perceptible structure. Unlike speech, writing typically maps onto language at a higher level of abstraction, fostering in literate minds a dichotomy between the abstract body of rules that constitute language and its surface manifestations that are visible (or audible) from day to day. In this chapter we shall see how this same process of abstraction serves to distance language from thought, in effect freeing the mind to engage in retrograde associative processes.

This observation brings us back to a hypothesis we touched on earlier, namely, Whorf's argument that language influences thought and different languages influence thought differently. While I am willing to entertain the possibility that a language's lexical items and syntactic structures have some effect on a speech community's characteristic modes of thinking, it would seem that the basic question to be addressed is not the influence a given language has on thought but the influence on thought of language in general. How are the two connected? Is thought simply inner speech, the mind talking to itself, or is there more to it? Finally, if creativity—a cognitive process—is realized only in the absence of language, does the ability that users of certain languages have to suspend language's grasp over thought qualify in a limited sense as an expression of Whorf's hypothesis?

The notion that language and thought are inseparable, or by some views identical, owes its modern incarnation to the same philosophical movement that claimed language is speech, that is, American behaviorism. Just as this school, in its effort to reduce all phenomena to measurable data, rejected those parts of language accessible through introspection for an approach that equated language with speech, so did it view all thought as a function of the same concrete behavior—speech, conducted inwardly. John Watson (1878–1958), behaviorism's main figure, believed that all human activity, including cognition, could be reduced to a series of stimuli and responses. He also claimed that thought and inner speech are identical. This interpretation was applied by Leonard Bloomfield to language, where it remained in vogue until the 1950s.

Having begun graduate school well after the Chomskian revolution had (mostly) driven this paradigm out of linguistics, I was spared its worst excesses, although some early visions of rats running through mazes still linger. Younger scholars raised on such modern day concepts as distributed intelligence, emergent properties, equilibrium, and spontaneous order have even less appreciation of how atomistic and unimaginative this earlier school of thought had been—a school that viewed cause and effect in the most stringent terms possible, as when one billiard ball strikes another, or an utterance is evoked in "response" to a linguistic "stimulus."

Ironically, former *Soviet* scholars, whom you would expect to have been in the vanguard of efforts to reduce thought and behavior to their lowest materialistic denominator, were among the first to see this approach as a sterile exercise. I have already remarked on Russian linguists' dismissal of American structuralism and its unsupported tenet that language "is" speech. More fundamental, however, was their unwillingness to accept the behaviorist belief that all forms of cognition could be reduced to something as facile as inner speech. Psychologist Lev Vygotsky is most commonly cited in this regard, but his ideas are representative of the Russian approach to psychology in general.

Vygotsky rejected the claim that language must be realized through speech noting, "In principle, language does not depend on the nature of its material. . . . The medium is beside the point, what matters is the functional use of signs" (1962:38).[1] I do not remember seeing this quote or any attribution to Vygotsky in my textbooks on generative grammar, which makes the same essential statement that language and speech are separate entities. Charles Hockett, who claimed somewhere that Chomsky coopted his own ideas about a distinction between deep and surface structure, also was unconvinced that the substance keeping morphemes apart *has* to be speech sounds (1947:229), although he acknowledged that sound plays the primary role. It hardly bears mention that scientists who have studied language acquisition by the deaf are aghast at the claim that the symbolism underlying linguistic operations is restricted to speech sounds alone.

I shall return to these ideas in the following sections where I discuss the relationship between concepts and words and the need to dissolve this relationship for creativity to proceed. I bring them up here to show that, if language is not speech but a set of relationships more abstract than speech, then it makes little sense to equate traces of speech with the whole of thought. Nor can the notion that language underlies all human cognition be entertained seriously. Vygotsky was adamant on this point:

Schematically, we may imagine thought and speech as two intersecting circles. In their overlapping parts, thought and speech coincide to produce what is called verbal thought. Verbal thought, however, does not by any means include all forms of thought or all forms of speech. There is a vast area of thought that has no direct relation to speech . . . thought can function without any word images or speech movements. . . . Nor are there any psychological reasons to derive all forms of speech actively from thought. (1962:48)

Vygotsky argued that the "fusion of thought and speech, in adults as well as in children, is a phenomenon limited to a circumscribed area. Nonverbal thought and nonintellectual speech do not participate in this fusion." Charles Darwin (1809–82), cofounder of evolutionary biology and an eclectic thinker in his own right, was also convinced of the separate origins of thought and language. According to Donald (1991:33), Darwin "assumed that knowledge was not primarily linguistic and that language was therefore not a world unto itself." Darwin believed that the "underlying concepts are not linguistic constructs but rather are based on a level of understanding that is logically prior in evolution." Donald summarizes Darwin's view by noting that "our linguistic skill skates on the surface of a highly developed, distinctly human cognitive capacity" that is independent of language (42–44).

Donald himself in presenting his own theory of mind centered on representation argues that prelinguistic children and illiterate deaf-mutes, that is, people who lack language, are "not incomplete. Even while isolated from symbolic use, they appear to be, quite literally, employing the cognitive skills of a different cognitive culture, one that, in its own way, is self-sufficient." Stripped of their symbolism, people survive "because a significant part of normal human culture functions without much involvement of symbolic language." Deaf-mutes who have not learned sign language are "fully aware in every sense of the term and comprehend and remember events with great accuracy." They have intact episodic memories and unimpaired consciousness (1991:166–67).

Oliver Sacks thoroughly examines the cognitive world of the deaf in his book *Seeing Voices*, in which he argues with Vygotsky, "It is clear that thought and language have quite separate (biological) origins, that the world is examined and mapped and responded to long before the advent of language, that there is a huge range of thinking—in animals, or infants—long before the emergence of language" (1990:40). Although Sacks, as we shall see presently, distinguishes sharply between preverbal thought and the advanced cognition that language supports, he has no illusion that language represents all thought. He states, "Language, as narrowly conceived, is not the only vehicle or tool for thought. . . . One does not think at the deepest level, in music or equations, nor perhaps even for verbal artists, in language either" (42).

Neuroscientist Michael Gazzaniga in his book *Nature's Mind* observes that

there is a good body of evidence to suggest that language can be dissociated from general purpose cognition. It is easy to show that you can have cognition without language. Animals, infants before they have language, [nonhearing] adults who grew up without sign language, or stroke victims who are aphasic, can all display some intelligence without the benefit of language (1992:79).

Gazzaniga makes the interesting point that the independence of language and thought works both ways: "Looking at it the other way around, patients who become demented are frequently able to speak relatively normally, but have little capacity to carry out the simplest problem-solving behavior." One patient he examined could speak impeccable Oxford English with "no grammatical errors even though her speech was absolutely devoid of content" (80). I personally know several people, including a former boss, who have this ability.

Other scholars with different methodological backgrounds have reached the same conclusion about the nonidentity of the two processes. Olson wrote, "there is no direct relation between language and thought. All language is related to thought or meaning only through an agreed upon or presupposed possible world" (1982:155). John Morton in his essay "An Information Processing Account of Reading Acquisition" argued for a cognitive division between visual and verbal semantics. The former mediates "between the visual world and action" so that "we can react to objects, parts of objects, or features of the environment without passing through a stage of verbalization, hypothesis formation, or other problem-solving activities." This allows us, for example, to "sit upon solid surfaces without identifying them as parts of tables" (1989:49).

Koestler built his theory of creativity on the idea that creative processes involve a temporary regression from verbal to visual symbolism, the latter being "an earlier form of mental activity" (1981:12). I shall have more to say about this phenomenon later. Meanwhile, Rex Li in his book *A Theory of Conceptual Intelligence* agrees that "there are overwhelming evidences that thought can exist independently of and without language" (1996:118). Li divides cognition into two types: "conceptual thought," which occurs through the medium of language, and "rudimentary thought," which operates on "prototypical images." These nonconceptual images "are mainly about objects and actions" and are "mostly visual" (119). Li's distinction between two types of thought processes, one linguistic and conceptual, the other visual and primitive, tracks perfectly with Koestler's verbal-visual dichotomy.

It is also consistent with Donald's distinction between "mimetic" and "symbolic" cognition, the former being visual and prelinguistic, the later emerging with the onset of spoken language. As Donald put it, "visual thinking is now seen as largely autonomous from language" (1991:167). Language, he explains, evolved to formalize and unify thought (216), but does not (literally) represent all thought. A significant amount of thinking goes on beneath the verbal threshold, including the associative processes responsible for the middle or integrative phase of creativity. Language, on the other hand, supports *conceptual* cognition and fixes the bounds within which symbolic thinking occurs (237).

The confusion of language with thought is an artifact of the need to use language to think about thought. The difficulty many people have, including the early Behaviorists, separating these two phenomena is symptomatic of the issue we are treating in this chapter, namely, the close link between language and conceptual thought, and the need to suspend this connection for creative associations to happen.

Words and Concepts

If thought is more than language, concepts are more than words. Happily, there is enough agreement in the technical literature on how concepts are represented in the brain to avoid laying out a theory of concept formation from scratch. There is also a fair consensus on how concepts relate to words.

Concepts, physically speaking, are semidiscrete networks of neural connections, grown from experience. Certain events occur in nature with enough regularity to warrant recording our observations of these events in the brain, in a manner that reflects their contiguity and salient characteristics. To put it more exactly, concepts develop "as one's global pattern of synaptic weights is gradually reconfigured in response to one's ongoing sensory experience" (Churchland 1995:279). By appropriately modeling the pertinent features of an environment, these synaptic activation patterns position themselves to be strengthened by ongoing stimulation from the same environmental sources. Accurate models persist, literally fed by their own success. Those that are less well structured compete unsuccessfully for stimulation and atrophy.[2]

Charles Lumsden describes the process as follows:

Human memory tends to organize both continuous and discontinuous impressions into discrete clusters. . . . [T]hese cuts are made around objects or abstractions that have the most attributes in common and share the fewest attributes with other objects or abstractions. They appear to be of a size that maximizes efficiency in storage and transfer of information. (1988:18)

Lumsden explains that these units of memory or "nodes" exist on at least three levels, the most elementary clusters being what we know as "concepts," which may or may not be "tagged" with words (18). Jason Brown (1997) in his essay on "Process and Creation" offers a similar explanation of concept formation:

Concepts arise in the subconscious of long-term memory organized around experiential and effective cores and traverse the dreamwork, images, symbolic and metaphoric relations, and the like, on the way to propositions and the rational or logical structures they instantiate as "facts" in the mind or world. (48)

Note Brown's use of the term "cores," which is consistent with Lumsden's idea of "nodes" or focal points *around which* these structures congregate. It is important to recognize that these foci are simply synaptic activation patterns that have a higher probability of occurrence than other, competing configurations. They are not set in stone. Although it is useful to think of concepts as "fundamental units of thought" (Mitchell 1993:231), without words they depend entirely on input from sense data to maintain their cohesiveness. Their foci shift with changes in a structure's relative synaptic strengths, induced by a changing environment. There is nothing to hold a configuration in place beyond the regularity of impulses channeled in from the senses. The structure is loose, self-organizing, and fluid.

On this point—the amorphous nature of pre-linguistic concepts—Hofstadter is unequivocal. He writes:

Although it is tempting to equate a concept with a pointlike node, a concept is better identified with this probabilistic "cloud" or halo *centered* on a node and extending outwards from it with increasing diffuseness. . . . [M]any diffuse clouds overlap each other in an intricate, time-varying way. (1995:215)

Hofstadter argues against both the localist and connectionist theories of mind, noting, "In localist networks, a concept is equated with a node rather than with a diffuse region centered on a node." In connectionist networks, however, "a concept is equated with a diffuse region but has no explicit core." His own view takes the middle ground (metaphorically and anatomically) of a "subcognitive superneural level at which it is realistic to conceive of a concept as having an explicit core surrounded by an implicit, emergent halo" (216).

Holland et al. likewise regard a concept as "a set of probabilistic assumptions about what features go with what other features and what consequences are to be expected given various antecedents." The mind forms a "virtual copy" of an entity or an event, which includes besides particular categorical information "information not explicitly stored at that node but nevertheless marked for ready access" (1986:17–18). This latter information corresponds to what Hofstadter calls "halos." Simonton treats concepts in much the same way—as a combination of loose aggregates and de facto foci, gaining or losing their sharpness according to input from the environment. As he describes it,

Configurations range from small, tidy collections of elements that act as a unit . . . down to more diffuse configurations, or near aggregates, with weak associative bonds between elements and with minimal separation from kindred configurations so that one concept easily flows into another. The act of consolidation serves as a sharpening process . . . producing configurations that are progressively more clear and distinct. (1988a:403)

These more tightly bound configurations, Simonton argues, act as units, which allows them to take up a place in a cognitive hierarchy for efficient organization of information, without which an organism could not survive. Although not directed by any outside agent, "the end result of this self-organization is a population of configurations that do not lend themselves to chance permutations, because of the dearth of interconnections among ideas" (403).

Not to chance permutations, perhaps, but the flexibility inherent in self-governing structures makes for weak configurations. It seems likely that here, as in all systems, specialization and adaptability work at cross-purposes. These neural configurations, on the one hand, must be able to shift foci with changes in the environment. The requirement presupposes a loose-ness in structure that, on the other hand, precludes the intense differentiation needed to catalog large amounts of discrete data.

Up to now, we have limited our inquiry to prelinguistic concepts, that is, to aggregates formed by a brain in response to natural stimuli from the environment, which persist, vanish, change, or merge with other patterns of neural activation depending on how successfully they model their environment. While it is clear that semistable patterns or "nodes" will emerge to the extent that the environment itself is stable, it is also evident that environmentally based reinforcement will not by itself lead to the number and type of distinctions needed to support all the high-end categories available to humans, many of which are abstract or lack a real-world analogue.

Moreover, *anchoring* these ephemeral assemblies within a sea of shifting patterns of activation cannot be done on the basis of what natural selection provides by itself. For this symbols are needed, extrinsic markers that point to unique patterns and lend them a measure of stability.

Here is where language comes in. As Lumsden noted, words "tag" concepts. Words allow concepts to keep their integrity when the environment that supports them is no longer apparent. By labeling concepts, words transform these amorphous structures into genuine units that are sustained by a self-fulfilling process. When a word is invoked, its semantic structure is invoked along with it. The internal bonds (its identity) are strengthened artificially, as it were, regardless whether the configuration is viable as a model of the world around us. As concepts become more abstract and the opportunities for direct reinforcement diminish, their dependency on words increases.

Beyond this passive role, words also promote the formation of concepts. When people acquire language, abstract concepts are not so much tagged by words as they are *introduced* by them. Words become more than labels for existing ideas. They shape the development of ideas by defining their parameters in advance. Knowledge acquired by past generations of "the categories and relations and dynamical processes that were found important" (Churchland 1995:269) is imbibed in prepackaged form, obviating the need to rediscover what past generations have learned, or think they have learned, of their environment. As Churchland describes it,

> The child still has to learn the relevant concepts or prototypes, of course, and that is emphatically not just a matter of memorizing vocabulary. It is a matter of repeated interactions with the world. But the vocabulary already in place and already at work in the local cognitive commerce forms an abstract template that shapes the infant's brain development by narrowing its search space during learning. (270)

While it is possible and—for creativity's sake—absolutely necessary to distinguish between high-level concepts and the speech sounds that hold them together, in practice these abstract concepts depend so heavily on words that separating the two becomes nearly impossible. A. N. Sokolov, who builds on Vygotsky's theory of language and thought, wrote in this context:

> thinking is not only expressed by but also fulfilled in speech, not only formulated by it but also formed in it. Early mastery of the verbal system of concepts ensures that virtually all other forms of thinking . . . will occur within the conceptual framework of language, i.e., on the basis of previously acquired concepts which are retained in memory and are subsequently actualized in the form of concealed, or inner speech. (1972:3)

Sokolov, like Vygotsky, denied that words and concepts are identical, but was compelled to point out that although concepts are free "relative to the concrete forms for their expression, still they cannot exist separate from their forms" (3). Donald, who is probably the last person on earth who would confuse language and thought, states nonetheless, "Language and advanced conceptual development on the symbolic level are so closely interdependent in the brain that they appear to be inseparable" (1991:237). Later he writes:

Once the mind starts to construct a verbally encoded mental "world" of its own, the products of this operation—thoughts and words—cannot be dissociated from one another. . . . [T]he models and their worlds are so closely intertwined that, in the absence of words, the whole system simply shuts down. There is no surviving "language of thought" from which the words have been disconnected. No symbols, no symbolic thought, no complex symbolic models. (253)

One measure of conceptual thought's dependence on language is provided by the prelingually deaf who have not learned to sign and lack the symbolic means to fix ideas. Although able to manage the routine tasks of life, people deprived of language have little or no ability to conceptualize beyond a basic level. Sacks, describing an eleven-year-old whose congenital deafness had not been diagnosed, noted the boy could solve visual problems, and

saw, distinguished, categorized, used; he had no problems with *perceptual* categorization or generalization, but he could not, it seemed, go much beyond this, hold abstract ideas in mind, reflect, play, plan. He seemed completely literal—unable to judge images or hypothesis or possibilities, unable to enter an imaginative or figurative realm. (1990:40)

People who lack language, according to Sacks and others who have studied the issue, cannot represent ideas or follow logical discourse. They have trouble separating one thought from another and are unable to "hold abstract ideas in mind." Even the low-functioning deaf "not only have difficulty in the understanding of questions, but refer only to objects in the immediate environment, do not conceive remoteness or contingencies, do not formulate hypotheses, do not rise to subordinate categories, and in general are confined to a preconceptual, perceptual world" (108). It is clear that, even if language is not needed for all forms of thought, language (or the symbolic activity it encapsulates) is a prerequisite for abstract conceptual thinking.

We seem to have come full circle. Earlier I argued that thought is not language, that concepts exist independently of their verbal labels, and that the two are distinct. Now I am saying that many concepts, particularly abstract concepts, depend on these labels for their identity. So which is it? Do concepts need words or not?

The confusion, I submit, is a measure of the torment creative thinkers face when blocked by this same dilemma, namely, the need to reconfigure concepts whose shapes are locked into place by the words that hold them together. Arthur Koestler addressing this issue observed that "the verbal symbol, which at the dawn of symbol-consciousness was at first no more than a label attached to a pre-existing conceptual schema, soon becomes its focal member, its center of gravity" (1964:600). Edoardo Bisiach in an essay titled "Language Without Thought" wrote in much the same vein that "linguistic icons might act as keystones supporting the assemblage of independent representations, and specifying the nature of their relations, in a conceptual act of thought" (1988:479).

My own view, from a linguist's perspective, is that a word is a fusion of a concept and a linguistic sign, a symbolic pointer whose structure includes *both* a referent *and* a set of extrinsic markers. The referent corresponds to a cascade of neural clusters whose signaling instantiates what we know as a concept; in a semantic context it becomes a "unit" of thought. The marker itself is made up of phonemes, graphemes, or the two together. "Words" without meaning are psuedowords, that is, legal phonological sequences that lack a referent. Meaning without words tends to be fuzzy, transient, and subject to multiple interpretations as, indeed, are the morphemes of which words are composed. Hence, although concepts can exist without extrinsic markers, their existence as *units* depends on these markers, which tend to dominate the structures after they are applied.

I need to bring one more qualification into the description of *word*, which impacts on the thesis that alphabets promote creativity. A word has been functionally defined as the smallest linguistic unit on which syntax operates.[3] This definition is not entirely satisfactory since it is circular: morphology, with its own set of rules, is distinguished from syntax because it functions within word boundaries. Ipso facto, words define what is syntax apart from morphology, and the two—words and syntax—end up defining each other. The confusion over the boundaries of words is adjudicated, however, not by linguists but by the consensus of literate users.

As I noted earlier, most types of alphabetic writing require that the community make decisions on what is or is not a word. I am unwilling to speculate on how far this formalization is reflected in the structure of an individual's mental lexicon, but one thing seems certain: this process of social ratification moves these linguistic structures beyond the realm of the personal and subjective and turns them into universal objects in a way that speech never could. What was invisible and hidden from scrutiny becomes a visible artifact revealed for the label that it is. The integral fusion of meaning and sound is found, via writing, to be composed of separable parts.

Given the role that orthography plays in defining words, I would have been happier if Pinker had included it in his own description of *word*, namely,

A word is a bundle of different kinds of information. Perhaps each word is like a hub that can be positioned anywhere in a large region, as long as its spokes extend to the parts of the brain storing its sound, its syntax, its logic, and the appearance of the thing it stands for. (1994:315–16)

What I do like about this description is its portrayal of a word, or more exactly its address, as a *pointer*. I am also intrigued by it being one of the few instances where Pinker, the localist, and Deacon, the connectionist, can agree. Here is what Deacon has to say about words: "Individual symbols are markers for points in a global pattern of relationships that are only quite indirectly reflected by individual instances" (1997:128).

Both scholars regard the physical symbol, or its mental trace, as a point of connectivity that leads to different areas of the cortex where the attributes associated with the word are "stored." This proposition makes a lot of sense. For one, it helps explain the dependency of concepts on words, particularly abstract concepts whose associations are remote. It also accounts for the hemispheric bias of language and the extreme localization of its phonological functions. Most importantly, for our purposes, it offers a clue to understanding the phenomenon that launched the present inquiry, namely, the ability of language to block creative cognition.

Linguistic Obstacles to Creativity

There is universal agreement among creativity specialists that verbalization interferes with creative thinking. This apparent contradiction—an affront to human intelligence or to the symbolic processes that we regard as the

epitome of intelligence—would be hard to countenance were the phenomenon itself not so common. But the history of science abounds with
reports of how language had to be set aside before novel solutions to a
problem could "emerge." Psychologists in controlled tests have duplicated
the inhibitory effects of verbalization on the reconfiguration of problem
sets. All of us, on a personal level, have experienced the need to suspend
linguistic *control* over our thoughts to escape what we refer to as "mental
blocks." This prescription also applies to the creative use of language itself.[4]

Now if creativity were contingent on the absence of language, then humans who lack language but possess all other cognitive faculties should be
among the most creative individuals on the planet. In a sense, this is exactly the situation we find. Sacks wrote in connection with what he described as "the deaf mind" of "an unusual number of deaf engineers, deaf
architects, and deaf mathematicians, who have, among other things, great
facility in picturing and thinking in three dimensional space, picturing spatial transforms, and conceiving complex topological and abstract spaces"
(1990:107). While these people assuredly do *not* lack language, language's
control over their cognitive activity is less restrictive.

Donald notes that humans without language who rely on the mimetic
system as their highest representational structure are able to carry on in society. "Their tendency to invent gestures and mime on the spot, in highly
creative ways" demonstrates developed intentional skills. "Their ability to
operate machines and invent solutions to practical problems" signifies
"generative praxic skills" (1991:167). Donald argues convincingly that
mimetic representation, which preceded the use of symbolism in the evolution of mind, was not supplanted by language but was *supplemented* by it.
As such, mimetic skills remain beneath the surface, available for use when
symbolic thought, for whatever reason, lapses. As he put it, if the linguistic
controller is "not engaged, control defaults to the next representational
level, the mimetic" (370). This protocol applies to everyone, not just to
those whose verbal capacities are impaired.

In describing mimetic culture Donald—apparently without trying—
outlines some of the same features that we associated in Chapter 5 with the
creative process. His comments about this preverbal level of cognition thus
are all the more striking. He notes, for example, that mimesis is not the
same as imitation, but "involves the *invention* of intentional representations." It "can incorporate a wide variety of actions and modalities to its

purpose" to produce "*creative, novel, expressive acts.*" And finally, "Mimetic representation involves the ability to '*parse*' one's own motor actions into components and then *recombine* these components *in various ways,* to reproduce the essential features of an event" (167–71, my emphasis).

Yet despite these observations about the unfettered, creative state that is possible through preverbal cognition, Donald points out that "in the absence of words and symbols, thought is pretty well limited to the act of event modeling and representation" (176). Sacks is also quick to acknowledge the "destitution of knowledge and thought" that characterizes the cognitive skills of the prelingually deaf who have not learned to sign (1990:14). If creativity requires a temporary regression to preverbal levels of cognition, it is also true that the cognitive structures on which one's creative skills operate depend on linguistic symbolism for their material. Creative advances in science cannot occur unless the concepts supporting them have been internalized through language.

And there is the basic dilemma. As I noted—indeed, emphasized—earlier, genuine scientific creativity presupposes the mastery of concepts and paradigms that are framed in linguistic terms. Yet these same linguistic constructs stand between what we know of a problem and that problem's solution. Somehow we must be able to use verbal symbols with a high degree of proficiency *and* suspend our use of them when the occasion calls for it. But how does one abandon the categories of a discipline that one has spent a lifetime building, that are enshrined in the words and phrases one uses to think?

This dilemma has drawn the attention of many thinkers and scholars. Koestler in *The Act of Creation* chronicled the testimony of one great scientist after another

that in order to create, they had to regress at times from the word to the picture-strip, from verbal symbolism to visual symbolism. . . . The necessity for this retreat derives from the fact that words are a blessing which can turn into a curse. They crystallize thought; they give articulation and precision to vague images and hazy intuitions. But a crystal is no longer a fluid. (1964:173)

Acknowledging that "words are essential tools for formulating and communicating thoughts" (174), he added that they "can become a screen which stands between the thinker and reality. This is the reason why true creativity often starts where language ends" (177).

Sokolov observed in the same vein that many competent researchers "frequently report that creative thoughts occur to them without words and that much effort is required to put them into verbal form" (1972:26). According to Sokolov, Albert Einstein (1879–1955) believed in

the great importance of images in the process of creative thought. During the first stage of problem solving, the essential feature for Einstein is the "combinatory play with images," directed by the desire to arrive at logically connected concepts which are formulated in words after the associated play, in the second stage of thinking, when words intervene at all, and the thinker hears them inwardly. (31)

Other scholars have expressed the problem in more technical terms. Stevan Harnad proposed a distinction between "bounded" and "unbounded" engrams (memory's representation of a real-world event), the former being highly reduced and used for "absolute discrimination," while the latter "blend continuously and namelessly into one another, preserving their irreducible uniqueness, but doing so anonymously, without benefit of absolute identity." These unbounded engrams "cannot have names" and "cannot be addressed readily" (1982:195–98). Findlay and Lumsden concluded their study of *The Creative Mind* by stating, "high entropy and *low semantic dominance* increase the probability of 'unconventional' links being established. For this to occur, conventions need not be *encoded explicitly* or set in the form of recallable declarative knowledge in the network" (1988:170, my emphasis). Johnson (1988) pointed out in his essay "Some Constraints on Embodied Analogical Understanding" that "the reason that our debates over the cognitive status of analogy and metaphor alike are interminable and typically inconclusive is that we continue to treat analogy as principally a conceptual and propositional structure that can be sequentially represented." Rather,

analogical and metaphorical projection is pervasive in human understanding at a level of meaning and reasoning below that of propositional relations. . . . [W]e don't have a fully adequate theory of analogical reasoning, because we haven't given sufficient attention to these preconceptual and nonpropositional levels of cognition. (1988:25–26)

Johnson puts his finger directly on the problem a little later on where he writes, "Our explicit reflective analogizing typically rests upon a massive interconnected web of experientially-embodied analogical connections and processes of which we are seldom aware. I would go as far as to claim that many of these connections and isomorphisms are unconscious processes to which we have *no direct access via propositional routes*" (39, my emphasis). Finke et al. in *Creative Cognition* concluded similarly "verbal labels can diminish the opportunity for subsequent reinterpretation of mental structures" (1996:196). Deacon wrote, "Only by shifting attention away from the details of word-object relationship is one likely to notice the existence of superordinate patterns of combinatorial relationships between symbols" (1997:136). Jason Brown, whose penetrating essay "Process and Creation" I have already cited, put it succinctly, "One could discuss creativity in terms of lexical concepts and still not tap the pre-lexical sources of the creative imagination" (1997:43).

Schooler and Melcher observed that "the nonreportability of creative processes suggests a rather intriguing hypothesis about the possible effects of language on creativity: if certain creative processes cannot be adequately captured in words, then attempting to articulate such processes may actually be disruptive" (1995:97). Earlier Schooler, Ohlsson, and Brooks (1993) had run a series of laboratory studies, cited in this essay, on "the effects of concurrent, nondirected verbalization on subjects' abilities to solve insight and noninsight problems," which showed "that concurrent verbalization markedly impaired insight problems while having no effect on the solving of analytic problems of comparable difficulty" (107). Subsequent testing by Schooler and Melcher revealed, "there is some truth to past suggestions that insight may be hampered by language." They further note, "it may be that verbalization primarily disrupts the search for alternative problem approaches (restructuring). Alternatively, verbalization may prevent subjects from disregarding the initial context-induced approach" (126–27).

Fiore and Schooler expressed similar conclusions based on empirical studies in an article written a few years later where they stated, "language may relate very differently to logical versus insightful problem solving. The processes associated with solving logical problems are readily verbalized and unhampered by articulation. In contrast, insight problem-solving processes are not well suited to verbal analysis and can even be disrupted by verbalization" (1998:353). To their enduring credit, Schooler and Melcher moved beyond the thesis that language (primarily a left-brain activity) disrupts creative thinking to the conclusion that the right brain (where the "insightful" stage of creativity is hypothesized to occur) can be denied a role in problem-solving by the left's ownership of the problem set (1995:128). Fiore and Schooler reiterated this thesis in their 1998 essay, noting that:

The LH, with its reliance on language processes, should be superior to the RH with respect to logical language-based problem solving. . . . [I]n contrast, the RH might actually have some advantages over the LH with respect to insight problem solving, a process less dependent on, and sometimes even disrupted by, language processes. (353)

Beeman and Chiarello (1998) in their "Concluding Remarks" to the same collection of essays endorsed Chiarello's (1998) proposal of "code-specific and code-independent semantic processors" to refer to the organization and retrieval of data in the left and right hemispheres, respectively. They argue that

in the LH, the code-specific processor commits to mapping word forms to meanings with some limited plasticity. In contrast, the code-independent processes (used by the RH for language) do not "commit" to processing one specific type of form-meaning mapping, and so concepts are more plastic in the RH and variable. (1998:381)

Recently, St. George et al. used functional magnetic resonance imaging to verify Beeman and Chiarello's hypothesis (whom they cite by name) that the right brain plays host to large semantic fields with great overlap, whereas activation in the left brain "is limited to the target [word] and its most closely linked associates." Their conclusion that "the right hemisphere serves to maintain the activation of distantly related concepts" (1999:1324) supports our earlier contention of a functional (and apparently physiological) distinction between concepts and words. It also strengthens our main premise, namely, that verbally based cognition, by virtue of its ability to manipulate well-defined units, is restricted to the knowledge available through existing concepts. Breaking these concepts of "limited plasticity" into primary components, and finding new ways to juxtapose the components by reference to generic concepts (engrams), means getting rid of the linguistic labels that hold these verbally based conceptual units together. The central question is: given what we know of language's grip on concepts, how is this latter task accomplished?

The ABCs of Creativity

It is done through linguistic awareness. As long as the labels binding concepts together are indistinguishable from the concepts themselves, the unified structure remains intact. For separation to occur, the labels must stand out as objects in their own right, apart from their semantic and pragmatic associations.[5] By becoming aware of words as words, one learns to discriminate between the linguistic structure representing a concept and the conceptual structure represented. Thoughts are cast off on their own, where survival is contingent on their inherent fitness instead of on the presence of linguistic signs.

Dissociating a concept from its sign is facilitated by the sign's visibility. If the concept has just one representation—usually speech—separation is hard to achieve since nothing contrasts with the marker on its own terms to draw attention to it. Speech by itself offers no hint of a distinction between sign and signified, as evidenced by the near absence of linguistic awareness among those unable to read. This circumstance is the most compelling reason for the conservatism of oral societies. Lacking a second point of reference, nonliterate cultures are less able to distinguish linguistic form from cognitive substance, and are more likely to hold on to obsolete concepts. *Writing* provides this distinction by offering an alternative system of addresses, which focuses attention on their existence as separate entities.

Although any system of writing will support this discrimination, alphabetic writing emphasizes it by displaying labels as discrete objects—as words, phrases, and sentences laid out in plain view. One's awareness of the linguistic mechanism, apart from its semantic content, is heightened by the ability to manipulate these abstract units *as if they had an existence of their own*. Nonalphabetic writing improves the situation only marginally because the linguistic boundaries are not depicted and must be inferred. Although it offers a contrast to speech, the contrast is minimized by its failure to identify phonemes and larger discourse structures.

Many of us accustomed to word division are surprised to learn that alphabetic writing, for much of its history, did not identify words or larger linguistic units either. Although phonemes were depicted in writing by 1400 B.C., word division used in combination with phonemic representation did not appear until well into the Middle Ages (500–1500), in some cases later. Paul Saenger explains:

Before the introduction of vowels to the Phoenician alphabet, all the ancient languages of the Mediterranean world, whether syllabic or alphabetical, Semitic or Indo-European, were written with word separation either by space, points, or both in conjunction. After the introduction of vowels, space between words was no longer necessary to eliminate an unacceptable level of ambiguity. (1991:207)

Both the Greeks and Romans continued for a while to separate words after vowels were introduced, but gave it up in favor of *scriptura continua* when the widespread use of vowels made word division unnecessary from an information processing view. This was a universal pattern for alphabetic writing in which vowels are depicted, including Sanskrit and Cyrillic.[6] According to Saenger, word separation was *re*introduced to Europe in the early Middle Ages to help make sense of Greek and Latin texts being recopied by scribes. By Renaissance times it had once again become the standard orthographic practice in Italy and France, and by the beginning of the seventeenth century it had entered the Slavic languages as well. The use of word division, in conjunction with fully phonemic alphabets, had a significant impact on European culture. As Saenger described it, word separation

freed the intellectual faculties of the reader, permitting him to read all texts silently and, therefore, more swiftly and in particular to understand greater numbers of intellectually more difficult texts with greater ease. . . . for these reasons, separated written text became the standard medium of written communication of a civilization characterized by superior intellectual rigor. (210)[7]

Ivan Illich noted that the reintroduction of word division into Europe made texts "visible," leading to other refinements such as titles and subtitles, paragraphs, tables of contents, and alphabetic indices, that conspired to make written texts much more than recorded speech (1991:37). Given the connection between Ancient Greece's use of a fully phonemic alphabet and the emergence of abstract science, it is hard to ignore the likelihood that this second major orthographic innovation is causally related to the explosive growth of creative inquiry that began in the late Middle Ages, in a way that goes beyond the effects that Saenger and Illich ascribed to the innovation, significant as they are.

In this context, Olson notes, "in the Middle Ages words, like images, were seen as having a natural connection to things [and that] both were seen as intrinsic parts of the object." However, by the seventeenth century when word division was once again in full bloom, signs were "no longer seen as natural to their objects but as conventions" (1994:167). This distinction, in the opinion of Olson and many others, was a major factor in the renaissance of scientific thought.[8] It would not have happened were it not for the contrast between words and their referents that word division helped make evident.

As I see it, the cognitive changes associated with word division are on a par with those brought about some two millennia earlier, when vowels were introduced to the alphabet. The depiction of word boundaries focused readers' attention on these signs qua signs, facilitating a distinction between label and concept. It also led to the depiction of phrases, sentences, and paragraphs, which tag propositions and whole schemata (Lumsden 1988:18). As these larger discourse units became visible, the identification with their cognitive antecedents grew weaker, freeing the way for conceptual restructuring.

Separating words from concepts is also facilitated by the atomistic nature of word addresses written alphabetically. Earlier we saw how an awareness of phonemes induced by alphabetic literacy serves as an analytical guide for cognitive activity in general. These analytical skills are used in the first stage of a creative act to scrutinize problems and reduce them to basic components, which are reassembled through right-track brain processes. The new constructs are evaluated by the same left-track skills fostered by use of an alphabet. Apart from this facilitation effect, phonemic representation also serves creativity by weakening the link between a sign and the signified concept.

Knowledge of a word's phonemes entails acceptance of its conventional nature. Being made up of a limited number of smaller units (letters) whose identities are assumed to be basic, the alphabetically written word is no longer seen as part of nature. Whatever can be composed at will by typing or spelling can be dismissed as invention, an expedient whose use is discretionary and not a necessary part of a cognitive structure. This impression is strengthened by the addition or substitution of letters within word boundaries to accommodate morphological variation. The flexibility of these word symbols, their looseness, divisibility, and changeability, convey a sense of transience.

Freed from any necessary connection with language, cognitive paradigms rest on their own. Their verbal scaffolding dismantled, these structures must be sustained by inherent logic. Words, of course, can change their meanings as new or modified patterns of thought seek linguistic expression. But for this "conceptual slippage" (Hofstadter) to occur at all, language must temporarily be set aside. The ability of alphabetic writing to make this happen is one of the system's greatest strengths.

The Tenacity of Character-Based Representation

Unlike alphabets, which overcome language's negative effect on creativity by helping one distinguish between sign and concept, East Asian writing does little to mitigate the problem. On the contrary, Chinese characters, on which all East Asian orthography is to some degree based, consolidate the link between sign and referent, strengthening this obstacle to creative thinking.

The problem begins with the scripts' depiction of phonology.[9] As de Kerckhove pointed out, syllabaries "emulate" phonology, they do not represent it (1986:284). Instead of depicting sounds discretely, the matching is done holistically. There is no discretion evidenced in the relationship: not at the level of sound, where the units are unanalyzed syllables; not within the grapheme, whose parts have no *discrete* relationship to the verbal sign; and not at the semantic level either, where the units (morphemes) are assumed to be indivisible wholes. This iconic relationship reinforces the link between linguistic and nonlinguistic phenomena, the opposite of what creativity requires.

Given its holistic mapping protocols, there is very little in Chinese character-based writing to suggest its conventionality. Although subcharacter components exist, they number in hundreds and are ill defined. Unlike the letters of alphabetically written words, which are limited in number and discernible as units, Chinese character components are not easily identifiable, nor *can* they be, given their greater number. East Asians as a consequence do not look at a character and read off discrete parts. They see the sign as a unit and analyze it, relatively speaking, with much more difficulty.

Moreover, Chinese characters do not reflect speech sounds in a principled manner. Instead of drawing attention to the linguistic sign (as distinct from the concept), both written and spoken signs lead to the concept independently. I mean this not only in a structural sense but also functionally. The alphabet's discrete representation of sound means that phonology is more likely to be invoked during reading, if not as a condition for lexical access then as an afterthought to aid short-term memory, or simply because users are used to making these associations. Access to a concept in alphabetic writing usually involves some phonologizing, which dilutes the immediacy of the connection. This feature helps keep the sign and its referent conceptually distinct.

Although Chinese characters can and often do invoke phonological associations, they are less prone than alphabetic scripts to do so given the lack of structural motivation. Their vague depiction of a word's sound means that readers are more likely to access a semantic referent "directly" without the prior or concurrent intervention of phonology. According to Tzeng and Hung, who studied the problem of lexical access in Chinese, there is "convincing evidence to support the hypothesis that logographic symbols are comprehended faster than phonetic symbols. Thus logographic symbols appear to allow more rapid access to meaning, whereas phonetic symbols allow more rapid access to verbal names" (1988:279).[10] Sign and meaning are more closely associated for readers of character texts. Separating the two, as required for creativity, is more difficult.

Unlike an alphabet, on whose units there is universal agreement, experts cannot agree on what constitutes a character component. The only area where minimal consensus is reached is the "radical" element of characters, which identifies broad semantic areas related to what a character means or at one time meant. Although the practical value of this device is overstated, the fact that these components can be identified at all is used by teachers and lexicographers to support learning and classification. Before *pinyin* and other notations were devised, Chinese dictionaries were arranged by these radicals. In school, teachers use them to simplify instruction and go out of their way to make associations between these parts of characters and their meanings, even where none exist.

Such practices are reinforced in daily life by East Asians' habit, born of necessity, of singling these elements out by name to make "sense" of a structure that has little apparent motivation. The upshot is that readers cannot help but associate the sign or parts of the sign with an *intrinsic* meaning. Unfortunately, these individual "meanings" interfere with one's grasp of the meaning conveyed by the whole. The interference results from the extraneous meanings that components impart to the character, and from the meanings that individual morphemes (represented by characters) impart to words (Hashimoto et al. 1987:55, 98–99).

Annoying as this effect is in the day-to-day task of language comprehension, its more debilitating consequence is the impact this imagined identity of sign and concept has on creativity. Coupled with the other factors just mentioned, East Asians face greater obstacles than Western readers do in distinguishing linguistic signs from the ideas they represent.

The problem doesn't stop there. By uniquely tagging morphemes, Chinese characters make a semantic statement that is much stronger than that evoked by the morphophonemic spellings of English, Tibetan, and other conservative phonetic scripts. It would seem, at first glance, that the characters *promote* creativity by presenting a collection of thought units that have already been divided and await reordering by the creative user. But such reasoning is misleading. The granularity represented by a few thousand morphemes does not begin to approach the level needed for genuine creativity. Morphemes are macrounits on the cognitive scale. Identifying them by a visual marker that is only remotely linked to a phonetic sign supports unity, not dissociation.

By the same token, semantic constructs are often keyed to larger structures, such as words and propositions, which cannot be easily identified by East Asians because they are not distinguished in the orthography. Alphabetic systems use word division as a source of redundancy, which puts the signal closer to the message. Dividing words also entails punctuating the larger structures in which words play a part. The two practices *incidentally* provide the cognitive focus needed to distinguish linguistic forms from underlying concepts. These practices did not arise in East Asia because Chinese characters, by depicting morphemes explicitly, obviate a functional requirement for word division.

It hardly bears mentioning that East Asian languages have words and syntax. What is missing in the tradition is an *awareness* of these structures. Although East Asians have a clear notion of morphemes because the orthography identifies them, they have greater difficulty grasping the notion of *words*. The same holds for phrases and sentences, which are punctuated poorly if at all. This fact is also noted by linguists who study the metalinguistic awareness of oral societies, namely, that people cannot identify linguistic units that their writing does not distinguish. With little support from the orthography, the task of separating sign from concept—the first step on the way to creativity—becomes more difficult.

This concludes my discussion of the primary obstacles character-based writing presents to creativity, namely, its failure to provide models of analysis and synthesis, and the difficulty East Asians who use these writing systems have separating the signs from the concepts they designate. In the next chapter I will consider some secondary or "macro" effects of East Asian orthography on the disposition of its users to create.

Chapter Ten
Chinese Characters and Creativity

All my life I have resented wasting hour after hour to master a decent
calligraphy, because I was aware that such formal exercises do not produce the substantive knowledge that is so desperately needed to rescue
China.

—Qian Wen-yuan

Why the Numbers Matter

The negative impact of character-based writing on creativity stems largely
from its failure to facilitate related cognitive processes. When people in
alphabetic cultures begin to read they are faced with two new conceptual
tasks. On the one hand, they must learn to distinguish abstract language
from the concrete speech to which they are accustomed. Since writing
maps onto language at a level deeper than the acoustic events used in
speech, literacy entails becoming aware of a body of rules kept beneath the
threshold of consciousness. The difficulty nonliterates have conceptualiz-
ing language and articulating its formal conventions is symptomatic of the
failure of speech by itself to inform users of its abstract foundations.

Learning a language's rules qua rules is one of the earliest steps a developing mind takes into the world of abstract thinking and is responsible for
what Ong, Olson, and others have broadly termed the "literacy effect." Beyond this, alphabetic literacy also requires that one learn to relate the concrete sounds of speech (syllables) to the abstract components of which they
are formed (phonemes). Overcoming this additional conceptual hurdle
leads, as we have seen, to an ability to identify abstract elements generally,
which underlies the creative act. The difficulty people have making this

transition from concrete sound to its abstract antecedents is evidenced in the evolution of writing across a variety of cultures, which typically pass through a protracted period when syllabic representation is the norm, and in the relative commonness of dyslexia among the alphabetic cultures of the West. Learning the alphabet's symbols, by contrast, is a trivial task.

When East Asians learn to read and write, they benefit from the same cognitive effect that accrues to literate speakers the world over. However, the crucial element missing in the East Asian learner's task, which has played an indispensable role in shaping the analytic spirit of Western culture, is any requirement to resolve speech sounds into abstract elements. Chinese characters and Japanese *kana* map directly onto natural syllables, obviating the need to relate these units to the smaller but psychologically remote set of phonemes that make up syllables. Although Korean and Vietnamese writing do identify phonemes, the tutorial effect is subverted by the orthographies' insistence on expressing the sounds in a syllabic format, which constitutes the basic psychological unit.

There are other ways Asian writing impacts negatively on the ability to create. An alphabet's abstract design enables one to express a large syllable set with a mere two dozen or so symbols. In the West, therefore, the difficult part of becoming literate lies not in learning the writing system's symbols but in grasping their cognitive import. In East Asia literacy has a different price tag. By foregoing the benefits of abstraction for concrete representation, Sinitic writing requires one to learn a symbol set some one hundred times larger. Eschewing one task, East Asians saddle themselves with another.

We noted that Chinese characters represent morphemes, the smallest units of linguistic meaning used to form words and syntactic elements. Given the characters' connection with morphemes, there are in theory as many tokens in the writing system as there are basic units of meaning. In practice, the system reduces this to a manageable (if onerous) figure by assigning multiple meanings to most characters, usually depending on the context of the word or phrase in which they occur. Many such meanings are the result of normal semantic development and often it is anyone's guess whether a Chinese character is representing one morpheme with extended meanings or more than one morpheme. Japanese goes further by attributing different sounds to a character depending on the status of its referents. This doubling up of sounds with characters is not uncommon in

Mandarin and Cantonese either, the difference being that in Japanese it is the rule whereas in Chinese it is supposed to be an exception.

Even with this mitigating device of assigning multiple meanings to characters, designating morphemes with unique symbols makes the number of tokens enormous, reaching into the thousands in Chinese. Since the number of characters available for use is cumulative, all 49,000 characters in the *Kangxi Zidian*, a Qing Dynasty (1716) dictionary regarded for many years as the standard, are potentially part of a learner's task. In normal practice, 6,000 or so graphs are in use today. A literate speaker in China or Taiwan can get by with a reading knowledge of 4,000 to 5,000. Japanese and Koreans learn about half that number, thanks to the availability of *kana* and *hangul.*

The number of *characters* one knows relates marginally to the number of words in one's vocabulary, since these symbols combine with other characters (morphemes) to form lexical items, just as in any language. Thus the claim that Chinese know only as many words as the characters they master is absurd. But there is little else in the way of combinatorial tricks to ease the memory burden. Although the characters can be reduced to components, most analyses yield figures of around 200 "semantic" signs and 800 or more semiphonetic indicators. Unlike the letters of Western words, which combine serially, these character components form geometric patterns that change when put together. Users must remember what components of a graph go where in relation to the others. These placement rules increase as the number of components used in the analysis decreases (as their stroke counts decline), with the result that the memory burden stays fairly constant no matter how the tokens are divided.

The fact that the number of character components varies with the analysis underscores their arbitrariness. The majority of Chinese characters *ideally* are composed of a semantic element that identifies a broad category of meaning and a phonetic element that equates holistically to a syllable sound. When new graphs are formed, these principles—when followed—lend the system a measure of rationality. But the associations are only approximate: the sound component (if there is one) usually has a range of phonetic associations. The meaning component is more tenuous. Its identification often depends on how a lexicographer interpreted the graph two centuries or two millennia ago. Whatever practical motivation a character had when it was formed is skewed over time by both semantic and phonetic change.

In the end, one can waste more time trying to elucidate rational correspondence rules between components and whole characters, with little gain in learning efficiency, than one can by simply plunging into the task to learn intuitively whatever correspondences seem to make sense. The situation is unlike that in alphabetic cultures, where learning time can be reduced drastically by tutoring in phonics. Learning Chinese characters means spending time—lots of time—memorizing graphic structures with no connection to anything in the real or psychological worlds. The task is entirely rote.

Instead of using their formative years to acquire real knowledge, East Asians spend their youth memorizing task-specific rules that pertain to an *instrument* for acquiring knowledge. Precious time that could be spent learning how to think or building a foundation for original thought is devoted to a menial task that has no application in any other cognitive area. Although children do show an early interest in the mechanics of character-based literacy, this interest wanes as the reality of learning thousands of symbols sinks in (Steinberg and Yamada 1978–79b:668–71), a task that continues through high school, college, and into one's adult life.

Some scholars argue that the requirement for universal literacy puts a strain on children asked to achieve this feat through character scripts, resulting in suicides and other malaises (Unger 1987:94–95). I personally think the argument is overdrawn but I agree that Chinese characters, coupled with other institutions that are part of the character-literate culture, represent forms of oppression that inhibit one's individual spontaneity. Class time used for drills in the writing system is obtained at the expense of other subjects that could provide a wider variety of source analogs for creative thinking. Or it is crammed into the curriculum in a way that makes learning an exercise in regimentation. Either way creativity suffers.

Worse than the time lost memorizing symbols is the impact of character-based education on people's attitude toward knowledge and creation. I have argued that learning to read and write in an alphabetic culture has cognitive effects beyond the goal of literacy. These effects entail not only an ability to engage in abstract and analytic thought, but also a disposition to view learning as a proactive process. For example, spellings of words must make sense (even in English) relative to their pronunciation and it is up to Mary or John to find these connections. Western children learn to expect a rational fit between the data of the two domains and to fulfill this expectation by seeking abstract correspondences. The process models the creative act.

What do East Asian children learn about creativity from the relationship of speech sounds to print? Two things. First, that there are no rational connections to be made between domains on an abstract level. Correspondences between sound and symbol are vague, haphazard, and poorly motivated in a discrete sense. While it is clear that associations are being made on some level as part of the learning process, the links between the two domains are concrete and holistic. The learner finds one set of data here (writing) that cannot be analyzed consistently, another set of data there (speech sounds) made up of concrete chunks, and correspondence rules between the two that are ad hoc. The lesson one draws is that different knowledge domains cannot be related by shared features, but conventionally if at all. There is nothing that hints of the bisociative act on which creativity is based.

The second thing East Asians discover is that learning is a passive act. Immersed in an environment where a large part of education consists of repeating meaningless facts, memorizing is seen both by student and teacher as the essence of learning. This attitude was characteristic of schooling in premodern East Asia and continues to color education there today, as evidenced by the dilemma of East Asians studying abroad who find themselves unprepared to participate in classroom discussions, challenge their instructors, or view instructional material critically. It is hard to ignore the likelihood that Chinese character-based writing is responsible for much of this passivity and for this willingness to accept "facts" as they are presented.

The Primacy of Process

Similarly, much of the formalism that characterizes East Asian society can be traced to the influence the writing system has on people's habits. There is so much more effort involved in learning a character-based system that users tend to regard it not as a means, but as an end. Writing, which should be a simple tool to express language, is elevated to an art form and revered as a cultural icon. The fierce attachment many East Asians feel toward the characters, including scholars who accept arguments against them on logical grounds, stems from this perversion of means and ends. Of course, focusing on outward form instead of inner substance and holding onto past practices for their own sake are hardly behaviors that support creativity.

No one denies that Chinese writing is an important part of East Asian culture. Indeed, it shaped the area's whole approach to creativity. As we shall see later, this unique system of writing affected not only its users' way of thinking but also many of their institutions. I will also agree that there are good reasons for retaining *any* functioning system as a bulwark against half-baked ideas that could have disruptive consequences. But there comes a time when dysfunctional practices must be set aside if a society is to remain competitive. Generally, such changes happen when the disutility of a traditional practice becomes apparent enough to move society past its inertia.

Yet, ironically, an attachment to the past for its own sake is one aspect of Asian formalism that is *abetted* by Chinese writing. It is not only habit that makes East Asians reluctant to give up this archaic system of writing; the characters themselves produce a collective disposition to value process over substance and thus perpetuate their own existence.

Just as Chinese characters have created a linguistic situation hospitable to their use by molding East Asian languages in such a way as to make them dependent on this form of representation, so have the characters shaped society's attitude toward form and tradition so that their continued use is guaranteed. Learning how to read and write consumes so much time and energy that one comes to accept ritual as a part of life. Schooled in this orthographic tradition, East Asians learn to value formality over utility. Means become ends.

Computer technology has done nothing to relieve East Asians of their attachment to formalism. If anything it has made matters worse by involving them deeper in character text manipulation. The chief difficulty is computer input, which is symptomatic of the issues East Asians face in dealing with a large character set. Let's examine this subject briefly.

There are three ways a character text can be rendered in digital form: by speech recognition, writing on a sensitized grid, or coding on a keyboard.[1] The first two techniques *in principle* are indifferent to the type of orthography, although some practical distinctions exist. Even if voice input software continues to improve (which I have to accept on faith, given my disappointing experience with these products), one still runs up against the fact that people do not speak the way they write.

Using this software requires one to speak artificially in a way that many people find awkward. That it works at all in English stems from the fact that alphabetical texts, like speech, depict a series of phonemes. Despite their different outward substance, both media—speech and alphabetical writing—encode language phonologically. A speaker who dictates to a voice recognition program is producing text in a style not far removed, in a relative sense, from what users of the language have set as the norm for writing. The redundancy is of the same type, if not of the same order.

Such is not the case with character-based text, whose graphic redundancy has little connection with sound. Chinese texts, even those written in the colloquial (*báihuà*) style, are difficult to comprehend when spoken aloud because their *visual* redundancy bears no relationship to the phonological redundancy speakers count on to ensure their message is understood. By the same token, East Asian text written with speech recognition software ends up being more redundant than what is appropriate for the character-based style if the spoken input is to be understood by the software. Editing this speech-like representation into a more concise text means spending more time on process. There is also the homonym problem that I will discuss in a moment. The upshot is that users are still occupied with the writing *mechanism* and are less able to focus on content.

Handwritten input in which the computer tracks the progress of strokes made on a pressure- or light-sensitive surface does, in a certain sense, put alphabetic and Chinese character text on the same footing by reducing both to the level of sophistication that existed before writing became mechanized. As with voice input, one must constantly check whether the system correctly interpreted the input. This peripheral task detracts from the primary goal of creating ideas.

I am not sure which obstacle to creative thinking is greater: having one's thought disrupted by mechanical tasks, or being lured into a false sense of accomplishment by the satisfaction one feels at having jumped successfully through the processing hoops. The dilemma applies especially to the third and most common way of inputting character text: typing on a keyboard.

Unlike alphabetic writing whose units consist of a few elements, Chinese characters must be input on large keyboards with several thousand key choices, or by pressing keys that correspond to character components. The first system typically puts several characters on each of a few hundred keys. One finds the right key, and then selects the proper character by pressing another key, like the function keying done on alphanumeric boards. If you have trouble remembering which functions are associated with the "Ctrl" and "Alt" keys on an alphanumeric keyboard, or lack the dexterity to execute these commands, multiply the confusion by a hundred to get an idea of the task users of large character keyboards face.

It is more efficient to use keyboards that identify components, which are assembled semiautomatically into whole symbols by the software. This procedure works well when the components are few and the target shapes are limited, as in Korean *hangul* inputting, whose final forms are expressed as syllables. One enters each component individually by pressing one of the twenty-six keys used for letters on a standard keyboard, with or without the shift key. The *hangul* letter appears in a small window. When a syllable is formed after two or more keystrokes, the complete graph reappears automatically on the text line and the window is cleared. The process is quick and intuitive.

Unfortunately, the elements that make up the Chinese character set are neither few nor well defined. Accommodating the commonly recognized components requires a keyboard of a thousand or more symbols. Of course, system builders take advantage of the fact that these components can be reduced to a smaller number of recurring stroke patterns and implement keyboard designs based on this. Depending on your ability to duplicate the software designer's analysis of character strokes and sequences, and the software's ability to recognize alternative analyses, for each character one wants to input one ends up with one or several characters displayed on a pop-up screen from which the proper one can be chosen. Unlike alphabetic keying, a lot of memorization and guesswork is involved simply to produce this *range* of choices. Once again the emphasis is on the process of creating individual character shapes rather than on the *content* of the message one wants to convey.[2]

Worse, the process corresponds to nothing in the real or notional worlds. It is wholly task-driven. Most people prefer *phonetic conversion* software, which is based on the sounds of syllables and words. Instead of reconstructing characters on a keyboard, one types a spelling for its pronunciation—*pinyin* for Chinese and *kana* or *rōmaji* for Japanese. The computer associates the input with a grapheme and displays it. Some programs take context into account in trying to produce the correct representation, thus greatly narrowing when not eliminating the range of possible choices. As far as Asian input systems go, this is the best of the lot.

However, practical considerations make phonetic input more difficult than one might expect. First, a given syllable in Mandarin and Japanese is almost always associated with several different characters. Typing *shi* on a keyboard gets you not only the symbol you want but also *every other* character with that sound, perhaps dozens. The computer normally presents these candidates in sets, prioritized by frequency. But you still have to shift from the mode in which you were thinking and acting to choose the correct character. Thought is diverted from the cognitive task at hand.

Dedicated "word" processing software reduces this ambiguity by considering the input in its syntactic and semantic contexts. One type of context is word boundaries, and the user can eliminate some confusion by inputting not individual syllables but words. As straightforward as this solution may seem, it is confounded by the fact that East Asian languages lack clearly defined words, since the writing system never required them. Moreover, even where word boundaries are agreed on, the incidence of homophony is high enough that the user must often select from multiple possibilities.

There are two points I need to make before moving on to the issue of spoken and written styles. In an earlier book (1997) I made the same complaint about the difficulty of inputting character-based scripts. Some reviewers felt that my skepticism betrayed a lack of familiarity with the technology. I would like to suggest to those reviewers—who are admirers of Chinese characters or developers of the next and best Asian software solutions—that they step back from the fascinating details of their projects and view the enterprise from a global perspective.

For the record, I work with Asian language software daily. I know what its use involves. I have sat on dissertation review committees for Chinese computational linguistics and subscribe to technical journals that treat character-based computing in detail. And I am as impressed as anyone with the ingenuity of the techniques being developed. But in the end, no matter how adept software becomes at divining a user's intent, there will always be an intermediate stage where one must confirm or revise the suggested text. This contrasts with alphabetically written languages, where the input *is* the final representation.

My second point refers to what I noted above about how people skilled at using Asian language software tend to confuse their adroitness at manipulating the system with the quality of the text they produce. Thanks to these computer input programs, one can find lots of excuses to play at writing while avoiding the trauma that afflicts writers elsewhere in the world, who know the value of what they have (or have not) written by what appears to the left of the cursor. With East Asian writing, there is plenty to do even if one creates nothing. Indeed, the software works best if you can anticipate what the *system* wants in input!

Focusing on form instead of content subverts the creative act. Character-based orthography—whether learning it or writing with it—requires that an inordinate amount of time be spent on processes that contribute nothing to content, and tend to act as a substitute for it. If alphabetic writing supports creativity by modeling its cognitive steps, character-based writing frustrates creativity by adding one more layer of formalism for the thinker to contend with.

Spoken and Written Styles

If the above arguments seem familiar to readers acquainted with the history of Asian writing reform, particularly with movements in the early twentieth century, this is because substituting form for content was an issue in East Asia long before computers were developed. The problem is as old as Chinese writing and is tied to it in a causal sense.[3] The complications associated with character-based software are simply a modern expression of a venerable paradigm, namely, the emphasis given to outward form, as evidenced in literary style.

As I noted earlier, "Chinese" refers to a family of related but mutually unintelligible languages, and to a system used alone or with subscripts to write the major East Asian languages. The term also denotes a style of writing (*wényán* in Chinese, *kambun* in Japanese, *hanmun* in Korean) that dominated literary art in East Asia through much of its history. Commonly known as "classical Chinese," the term is misleading since it implies that the language reflected in these texts was at one time spoken, when it probably never was.[4] "Literary Chinese" is also a misnomer because it suggests that this stilted medium was the only venue available to writers. In fact, a written style closer to speech coexisted alongside the formal style but lacked its prestige, being Buddhist-inspired and out of step with state ideology in content and spirit. Perhaps the best way to refer to this formal style of writing is by the Chinese term *wényán*, which means "written language" but is understood universally in this more restricted sense.

Wényán takes advantage of Chinese characters' visual redundancy by eliminating most polysyllabic expressions used in speech and colloquial writing. For example, instead of writing the two characters 時候 pronounced *shíhou* ("time"), one writes the first character 時 only, which is enough to convey the idea. The style uses a rigid grammar that includes restrictions on "word" order and the presentation of ideas to achieve further succinctness. Finally, *wényán* attains its brevity through nuance. Writers—highly educated literati who spent their lives poring over approved classics—counted on their readers' familiarity with these works to allude with a few characters to a whole train of ideas—ideas rooted in tradition and in the past. Given this kind of conciseness, when read aloud *wényán* cannot be understood orally, outside the restricted medium in which it was composed.

Wényán contrasts with *báihuà* ("plain talk"), a written style that is supposed to approximate speech more closely. There are problems with this dichotomy, however, the first being that writing in any culture rarely mirrors speech. This gap is a function of the two media's technical characteristics and the nature of the demands put on them by users. Thus *báihuà* also differs significantly from speech, albeit less dramatically than *wényán*. Second, *wényán* itself changed in the course of its 3,000 years of use. These changes followed their own dynamic independently of changes the spoken languages underwent. Depicting *wényán* and *báihuà* as the formal and colloquial versions of each other obscures the fact that the two portray entirely different languages.

Third, much of the writing done in China today is neither *wényán* nor *báihuà* but a mixture of the two. Even a thoroughly modern book such as *Chāoxiàn Zhàn* (*Unrestricted Warfare*), published by two army officers (Qi Liang and Wang Xiangsui 1999), is full of literary allusions that seem out of place in a book dealing with computer hacking and state-sponsored terrorism. Early twentieth-century supporters of China's *báihuà* movement, who sought to replace *wényán* with this more speech-like style of writing, also were unwilling to purge their own writing of these traditional forms. This tendency to use *wényán* elements in colloquial writing has been inherited by younger Chinese over the past two or three decades, which suggests that the roots of this genre go beyond tradition and relate to the nature of the writing system itself.

Chinese script and *wényán* have in common the fact that they are both worlds apart from the living spoken language. *Wényán*'s pithy, truncated style depends entirely on the availability of the character script, whose visual redundancy is greater than the phonological redundancy of the sounds it encodes. By the same token, economy of expression, which accounts for a large part of good taste, encourages writers to take advantage of the visual redundancy characters offer to compress their ideas. Just as Chinese characters distance themselves from speech by depicting language at the morpheme level, so has the culture's literary style evolved in a *non*-speech-like manner consistent with the information-bearing characteristics of the medium. Chinese writers have difficulty writing in *báihuà* because the technical qualities of the script work against it, and because the literary ethic that has grown up around *wényán* infused itself into the language and culture.

What do these facts imply for creativity? Several scholars of Chinese thought have pondered the relationship between *wényán* and East Asia's scientific development. Schwartz (1964), Needham (1969), and Sivin (1977), while acknowledging the writing system's difficulties, did not regard the script and its literary protocols as absolute impediments to scientific development. Others such as Qian (1985) and Bodde (1991) disagree. Although Bodde allows that *wényán* may not be "hopelessly ambiguous," he notes "the unnecessary burden of time and energy such imprecise writing imposes on the reader by obliging him or her to focus on the text's *externals rather than its inner content*" (37, my emphasis).

This observation leads back to my comment about how Chinese characters shift a writer's attention from content. Not only is creativity frustrated by the emphasis the orthography places on form; it is also diverted by the formalistic nature of the style that goes with it. Add to these factors the psychological impact of a system whose phrases are based on allusions to historical events and the barrier posed to creative thinking becomes formidable.

Early reformers understood the stultifying effect of *wényán* on the genesis and transmission of new ideas and campaigned actively to replace the style with one closer to speech. In China the effort became known as the *báihuà movement*. In Japan it was called *gembun-itchi* ("unification of the written and spoken language").[5] In both countries the outcome was a written style that, by and large, follows modern grammar and can mostly be understood when read aloud. These developments were comparable to the transition that occurred in Europe between the fourteenth and seventeenth centuries when Latin was replaced by written vernaculars. The parallel is close enough for one of the *báihuà* movement's founders, Hu Shi, to have called it the "Chinese Renaissance."

I am not sure the move to unify written and spoken languages has been justified in terms of its potential impact on creativity, other than as a retrospective judgment of developments in Renaissance Europe. Indeed, the notion that writing the same language one speaks facilitates the free flow of ideas and therefore supports creative thinking contradicts what I said earlier about how language inhibits creativity in its critical stage. Yet the belief that writing in the vernacular supports creativity is common enough to justify some speculation on its probable causes.

Two such linkages come to mind. I have argued that literacy promotes creativity by casting language apart from the ideas it represents. Expressing one's ideas solely through speech offers no basis for distinguishing linguistic form from semantic content, as evidenced by the near lack of linguistic awareness in nonliterate societies. It is only when an alternative medium is available—writing—that a contrast can be made between the two forms of language, leading to the identification of language as an entity itself. This awareness enables one to suspend the bond between language and its content, exposing the content to creative reordering. For the effect to work, however, the same language must be represented, in both speech and writing.

Now as Gelb (1962), DeFrancis (1989), and others pointed out, there is no such thing as a "pure" writing system. Systems based on phonemic alphabets often have large morphophonemic components through which meaning plays a role in determining what graphemes are used to represent sound in a given environment. English spelling is a famous example. Hence it is better to speak of a *gradient* of script types, some more phonetic than others, some whose graphemes are keyed more to meaning. I should add that, owing to its permanency, all forms of writing, not just Chinese, compress language beyond what is normal for speech.

These caveats aside, phonetic writing systems—alphabetic writing in particular—are prevented from *unduly* compressing texts by the need to maintain word boundaries. One can use longer words, fewer words, or even uncommon words, but as long as the writing is phonetic, a text will preserve its phonetic intelligibility by virtue of the fact that full words are written. There is a limit therefore to how far Western language texts can diverge from the spoken style. Although the spoken and written styles are not identical (nor should they be given the need for contrast), both focus on a single language, highlighting one's awareness of that language as distinct from the ideas expressed in it.

These conditions did not exist in pre-Renaissance Europe, when people wrote Latin and spoke their own vernaculars. Nor did any such unified focus emerge in East Asia, where writing was done in *wényán*, a language that shared little with the vernaculars. This same situation exists in Asia today, albeit with less severity. Users of character-based scripts pay less attention than alphabet-literate Westerners to the phonological aspects of their writing, which isolates the two media from each other. Furthermore, the characters encourage use of a style that compresses language beyond what a phonetic script is capable of, bifurcating the two media. The much touted "density" of character-based texts turns out to be one of its greatest liabilities.

The second link between creativity and "unified" writing and speech relates to a tutorial effect set up through the cognitive exercise of shifting between the two media—a process that parallels the shuffling one does between disciplined thought and free association in the act of creating something. Writing causes one to focus on the idea at hand, expressing it in terms of defined protocols, which when properly executed ensure that one's thought makes sense (in terms of the usual grammar). Speech by contrast is less rigid. Although we do not perceive it as disjointed, transcribed specimens of speech across a variety of cultures reveal an incredible lapse of "good" grammar, or, as I prefer to think of it, a loss of inhibition that is closer in style to the subvocal speech we use in our thoughts. To the extent that we learn to bridge this gap between free and disciplined thinking, exemplified by the contrasting styles of the two media, we model the processes used in the creative act.

This model is valid only if speech and writing express two forms of one language that are close enough to permit bisociation, but sufficiently distinct to allow for a creative tension. A close analogy is found in electricity, where two poles either too near or too far apart will not conduct a spark. Similarly, creative thinking is not stimulated when the spoken and written styles are identical (the limiting case being the absence of writing), nor when they diverge radically, as in the pre-Renaissance West and in East Asia even today.

Ordering Knowledge

Derk Bodde, the China classicist, has argued that Chinese writing inhibits science by making it difficult to order information. Professor Bodde summarizes his view as follows:

As the daily users of alphabetic scripts, we Westerners are scarcely aware, because they are so ubiquitous, of the enormous benefits that are ours because of the principle of alphabetization. In dictionaries, encyclopedias, library catalogues, indexes, telephone books, and countless other media, this technique for classifying words has so transformed our lives that it is impossible to visualize our civilization without it. Yet the technique was by no means always exploited in the alphabetic civilizations, nor of course is it available in nonalphabetic China today. (1991:64)

These disadvantages were compounded, Bodde notes, by a lack of punctuation in traditional Chinese texts and "the partial or total neglect of such simple typographical devices as continuous pagination, paragraphing, subtitles, catchwords, and the like" (72–73).

Now East Asian writing has come a long way from when the correct segmentation of a text was subject to multiple interpretations. Unlike premodern texts, which were unpunctuated, Asian writers today use periods, quotation marks, colons and semicolons, two types of commas, serialized headings, and most of the other extrinsic cues that lend order to Western texts (except italics and upper case letters). However, vestiges of the earlier lack of markers to guide a reader from one thought to the next are still evident. Punctuation can be very ad hoc, as if writers have not mastered its use or the logic behind it.

Run-on sentences in particular are common even in Vietnamese, which abandoned characters more than a century ago. If this laxity were confined to imaginative genres, one could excuse it as literary license. But it is not. Sentences that continue for twenty lines or more can be found in scientific literature, compounding its inherent difficulty. Professional translators of Chinese technical materials, who are native speakers working within their areas of expertise, have confided to me their inability to understand some of these long passages. The difficulty, in their view, lies not in translating the text into English but in making any sense of the original.

The unwillingness of many East Asian writers to express their thoughts in a reader-friendly manner is a function, in part, of the character script, which imposes few obligations on writers to write coherently. The problem begins with the nature of the graphic unit. Although alphabetic texts usually include word division, Chinese character-based writing gets by without identifying word boundaries because the characters provide a semantic analysis of their own. While limited in scope, enough meaning is conveyed by characters individually to make word marking unnecessary. There is enough redundancy, in *báihuà* at least, for readers to figure out—with more or less effort and success—which characters group with which others. Consequently words remain unmarked in Chinese, Japanese, and Vietnamese.[6]

The definition of "word" is elusive and has long troubled linguists, their confusion abetted by the fact that nonliterate speakers typically are unaware of the concept, in contrast to literate speakers who know intuitively what a word is (even if they cannot define it). "Word" accordingly is regarded by many linguists as an artifact of literacy or as "what exists between two blank spaces." Literate people determine through their orthographic habits what a language's words are. Their decisions become part of the speech community's competence. The absence of a clear notion of word among East Asians, whose written languages do not use word division, supports this hypothesis.

Linguists also define word as the unit on which syntax operates. Since nonliterate speakers use syntax to form utterances, the notion that words depend entirely on an orthographic tradition is misleading. But the issue here is *awareness* of words and how this faculty translates into preferences for generating orderly discourse structures, such as distinct sentences and rhetorical units. I would suggest that the absence of punctuation in early Chinese texts and the difficulty East Asians have today using punctuation to structure their writing result from a diminished awareness of words, which is traceable to the character script.

This leads to a larger issue. Given the connection between language and knowledge in general, and the possible effects of language on the way people think (the weak Whorfian hypothesis), the propensity to think in ordered categories may owe something to one's linguistic exposure. To the extent that a language and its orthographic rules cause people to organize linguistic units into distinct categories, so might that experience induce thinkers to organize their thoughts in a similar fashion.

This same argument has been made regarding the impact of phoneme analysis—a product of alphabetic literacy—on cognitive habits. And in both cases the connection with creativity is the same: perceiving wholes as a collection of distinct parts figures importantly in the creative act. Not only the alphabet, but also the writing conventions that alphabetic literacy generates, train one to seek out and identify the abstract constituents of wholes, laying the groundwork for their emergence in new configurations.

But we need not theorize about creative cognitive processes to grasp that the alphabet, by providing a standard for indexing language, ipso facto offers a fixed and ready means of ordering knowledge. Representing words by conventional spellings allows us to treat information uniformly, without reference to its content. By following a rule readily mastered by preschoolers, information is stored and retrieved in alphabetical order. There is no need to learn anything beyond what is needed to read and spell to use this device.

Westerners are so accustomed to using alphabets to organize data that they are little aware of the benefits they provide. These benefits have increased with the growth of information and use of computers. By the same token, it is probably not coincidental that computer technologies were developed first in the West, given the ease with which alphabetic texts can be adapted for use with digital equipment. Software development in particular, an area where East Asia (but *not* India) lags seriously behind the West, is based on alphanumeric instructions.

East Asians can and do use alphabets to represent information. As I noted earlier, China, Japan, and Korea each have alphabetic notations whose use is driven in part by the need to index data and represent it in machine-usable format. But these notations perform auxiliary roles only. East Asians in most applications use the indigenous character-based scripts, whose units cannot be parsed systematically. Nor is there any standard for determining what components follow what others, to the extent that they are even identifiable. The closest East Asia came to a universal index was the 214 "radicals" in the *Kangxi* Dictionary.

The lack of a simple, intuitive indexing protocol has degraded East Asians' ability to handle information, as evidenced in low office productivity, underdeveloped library systems, and clumsy retrieval software. James Unger correctly blames this situation on the character writing system. As he put it,

Indexing is perhaps the most common and economically important example of large-scale list making. Without indexes to serial publications, abstracts of reports, and other synoptic aids, especially in the hard sciences, a modern researcher simply cannot cope with the flood of information in his or her field. (1987:55)

Which brings us to the heart of the matter: if creativity is 10 percent inspiration and 90 percent preparation, then *access* to information must be crucial in determining creative outcomes. Specialists agree that mastery of a discipline is an absolute prerequisite for creative work within any field. This presupposes full access to the thoughts of those working in one's field of study, including minority views that are expressed outside common channels. Tapping this knowledge is facilitated by efficient indexing and inhibited if the indexing system is hostile to users, as in Asia.

This simple fact—the disadvantage East Asians have relative to their Western counterparts in obtaining information—figures into the present book's thesis in yet another way. Most educated East Asians, particularly those in the sciences, have some facility with English or another Western language, including reading skills in their areas of expertise. Given the ease with which alphabetically arranged materials are retrieved, East Asian scientists are better able to access Western language data than they are materials in their own languages.[7] Hence West-to-East technology transfer is promoted by the same mechanism that played a major role in fostering the West's creative preeminence.

The Sterility of the Elite

Chinese characters and the *wényán* style of writing also harmed Asian creativity by restricting literacy to the social elite—the group least disposed to creative change. Bodde put his finger on part of the problem:

if science prospers in an atmosphere of intellectual diversity, one might argue that the cultural uniformity that was encouraged, especially on the level of the ruling elite, by use of a common literary language, could well have been unfavorable to original scientific thought. (1991:31)

Later in his book Bodde raised the diversity theme again, noting, "Chinese writing and the literary language . . . made the entry of foreign ideas into China difficult, slowed down change, and discouraged cultural variation, especially within the small but dominant literate minority" (90). Educated on the basis of an identical curriculum meant to produce a homogeneous cadre of bureaucrats, East Asia's Confucian elite was the very opposite of the diverse group of thinkers creativity requires. Far from encouraging original thought, traditional education deprived free thinkers of a forum to promote change. Indeed, the notion that change could be beneficial was alien to Confucian beliefs.

Scholars who passed through the educational sieve and became officials acquired a vested interest in preserving their positions, which meant maintaining the status quo on all fronts. In literary terms, intellectual conservatism took the form of support for Confucian orthodoxy and for the *wényán* style in which these standard works and commentaries were written. Popular Buddhist- and Taoist-inspired literature was seen as subversive of the official order. The elite defended their roles, in part, by writing calligraphy and obscure characters, making a difficult writing system even harder.

I am tempted to speculate on the course of events if East Asia had more

efficient writing systems devoid of the embellishments that amused generations of traditional scholars. It is known that functional, shop-based literacy
was widespread in East Asia, despite the difficulty of the character script.
Records of technical accomplishments were also passed down through
texts, which, though terse and ambiguous, testify to the ability of traditional society to communicate science through writing. What if full literacy,
defined as ready access to society's leading intellectual paradigms, had
been in the hands not only of the elite but of this middle stratum of the
population, who were responsible for the incremental and often ingenious
changes to technology that had kept Asia prosperous for so many years?

And what would the effect have been of writing in the vernacular, that is,
the local languages in which artisans and manufacturers thought, which
have been disparaged (then and now) as dialects? With speech-based literacy on tap, would the concrete mentality on which East Asian science was
based have been able to resist an imaginative component?

Marxism treats monopoly of the means of production as the path
through which a ruling class maintains power. We should also acknowledge
the effect that maintaining a character-based orthography has had (and
continues to have) on society, along with its impact on society's ability to
create. The next chapter explores this relationship between creativity and
Asian society in more depth.

Chapter Eleven
Creativity and East Asian Society

> The term "brain drain" is not fully appreciated. The drain is not from one country to another. . . . The real drain is the loss of creativity that stays at home but is not employed properly. And that is a worldwide waste.
>
> —Frank Barron

Society and the Creative Process

We saw how East Asian writing hinders scientific creativity through its effects on thought processes. The concrete syllabic writing systems used in China, Japan, and to a great extent in Korea do not provide a model for analysis. Phonology is assimilated in East Asia, as in oral societies everywhere, nondiscretely, in lumps. As such, East Asians miss an early opportunity to develop the analytic habits of thought that are forced on Westerners. Without these skills Asians are less prone or less able to dissect intractable problems into their abstract antecedents, which is the first step toward creative reordering.

More problematic is the difficulty Asians have distinguishing sign from concept. The holistic nature of character-based representation obscures the difference between signifier and signified, merging the two in people's minds in a way reminiscent of oral societies. Abstract concepts and beliefs, which depend as much on verbal labels as they do on their inherent fitness, tend to remain intact in East Asia even after their justification is no longer apparent. Of course, maintaining the integrity of a concept in the absence of direct environmental stimulation is exactly what symbolic language is meant to do. But there comes a time when language must relax its grip over thought to let new patterns emerge. Alphabets facilitate this process by focusing awareness on a sign's elements, demonstrating its artificiality. By contrasting with speech on the same plane, alphabets draw attention to the sign apart from its meaning. Without a sign, a concept must stand on its own merit or be subject to reappraisal, unlike character scripts whose concrete signs foster conservative thinking by their tighter grip on meaning.

Thinkers literate in character-based scripts who overcome this formidable obstacle to creativity and assimilate analytical skills without the aid of an alphabetic model still face the problem of synthesizing novel structures and coordinating the exchange of data between brain hemispheres. Just as the alphabet offers a model for analysis, so it provides an early example of the synthetic operations believed to underlie creative thinking, that is, composing wholes from abstract parts within the limits of plausible constraints. Also, the alternation between discrete consonant and diffuse vowel phonemes, and between analysis and synthesis, that occurs while using an alphabet acclimates the user to coordinating left and right track brain processes. There is nothing comparable in the use of Chinese character-based writing.

On another level, we saw how secondary issues associated with Asian orthography also inhibit creative thinking. These problems include an excessive gap between speech and writing, the effect of rote memorization on thought, the time wasted learning the complicated writing systems, a preoccupation with the mechanics of writing, difficulties indexing and categorizing, emphasis on process over content, and denial of literacy to those groups most disposed to create. These issues relate to the impact of character-based writing on the cognitive habits of individuals. It is now time to look at society's role in creativity, regarded by some as a fifth stage in the process. Specifically, we need to consider the impact of social norms and customs on the ability of individuals to create, and on society's capacity to assimilate these creations.

We begin by considering the environmental requirements for creativity. Many can be cited. I will not pretend to rank them in any particular order of importance, for two reasons. First, to my knowledge no methodology exists for evaluating the relative significance of one factor over another. It has only recently become possible to describe systematically the cognitive aspects of creativity. We are far from being able to treat creativity's social dimension at the same level of detail. That said, the attempt to link creativity with gene-culture coevolution (discussed below) is an important step toward understanding the actual mechanisms that account for society's impact in this area.

Second, what seem to be individual predictors of creativity are likely parts of a *complex* of factors that reinforce one another. In such an integrated system one element is both the cause and the effect of all other elements, making the isolation of any single factor an arbitrary exercise. The interaction of these elements tends in time to produce an equilibrium that defines the society as a whole. It is possible, of course, for one society to be more or less creative than another. But given the imperative to adapt to change, only two *basic* strategies are available: to manage change proactively—the dynamic society that Kelly (1994) and others describe—or to use borrowing as an evolutionary strategy.

In a dynamic society, creativity is expressed by the ability to navigate the two hazards of "dangerous innovation" and "business-as-usual conservatism" (Calvin 1996:154–55). This balance, while difficult to maintain, is the hallmark of all adaptive systems—physical, biological, social, and intellectual—and, indeed, has supported the shift from one level of organization to the next (Pirsig 1991). Successful dynamic systems negotiate a compromise between unrestrained innovation (chaos, the absence of structure) and the inability to innovate altogether (the triumph of form over function). The similarity between this rule and the model for individual creativity described earlier, characterized by the need to temper intuition with logical restraint, is apparent.

Joseph Agassi expressed this theme on a personal level with his observation that some people view every hypothesis as immoral while others "think every hypothesis is welcome" (1988:401). It is too much to hope that all individuals escape these extremes, but while awaiting that day a good interim strategy is found in societies that tolerate both personality types, so that the aggregate effect works out to be the same. The need to temper innovation with skepticism is why some creativity specialists include peer recognition as part of the creative process. On the other hand, the willingness of society to support creative types is where innovation begins.

In a creative society, people must have the latitude to display different habits and personality traits so that a variety of source models are available to choose from (Findlay and Lumsden 1988:27). Both visionaries and cynics are needed to achieve the aforementioned balance. However, while recognizing a role for the critic, most creativity theorists emphasize the need for society to minimize repression to allow the free expression of alternative ideas. This applies not only to the authoritarianism practiced by governments;[1] it also includes *social* constraints "in the form of a regulated status quo" (173).

Uniform education meant to "socialize" citizens and inculcate them with the state's values can hardly be construed as supporting the requirement that "knowledge acquisition be unstructured in a well-defined sense" (173). Western educators began to recognize the need for curricular diversity decades ago to nurture creativity in the young. Some would say that this liberalization happened at the expense of basic skills, although those concerns seem to have been laid to rest by advances in technology that were fueled in part by the creativity of that same generation. Others argue that academic liberalization is a sham, and that institutional values, while different from before, are as rigorously enforced as ever. Still others question the meaning of diversity within the intellectual straitjacket that state-subsidized education imposes.

These comments also apply to higher education. While it is commonplace to praise the academic freedom that is supposed to characterize university life, the reality is that conformity often reigns. Scholars and scientists whose careers are linked to particular intellectual paradigms have little incentive to embrace conflicting views. This is an old problem, described by Kuhn (1962), which has inhibited science throughout the ages. Happily the situation seems to be changing. There are several trends working against ivory tower conservatism today, including a competitive market for intellectual products, a growth in the types of venues through which intellectual activity is rewarded and—for the first time—the availability of free and universal fora to share ideas with diverse groups of thinkers.

What is true in the intellectual realm is also true of culture, and ethnic composition in particular. A lack of diversity within a society diminishes the opportunities for its members to access nonstandard models on which creative discoveries depend, at the same time that it works against the transmission of these discoveries. Although I generally find little value in the insipid rhetoric of America's cultural elite, this is one argument that makes sense, as evidenced by the adoption of the diversity agenda by businesses, and by the U.S. preeminence in creative science.[2] In the long run, there is no conflict between moral imperatives and practical behavior.

It must be remembered, however, that creativity is an individual act. Environmental stimulation may support creativity, but beyond a point creativity requires that one be insulated from the environment, both metaphorically and literally. People must be accorded solitude to contemplate problems (the preparatory stage) and to recognize solutions when they emerge. Tolerating unusual individuals and their alternative lifestyles can challenge the endurance of polite society, but it is part of what a culture pays to stay on the leading edge.

As a final note, the prominence of the ego in the creative act is explained by the need for thinkers to set aside dominant views and follow their own hunches, however much they conflict with the opinions of others. The psychology needed to support this attitude almost guarantees a degree of insensitivity to one's social environment that others may find hard to countenance. Looked at the other way, being different entails feelings of alienation that only a strong sense of personal identity can overcome. A creative society thus requires the elaboration in some form or other of an egocentric ethic, honored in principle if not always in practice, to sustain the individual in search of new truths.

Social Impediments to Creativity

"You have too much freedom in the West." The first time I heard this, some decades ago in Taiwan, I dismissed it as sour grapes. What *can* he say? He lives here and I'm just passing through. But after hearing the remark several times in different Asian countries, I began to suspect a common sentiment. Moreover, criticisms Asians share with me of their own institutions focus less on freedom and more on the nature of political processes: *how* to get the thieves out of government and what *measures* can be taken to make the new bosses responsive to public needs. I hear fewer complaints about paternalistic government or about authoritarianism as a social norm. On the contrary, bureaucratic control, reviled in the West, is accepted in East Asia as the natural way to get things done.

The above observation is consistent with scholarly accounts of East Asia's attitude toward government and the ideal society. Good government in Confucian societies and their modern incarnations rests on benevolent administration, that is, not what the government does but how it does things. Only recently did East Asian countries, under competitive pressure from the West, begin to divest, or try to divest, private enterprise from state-run businesses—including companies directly under government control in China and Vietnam and those under de facto control through "administrative guidance" in Japan and South Korea—or even question the size of the public domain. Indeed, the very idea of distinct public and private sectors equivalent to what is owed to God and Caesar in the West did not exist.

East Asians' belief that economic activity falls within the purview of the state coincides with a willingness to subject aspects of their personal lives to government control that most Westerners would find intolerable. I recall how shocked my Chinese students were to learn that Americans have no national ID cards. The typical reaction was, "How do the police know who you are?" Indeed, how? In China, political authority extends down to the city block and is invasive to the point where local cadres are privy to the details of family and personal events. In Japan similar powers are exercised by neighborhood police operating out of their ubiquitous "boxes." I will grant there is some scope in East Asia for local organizations acting on behalf of community interests. But where in Asia can one find institutions willing to support *individual* rights at any cost? The distrust Americans have of government is not shared by Asians, who view government and its officials as the natural arbiters of social norms.

Given the scope of government in East Asia, the goal has been to moderate government (not limit it) and get a piece of it for one's self in the bureaucracy or hierarchy of sanctioned political-economic relationships. Although East Asians, now and in the past, have circumvented the state in pursuit of gain, these individuals are tolerated at best, not welcomed. Until recently entrepreneurship was viewed there as disruptive of the social order—which indeed it is anywhere. But the critical issue is whether a political culture can accept change and the individuals who bring it about. In East Asia, the balance has always been skewed against innovators and for the existing order.

The different conceptions East Asians and Westerners have of government's role in society are reflected in the status granted to members of occupational groups. In the West, status is more likely to be accorded to corporate executives or to people in the professions. Evidence of a Western preference for the private success model is abundantly available in folklore. Curiously, it is also apparent in the pretentious use by government bureaucrats in the United States of business metaphors and titles to describe their own activities, as if importing the vocabulary of the market somehow lends more dignity and credibility to their jobs.

In East Asia government officials (Chinese: *guān*) enjoy the highest prestige, not because they are any better than their Western counterparts but because they have been more successful at promoting their image as custodians of social order. This was achieved in part by force ("the barrel of a gun") and in part by centuries-old propaganda that places bureaucrats at the top of the hierarchy and "people" (i.e., everyone else) somewhere below them depending on their occupation. Farmers and workers ranked higher than merchants since neither of the former groups directly threatened the regime. According them nominal status was a cost-free gesture meant to debase those with entrepreneurial talents, who *are* a threat.

Artisans, who contributed most to technological progress, were ridiculed by bureaucrats for possessing "small skills" (*xiǎojì*), not comparable to the skills needed to manage affairs of state. For that lofty task higher talents were needed, such as those achieved by reading and writing poetry and by memorizing passages of the Confucian canon, so as to be better acquainted with the way things supposedly were done in the past. Instead of contemplating the future, East Asian scholar-bureaucrats looked to the imagined past for guidance. There was little room for innovation in such an environment.

Authoritarian rule is wielded in East Asia intensively and extensively. Just as government has exerted its power over individuals, constraining choices to the point where change is hard to conceive, let alone effect, so has it managed to corral large populations into centralized states, which by nature tend toward uniformity. Long before scientists began to explore the cognitive requirements of creativity, students of Chinese history had noted a correlation between innovation and the degree of political fragmentation. The lesson drawn was that creativity and government work at cross-purposes, the former declining whenever the state consolidates its grip on society.

Yet unity is the goal of every Asian government. It is treated in official histories as the best of times, in contrast to "periods of disunity" held to be akin to dark ages. The motive for seeking national unity—and for this distorted account of history—is apparent: by bringing large areas under its control, the ruling class could stave off challenges from the hoi polloi by stifling innovation on a universal scale and eradicating the source of creativity that resides in access to alternate models. Recognizing the prerequisites for its survival, the authoritarian state instinctively seeks uniformity in all dimensions. This fact explains why East Asian regimes have alternately sought to expand their territory or close the country to foreign contacts. New ideas from within or afar threaten existing order and the privileges of the those who identify with it.

Authoritarianism is supported in Asia by a state ideology that extols obedience, portrayed as a set of reciprocal relationships. Subordinates do as they are told, and government officials or dominant males in general are expected to moderate their demands and attend the needs of the weaker party. Society functions to the extent that these norms are internalized by all concerned. Beyond this, the Confucianism that guided East Asia through much of its history promotes vertical channels of exchange, a static worldview, and the past as a model, all of which work strongly against creativity. Most damaging, in my view, is its elevation of the generalist over the technical expert ("a gentleman is not a tool"),[3] shades of which were evident in the "red versus expert" debacle during China's Cultural Revolution (1965–75).

As noted early in this book, scientists are adamant on the need for creativity to be preceded by mastery of a discipline, which in East Asia has always been undermined by official ideology. The frantic efforts made now in China to reverse the situation by according status to the technical cognoscenti demonstrate how perverse the problem has become. Korean thinkers, for their part, rail at the *yangban*[4] mentality that leads the best minds in the country to pursue a government sinecure instead of productive work. Evidence that this is changing is scant. In Japan, where the state is probably the least invasive, success is demonstrated by graduating from a national university, preferably the law department at Tokyo University, and taking a post in a government ministry.

In East Asia, the struggle for status starts early in life with relentless cramming for college entrance examinations. There is nothing comparable to this institution in the West. Today's exams, successor to the traditional civil service exam, differ from the earlier system in content but not in approach. In imperial China a candidate for a job in the bureaucracy spent his youth learning to recite from memory a handful of classical texts and approved commentaries. The intention was to deprive the intelligentsia of the capacity for independent thought, inculcate them with a conservative outlook, and ensure that inductees identified with the existing order.

This traditional view of learning as a synonym for memorization and thought control has been carried into the present with predictable effects on creativity. Middle-class East Asian students from the time they enter elementary school (and for children of affluent parents even earlier) begin the arduous task of preparing for the event at the end of high school known as "Exam Hell." Like the state exams of the past, these tests are designed to measure one's mastery of approved material. It is the pivotal event of a lifetime, through which one's placement in the hierarchy of universities and, ultimately, society is determined.

Students who pass the exams are given a four-year vacation at a national university, where they are free to riot or relax, and to release a lifetime of pent-up frustration (in an institutional setting) with no fear of being dismissed, no matter what sort of academic performance is turned in. And why not? The goal of the education has been achieved—twelve years of strict regimentation have rooted out most unorthodox impulses. East Asians are aware of the system's debilitating nature and many emigrate to spare their progeny what they suffered themselves. Yet efforts to mend the system generally fail, because the habits and institutions that complement the system are still in place.

The negative impact of East Asian culture on creativity is also apparent in family behavior. Preschoolers are given what most Western parents would consider enormous latitude to do as they please, on the grounds that life will get hard soon enough. Discipline is seldom required of a child in its first few years. As a consequence, East Asians do not acquire the same distaste for authority that impels Western youngsters to rebel against the status quo. By the time East Asian children enter school, they lack the skills and spirit to reject the demands for conformity that the educational system is set up to impose.

Another trait with negative consequences for creativity is the emphasis put on familial relations and the deemphasis of personal identity. East Asians give titles to each member of the extended family, based on generation, gender, and order of birth, which are used in lieu of personal names. Children thus regard themselves less as individuals and more as members of a structured caste. Egocentric behavior also tends to go unrewarded. In contrast to the West's concern for privacy, the right to which the most meddlesome Western parents will grant in principle, East Asians consider the concept perverse and until recently did not have a word for it. "Individual" (Chinese: *gèrén*) also has a negative connotation akin to selfish.

The subordination of individuals to the group continues outside the family into the workplace, where strong ties of affiliation further detract from personal autonomy. When I make a phone call to someone in China or to a Chinese who has recently moved to the United States, even after working hours, I am as likely to hear "What unit are you?" (*Nǐ shì shénme dānwèi*) as "Who are you?" (*Nǐ shì shéi*). The commitment Asian companies expect of employees is well known and needs no elaboration here, other than to note that it is consistent with a tradition of requiring the surrender of personal interests to those of the group, which is not a recipe for creative thinking.

On a philosophical plane, Derk Bodde noted that "Confucianism very rarely looks at the human individual simply qua individual. Almost always it sees him or her as functioning within a series of concentrically larger social units" (1991:194). Bodde regarded the absence of individualism as a major factor in East Asia's failure to develop abstract science. If individual autonomy is constrained on the social level, self-awareness—another trait associated with the creative mindset—is not supported by the culture either: not in literature, whose themes tend to be other-directed; not in art, where the individual is reduced to a pinpoint in a landscape; and not in the language, where first person pronouns and grammatical subjects are often omitted.

Finally, East Asians exhibit a degree of ethnocentrism that is out of step with the needs of creativity and expectations of global society. The link between Japan's tendency to exclude *gaijin* (foreigners, but literally "outside people") and the country's poor showing in basic science was acknowledged in the "Report of the Prime Minister's Commission on Japan's Goals in the 21st Century" (February 9, 2000), which recommended opening immigration and "making a strength of diversity" to remedy the effects of an insular mentality on creativity. Koreans, obsessed with their national identity, show even less interest in opening their hearts to foreign and especially non-Asian people.

China, on the other hand, has always boasted of its willingness to accept people of any ethnicity *if they adopt the elements of Chinese culture.* But isn't that the whole issue? Diversity promotes creativity not because people look different but because they think and act differently. Learning to accept differences instead of "sinicizing" them out of the population will prove to be difficult for a people who, after a century of humiliation by the West, still seem unable to fathom that some aspects of their culture may be in need of change.

Gene-Culture Coevolution

As the above sketch suggests, the social and cultural requisites for creativity found to varying degrees in the West are largely absent in East Asia. Through most of its history, East Asia has been governed by an authoritarian ethic that coopted society's literate elements to suppress change. It was not just a case of a few despots, fretful of innovation, who prevented society from evolving in new directions. Rather, the culture seems to have been designed to perpetuate itself without altering its basic characteristics.

A disposition to thwart creative impulses is evidenced in every nook of East Asian society: in the structure of the family, the low value given to freedom and personal autonomy, the predatory behavior of the elite, paternalistic governments, a tendency toward uniformity and centralization, the use of education for social control, and a tradition of viewing change as synonymous with chaos. These traits are in addition to characteristics I discussed earlier concerning a disposition to shun logic, to think in concrete terms, and to view reality in wholes instead of parts. We are looking not just at a few separate areas where the expression of creativity has been impaired, but at a whole complex of related factors that collectively drive East Asia away from radical creation. Moreover, it has existed for two millennia.

This observation leads to what will probably be regarded as the most controversial aspect of the present book's thesis, namely, that the shortage of creativity in East Asia is in part a function of the interaction between genes and culture. Let me emphasize at the outset, in deference to most of my colleagues in the humanities, who view genetic arguments with horror, and to my own disposition to regard such arguments as highly suspect, that I would be amazed if geneticists were to discover a gene or set of genes that "control" an individual's or a society of individuals' ability to create. Creativity as we have seen is a *process* that depends on many factors including intangibles that cannot be personally inherited, such as a critical knowledge base, access to alternative paradigms, and the availability of models that emulate creative cognitive processes.

What *can* be inherited, apparently, is a disposition to react to the presence of features in the environment. As Charles Lumsden pointed out, there are three possible ways for culture to be learned by a developing organism: pure genetic transmission, pure cultural transmission, and gene-culture transmission—the last being a hybrid strategy that Lumsden and others believe is the primary mechanism used to sustain human culture (1988:20). As he explains it, gene-culture transmission "describes the presence of epigenetic[5] rules that predispose mental development to take certain specific directions in the presence of certain kinds of cultural information." Genes, by this account, do not determine the mind's development. Rather, they guide and shape it in the context of a particular environment. Information obtained while interacting with the environment determines the mind's specific content (19–20). In Lumsden's words:

In a cultural species the genetic fitness of an organism is affected not only by its genotype but also by its cultural heritage as expressed by a subset of cultural information that is allowed to affect development. The genetic fitness is influenced by the pathway of enculturation that the organism follows, and is enhanced by any tendency of mental epigenesis to use culturally transmitted information that confers greater relative genetic fitness. (22)

Culture exists as a road map for survival and individuals disposed to tap into it have an advantage. Thus culture itself, in a sense, is genetically transmitted as the genotype coevolves with its environment. As Lumsden put it: "The innate epigenetic rules of gene-culture transmission provide this capability, guiding the organism to incorporate or respond to sets of relatively advantageous information more often than sets that are relatively deleterious." Tabula rasa organisms, those that are genetically *un*biased, lack these guideposts for distinguishing aspects of the culture that are more or less advantageous. Over generations, they are "unstable against invasion by genetic mutants that set innate biases toward adaptive culture traits" (22).

According to Michael Gazzaniga, neuroscientists prefer this "interactionist" theory of cognitive development that places selection over instruction.[6] Instead of telling an organism how to behave, genes are configured to allow selection of a preexisting capacity in response to a particular environment. The brain therefore is "not a blank slate" (1992:3). Gazzaniga clarified his statement by noting, in terms similar to Lumsden's, that "brain development requires a key signal from the environment if normal connections are to occur. This does not mean that brain development is not driven by genetic factors. What it does mean is that the developing brain has evolved in the context of a particular environment" (37).

Environment impacts the development of cognitive structures in three ways, according to Lumsden: by "sensory screening, which limits perception to narrow windows opening on the vast array of physical stimuli impinging on the body"; by "a tendency for certain node-link structures to take form and link preferentially with others in semantic memory"; and through "constraints on achievable cognitive design," which bias "development toward certain parameters of information processing capacity rather than others" (1988:23). Predisposed by one's genes to respond to features of the physical, intellectual, and social environments, synaptic patterns are laid down that reflect these particular cultural characteristics.

These processes relate to the brain's ontogenetic development. Feedback to the genotype is a function of standard Darwinian evolution: individuals who make the best use of these rules adapt more quickly and fully to the environment, they reproduce more often, and the genetic traits that led to their relative success are transmitted through the population. Successive generations thus share not only a disposition to respond to an environment, but the expectation of encountering a particular environment, and, in a classic case of self-fulfilling prophecy, they behave in such a way as to bring these expectations about.

Now there are some drawbacks to this arrangement, beginning with its assumptions that the environment is stable and the strategies that evolved to deal with it are viable. But in East Asia such conditions did obtain for most of two millennia. Chinese culture became dominant because it was superior to everything it encountered. The amalgam of technological, intellectual, and social structures that made up Sinitic culture was adequate to sustain its members against most challenges.

One might even argue, as Mark Elvin (1973) has, that Sinitic culture was a victim of its own success. Chinese agriculture and water management— and the social and cognitive infrastructure that grew up around these technologies—were so well suited to the physical environment that there was no incentive to invest effort and resources in new modes of production. By the same token, threats from competing non-Sinitic civilizations were too unsophisticated to matter. Even when, through a combination of internal corruption and external political changes, foreign groups were able to overcome China militarily, the invaders were forced by the same geophysical circumstances to adopt the Sinitic culture that evolved with that environment, in effect becoming Chinese themselves.

There was little pressure, accordingly, for China and other East Asian countries that were part of the Sinitic metaculture to change. Given the way gene-culture coevolution operates, advantages accrued to everyone able to embrace that culture and expedite its adaptation. There seems to be no delicate way for me to state what these facts imply for East Asian creativity, so I will let Dean Simonton spell it out:

> Now let us take the case of a sociocultural system that has been occupying the same ecological niche for centuries, perhaps millennia. Under such circumstances, the repertoire of cultural traits should provide highly efficient functioning for the culture's membership, making it highly probable that the kind of conceptual or behavioral variations that we call "creativity" would most likely be useless, even detrimental. Would gene-culture coevolution accordingly reach a new equilibrium point between variation and retention such that variation is minimized? More baldly put, would those from "traditional" societies of long standing be biologically predisposed to be less creative than those from less static cultures? From the sociobiological perspective, this conclusion appears reasonable. (1988b:153)

Changes are conceived and entertained when the strategies for coping with one's environment become untenable. Otherwise people follow the commonsense maxim of "If it isn't broken, don't fix it." Arguably, open systems should have evolved a mechanism that anticipates the vulnerability they encounter through long-term success, and periodically engineer artificial mini-crises to keep creativity intact. Perhaps they have and we are too immersed in details to notice. But I am unwilling to credit evolution with this much prescience, and so I see the process in simpler terms as a combination of statistics and dumb luck. This leads to the second downside of gene-culture coevolution: its outcome is not always the most desirable. As Lumsden explains,

> because people use the decisions and behaviors of others as part of their own deliberations, natural selection of genotypes during gene-culture coevolution is in general frequency dependent: its direction and intensity are determined in part by the number of individuals using alternative culture traits and thus by the relative frequency of competing gene variants. (1988:30)

Thus "selection may not lead to the optimization of a fitness measure at all" (30). Instead, socially prevalent behavior works its way into the genotype whatever its absolute viability is, particularly under conditions where the culture lacks serious challenges or is intolerant of diverse behavior. Creativity, in a sense, was not only unneeded in East Asia, it upset the stable constellation of social, economic, and political structures that evolved around a successful paradigm. In the face of indifference or outright hostility to new ideas, the inclination to create disappeared in East Asia, if not from the genotype then from the culture to which the genotype looks for its cues.

Borrowing as an Evolutionary Strategy

Claiming that creativity has been bred out of East Asian culture is a far cry from denying the potential for its realization among East Asians themselves. It is clear to anyone who has spent time in an American institution of higher education or has interacted with the staff of high-tech start-ups that a large proportion of those engaged in creative scientific work in the United States are of East Asian ethnicity. But this phenomenon only supports my argument that Sinitic culture is hostile to creativity.

First, gene-culture coevolution requires that the two elements act in tandem. The disposition to create (which, as I have argued repeatedly, does not correlate with IQ or other measures of overall mental capacity) depends on the genotype's ability to seek out cues in the environment that may or may not be present. In East Asia these cues mostly are not present, so it is hardly surprising that the trait is not expressed widely by individuals born and living there. Bitter experience, such as that suffered by China's intellectuals during the "Hundred Flowers" campaign in 1957, the Cultural Revolution, and countless other "struggles" against deviant behavior, have taught those blessed with creative potential that such expressions must always be guarded.

Second, it is probable that many East Asians who emigrate do so out of conviction that life in one's native country offers fewer prospects for success. Emigration throughout history has acted as a sorting mechanism to separate people disposed to find fault with the status quo (a predictor of creativity if there ever was one) from regimes managed by elites who are inclined to view the current state of affairs favorably. Émigrés by nature are misfits who do not blend in with society. The creativity that East Asian emigrants display in the West is the expression of a fringe group that, almost by definition, is not representative of the culture as a whole. That so many of these émigrés have distinguished themselves in creative science is exactly what one would expect.

The movement of Asian scientists to the West, and to the United States in particular, is usually portrayed as a "brain drain," the implication being that Western countries are siphoning off the best minds of the East. Unable to offer their brightest people the rewards available in "the advanced countries of the West," East Asia suffers a loss of creative talent. Smart enough to master a science and lucid enough to distinguish between patriotic hype and benefits to one's self and family, many of East Asia's intellectuals abandon their homelands in search of a better life. The rich nations, by this argument, get richer, while "developing" East Asian countries scramble for ways to stem the outflow of talent.

I certainly bear with all Americans a debt of gratitude for the diaspora of Asian intellect to Western shores. This influx of talent benefits the West not just in scientific expertise but, more crucially, through the creative advantages associated with diversity. I am less certain, however, that blame for the "brain drain" should be placed on the West, or even on the principals themselves. Leaving one's country of birth is a wrenching experience undertaken out of frustration at being unable to find a venue for one's talents at home. Although economics accounts for part of it, sociopolitical considerations play a large role too, which is simply another way of saying that the governments voicing these complaints have themselves to blame.

But are they complaining? Every year the Chinese and Korean media dutifully publish statistics about the number of students who go abroad and fail to return. Editorials appear, especially in the English language papers, about how "measures" are needed to keep the talent at home. My own reading of vernacular media not aimed at international audiences, however, has persuaded me that East Asian governments came to grips long ago with the impossibility of stemming the exodus of creative talent and, what is more, regard this situation not only as acceptable but as the best of all possible worlds.

Behind its stoic attitude toward the loss of scientific talent (Chinese: réncái) lies more than recognition of the state's impotence in the face of a universal quest by individuals to better one's own lot. East Asian policy makers, I submit, are willing to let the brain drain continue because retaining these people would require restructuring society and its political institutions from the ground up—assuming that such a reform could be carried off in the first place. Moreover, keeping the talent at home *is unnecessary*, since their knowledge can be funneled back home to good effect without exposing society and government to the "unhealthy" habits that accompany creative thinking.

Earlier in this book I documented how China and South Korea exploit the ethnic sensibility of émigré scientists to transfer foreign technology.[7] These governments go to extraordinary lengths to keep tabs on the whereabouts and activities of expatriate scientists and engineers: entering their names and personal information into databases; linking their talents by specialty for efficient "outsourcing"; organizing them by region and occupational expertise; funding return visits under one guise or another (including get-acquainted junkets for kids who show academic promise); and debriefing them in subsidized collection centers both at home and in the United States.

Korean officials are not reticent about discussing these programs in open fora, particularly those that support solutions to the national "creativity problem." It is as if they cannot imagine anything unethical about the activities, or that the host country might care about having its technology expropriated, or that second- and third-generation Korean Americans may be indifferent about where their parents or grandparents came from.

Information on China's similar programs is not much harder to come by, probably for the same reason—the Chinese government sees no wrong in attempting to exploit the expertise of its "own" people, many of whom never saw China and speak English better than I do. Every year for the past several years the Chinese Academy of Sciences has run overt recruitment campaigns to attract ethnic Chinese scientists "back" to the homeland, for either short informational exchanges or long-term residency as lecturers and leaders of research teams. The scientists are expected to share with their colleagues in China knowledge obtained while abroad. Paralleling these efforts are those by overseas Chinese groups, which receive subsidies, tasking, and guidance through parent organizations headquartered in Beijing.

These examples refer to open recruitment activities acknowledged by the public media and government websites. Covert recruitment of expatriate scientists, of course, has been a priority of both countries for decades.[8] Inevitably it is this latter aspect of the transfer process that captures the attention of the Western press, which is unfortunate since it accounts for only a fraction of what actually goes on, the rest being open and mostly legal.

Nor does exploitation of expatriate scientists account for more than a part of the effort that goes into acquiring Western scientific knowhow. As we have seen, East Asian nations operate a variety of collection venues to compensate for their lack of creativity. These transfers cost far less than the expense of creative research and entail none of its social costs. Knowledge created by others is imported without threatening traditional institutions.

Considered in the larger scheme of things, there is nothing irrational about East Asia's dependency on Western creativity. It is an effective survival strategy that attenuates the risk of innovation while allowing East Asia to continue operating as it has in the past. As Findlay and Lumsden noted:

> If conspecifics can accrue benefits simply by adopting discoveries originally formulated by others (for example, through observational learning), then the creative process can face substantial opposing selection pressures, especially if it entails some cost. . . . as discoverers become more frequent, the selective advantage of the innovator alleles decreases since parasitic non-innovators enjoy the benefits of innovativeness without suffering any of the associated costs. (1988:19)

As long as their hosts acquiesce in the unrequited transfer of intellectual property, there is little incentive for the borrowing parties, especially their elite, to introduce *institutional* changes: not to the authoritarian government, not to education, not to the socialist or quasi-market economies, and, not least of all, not to the archaic system of writing, which, in my estimate, underlies much of the creativity problem.

Writing and the Evolution of Sinitic Culture

What role has Chinese writing played in the development of East Asian culture? Beyond the literacy effect produced by any form of writing, I maintain with de Kerckhove and Lumsden (1988) that the particular form of writing used by a people can shape their apprehension of the environment, at the same time it affects the evolution of the culture. This applies generally and to Asian writing specifically.

I began my inquiry into the relationship between writing and culture by asking, do Chinese characters shape Asian culture by affecting the cognitive outlook that supports and sustains it? Or is it the other way around? Does culture bias people toward a concrete system of writing and cognitive outlook consistent with survival in that milieu? The answer, of course, is both. The relationship between the cognitive aspects of Chinese character-based writing and the culture that grew up around it is a perfect example of how gene-culture coevolution works.

De Kerckhove and Lumsden, whose views on Western orthography and cultural evolution have influenced my thinking on the East Asian issue, are adamant about the impact of writing on both culture and the genotype. They argue that cultural conditions lead to cultural

selection, which eventually over generations of culturally conditioned populations, will find its way into the genotype. . . . Writing, as a significant modifier of the cultural domain, can be expected to affect culture sufficiently to create conditions of gene-cultural selection. (1988:6)

A standard objection to claims that writing, like spoken language, affected the evolution of the brain is that writing's recent appearance has left insufficient time for selection to operate. As Goody put it, "The late advent of writing means that any influence on the physical structure of the brain is likely to be negligible" (1987:249). Given the limits of pure Darwinian evolution and the "mere" 3,000 or so years that fully developed writing has existed, there is no way, it is argued, that writing could impact the permanent structure of the brain. A second objection centers on the "unnaturalness" of writing expressed in the difficulty people have mastering it. Finally, it is argued that writing for much of its existence belonged to a minority of people and hence could not have influenced society as a whole, much less an entire genotype.

If these arguments sound like an extension of the writing-is-merely-a-device-for-recording-speech theme that I and most other linguists today treat with the same respect cognitive scientists have for other simplistic forms of reductionism, I will have succeeded in drawing attention to the importance of this basic issue, which has implications beyond academic linguistics. Let's look at these claims about the impossibility of writing affecting the brain.

David Olson's work on the relationship between literacy and culture has taught us that one need not be literate to view language in the same way as literates. Just being part of a literate culture can influence one's responses to the real and cognitive environments defined by the "metalanguage," which is shaped by a particular system of writing (1991:262–63). The cognitive benefits of literacy are powerful enough to confer selective advantages to members of a population exposed to writing only at its fringe.

The fact that most humans speak but only a subset of speakers learn to read and write suggests to some that the "innate" capacity people have for spoken language does not extend to its visual component. However, a disposition to acquire elements of culture is not realized independently but through exposure to environmental cues that are present at critical junctures during epigenesis. The timing and nature of literacy acquisition may be the result of factors unrelated to the heritable trait itself. Moreover, a disposition to read and write may exist in the form of instructions more general than the particular expression. Deacon makes this argument with regard to language's spoken component, namely, that it evolved to fit general cognitive capabilities[9] and there is no reason to deny application of the principle to writing as well.

Literacy involves more than an ability to manipulate "secondary" symbols of speech. If that were all there is to it, people would learn to read as early and easily as they learn to speak. The reason literacy is acquired later in life is because it involves the use of abstractive skills that cannot be exercised until the growing brain has become more structurally sophisticated. This is why societies the world over delay formal (literate) education until the child's sixth year, when the brain is physically able to assimilate abstract knowledge. Thus the primary skill being actualized probably is not literacy at all, but the potential for abstract thinking on which literacy depends.

If writing acts as a cue to promote the realization of latent (genetic) capabilities for abstract thinking, the type of writing that serves as its cue gauges the degree to which these capabilities are brought forth, stimulating the brain to invest cognitive resources toward a particular task, namely, literacy in a given script. Success at this task leads to other cognitive achievements of commensurate abstractness, which become part of the local culture to which generations adapt. Locating these epigenetic rules in the culture instead of the genome is more efficient, since it makes no sense for the brain to invest in cognitive structure that the culture may not require.

This formulation neutralizes the criticism of insufficient time for writing to have an impact on the brain's heritable structure. What the genotype most likely encodes is not the capacity for a particular writing system or even for writing in general, but a propensity to seek cues that enable deployment of the latent capacity to think abstractly. Although writing and other modern tasks maximize use of the brain's abstractive capabilities, the potential for abstract thought is a function of neurophysical infrastructure mapped out long ago, which serves as the basis for multiple cognitive tasks. The inclination to tap culture for epigenetic cues is, likewise, a general mechanism established in the genome long before writing or perhaps even before language appeared on the scene. Neither mechanism, in other words, owes its origin to writing. But since writing triggers and maximizes this potential, the effect works out to be the same.

The distinction between what is inherited through pure culture transmission and what is coded in the genome is, from a functional perspective, arbitrary. The two bodies of rules act in tandem to guide cognitive development. That creative thinking and the cognitive processes that support it play less of a role in East Asia than they might can be explained, in part, by the fact that Sinitic culture went unchallenged for ages. Impious impulses to alter the successful model became unwelcome, and remained unwelcome for so long that the culture lost the capacity for radical change. More than one historian has pointed out the similarity between East Asia's past and present institutions.

Sinitic writing, as a key component of that culture, sustained the traditional nexus of gene-culture relations by failing to provide the cognitive cues that enable a society to break free of its past patterns. Wedded to concrete representation, East Asian writing prompts its users to assimilate only a part of the abstract tools available to literate Westerners and little of their analytical propensity. Thus not only was the motive for creativity lacking in Asia, so was the potential. The dependency of East Asia today on Western basic science is a measure of this lack of creativity and, to that extent, of the failure of Chinese character-based writing.

One of the more thoughtful reviewers of my earlier book on Asian writing called me to task for not recognizing the relationship between a writing system and the culture that surrounds it, which stands in the way of any purely logical attempt to reform writing or put it on a rational footing (Gottlieb 2000).[10] The present chapter corrects that oversight. There are intimate links between an orthography and the nature of the society using it, links that extend beyond habit and aesthetic preference to the dynamics of gene-culture coevolution. But insofar as the process *is* dynamic, it is not unreasonable to view reform as within the realm of possibility.

Chapter Twelve
Conclusion

You can't be serious. If we tighten controls, they may end up fixing their creativity problem. What then?

—U.S. Department of Commerce official

A Catechism of Complaints

This study began by noting that the East Asian countries, the "Chinese character nations" (*kanji minzoku*) of China, Japan, and Korea, suffer a creativity deficit, evidenced by an insatiable quest for Western wellspring technology. This inability to make radical breaks with the past in science and thought, which drives East Asia's dependence on Western creativity, is a function of the type of writing used there. Without the incentive alphabetic writing provides to think analytically and abstractly, users of Chinese character-based scripts are at a handicap vis-à-vis the West in their capacity to generate new ideas and create entirely new technologies.

Neither of these propositions—that East Asian nations depend heavily on Western scientific innovation and that alphabetic writing biases its users to analytic habits of thought—is original. Both arguments were made by others with specialized backgrounds. What the present study provides is a link between these two phenomena that takes into account facts discovered about the cognitive processes used in creative thinking.

Although the connection between East Asia's borrowing and the use of character-based orthography seems clear to the present writer in light of what is known of the requirements of creativity, this thesis will be hard for some to accept, if not on intellectual grounds, then for practical or emotional reasons. Acknowledging that East Asia informally transfers technology created by others entails an obligation for the responsible parties to curtail the practice, and for the governments of countries victimized by these attacks to prevent them. These "gray" transfers have been going on for decades. Stopping them will require adjustments on both sides.

Beyond this, few icons of traditional culture are accorded as much sanctity in East Asia as character-based writing. Residual attachment to a writing system exists in any literate community, but in East Asia the linkage is especially close, both to the languages which evolved *around* the writing, and to the culture at large, which is defined in part by the orthographic tradition. Given these connections, it is not surprising that feelings run strongly against proposals to replace Chinese writing and its derivative scripts with systems based on alphabetic principles. Challenging the validity of character-based writing almost guarantees a negative response from people attached to the script by habit and sentiment.

Given the reaction these arguments may produce among some readers, it occurred to me that instead of summarizing statements made in earlier chapters, it might be more useful, and more entertaining, to address some complaints in advance of their actual appearance. The utility of this catechistic approach as an instructional tool is well attested and is meant, not to deflect criticism, but to focus it on these critical issues. The following sets of points, arranged in no special order, pertain.

1. *The argument is a rehash of Whorf's discredited claim that different languages have different effects on thought.*

Let's not mix apples and oranges. The Whorf-Sapir hypothesis applies to the effects different *languages* supposedly have on the way people parse reality. The present thesis deals with the impact of *literacy* on thought, in particular, with the effects of an analytically oriented writing system on people's ability to think analytically.

2. *The claim that alphabetic writing is superior to other types conflicts with the linguistic maxim that all systems are equal.*

I am not sure this assertion has been proven, although I have heard it many times. Still, it is beside the point. *Writing,* which is the issue here, evolved along a well-defined path from iconic to phonetic representation and can be judged, if one so wishes, by its progress along that continuum. The alternate claim—that East Asian writing is well suited to the languages it represents—is empty, given that the languages developed under the character script's tutelage.

3. *The book puts too much emphasis on the importance of writing. Humans have had speech for some 50,000 years and writing for one-tenth of that time.*

Have you ever wondered what triggered the shift in the human condition that began some 5,000 years ago, the beginning of the asymptotic rise in technical knowledge that changed everything? Writing, besides helping to record information, also decontextualized it, opening it for inspection and manipulation, and transforming the way we think about our surroundings and ourselves. Whether linguists, for their own reasons, choose to include writing within their field of study has no bearing, or for that matter any impact at all, on the effect writing has on culture and thought.

4. *Linguistics is supposed to be descriptive. The author uses it prescriptively, displaying his contempt for the discipline.*

Find a scholar, from physicist to psychologist, who has not made normative statements at one time or another. If a writing system has demonstrably ill effects on the welfare of its users, it is incumbent on those familiar with the issue to make that knowledge public. Linguists cannot prescribe national policy, but they can describe with some precision the effects of policies.

5. *The author's hostility toward character-based writing stems from his non-native familiarity with the languages involved.*

You can get into as much trouble making claims about your native language as you can about one learned later in life. In any case, there are active movements to replace Chinese characters led by native speakers, who cite numerous practical problems with the traditional script. The present study focuses on the cognitive issue.

6. *American children learn to read by the whole word method; they do not analyze phonemes. Korean writing, on the other hand, is alphabetic (phonemic), offering the same facilitating effect the author claims for Western orthography.*

There is more to the Western alphabetic tradition than English orthography and the misguided attempts of some to bypass phonics. Nonetheless, English readers make substantial use of phoneme-letter correspondences in spelling exercises, "sounding out" unfamiliar vocabulary and typing. Koreans, for their part, undermine the cognitive facilitation *hangul* could provide by using it as a syllabary in the final design of its graphemes and in the way the units are taught and perceived.[1]

7. *East Asian writing is not syllabic, nor are Western alphabets phonemic.*

Although there is no pure writing system, typologies are based on the predominant relationship of meaning to sound. The most convincing typology, proposed by DeFrancis (1989:58), classifies Chinese characters and *kana* as "syllabic systems" distinct from the consonantal and alphabetic systems used in the West. *Hangul* is classified with English as "morphophonemic." Since I am concerned with the system's operation, I treat it as a *functional* syllabary. Should *hangul* abandon its syllabic format, I would be the second (after Ch'oe Hyon-bae, who made the same argument) to applaud the development.

8. *The book betrays a Westerner's insensitivity to the cultural significance of character-based writing.*

Quite to the contrary, one of this book's cardinal points is that Asian writing connects to the culture on multiple levels. Authoritarianism, concrete thinking, borrowing, and excessive attachment to the past, all elements of East Asian culture, are abetted by the use of character-based writing. Given this relationship between writing and culture, and the goal of Asian policy makers to overcome anachronistic features of traditional society, it behooves those interested in effecting cultural change to consider the problem in all its dimensions.

9. *There is little appreciation shown for Asia's intellectual tradition.*

The argument made here about the difficulty East Asians have rethinking issues from the ground up is accepted by many scholars, including Joseph Needham, who cannot be accused of slighting Chinese science. There is no disputing the richness of East Asia's intellectual heritage, the beauty of its art and literature, and the subtlety of its philosophy. These accomplishments, however, are products of a concrete mindset that reluctantly examines the abstract nature of phenomena.

10. *Claiming East Asians lack creativity is an affront to a people's dignity, whose superiority in intellectual pursuits is amply demonstrated.*

I have dealt with this issue in detail but it bears repeating: there is no connection between IQ and creativity. Although average or better than average intelligence is needed to master the concepts of a discipline, generating new ideas is an independent skill. Experts concur that beyond IQ 120 or so the correlation between intelligence and creativity vanishes.

11. *The basic problem is cultural, not cognitive. Asian scientists are creative in the West.*

This is precisely my point! East Asians who have emigrated to the West are using English and other alphabetically written languages. More broadly, they are working in an alphabetic culture whose norms support creative enterprise. Looked at the other way, East Asian culture rejects individuals who are apt to disrupt the status quo with creative ideas, filling the emigrant pool with a large number of creative types.

12. *The notion that culture itself can be inherited harks back to the Lamarckian view on evolution, long since discredited.*

Sociobiology discounts Lamarck's views as simplistic. Cultural traits per se are not inherited. What is inherited is a disposition to react to cues in the environment present in the form of culture.

13. *The book puts too little emphasis on creativity's social aspects.*

The insight stage of creativity is a profoundly personal act, although clearly there is more to the process. I agree that creativity should be treated in the context of gene-culture coevolution, and go as far as to include peer acceptance as a fifth stage, in recognition of society's role in generating the conditions that make creativity possible (or impossible).

14. *Granting the existence of a creativity deficit in East Asia, the book neglects other factors responsible for the problem.*

Such as bureaucratic obstructionism, cronyism, a risk adverse culture, low-trust environment, a shortage of venture capital, inadequate legal protection, and so on. Cultural evolution makes it difficult to pinpoint the source of a particular problem from the empirical data alone, since the cause and its consequences interact. By focusing logically on the cognitive requirements of creativity, one has a better chance of isolating its roots.

15. *The author does not give due credit to East Asia's indigenous S&T accomplishments.*

I acknowledge East Asians' incomparable skill at improving technology incrementally. Just as alphabetic writing promotes revolutionary creative skills in the West, a case could be built around the notion that the gradual evolutionary progress East Asia favors is fostered by thought processes associated with character-based writing. My unwillingness to credit East Asia with significant achievements in breakthrough science is shared by Asia's own S&T managers.

16. *All countries borrow technology. East Asians are more successful at it.*

It is a matter of degree. The first several chapters of this book demonstrate how far this pattern of borrowing and adaptation has gone in East Asia—clearly beyond anything done in the West. Given this manifest interest in technology, it is doubly striking that East Asians have not shown more initiative in creating it.

17. *The allegations of industrial espionage could usher in a new era of McCarthyism.*

Asia's S&T collection against Western targets has been tracked for decades by counterintelligence organizations on the national and corporate levels. Discussion of the issue entered the public arena long ago. The present book contributes to an understanding of the problem by offering corroborating data provided by the principals in their open media.

18. *At this critical juncture in East-West relations, we need cooperation and under-standing, not another inflammatory attack on East Asian culture.*

Cooperation, as in "strategic cooperation," has been a euphemism for one-sided "exchanges" that result in Western technology being transferred to the East at a fraction of its value. Ignoring the problem contributes to an unwillingness to address it at its source.

19. *Most of the linguistic issues associated with character-based writing have been resolved by computers.*

Computers *exacerbate* the problem by amplifying inequities between character-based and alphabetic writing, particularly in input. Computerization does not solve the cognitive issues that led to a creativity deficit.

20. *Replacing character-based writing is a cure worse than the disease.*

Reform need not be sudden or catastrophic. Koreans already use an all-phonetic script and have enacted more legislation than I can keep track of for this or that alphabetic notation. Chinese *pinyin* and Japanese *rōmaji* act as full-fledged orthographies in certain applications. Allowing two systems to coexist in a state of *digraphia* for an indefinite period would ease any transitional discomfort.

21. *Writing reform is a ploy to subvert East Asian civilization.*

If that were my goal, this book would be unnecessary. The shortcomings of traditional East Asian civilization as they pertain to creativity have long been recognized by Asia's political leaders. More recently, measures to overcome these obstacles were laid out in an official report on Japan's goals for the twenty-first century, which I shall discuss presently.

Toward a Creative Culture

There is no doubt that East Asia engages in sweeping efforts to acquire Western technologies. The fact is hardly news. It is known by the principals involved in these transfers, who until recently had few qualms about discussing them in their domestic media. It is also known by counterintelligence specialists, who have gone public with the facts to alert corporations to the danger. Documenting these infractions of what Westerners regard as ethical business practice has been easy.

Explaining this behavior is more challenging. My first hint that something was amiss in all this borrowing—beyond its sheer scale—came from the level of technology sought. Japan, South Korea, and increasingly China seek access not to proven technologies but to *ideas*, promising concepts that have not yet been realized as products. This preference reflects East Asians' practical skill at commercializing innovations and improving existing techniques. But the main reason East Asians transfer wellspring technology is to compensate for their difficulty creating new things. There is ample evidence that East Asians are aware of this problem but few signs they are addressing it at its core.

Part of the fault lies with the Western countries themselves, which through negligence and sloppy business practices deprive East Asians of any incentive to rectify the situation. The United States in particular seems unable to recognize the value of its creative talent. While going to extraordinary lengths to protect software patents and the recording industry, scientific discoveries of commercial and military value are shared like water. Universities and research institutes that depend on outside funding are the most heavily targeted and are also the least disposed to protect their discoveries from being exploited abroad.

The problem involves more than economics. Scientists, who count on the free flow of ideas, are reluctant to support measures aimed narrowly at America's military needs and economic well-being. Recent disclosures of security lapses at national labs, while bad enough, only highlight a general disdain among thinkers for secrecy agreements that block the exchange of knowledge.[2] This aloofness from practical matters may be unavoidable, given the nature of the creative mind. It also serves as a check against bureaucracy's instinct to control and suppress. Still, there are plenty of historical and contemporary examples that point to the peril of ignoring these domestic concerns. Our open society could do a better job watching its back door.

Another way the West abets the hemorrhaging of its creative ideas is by neglecting commercialization. As demonstrated by the plight of many online businesses, ideas devoid of *content* have little lasting value. The notion

that Western countries could go on trading thoughts for tangible substance has left them without the means to protect their technology and
benefit from it. For decades businesses have found it easier to produce off-
shore than to cope with regulations and workers' aspirations to the extent
that their ability to implement new concepts has been "hollowed out."

As was emphasized throughout this book, validation of ideas is both the
end point and beginning of creativity. If the benefits of creativity are to be
enjoyed by those who through their taxes and forbearance support the culture that makes their societies creative, then a capacity to translate radical
ideas into salable products must remain part of the chain, both as a measure of the idea's value and to support creative thinkers' livelihoods. Clos-
ing the circle would also compel Asian countries to look harder at ways to
reduce their creativity deficit.

Efforts to resolve some of the factors causing this creativity deficit are already afoot. According to a document released by the Japanese government in February 2000 titled "Report on the Prime Minister's Commission
on Japan's Goals in the 21st Century," Japan accepts that it can no longer
rely on "ready-made models" to stoke its economic development. Creativity
must be encouraged, the report says, by changing traditional norms and
institutions, including neglect of the individual, an intolerance of diversity,
the outdated educational system, a penchant for top-down regulation, state
control of economic and social affairs, and the quest for harmony above all
else. The aim is to infuse society with a pioneer spirit.

A month later Li Xueyong, PRC vice-minister of science and technology,
aired the outline of China's program "to improve the country's overall creativity and nurture high-quality personnel in basic research."[3] Li called for a
shift in emphasis to creative research aimed at breakthroughs in half a
dozen key sectors. He acknowledged that only 5 percent of China's "basic
scientific research can compete with the world's advanced countries, because of problems including the lack of creativity and insufficient funding."
Although Li stopped short of describing exactly how China would achieve
its goal, his frank admission that China faces a creativity problem opens the
door, perhaps, to the appearance of long-term solutions.

A Plea for Orthographic Reform

For me, the most intriguing part of the Japanese report is its call for global
literacy to be met by making English an official second language. Acknowl-

edging a shortage of communication skills, the report argues, "We should also think about requiring the central government, local governments, and other public institutions to produce their publications, and home pages, in both Japanese and English." The goal is to give people better access to global information and a venue to share their values with the world community.

If Japan institutes a serious program of bilingual education, it could end up solving gratuitously the problem that has been our concern throughout this book, namely, the need to model the cognitive stages of creativity through use of an alphabet. The phenomenal spread of English in Korea and Chinese-speaking areas could also have this effect. However, a word of caution is in order.

As long as character-based scripts remain the *primary* channel of literacy for East Asians, the cognitive effects associated with these systems will weigh on their users as before. Not only will East Asian children continue to waste their formative years on rote tasks; their linguistic competence will be split between two languages that have no shared focus and little in common. There is nothing in the creativity literature that suggests bilingualism, like literacy, facilitates creative acts. Indeed, true bilinguals seldom achieve greatness in either language. For literacy in English to have a significant reordering effect on East Asians' minds, a level of mastery may be required that inhibits development of the main language, with full proficiency attained in neither. This, in its own way, could be worse than the creativity problem.

How much simpler it would be if East Asians were to accept what many of their own best thinkers have argued for nearly a century, namely, that character-based writing, practically speaking, is bankrupt and should be replaced with an alphabet. There is no reason why the alphabetic notations now used in China, Japan, and Korea cannot assume a wider role in the orthographic lives of East Asians. Allowing the two writing systems to vie in representing the national language would eliminate transitional problems by substituting user choice for government fiat. Animated by its proximity to speech, the literary norm would adapt on its own to the needs of phonetic writing, freeing East Asians from the anachronism of character-based writing and removing this obstacle to creativity.

Or perhaps I am misreading history's course. Chinese characters and the syllabic writing systems derived from them have hobbled the growth of East Asian languages for millennia by distorting the shape of new expressions and isolating the languages from direct contact with the world community. Could the spectacular rise of English in East Asia be a consequence of the failure of indigenous languages, under orthographic constraints, to adapt to modern needs? Will the ultimate effect of Chinese characters be to deprive East Asians of their own languages? As a linguist, I cannot imagine a greater tragedy.

Notes

Introduction

1. *Kodak vs. Fuji Film* case before the World Trade Organization, briefs filed on behalf of Kodak by the U.S. Trade Representative, February 20 and May 20, 1997.

2. Seoul, *Chonja Sinmun*, "No Cuts Foreseen in R&D Investment," December 11, 1997, p. 2.

3. Tokyo, *Nihon Keizai Shimbun*, "Proper Distribution of Increasing Research Budget Urgently Needed," March 29–April 12, 1997, pp. 13, 11, 10.

4. Tokyo, *Kagaku Gijutsu Janaru*, "Basic Research Programs Under Japan Science and Technology Corporation," April 1997, pp. 16–17.

5. Science and Technology Agency, "1997 Science and Technology Indexes," May 22, 1997, reported in Tokyo, *Nikkan Kogyo Shimbun*, May 23, 1997.

6. Tokyo, *Nikkan Kogyo Shimbun*, "STA Survey: Japan Research Activities Fall Further Behind US," June 27, 1997, p. 7.

7. Tokyo, *Kagaku Kogyo Nippo*, "MITI's AIST to Revise Industrial Science and Technology Frontier System," January 17, 1997, p. 1.

8. Beijing, *Xinhua*, "Li Lanqing Pushes High Level of Scientific Research," June 2, 1997.

9. Beijing, *Xinhua*, "Jiang Zemin Stresses Basic Scientific Research," August 25, 1997.

10. Beijing, *China Daily*, "Beijing Research Center to Stimulate Innovation," August 2, 1997, p. 2.

11. For example, Sansom (1928) and DeFrancis (1950).

Chapter 1

1. Nakamura (1964:5–6) wrote: "Language is basic to the cultural life of a people; so basic that when a special language system comes into being, we may say that a people has come into being. . . . Forms of linguistic expression become, in the inner consciousness of people, norms for psychologically ordering in a fixed pattern and carrying to conclusion the operation of thought."

2. For example, Alfred Bloom (1981).

3. Richard Bloom (1998). See also Ji Fengyuan (forthcoming).

4. Patricia Ellen Grant (1988) argued that "the extent to which the language shapes the mind, as opposed to the mind influencing the language is difficult to determine. Their interdependence results in a mutual development."

5. For example, Bylinski (1978); Nicholson (1982); Dreyfuss (1987).

6. Schweizer (1993:82) noted that a 1981 list of registered foreign agents compiled by the U.S. Justice Department ran to forty-four pages for Japan, compared to twenty-three and seventeen pages for Great Britain and Germany. The success of the Japan lobby at influencing U.S. policy and public opinion has not been lost on other countries. The director of the U.S. office of the Korea Trade Promotion Corporation, in an article published by Seoul's *Hanguk Kyongje Sinmun* on February 22, 1993, recommended that South Korea model its efforts on those of Japan, which he said employs hundreds of lobbyists and lawyers at a cost of over $100 million annually, including "Americans who have gone on to become prominent trade officials."

7. Professor Angel analyzes the influence of the U.S. Japan lobby in a forthcoming book.

8. Robert Angel, personal communication, July 12, 1998. Hall (1998:167) writes that Angel eventually had misgivings about the biased representations his employer expected of him and returned to his academic post to continue "his critical analyses of Japan." Angel's defection won him the enmity of Japan's U.S. apologists. He refers to his residence in Columbia, South Carolina, as "Dazaifu," a traditional place of exile in Japanese history.

9. Lois Peters states in *Technical Networks Between U.S. and Japanese Industry* that "Japanese capability for absorbing technical know-how generated beyond its borders is legendary" (1987:5). Peters does a credible job describing some of Japan's favored transfer venues but manages to portray these "exchanges" as a bilateral benefit worthy of preserving. Peters's study was published by Rensselaer Polytechnic Institute, whose faculty have been prominent organizers of symposia for international S&T cooperative exchanges. She acknowledges her gratitude "for the support of the Japan Society for the initial phases" of her book project.

10. Hansen similarly found that Japanese competitive intelligence "relies primarily on open-source information available in the public realm" (1996:1).

11. Japanese *kana*, a syllabic script that evolved from shortened and stylized Chinese characters used purely for their phonetic value, may not have been wholly

indigenous. Several of the forms were shared by early Korean scripts. *Kana*, moreover, was an incremental, not a discontinuous development. Typical of Japan's approach to innovation, the system cannot be considered "creative" in the Western sense.

12. Some linguists, beginning with Suzuki Takao (1975) and Kato Hiroshi (1979), claim that learning individual Chinese characters (*kanji*) gives Japanese readers a unique insight into the meanings of words written with a combination of such characters. I have argued elsewhere that this view is overdrawn and misleading (1997:144–50).

13. *Gairaigo* dictionaries, with 50,000 or more entries from English and European languages, are obsolete the day they are published, so quickly do these new adaptations occur. Professional translators generally find it more expedient to sound out the *katakana* word until the English equivalent pops into mind. The dictionaries are useful for established English borrowings, especially those that have been truncated so much that they no longer resemble the original term.

14. The present practice of relying heavily on English loanwords has generated a backlash among Japan's more nationalistic thinkers, including some linguists. See, for example, Suzuki Takao (1987:140, 170, 183, 324–25).

15. Material for this section is based on Bylinski (1978, 1987); Dalton and Genther (1991); Dalton and Serapio (1995); DeLuca (1988); Dreyfuss (1987); Duggan and Eisenstodt (1990); Fialka (1997); Gertz (1992); Glickman and Woodward (1989); Halamka (1984); Hall (1998); Hansen (1996); Herbig (1995); Kahaner (1996); Katzenstein (1996); Kolata (1990); Levine, Gross and Carey (1989); Meyer (1987); Morishima (1982); Murray and Lehner (1990); Nicholson (1982); Okimoto (1989); Peters (1987, 1993); Porter (1990); Prescott and Gibbons (1993); Prestowitz (1988); Reid and Schriesheim (1996); Rosenberg and Steinmuller (1988); Rosenberg, Landau and Mowery (1992); Roukis, Conway and Charnov (1990); Samuels (1994); Schweizer (1993); Teece (1987); van Wolferen (1989); Yoder and Lachica (1988); and my own research.

16. Herbig states, "If one can view databases as a technological transfer vehicle, the differences become apparent: Nearly 2,000 U.S. databases are accessible in Japan; however only eighty-three of Japan's domestic databases are available abroad, and only twenty are in science and technology" (1995:223).

17. Described by Schweizer (1993) and by Eftimiades (1994).

18. The Science and Technology Agency has metamorphized into the Ministry of Education, Culture, Sports, Science and Technology or MEXT.

19. Renamed the Ministry of Economy, Trade and Industry (METI) in 2001.

20. Successive CIA directors have flatly rejected the idea of the U.S. government engaging in industrial espionage. Former DCI Robert Gates is on record as stating that "the US intelligence community does not and will not engage in industrial espionage." James Woolsey was even more emphatic: "Let me be quite clear about this. The CIA is not going to be in the business that a number of our friends' and allies' intelligence services are in—spying on foreign corporations for the benefit

of domestic business." John F. Quinn (1998) posted at <www.ccnet.com/~suntzu75/jindesp.htm> and visited December 16, 1998.

21. The two reporters offered the example of Corning Glass Works, an American manufacturer of fiber optic cable, which applied for a patent in the United States and got it two years later; in 1975 it applied for the same patent in Japan and received it in 1985.

22. A paper by Keith Maskus and Christine McDaniel (1999) on "How Japan's Patent System Encourages Incremental Innovation" argues that "Japan's early disclosure and narrow claim requirements increased technology diffusion and contributed to technological 'catch up' with the West" and that the same system also inhibits "incentives for fundamental invention" (6).

23. Teece observes that patents are notoriously weak guarantors and other companies can usually "invent around" them. "As technology becomes more public and less proprietary through easier imitation, strength in manufacturing and other capabilities is necessary to derive advantage from whatever technological advantages an innovator may possess" (1987:214).

24. <www.jetro.go.jp>, visited October 23, 2000. Quinn (1998) counted 76 JETRO overseas offices and centers in 1998 with "a total staff of approximately 1,200 people."

25. Katzenstein observed, "Each of the nine major trading corporations is active in more than a hundred countries; sends 600 to 1,000 Japanese employees abroad and hires an additional 1,500 to 3,000 overseas; operates across a broad range of economic sectors; and relies on diverse sources of information including business partners, foreign governments, local financial firms, other trading companies, and domestic and foreign press and intelligence agencies" (1996:37).

26. *High Technology Careers Magazine*, October–November 1995, pp. 44–49.

27. Herb Meyer, former vice-chairman of the U.S. Central Intelligence Agency's National Intelligence Council, is quoted by Schweizer (1993:66) as having said, "The only thing unusual is [Hitachi] got caught."

28. Fallows (1995:91) described a meeting he had in 1992 with a Japanese official charged with "coordinating the 'mutual' exchange of scientific information between Japan and the United States." The official "spent a long time describing all the projects the Japanese government and Japanese companies had launched to understand American science, to observe American research, to learn from American techniques. At the end he was asked about the other side of his job—encouraging the flow of information out of Japan. 'Actually, nothing formal has been established as of yet.' "

29. Sakakibara and Westney's (1992) remarks on local R&D centers support this thesis, albeit reluctantly. In their words, Japanese still tend "to treat the developing research center as a 'listening post' whose function is to report on local developments in technology and to host *visiting technology scanners*" (333, my emphasis).

30. Peters, who surveyed individual Japanese companies on their plans to outsource creativity, reported that "Most Japanese executives say they expect their

companies to conduct more research in the United States in the future, and at the same time to increase their ties to U.S. research universities" (1993:229).

31. Fialka (1997:154) adds that in the late 1980s MIT was receiving over half a billion dollars annually of federal money for research programs that were being used primarily by Japan.

32. Herbig notes that between 1986 and 1989 Kubota invested $190 million in five Silicon Valley high-tech firms, Hitachi put $160 million into a U.S. computer printer developer, and NKK bought 5 percent of Silicon Graphics for $35 million (1995:220–21).

33. Complaints from U.S. firms prohibited from marketing their products in Japan without some form of technology sharing are legion. Herbig cites the case of IBM, which was forced to license key technologies for permission to sell computers in Japan. "MITI told IBM it would take every measure possible to obstruct the success of its business unless IBM licensed its patents to Japanese firms and charged them no more than a 5 percent royalty." Texas Instruments found itself in a similar bind (1995:37).

Chapter 2

1. Known as the Cox Commission Report after Representative Christopher Cox, chairman of the House committee charged with investigating China's illicit technology transfers. The top secret report was published in January 1999; a redacted, declassified version was released by the U.S. Government Printing Office five months later in May.

2. Simon and Goldman observed (1989:20): "The real problem is the overriding political system whose controls, while somewhat lessened by the reforms, still do not allow this talent the freedom of action and flexibility to develop beyond the physical manifestations of a modern research system. Unless this weight is lifted, China of the twenty-first century may achieve a modicum of scientific stature, but will be unable to achieve the global technological leadership to which it aspires."

3. Although the Cox Report highlighted China's theft of advanced weapons technology through clandestine means, it acknowledged that covert action is just one of many tools used by the PRC to obtain U.S. military technology. In the Commission's words: "Professional intelligence agents from the MSS and MID account for a relatively small share of the PRC's foreign science and technology collection. The bulk of such information is gathered by various non-professionals, including PRC students, scientists, researchers, and other visitors to the West" (1999:19).

4. According to Kahaner, China's poorly developed information infrastructure leads the country to "engage in state-sponsored industrial espionage activities" (1996:199). I am not sure I agree with this negative assessment of China's ability to glean intelligence through benign methods, particularly in light of recently available information on the PRC's open source collection effort (see Huo and Wang 1991).

5. Lee Livingston, former Defense Intelligence Agency counterintelligence expert, personal communication, 1998. See also Daniel Yi, "Scientist Sentenced to Halfway House in Chinese Espionage Case," *Los Angeles Times*, March 27, 1998.

6. Comments attributed to PRC Foreign Ministry spokesperson Zhu Bangzao by *Xinhua* on January 7, 1999 and to Foreign Minister Tang Jiaxuan by a Hong Kong AFP dispatch on March 7, 1999.

7. Hong Kong *Ta Kung Pao*, March 18, 1999.

8. Cited by Elisabeth Zingg, Hong Kong AFP dispatch, May 26, 1999.

9. The Chinese phrase is *qíngbàoxué*, literally "intelligence science." Qíngbào (*jōhō* in Japanese) is translated into English as "intelligence" or "information" depending on context. In East Asia the one term covers both concepts. Although there are other words in Chinese for "information," such as *zīliào*, *xìnxī*, or *xùnxī*, "intelligence" (in the sense of information communicated) is translated only by *qíngbào*. By contrast, "information science" is rendered in *A New English-Chinese Dictionary* (Ge Chuan'guei et al., rev. ed., [Seattle: University of Washington Press, 1988], p. 649) straightforwardly as *zīliàoxué* and is explained as "the discipline of collecting, analyzing, and storing research material." The main objection to translating *qíngbào* as "intelligence" in all its appearances is that the word is used more commonly in Chinese than "intelligence" is in English. But this fact may only reflect the difference in East Asian and Western attitudes toward use of others' intellectual property.

10. Tang (1984:20) and Miao (1993:49). The institute, currently called Zhongguo Keji Xinxi Yanjiusuo, used *qíngbào* ("intelligence") instead of *xìnxī* ("information") in its original name, according to Tang.

11. ISTIC today presents itself to the world as a "national comprehensive information center" for "disseminating and popularizing national S&T information," although its primary function as a collection facility is evident in the introduction to its Information Service Center, which states, "With the collection and processing of Chinese and foreign S&T information resources, and the providing of comprehensive document services to the public, as its main task, the Center commands a rich collection of S&T documents covering a wide range of disciplines" <www.istic.ac.cn>, visited September 22, 2000).

12. Bruce Gilley's review has made it nearly impossible to obtain an original copy of the book, although I did find one at the Library of Congress. Gilley attributes the release of this extraordinary book to an "oversight," noting that it could not be published in the atmosphere that prevails today. I believe the explanation for the book's appearance is more facile and disconcerting: China's commitment to exploiting foreign technology is so much a part of its R&D culture that the authors simply took acceptance of this behavior for granted.

13. The unclassified 1999 "Report to Congress on Chinese Espionage Activities against the United States," an annual review submitted to Congress jointly by the CIA and FBI, observed, "Because the Chinese consider themselves to be in a developmental 'catch-up' situation, their collection program tends to have a compara-

tively broad scope. Chinese collectors target information and technology on any-thing of value to China, which leads them to collect open-source information as well as restricted/proprietary and classified information."

14. The acronym "AD" derives from the original name "Armed Services Tech-nology Information Agency (ASTIA) Document," available through the U.S. De-partment of Commerce's National Technical Information Service (NTIS).

15. Xu Hongying (1996); website visited March 23, 2000.

16. According to its website (<www.china-jeti.com>, visited January 21, 2002), the institute was founded in 1978 "as the first large sized institution specialized in tech-nical and engineering translation in China." It reportedly has 250 full-time staff members.

17. Jia and Rubin (1997); website visited August 17, 2000.

18. Some 90,000 individuals left Taiwan between 1949 and 1983 to study abroad, according to the August 1999 issue of *Zhongguo Rencai*.

19. "On China's Brain Drain Problems and Responses," *Zhongguo Rencai*, Novem-ber 1999, pp. 47–48.

20. Ibid.

21. Guo Dongpo, "A Promising Undertaking," in *Renmin Ribao*, August 25, 2000. Jon Sigurdson argued, however, that by 1975, China's S&T managers had conceded that scientists trained after 1949 were of limited value; those sent abroad for train-ing from 1978 on were to become the main force in building up China's S&T es-tablishment (1980:15).

22. O. Schnapp (1989:180–81). Chinese media reports acknowledge overseas training as being the major noncontractual means of obtaining foreign technology. According to the December 1997 *Kexue yu Kexue Guanli*, returned students make up the backbone of all fields of Chinese science. The June 22, 1998 *Keji Ribao* af-firmed that training Chinese specialists in advanced science is "the most important aspect of Sino-American S&T cooperation," adding that 70 percent of China's lead-ing scientists studied in the United States.

23. *Kexue yu Kexue Guanli*, December 1997. The journal also suggested that China's own research priorities are adjusted according to the information these overseas scholars can provide, noting that "an effort is made to combine domestic requirements with the capabilities of those doing research abroad."

24. *Zhongguo Jingji Shibao*, February 13, 1999.

25. *Xinhua*, August 24, 1999.

26. *Xinhua*, September 29, 1999.

27. *Xinhua*, October 18, 1999.

28. *Xinhua*, November 3, 1999.

29. *Xinhua*, June 5, 2000.

30. *Xinhua*, July 6, 1999 and April 20, 2000. CAS vice-president Bai Chunli told *Kexue Shibao* (a newspaper on science published by the CAS) on July 12, 2000, that his academy would seek "300 outstanding overseas Chinese scientists" to participate in "national innovation projects." Besides their scientific expertise, the candidates

would need organizational skills "to guide research and train a cadre of new scientists."

31. *Guoji Shangbao* (a newspaper published by the Ministry of Foreign Trade and Economic Cooperation), January 21, 2000.

32. *Jingji Cankao Bao* (an economic newspaper published by China's official *Xinhua* News Agency), April 8, 1998, and *Wen Hui Bao* (a nationally prominent daily newspaper for intellectuals), July 13, 1999.

33. *Kexue Shibao,* June 14, 1999.

34. *Xinhua,* August 18, 1998.

35. *Xinhua,* June 5, 1998.

36. *Xinhua,* January 23, 1998.

37. *Guoji Shangbao,* January 21, 2000.

38. Guo Dongpo, "A Promising Undertaking," in *Renmin Ribao,* August 25, 2000.

36. *Xinhua,* January 20, 2000.

40. *Xinhua,* February 7, 2000.

41. <www.qiaolian.org>, visited in November 1999. In addition to information about the aims of the organization, the website includes hotlinks to eighty-three overseas Chinese associations and individual database entries on overseas Chinese who have scored "glorious achievements" for China.

42. <www.coea.org>, visited in January 2000. Online references to the COEA in both Chinese and English disappear after 2001, which suggests to me that the group has been renamed or reorganized.

43. The more important ones are the Asia-Silicon Valley Connection, the Chinese Information and Networking Association, the Chinese Software Professionals Association, the Chinese-American Semiconductor Professional Association, the Silicon Valley Chinese Engineers Association, the Silicon Valley Chinese Overseas Business Association, and the Silicon Valley Chinese Wireless Technology Association.

44. According to information posted on the Chinese Technology Innovation Information Net <www.ctiin.com.cn>, visited in November 2001.

45. According to Minister of Science and Technology Zhu Lilan in an interview with the Beijing *China Daily,* March 30, 1998. Wu Duanmin reports a total of 154 countries in his article "The 21st Century: the Time When China Will Snatch Nobel Prizes," in *21 Shiji,* June 1997, p. 13.

46. U.S. Congress, Office of Technology Assessment (1987:8).

47. According to (then) State Science and Technology Commission Vice-Minister Hui Yongzheng, cited in the Beijing *China Daily,* November 19, 1997.

48. *China Daily,* March 30, 1998.

49. *Keji Jinbu yu Duice,* March 1998.

50. *Zhongguo Maoyi Bao,* April 16, 1998.

51. *Xinhua,* December 8, 1998.

52. Fialka (1997:32). Joseph Kahn in the May 22, 1996, *Wall Street Journal* described how Douglas was cowed into "one of the largest technology transfers in history" in connection with its sale of MD-82 civilian jet aircraft to the PRC. China

walked away from the deal with the equivalent of "80 years of accumulated aircraft manufacturing experience" and the ability to manufacture "nearly all major plane parts."

53. *Kexuexue yu Kexue Jishu Guanli*, December 1997. Simon (1989:300) wrote, "Foreign investment abroad by Chinese organizations has also become an attractive mechanism for gaining access to foreign technology. . . . The Chinese see these as technology listening posts as well as opportunities to train technical personal."

54. *Keji Ribao*, May 13, 1996.

55. Hong Kong *AFP* dispatch, June 3, 1996.

56. *Zhongguo Maoyi Bao*, November 19, 1998.

57. *Keji Jinbu yu Duice*, May 1998.

58. Occasional admissions can be found. For example, on January 13, 2002, *Xinhua* published a "Commentary on Change in China's S&T Strategy" in which it stated "the absence of any state first prize for natural science for three successive years reflects the embarrassing fact that China lacks major original innovations."

Chapter 3

1. *Hanguk Kyongje Sinmun* (*HKS*) is one of Seoul's three main business newspapers, along with *Maeil Kyongje Sinmun* (*MKS*) and *Seoul Kyongje Sinmun*.

2. *HKS*, December 22, 1995.

3. *Seoul Kyongje Sinmun*, November 30, 1995.

4. *Seoul Kyongje Sinmun*, October 27, 1995.

5. *Sanhagyon 21* is a monthly journal of high-tech Korean industry that promotes cooperation between industry, academic institutions, and national laboratories.

6. *HKS*, January 25, 1994.

7. *Chonja Sinmun*, March 16, 1994. *Chonja Sinmun* is a daily newspaper of the electronics industry serving the science and technology community in general.

8. *HKS*, October 7, 1994.

9. A survey of South Korean businesses' attitudes toward foreign cooperation, reported in the September 9, 1993, *MKS*, showed that ROK firms were losing interest in Japan, traditionally South Korea's main technology source, due to Japanese efforts to control advanced technology exports.

10. *HKS*, March 25, 1993.

11. *MKS*, October 19, 1994.

12. The ministry's name and its English acronym have changed several times over the past decade.

13. *MKS*, January 31, 1994.

14. *MKS*, June 19, 1996.

15. *HKS*, May 17, 1993.

16. *Chugan Maegyong*, March 9, 1994. *Chugan Maegyong* is a weekly business magazine published by the newspaper *Maeil Kyongje Sinmun*. South Korean newspapers

leave little doubt about the purpose of these overseas facilities, as when *MKS* reported on February 7, 1994, that Pohang Iron and Steel would use its Delaware subsidiary to "engage in technical information collection activities."

17. *MKS*, March 1, 1995.

18. *MKS*, November 12, 1994.

19. *MKS*, September 25, 1995.

20. *MKS*, April 25, 1995.

21. *Chugan Choson*, April 15, 1993.

22. *Chugan Choson*, August 1, 1993.

23. *MKS*, January 28, 1994.

24. *HKS*, January 16, 1995.

25. LG established the lab "on the assumption that it would be difficult to remain competitive under the present system of depending on foreign companies for well-spring technology" (*Chonja Sinmun*, April 21, 1995).

26. *MKS*, March 15, 1995.

27. *HKS*, January 12, 1995.

28. *HKS*, May 14, 1995.

29. Published in *Chonja Sinmun*, September 18, 1995.

30. *HKS*, November 18, 1995.

31. *HKS*, September 22, 1995.

32. *HKS*, February 13, 1996.

33. *MKS*, October 7, 1995.

34. *MKS*, March 27, 1996.

35. *MKS*, April 19, 1996.

36. *MKS*, May 2, 1996.

37. *HKS*, July 24, 1996.

38. *HKS*, November 30, 1996.

39. *KITA Bulletin*, August 30, 1996.

40. Ministry of Science and Technology press release dated August 28, 1996.

41. *HKS*, December 28, 1995.

42. *Chonja Sinmun*, October 21, 1996.

43. *Chonja Sinmun*, August 5, 1996.

44. Press release, August 28, 1996.

45. *HKS*, February 1, 1966.

46. As reported by the semiofficial ROK news agency *Yonhap* on December 3, 1996.

47. *HKS*, September 27, 1997.

48. *MKS*, October 3, 1995.

49. *HKS*, July 13, 1994.

50. *HKS*, January 23, 1995. The newspaper said that South Korean businesses are expanding their links with foreign universities because they "enable the companies to rapidly acquire advanced technology and raise the skills of their research personnel."

51. *Chonja Sinmun*, January 18, 1996.

52. *MKS*, February 22, 1994, and September 16, 1994. On October 13, 1998 *Yonhap* reported a deal between the ROK Ministry of Information Communications and Stanford University to train Korean specialists in information technology and facilitate bilateral cooperation between U.S. and South Korean firms. According to *Yonhap*, the idea for the project arose when the head of an ROK venture company in Silicon Valley donated $2 million to Stanford.

53. *HKS*, June 25, 1994.

54. *Korea Herald*, January 14, 1995.

55. *HKS*, June 25, 1994.

56. *Chonja Sinmun*, March 19, 1994.

57. *Seoul Database World*, August 19, 1994.

58. *Chonja Sinmun*, August 19, 1994.

59. *Chonja Sinmun*, September 2, 1995.

60. *Chonja Sinmun*, December 1, 1994.

61. *MKS*, April 17, 1995.

62. *HKS*, March 27, 1996. The site was visited at <irtech.kordic.re.kr/~kristal>.

63. *Chonja Sinmun*, August 14, 1995.

64. <www.korbiz.or.kr/kufit>, visited May 1997.

65. *Chonja Sinmun*, March 28, 1995.

66. *MKS*, May 25, 1994. The forum hosted a "technology networking room" to promote the "exchange of data, human resources, and technology."

67. *Chonja Sinmun*, September 29, 1995.

68. *MKS*, June 13, 1995.

69. *Chugan Choson*, August 1993. *Chugan Choson* is a weekly magazine published by the Seoul daily newspaper *Choson Ilbo*.

70. Ibid.

71. *Chugan Maegyong*, February 28, 1994.

72. *Hangyore Sinmun*, July 29, 1993. *Hangyore* was South Korea's leading dissident newspaper.

73. *Choson Ilbo*, November 18, 1994.

74. *Sisa Journal*, August 26, 1993. *Sisa Journal* is a weekly news magazine published in Seoul.

75. *Chugan Choson*, December 24, 1992.

76. *Chugan Maegyong*, January 9, 1994.

77. *Sisa Journal*, January 27, 1994.

78. *Chugan Maegyong*, January 9, 1994. "Technical consulting" with the former employees of foreign companies is common enough among ROK corporations to have become computerized. According to the August 28, 1995, *MKS*, an organization called "Korea Efficiency Association Consulting" offers through its "Technology Benchmarking Center" the services of some 2,000 retired technicians around the world to solve "technological bottlenecks" that cannot be overcome with indigenous know-how. Included in the center's "specialized technology consultant

bank" are the names of another 20,000 Japanese, American, and European experts in semiconductors, electricity, electronics, chemistry, construction, and other industrial fields. A company official explained that the service is used by ROK firms that run up against technological problems, or where "technology development is impossible because of the burden of royalty payments." Clients include Samsung, Daewoo, Hyosung, and others.

79. *HKS*, January 9, 1994. Iljin's damage control efforts were ludicrous. Shortly after the case broke, the group ran full-page ads in the major Seoul dailies extolling its "indigenous" research capabilities. GE, vilified by the ROK press for its "monopolistic" practices, eventually buried the hatchet and entered into a series of cooperative arrangements with Iljin and other ROK corporations.

80. *MKS*, June 20, 1995.

81. After several reorganizations and name changes, KOTRA in 1996 finally acknowledged its status as a formal ROK government institution.

82. *MKS*, December 22, 1993.

83. *MKS*, December 30, 1993.

84. *MKS*, May 23, 1996.

85. *MKS*, May 27, 1996.

86. *MKS*, September 7, 1994.

87. *MKS*, October 16, 1996.

88. *HKS*, October 21, 1996

89. KOSEF reiterated this goal on page 11 of its 1996 brochure under "Securing R&D Bases in Advanced Countries."

90. KOSEF, brochure, p. 33.

91. *MKS*, March 17, 1994.

92. *MKS*, December 8, 1995.

93. *MKS*, May 11, 1995.

94. *Chonja Sinmun*, September 29, 1995.

95. *Chonja Sinmun*, September 19, 1995.

96. *Yonhap*, June 27, 1996.

97. *MKS*, June 25, 1996.

98. *Chonja Sinmun*, September 14, 1995.

99. *MKS*, June 25, 1996. The paper said that during the conference the foreign scientists would "link up with the permanently operating 'Center for Attracting Overseas Scientists and Engineers.' Seminars, special lectures, consulting, informal talks, and *on-site technical guidance* were to be carried out at industrial companies, research organizations, and universities" (my emphasis). Some 3,500 domestic S&T personnel were on hand to benefit from this "important opportunity to transmit the latest trends in advanced science and technology to South Korea's scientific community."

100. Ibid.

101. *MKS*, January 25, 1994.

102. *MKS*, June 10 and December 3, 1994. On March 29, 1995 *MKS* advertised a second "brainpool" recruitment drive aimed at "inviting superior overseas scientists

and engineers to Korea to work in research and development, in order to achieve the supreme national task of helping Korea enter the ranks of scientifically and technologically advanced countries by 2000." The phrase "overseas ethnic Korean and foreign scientists" appeared in the ad three times.

103. Brochure distributed by the Korea-U.S. Science Cooperation Center, Inc., 1952 Gallows Road, Vienna, Virginia, at its opening ceremony on February 20, 1997.

104. *MKS*, February 21, 1997.

105. The memorandum was one of several internal Korean language documents leaked by KSEA in 1996 in connection with a dispute over managerial rights. The dispute was more bureaucratic than substantive, since no one questioned the propriety of using ROK government funds, nor was there any quibble over the center's stated function. Whereas KOSEF wanted to establish it "as a local corporation, in accordance with the basic plans of the ROK government," KSEA argued for more autonomy to "avoid the impression that the South Korean side is able to control the board of directors at will," adding nonetheless that "the viewpoint of the ROK government will be reflected fully." KSEA also evinced concern that the center might be poorly received "by Americans in general" if its direct connection with Seoul were manifest.

106. <www.phy.duke.edu~myhan>, visited September 1998.

107. <www.AKPA.org>, visited May 1998. The labs include Argonne, Brookhaven, Fermi, Lawrence Livermore, Los Alamos, Oak Ridge, and Sandia National Laboratories, the Jet Propulsion Laboratory, and the Naval Research Laboratory.

108. *MKS*, June 16, 1994.

109. Ministry of Science and Technology press release August 28, 1996.

110. The Korean phrase is rendered into English parenthetically in the report as "strategic global sourcing of human resources."

111. *Chonja Sinmun*, October 9, 1997 and January 10, 1998.

112. *Chonja Sinmun*, September 30, 1997. The newspaper noted that Daewoo "is securing competent employees overseas by using Korean students studying abroad on company scholarships, its overseas branches, and its own research institutes established in the U.S., Japan, and Europe as information networks."

113. Cited by *Chonja Sinmun*, December 10, 1997.

114. Ibid.

115. My translation. Chong Ch'ang-hun, the author, was the newspaper's top S&T reporter at the time. His articles tracked consistently with government policy announcements and events. The Chief of MOST's Science and Technology Cooperation Division also served as director-general of the Korea-U.S. Science Cooperation Center.

116. *Chonja Sinmun*, July 15, 1998.

117. *Tonga Ilbo*, January 19, 1994.

118. *Yonhap*, December 26, 1997 and December 29, 1997.

119. *Korea Times*, March 12, 1998 and *Hanguk Ilbo*, April 28, 1998.

120. *Sindong-a*, July 1, 1999.

Chapter 4

1. See, for example, Sivin (1977, 1980), Qian (1985). Progress need not be measured in terms of scientific knowledge and exploitation of material resources alone. Human values can also be the yardstick of success. I personally see no conflict between the two and would argue that the one entails the other.

2. Chinese characters simultaneously represent syllables and morphemes, unlike Japanese *kana* and (formatted) Korean *hangul*, which primarily designate syllables and take up the same space as a character. Because of the large number of referents the Chinese character set must identify, they bear a commensurate degree of graphic redundancy well beyond what is needed to convey an individual syllable sound. When Chinese characters are used solely for their phonetic value their complexity is wasted, yielding one-character-per-syllable sequences that are more complex than needed for the amount of information conveyed.

3. Character shapes underwent different changes in China and Japan, making many of them unrecognizable to users of the other language and to Koreans, who mostly kept the original characters, when they use them at all.

4. Herbig (1996:73–74). Herbig also points out that "Only five Japanese scientists have ever won Nobel prizes . . . and most of the winners did their prize-winning work elsewhere. . . . The few Japanese Nobel Prize winners have few kind words to say about Japan" (64).

5. *Association of Korean Physicists in America Newsletter* 15, 3 (January 1994), reprinted with commentary in the online *Korean American Science and Technology News*, Issue 96–30 (August 7, 1996), visited October 1, 1996, at <www.phy.duke.edu~myhan>.

6. This term (*chojŏng* in Korean) is a genuine nuisance for translators, because it is used far more often in East Asian texts than is appropriate in a Western context. Also there are times when none of the standard English translations of "regulation, adjustment, co-ordination, control, or modulation" seems to apply. Often the best translation is simply "improvement."

7. Needham's own style approximates that of his subjects: strong in assembling concrete data but weak in theory and interpretation. Qian's observation that "Needham must be appreciated as a remarkable encyclopaedist, but not as a great philosophical historian; someone who raised many more important questions than he could satisfactorily answer" (1985:131) could apply to the history of Chinese science.

8. Needham's and other historians' views on the institutional causes of the problem are examined in Chapter 11 of the present book.

9. I am aware of the exceptions, such as the syllabaries used in Africa and the Americas, Tibet's pseudo-alphabet, and other intermediate types such as Semitic consonantal orthography. I take them up in later chapters.

10. Nakamura states, "There is a definite limit to the force of artistic imagination of the Chinese. Their attitude of observing only those things that can be concretely

experienced, that are grasped specifically through sensory effects directly perceived, weakens their power of imagination." They produced novels and dramas, but no epics. Chinese wrote "excellent poems, but most of the ideas expressed were concrete and stayed within the natural laws of time and space" (1964:217).

11. Bertram Russell wrote in *The Problem of China* (1922:194), "The distinctive merit of our civilization, I should say, is the scientific method; the distinctive merit of the Chinese is a just conception of the ends of life." Nathan Sivin also seems to regard the philosophical emphasis on moralism as part of the reason modern science failed to develop in China. Sivin notes that Chinese philosophy "tended to center on the problem of moral self-cultivation" and could not provide the same integration to science as happened in Europe. (1977:xvii). Chinese, according to this argument, put all their energy into finding the good within themselves and *consequently* were less concerned with material development. Qian Wen-yuan (1985:103) considers this line of thought one of two traditional (and false) explanations for the failure of modern science to develop in China (the other being political constraints).

12. It is amusing to note the appearance over the last few years of the term "sustainable development" (*kěchíxù fāzhǎn*) in Chinese S&T publications. The term—an English language loan translation—like the concept itself was introduced to the PRC scientific community from abroad through theoretical journals and is just now working its way into mainstream discourse. Chinese scientists and science managers have only recently begun to show concern for the country's natural environment, which by all accounts is in a deplorable state. Westernization only hastened a centuries-old disregard by China for its natural heritage, with deforestation, soil erosion, and pollution of inland waterways endemic throughout most of China's history. Two of my colleagues, both avid environmentalists, got their interest in the subject after extended tours in the PRC. Taiwan kindled my earliest awareness. I will leave it to someone else to fit these *concrete* facts into China's alleged efforts "to maintain the primordial unity."

13. Nakamura notes that "Diversity rather than similarity characterizes the realm of phenomena. Consequently, the Chinese, who depend upon perceived phenomena and value particulars, are naturally sensitive to the multiplicity of things, and rarely attempt to think about the universal validity of laws which regulate this multiplicity of things" (1964:217).

14. "Phonology" in Chinese is *yīnyùnxué*, literally "the study of rhymes." Yīn-wèixué, "the study of phonemes," is a more recent coinage. Chinese phonology did, of course, distinguish syllable "initials" and "finals" through *fǎnqiè*, a system of analogical spellings that grouped characters by rhyme. Their rhyming dictionaries also made provisions for different medial vowels. There was no attempt to define the segments of complex finals nor any effort made to symbolize the categories that were identified.

15. *Hangul* does identify phonemes and goes a step further by basing many of its letter shapes on a distinctive feature analysis. The effect of this remarkable

achievement was mitigated by *hangul*'s preservation of the orthographic syllable as the frame of reference (letters change size and shape depending on where they are in the written syllable), its co-use with Chinese characters, and the marginalization of *hangul* through most of its history by the educated classes.

16. Again, *hangul* texts are exceptional. Korean editors, publishers, linguists, and lexicographers have busied themselves over the past several decades creating the rules for word division needed by an all-*hangul* orthography. The results are still spotty and at times seem ad hoc.

17. This hypothesis, drawn from my understanding of linguistics, was stated earlier by Qian (1985:144), whose background is physics and historiography. According to Qian, "Methodologically . . . analysis must precede synthesis. Neither incompetence by the human intellect in analysis, nor a personal 'keen propensity for synthesis,' comprises a valid excuse to change this general rule of epistemology."

18. Nakamura likewise had little patience with the East Asian style of discourse, and ran afoul of linguists with statements like "Indifference to or lack of consciousness of the necessity for rules of language meant that the grammar was not developed" (1964:189). I'm not sure the grammar per se was undeveloped, but I do agree with the first part of his statement as pertains to usage.

Chapter 5

1. Churchland later offered a technical definition of creativity as "the capacity for the novel deployment and extension of existing activational prototypes in the face of novel or problematic phenomena, by means of vector completion and the recurrent manipulation of one's neuronal populations" (1995:279).

2. "The analogy mechanism is most likely to come into play when initial solution efforts based on available diachronic rules that describe the behavior of the target domain fail to generate an acceptable solution plan, resulting in an impasse" (Holland et al. 1986:307).

3. "The mind, owing to its hierarchy organization, functions on several levels at once, and often one level does not know what the other is doing; the essence of the creative act is bringing them together" (Koestler 1964:625).

4. Mitchell, who follows Hofstadter's model, also regards analogy as a special case of categorization: "Very similar, if not identical, mental mechanisms seem to underlie analogy-making, recognition, and categorization." All involve similarity comparisons. The difference may only be that categorical connections are more deeply entrenched (1993:3–5).

5. The psychologist William James wrote in 1890 that man "owes his whole preeminence as a reasoner, his whole human quality of intellect, we may say, to the faculty with which a given mode of thought in him may suddenly be broken up into elements, which recombine anew" (368). Deri (1984:37) observed similarly that "We have seen that productive, creative gestalt formation involves the capacity to

break up an existing gestalt into its elements and to use these for the organization of a new one." Brown (1997:47) wrote "the decomposition of wholes into parts . . . characterizes intuition and naive induction and is the basis of novel concepts in scientific and other forms of creative thought."

6. Robert W. Weisberg (1995:163) stated that "Insight occurs when a problem is solved through restructuring: That is, if we compare the initial solution attempt(s) with the insightful solution, they must be the result of different analyses of the problem." Kenneth S. Bowers, Peter Farvolden, and Lambers Mermigis (1995:31) wrote that "it is not the case that a hypothesis or full-fledged solution occurs unconsciously and then is simply transferred to consciousness. Rather, the very notion of a hypothesis or solution implies conscious appreciation of how a particular thought or idea organizes or fits the pattern of clues."

7. Edelman and Tononi argue in a recent book for distinct "primary" and "higher-order" conscious states, the latter one being symbolic, linguistic, and peculiar to humans. In their estimate, "neural changes that lead to language are behind the emergence of higher-order consciousness" (2000:193).

8. Blandshard wrote in 1939 that "the laws of deductive logic and even the canons of induction are tests for theories already achieved rather than devices for achieving them" (147).

9. As Brown noted, "creativity is a flight from deliberation in the service of novel concepts. The withdrawal from objects to their anticipatory constructs in spatial and imagined thought allows a more generic concept, i.e., one with the potential to develop into different modalities, to be realized in a specific cognitive domain" (1997:48).

10. The phenomenon is real enough to have commercial applications. In 1991, IBM began marketing a product called Visualization Data Explorer, which renders data-based problems into visual images to facilitate insightful solutions. According to the company, "This software can transform incredibly complex information into 3D images that make it easier to analyze data—to uncover patterns, identify trends, and model 'what-if' scenarios" (<www.research.ibm.com/dci/dx_release.html>, visited May 24, 1999).

11. Handedness was believed to predict hemispheric dominance, but the issue has turned out to be more complex. According to Calvin and Ojemann, "About 5 percent of all people have language in the right brain and another 5 to 6 percent have significant language functions in both halves. Although left-handers are found more often in the reversed-dominance and mixed-dominance groups, no pattern of hand use reliably predicts the side of the brain where the major language area resides" (1994:43).

12. The point is made by Fiore and Schooler (1998:349).

13. Bellugi et al. (1989:145–46, 164) note similarly that signers with left hemisphere lesions exhibit linguistic impairments analogous to those shown by speakers with such lesions. On the other hand, "signers with right-hemisphere damage were not aphasic. They exhibited fluent, grammatically correct, virtually error-free signing." But they

did show "the classic visuospatial impairments seen in hearing patients with right-hemisphere damage." Pinker also observed that "language, whether by ear and mouth or by eye and hand, is controlled by the left hemisphere" (1994:306).

14. Calvin and Ojemann found some electrical activity in the right hemisphere on language-related tasks, just as some neural activity was found in the left hemisphere during spatial tasks. But the *earliest* electrical activity appears in the left hemisphere for language and the right for shapes (1994:226).

15. Kevin Kelly discusses the theory that evolving systems are perpetually "balanced between rigidity and chaos." According to Kelly, the number of systems— physical and biological—that are "poised on the edge" is large enough to suggest that the phenomenon is universal. Viable systems are those that have learned to tread the thin line between repetition and randomness (1994:402–3).

16. Several years ago I had the unenviable job of assessing letters written by people from different East Asian countries that warned of UFO threats, global conspiracies, and other weird subjects which I won't get into. Some of these writers were privy to voices, which brings Jaynes's (1976) right hemisphere theories to mind. Handwriting aside, the grammar and word choice of most writers (they tended to be the same individuals) were no worse than average, so that the linguistic challenge was following the logic, as it were, from one thought to the next. At first I thought the letters were humorous. Then I found myself fighting off sadness and pity. Finally, when they started getting interesting, I knew I had enough. Schizophrenia is universal.

17. Interestingly, these orientations are reversed in the political terminology. The left brain's control of the body's right, and viceversa, were unknown through most of human history.

Chapter 6

1. I discussed the emergence of these schools of thought earlier (1997:236–37).

2. Readers typically access words or parts of words directly, through a visual pathway, and optionally retrieve a pronunciation from the lexical store for use as a mnemonic to hold the word in memory until its meaning can be integrated into the wider discourse. Phonology is literally added on as an afterthought, after the word has been accessed by a visual route. Thus the detection of phonological reflexes in various types of reading experiments cannot be relied on to indicate that phonology plays any role in the initial stages of the process, when lexical items are first addressed. Psycholinguists for the past two decades have been aware of this critical distinction between pre- and postaccess phonological coding and control for it, although their work seems to have escaped the notice of diehard structuralists who see the presence of phonology at any stage as evidence of its functional "primacy."

3. I except here the Chinese character-based scripts of East Asia, which com-

pound the conceptual hurdles that learners face with logistical problems far in excess of that presented by alphabetic orthography.

4. Andre Lecours (1989:34–36) in his studies of literate and illiterate stroke victims noted that the two groups are equally impaired by left-hemisphere damage, which he interpreted to mean "left cerebral dominance for language does not depend primarily on literacy." However, he also found in right-hemisphere stroke victims that linguistic impairment for illiterate people is worse than for literate people, which suggests that left-lateralization of language is accelerated by literacy.

5. Summarized by D'Angelo (1982:157).

6. Summarized by Goody (1987:205).

7. H. Innis, *Empirical Communication* (1950:10), cited in Robert Logan (1986).

8. Olson (1982:151–61); (1986:302–17).

9. Olson agrees that the causation was from alphabet to abstract thought, not the other way around. "Again, the point to note is that such a theory does not require the assumption that the Greeks attempted to represent phonemes; it does not assume the availability to consciousness of the phonological structure of language. Rather, the script can be seen as a model for that structure" (1994:85).

10. According to Yukawa, "Science developed mostly in Europe. Greek thought, it is often said, served in the broad sense as a basis from which all science was to develop. . . . [W]here there was no influence from Greek thought science underwent no development. Historically speaking, this is probably correct. Even in the case of Japan since the Meiji Restoration, the direct influence of Greek thought may have been small, yet indirectly at least it has provided the starting point for her adoption of the science developed in Europe" (1973:66).

11. Vygotsky (1962:99) observed that "Writing also requires analytical action on the part of the child. In speaking, he is hardly conscious of the sounds he pronounces and quite unconscious of the mental operations he performs. In writing, he must take cognizance of the sound structure of each word, dissect it, and reproduce it in alphabetical symbols, which he must have studied and memorized before." Alphabetic literacy becomes the model for abstract analysis. Logan (1986:19) agrees that "The information that is coded is not important; it is the act of coding itself that has been so influential and acted as a springboard for new ideas."

12. Generative grammarians have made something of a fetish over how a limited number of rules can be used to generate an unlimited number of sentences, but the principle is worth invoking in this context. It is also necessary to bear in mind that the absence of rules does not produce novelty; it yields chaos. Due largely to their character-based orthographies, East Asians freely juxtapose one morpheme with another on the basis of subjective criteria, without regard to precedent or intelligibility. This would seem to encourage creativity, were it not for two critical facts: (1) the same holistic syllable-morphemes are reshuffled. There is no modeling of analytic processes. (2) If everything is connected, nothing is. Connections imply the *absence* of links between some elements of the set. I am grateful to Dr. Marc Damashek, a specialist in n-grams and data mapping, for pointing this out to me.

13. A morpheme is defined as the conventional interface between language and thought. It can be thought of as a two-sided structure with meaning on one side and a linguistic address on the other. The address is in the form of a speech code or, for literate persons, a speech and an orthographic code.

14. According to M. Martin Taylor, "Always the RIGHT track provides alternatives, multiple interpretations and various viewpoints, while the LEFT track checks the logical relations that preclude or favor various of these interpretations" (1988:324).

15. Gazzaniga summarized neuroscientists' opinion on the issue as follows, "certain universal aspects of human behavior, such as our capacity for language, are largely determined by genetic processes, while variations in our capacities are shaped by the environment. . . . Taken together, today's prevalent views argue for genetic constraints with plenty of leeway built into the brain to allow for modification of behavior through learning" (1992:2).

16. Deacon later argues that language produced the human mind. "And I don't mean this in a figurative sense. I mean that the major structural and functional innovations that make human brains capable of unprecedented mental feats evolved in response to the use of something as abstract and virtual as the power of words. Or, to put this miracle in simple terms, I suggest that an idea changed the brain" (1997:322).

17. Calvin explains that "even a cortical area with 'expert' long-term ruts could serve as a work space, using overlaid short-term ruts to bias competitions" (1996:140).

18. Bellugi, Tzeng, Klima, and Fok (1989).

Chapter 7

1. A short list includes William G. Boltz (1994), John DeFrancis (1977, 1984); Yaeko Sato Habein (1984); William C. Hannas (1997); Michel Paradis et al. (1985); Young-Key Kim Renaud (1997); Insup Taylor and Martin M. Taylor (1995); and J. Marshal Unger (1987). These books differ on points of interpretation but their reporting of facts is generally reliable.

2. *Liè* additionally means "sound of the wind" when reduplicated.

3. This is not to say that all *words* are monosyllabic, any more than English words are. Single-syllable morphemes in Chinese Mandarin combine to form polysyllabic words.

4. The language itself is called *Wú* and has no common English translation. Shanghainese is its most prestigious dialect.

5. A proper translation of *fāngyán* is "topolect," defined as "A set of similar dialects constituting any of the larger distinct regional varieties of a language" (*American Heritage Dictionary*, 4th ed., 2000).

6. Cantonese has a minor orthographic tradition carried on locally in signs, informal writing, textbooks, and some newspapers. Lately there have even been sev-

eral moderately popular novels written in Cantonese. Its texts are largely illegible to Chinese literate only in the standard Mandarin-based script.

7. Although the characters do not depict sound discretely, substructures loosely associated with certain syllables reappear throughout the corpus with enough regularity for users to exploit. However, sound mergers and splits distributed the relationship between phonetic sets (characters with the same substructure) and pronunciation differently by language, further reducing the characters' transitivity across Sinitic languages.

8. *Pinyin* is China's official alphabetic notation used in conjunction with (not as a substitute for) character writing. Since the demise of China's writing reform movement some three decades ago, PRC linguists have been careful not to use the term "script" (*wénzì*) to refer to their national alphabet.

9. Phonetic change, including the loss of all but two final consonants, reduced that figure in modern Mandarin to 1,280 syllables (including tone).

10. The vocalic elements of the four quasi-syllabic forms -*ki*, -*ku*, -*ti*, -*tu* that were added to capture original Chinese consonant endings are deemphasized in speech, so the *onyomi* largely retain their monosyllabic characteristic.

11. By the fourteenth century a restricted set of characters, severely reduced in form, was used in Korea to gloss Chinese texts with Korean grammatical inflections, enabling Koreans to read the Chinese as if it were Korean. Known as *kugyŏl*, the system would not have worked were it not for the many Sinitic borrowings that made much of formal Korean read like Chinese. In Japan the same practice of lacing Chinese texts with enough hints through *katakana* and diacritics to make it read like Japanese was called *kambun*. In both countries the practice effectively removed the distinction between Chinese and borrowed Chinese vocabulary.

12. The *han* in *hangul* means "Korea." It is a different morpheme from the *han* used in *hanja* meaning "Chinese."

13. Ko Yong-gun (1989); Kim Min-su (1989).

14. Detailed information on East Asia's writing reforms can be found in the following sources: Blank (1981); DeFrancis (1950); Gottlieb (1996); Hannas (1997); Martin (1982); Seybolt and Chiang (1978).

15. The proposal was made by Mori Arinori (1847–89), who later became Japan's Minister of Education.

16. The term is translated by DeFrancis (1977) as "demotic script" in recognition of its function as a vehicle to write the popular language. Chinese language and writing (called *chū nho* or "scholarly writing") was preferred by the educated elite.

Chapter 8

1. Grassroots reforms during China's Cultural Revolution (1965–75), and in some cases earlier, produced a few hybrid characters that stand for multisyllable words and expressions. They number about a dozen.

2. The Sinitic formula's strict iconicity, where each element of the linguistic sign is a single, unanalyzed unit, is hardly conducive to creative thinking and surely has a numbing effect on the psyche at some level. As Koestler wrote in his book on creativity, "When rhythm assumes a rigidly repetitive form it no longer recalls the pulsation of life, but the motions of an automaton; its superimposition on human behavior is degrading" 1964:132). What rhythm could be more "rigidly repetitive" than an endless procession of monosyllabic morphemes? Every printed unit in Chinese is the same size. When the units are pronounced, they are the same length (one syllable). Words are minimally differentiated, the vast majority consisting of one or two syllables.

3. George Sansom, who can hardly be accused of not knowing Japanese, wrote, "One hesitates for an epithet to describe a system of writing which is so complex that it needs the aid of another system to explain it. There is no doubt that it provides for some a fascinating field of study, but as a practical instrument it is surely without inferiors" (1928:44). An Australian reviewer of my earlier book (1997) suggested that my failure to appreciate the character writing system and much of its historical content be attributed to poor Chinese language skills. I wonder what he thinks of Lu Xun's ability with Chinese or Hu Shi's, both of whom backed writing reform and separating the modern language from the classical. Did Ch'oe Hyonbae and Ho Ung show ignorance of their native tongue by trying to get Chinese characters out of Korean? There are thousands of East Asians who detest the character writing system and its cultural legacy enough to have organized movements against it. Dismissing the argument for writing reform on this basis won't work.

4. Vietnamese historically aimed at this very effect by distorting the Roman letters that made up a written syllable and compressing them into a single, character-like block. The practice survives today in funerary inscriptions.

5. I have read experimental texts written in this manner and can attest that there is something psychologically different between them and normal Vietnamese writing. Although establishing universal conventions for word division will take time, there seem to be no technical obstacles to its realization. The aesthetic effect is also quite stunning.

6. The non-Mandarin Chinese languages, which historically and even today make up a significant part of the Chinese that is spoken, are generally not written. Speakers of these languages read Mandarin materials as a bilingual exercise.

7. Lee Ki-mun (1977:60), Kontsevicha (1979:28).

8. According to Gleitman and Rozin, "At least 7 ancient societies independently invented syllabary notations, and there are some modern instances. . . . In contrast, to the best of our knowledge, an alphabetic system was invented only once, and even this once not by a clear and exhaustive insight into the phonemic notion: development . . . took hundreds of years" (1973:463).

9. Vietnamese *ng-* and *tr-* initials are orthographic conventions for single-consonant phonemes.

10. According to Yunsook Hong, "the surface form of the syllable structure is

confined to (C)V(C). . . . In the coda structure of C1C2, either C1 or C2 must be deleted while the other member of the cluster is retained. This condition is obligatory" (1991:90).

11. The letters -c and -t in final position are realized as a coarticulated bilabial stop ([k] and [p] pronounced simultaneously) after back vowels in Southern Vietnamese.

12. The Beijing and Tianjin variety of Mandarin has an additional final consonant [r] added to some words as a diminutive. Its use outside the capital area is mostly affected.

13. Steinberg and Yamada (1978a) in a much maligned article also demonstrated the practicality of introducing reading to problem learners through syllables. Their use of Chinese characters as a syllable medium, chosen for reasons of availability, was seized by supporters of the character script as "proof" of its superiority, and misconstrued by others as an endorsement of character-based orthography. In fact, Steinberg and Yamada claimed nothing about the efficacy of characters per se, and noted that their complexity very quickly became "intrusive."

14. An exception was Dr. Yu-chen Fan, author of a recent dissertation on Taiwanese case grammar (Georgetown University 2001), who was far ahead of me in analyzing the phonology of her own language.

15. Most accounts list thirty "consonant" letters, but two of them are for the vowel [a] in upper and lower tone. Tibetan orthography has also been criticized for not reflecting tonal distinctions, but this is untrue. Tibetan tones (there are only two of them) are mostly a function of the segmental phonology and are predictable on that basis; in those few cases where there is overlap, i.e., [sha], [sa], and [a], different letters are used.

16. Goody wrote, "the notion of literacy . . . having a direct, precise, immediate and unmediated effect on general cognitive abilities in a specific psychological sense is a non-starter" (1987:216–17). D'Angelo conceded that "disturbing questions about the relationship between literacy and cognitive development" were raised (1982:167).

17. Scribner and Cole agree that "the relationship between word concepts and rules of graphic representation (segmentation of script into word units) merits further exploration" (1981:157).

18. Another gem buried in Scribner and Cole's study that has been overlooked by adherents of the language-as-speech school concerns the effects of writing on speech. The authors noted, "Studies of the relationship between oral and written language . . . have been predominantly concerned with examining the influence of speech on writing. Yet, in the auditory integration task, we found evidence suggesting that influences may operate in the other direction. . . . Specifically we make a case here that changes in word pronunciation and word reference are both due to the same underlying mechanism—namely, that literacy alters individuals' internal representations of language, and these representations mediate the differences we observe in speech characteristics" (1981:187).

19. I am indebted to Nate Y., physicist, native Chinese speaker, and accomplished translator of technical materials, for pointing this out to me.

20. Needham's chronology of Chinese scientific achievements is paralleled by an extensive list of technological innovations that Donald argues preceded *any* form of writing. As Donald put it, "The complex technological and social developments that preceded writing might suggest the existence of some apparently analytical thought skills that contained germinal elements leading to later theoretic development. However, early inventions were pragmatic and generally not far removed from nature. . . . These pragmatic developments, impressive as they were, lacked the essentially reflective and representational nature of theory" (1991:333–35).

Chapter 9

1. Lev S. Vygotsky's (1896–1934) translated works were collected and published posthumously by MIT Press in 1962.

2. Calvin (1996) provides a more sophisticated description of this "Darwinian" competition for synaptic resources, which accounts for much of our cognitive structure.

3. Pinker suggests as one definition of *word* "a linguistic object that . . . behaves as the indivisible, smallest unit with respect to the laws of syntax" (1994:48).

4. Donald observes that "The purely linguistic act of instantiating a given literary idea under the guidance of a particularly mythic mode may be a more technical, or 'front-end,' matter, but the driving forces behind the products of the literary imagination go much deeper, to the author's perceptions of large-scale literary themes, whose cognitive roots are ultimately mimetic" (1991:170).

5. Olson (1994:242) captured this point succinctly, "Consciousness of words permits their distinction from the ideas that words express."

6. Semitic languages written without vowels have always used word division to compensate for what the orthography does not specify on the phonological level.

7. Saenger expands these observations in his 1997 book *Space Between Words: The Origins of Silent Reading.*

8. Olson (1994:164) cites passages by late Renaissance thinkers that demonstrate a clear awareness by this time of the difference between words and concepts. Francis Bacon (1561–1626), for example, wrote, "A syllogism consists of propositions, a proposition of words, and words are the counters or symbols of notions or mental concepts," *Cogitata et Visa*, in *The Works of Francis Bacon*, ed. James Spedding, Robert Leslie Ellis, Douglas Denon Heath, and William Rawley (Boston: Brown and Taggart, 1860–64), 7:125.

9. Hangul, of course, is an exception. However, the problem affects South Koreans inasmuch as Chinese characters constitute a significant part of the orthography. Recent media reports show the pendulum of government support, which

oscillates between reform and tradition, swinging back in favor of the characters, for now anyway.

10. "Orthography, Reading, and Cerebral Functions," in de Kerckhove and Lumsden, eds., *The Alphabet and the Brain* (1988). Tzeng and Hung agree with my position that phonological recoding is not necessary for reading "a large number of words" in alphabetically written languages. They also agree with the thesis that Chinese *can* be read by phonological codes (276). This issue here is one of relative tendencies.

Chapter 10

1. I exclude optical character recognition because the main problem is how text is generated in the first place. OCR technology potentially puts character-based and alphabetic text on the same footing *only for text that has already been written*, although software costs will continue to be higher for East Asian languages due to the complexity of the character set.

2. Professor Victor Mair (personal communication, September 15, 2000) points out that in China the computer input system pushed by the government consists of completely arbitrary sequences of keystrokes assigned to each character. The system is suitable only for professional typists who *copy* from written or printed texts. Even with their years of training and experience they often have to look up the codes for characters beyond the 5,000 or so most common ones, or resort to *pinyin* input to call them up.

3. The genesis of the script in oracle bone inscriptions bears this out: they were formulaic in the extreme.

4. There are two views on this issue. One view, advanced by Swedish linguist Bernard Karlgren, holds that the greater number of phonetic distinctions in the ancient language made the monosyllabic texts phonetically intelligible. Language spoken in the same manner could be understood. The other view, which I find more plausible, is that written Chinese originated as an abbreviated code that developed more or less independently of the spoken languages, borrowing from them as needed, but never in its *wényán* form representing any spoken variety.

5. In Korea the movement took the form of a struggle between supporters of the mixed Chinese character-*hangul* script, which tends to follow the elliptical style of formal literary Chinese, and the all-*hangul* script, which being entirely phonetic must approximate speech to be understood. Early attempts to translate classical Korean into all-*hangul* by transcribing the original characters with phonetic symbols were notorious failures.

6. Korean's use of word-division resulted from a conscious decision by language planners decades ago to facilitate all-*hangul* writing.

7. Evidence for this claim in found in *Sources and Methods of Obtaining National Defense Science and Technology Intelligence*, whose authors complain about the poor

diffusion of Chinese language S&T materials within China. The book is primarily a guide to exploiting defense-related scientific documents in Western languages. It includes several alphabetical indexes of Western publications.

Chapter 11

1. Findlay and Lumsden regard decentralized government as "the single best political predictor of creativity" (1988:27).

2. Robert Pirsig's (1974, 1991) fascination with the Native American influence on European civilization brought into the United States stems in part from its democratizing effect on Old World culture, expressed as a shift from top-down to lateral thinking. The mingling of diverse cultures in the United States strikes me as a textbook case of the dynamic interaction that supports creativity.

3. The Confucian "gentleman" (*jūnzi*) was the fungible generalist par excellance. According to Bodde (1991:213), scholars were encouraged to concentrate on "broadly humanistic studies—the classics, the major histories, the major literary works—at the expense of other more specialized and more scientific subjects. . . . Thus the overwhelming majority of educated men who entered the civil service did so on the basis of what would today be called a 'liberal arts' education."

4. Literally, the "two [upper] classes" of the Korean aristocracy or nobility.

5. Lumsden defines "epigenesis" as "the total process of interaction between genes and the environment during development" (1988:19).

6. Frans de Waal in "The End of Nature Versus Nurture" (1999) argues similarly for a convergence of views by biologists, who have been prone to see genetic causes for everything, and social scientists "who have flocked to the opposite position: that we are fully and entirely our own creation, free from the chains of biology." He explains, "genes, by themselves, are like seeds dropped onto the pavement: powerless to produce anything. When scientists say that a trait is inherited, all they mean is that part of its variability is explained by genetic factors. That the environment usually explains at least as much tends to be forgotten" (98). Matt Ridley also accepts the basic tenets of gene-culture coevolution, as evidenced in the following passage: "After two million years of culture, in which our ancestors passed on learnt local conditions, human brains may have acquired (through natural selection) the ability to find and specialize in those particular skills that the local culture teaches, and that the individual excels in" (2000:90).

7. Japan has moved beyond targeting its own expatriate nationals and is less discriminatory about whom it approaches for informal IPR transfers.

8. See Eftimiades (1994) and Schweizer (1993). The U.S. Central Intelligence Agency and Federal Bureau of Investigation are required by law to issue an annual report on Chinese espionage activities directed at the United States, which is publicly available through the U.S. Government Printing Office.

9. The seat of the human capacity for language learning is uncertain. Generative

grammarians and cognitive scientists under their influence believe the brain developed an innate mechanism for learning language, which they call, somewhat unimaginatively, a "language acquisition device." The universality of speech and the ease with which it is acquired are cited in support of this "nativist" view. As I noted earlier in this book, Terrence Deacon (1997) argues from the opposite perspective, namely, that *language* evolved to match preexisting cognitive categories.

10. Read May 2, 2000.

Chapter 12

1. South Korea's Ministry of Education publishes charts of *hangul* consonant and vowel combinations arranged in a grid to show their application as syllables. School primers typically drill the sounds and letters in syllabic contexts.

2. Scientists at U.S. nuclear labs reportedly call recent efforts by security personnel to clamp down on abuses "the revenge of the C-minuses."

3. *Xinhua*, March 27, 2000.

Bibliography

Abra, Jock. 1988. *Assaulting Parnassus: Theoretical Views of Creativity.* Lanham, Md.: University Press of America.

Agassi, Joseph. 1988. "Analogies Hard and Soft." In Helman, ed. (1988).

Aitchison, Jean. 1987. *Words in the Mind.* New York: Basil Blackwell.

Amabile, Teresa M. and Jonathan M. Check. 1985. "Commentary." In Findlay and Lumsden (1988).

Amirova, T. A. 1977. *K istorii i teorii grafemiki (On the History and Theory of Graphemes).* Moscow: Akademia Nauka.

———. 1985. *Funktsional'naya vzaimosvyaz' pis'mennogo i zvukovogo yazyka (Functional Interdependence of Written and Spoken Language).* Moscow: Akademia Nauka.

Andersson, Ake E. and Nils-Eric Sahlin, eds. 1997. *The Complexity of Creativity.* Dordrecht: Kluwer Academic.

Baum, Richard. 1982. "Science and Culture in Contemporary China." *Asian Survey* (December).

Beeman, Mark. 1998. "Coarse Semantic Coding and Discourse Comprehension." In Beeman and Chiarello, eds. (1998).

Beeman, Mark and Christine Chiarello. 1998. "Concluding Remarks." In Beeman and Chiarello, eds. (1998).

———, eds. 1998. *Right Hemisphere Language Comprehension.* Hillsdale, N.J.: Lawrence Erlbaum.

Bell, Alan and Joan B. Hooper. 1978. "Issues and Evidence in Syllabic Phonology." In Bell and Hooper eds. (1978).

———, eds. 1978. *Syllables and Segments.* Amsterdam: North-Holland.

Bellugi, Ursula, Ovid Tzeng, Edward S. Klima, and Angela Fok. 1989. "Dyslexia: Perspectives for Sign and Script." In Galaburda, ed. (1989).

Bernstein, Richard and Ross H. Munro. 1997. *The Coming Conflict with China.* New York: Alfred A. Knopf.

Bertelson, Paul and Beatrice De Gelden. 1989. "Learning About Reading from Illiterates." In Galaburda, ed. (1989).

Bisiach, Edoardo. 1988. "Language Without Thought." In Weiskrantz, ed. (1988).

Blanshard, Brand. 1939/1969. *The Nature of Thought.* London: George Allen and Unwin.

Blank, Lenore Kim. 1981. "Language Policies in South Korea and Their Probable Impact on Education." Ph.D. dissertation, University of San Francisco.

Bloom, Alfred. 1981. *The Linguistic Shaping of Thought: A Study in the Impact of Language in Thinking in China and the West.* Hillsdale, N.J.: Lawrence Erlbaum.

Bloom, Richard. 1998. "The Alphabet and the Ideograph: The ABCs of Political Conflict." *International Bulletin of Political Philosophy* 4, 15 (April 17). Posted to <www.pr.erau.edu>.

Bloomfield, Leonard. 1933/1984. *Language.* Chicago: University of Chicago Press.

Blumstein, Sheila. 1978. "Segment and Structure and the Syllable in Aphasia." In Bell and Hooper, eds. (1978).

Bodde, Derk. 1991. *Chinese Thought, Society, and Science.* Honolulu: University of Hawaii Press.

Boden, Margaret A. 1991. *The Creative Mind: Myths and Mechanisms.* New York: Basic Books.

———, ed. 1994. *Dimensions of Creativity.* Cambridge, Mass.: MIT Press.

Bogan, Joseph E. and Glenda M. Bogan. 1976. "Creativity and the Bisected Brain." In Rothenberg and Hausman, eds. (1976).

Bolinger, Dwight. 1968. *Aspects of Language.* New York: Harcourt, Brace and World.

Boltz, William G. 1994. *Origin and Early Development of the Chinese Writing System.* Ann Arbor: American Oriental Society.

Boodberg, Peter A. 1937. "Some Proleptical Remarks on the Evolution of Archaic Chinese." *Harvard Journal of Asiatic Studies* 2:329–72.

Bowers, Kenneth S., Peter Farvolden, and Lambers Mermigis. 1995. "Intuitive Antecedents of Insight." In Smith, Ward, and Fink, eds. (1995).

Brick, Ingar. 1997. "The Gist of Creativity." In Andersson and Sahlin, eds. (1997).

Brown, Jason W. 1997. "Process and Creation." In Andersson and Sahlin, eds. (1997).

Bylinski, Gene. 1978. "The Japanese Spies in Silicon Valley." *Fortune*, February 27, 74–79.

———. 1987. "Trying to Transcend Copycat Science." *Fortune*, March 30, 42–47.

Calvin, William H. 1996. *How Brains Think.* New York: Basic Books.

Calvin, William H. and George A. Ojemann. 1994. *Conversations with Niel's Brain.* Reading, Mass.: Addison-Wesley.

Capra, Fritjof, 1985. *The Tao of Physics.* Boston: New Science Library.

Chen Hsuan-chih, ed. 1997. *Cognitive Processing of Chinese and Related Asian Languages.* Hong Kong: Chinese University Press.

Chen Hsuan-chih and Ovid J. L. Tzeng. 1992. *Language Processing in Chinese.* Amsterdam: North-Holland.

Chiarello, Christine. 1998. "On Codes of Meaning and the Meanings of Codes: Semantic Access and Retrieval Within and Between Hemispheres." In Beeman and Chiarello, eds. (1998).

Ch'oe Hyon-bae. 1946. *Kŭlja ŭi hyŏngmyŏng (Revolution in Writing).* Seoul: *Chŏng'ŭm* Sa.

Chomsky, Noam. 1957. *Syntactic Structures.* The Hague: Mouton.

———. 1965. *Aspects of the Theory of Syntax.* Cambridge, Mass.: MIT Press.

Churchland, Paul M. 1995. *The Engine of Reason, the Seat of the Soul.* Cambridge, Mass.: MIT Press.

Congress of the United States, Office of Technology Assessment. 1987. *Technology Transfer to China.* Washington, D.C.: U.S. Government Printing Office. OTA-ISC-340.

———. 1999. *Report of the Select Committee on U.S. National Security and Military/ Commercial Concerns with the People's Republic of China.* Washington, D.C.: U.S. Government Printing Office.

Copp, Newton and Andrew Zanella. 1993. *Discovery, Innovation, and Risk.* Cambridge, Mass.: MIT Press.

Crichton, Michael. 1992. *Rising Sun.* New York: Alfred A. Knopf.

Csikszentmihalyi, Mihaly and Keith Sawyer. 1995. "Creative Insight: The Social Dimension of a Solitary Moment." In Sternberg and Davidson, eds. (1995).

Dalton, Donald H. and Phyllis A. Genther. 1991. *The Role of Corporate Linkages in U.S.-Japan Technology Transfer.* Washington, D.C.: U.S. Department of Commerce.

Dalton, Donald H. and Manuel G. Serapio, Jr. 1995. *Globalizing Industrial Research and Development.* Washington, D.C.: U.S. Department of Commerce.

D'Angelo, Frank J. 1982. "Luria and Literacy: The Cognitive Consequences of Reading and Writing." In Raymond, ed. (1982).

Deacon, Terrence W. 1997. *The Symbolic Species.* New York: W.W. Norton.

DeFrancis, John. 1950. *Nationalism and Language Reform in China.* Princeton, N.J.: Princeton University Press.

———. 1977. *Colonialism and Language Policy in Vietnam.* The Hague: Mouton.

———. 1984. *The Chinese Language: Fact and Fantasy.* Honolulu: University of Hawaii Press.

———. 1989. *Visible Speech.* Honolulu: University of Hawaii Press.

de Kerckhove, Derrick. 1986. "Alphabetic Literacy and Brain Processes." *Visible Language* 20, 3:274–93.

———. 1988. "Inventio." In Findlay and Lumsden (1988).

de Kerckhove, Derrick and Charles J. Lumsden, eds. 1988 *The Alphabet and the Brain: The Lateralization of Writing.* Berlin: Springer-Verlag.

DeLuca, John. 1988. "Shedding Light on the Rising Sun." *International Journal of Intelligence and Counterintelligence* 2, 1:1–20.

Deri, Susan K. 1984. *Symbolization and Creativity.* New York: International Universities Press.

de Waal, Frans B. M. 1999. "The End of Nature Versus Nurture." *Scientific American* 281, 6:94–99.

Di Sciullo, Anna-Maria and Edwin Williams. 1987. *On the Definition of Word.* Cambridge, Mass.: MIT Press.

Dennett, Daniel C. 1996. *Kinds of Minds.* New York: Basic Books.

Donald, Merlin. 1991. *Origins of the Modern Mind.* Cambridge, Mass.: Harvard University Press.

Doremus, Paul N., William W. Keller, Louis W. Panly, and Simon Reich. 1998. *The Myth of the Global Corporation.* Princeton, N.J.: Princeton University Press.

Dreyfuss, Joel. 1987. "How Japan Picks America's Brains." *Fortune,* December 21, 79–89.

Duggan, Patricia and Gale Eisenstodt. 1990. "The New Face of Japanese Espionage." *Forbes,* November 12, 96.

Dunbar, Kevin. 1995. "How Scientists Really Reason: Scientific Reasoning in Real-World Laboratories." In Sternberg and Davidson, eds. (1995).

Du Ponceau, Peter S. 1838. *A Dissertation on the Nature and Character of the Chinese System of Writing.* Philadelphia: McCarty and Davis for the American Philosophical Society.

Dutton, Denis and Michael Krausz, eds. 1981. *The Concept of Creativity in Science and Art.* The Hague: Martinus Nijhoff.

Eccles, John C. 1989. *Evolution of the Brain: Creation of the Self.* London: Routledge.

Edelman, Gerald M. and Giulio Tononi. 2000. *The Universe of Consciousness.* New York: Basic Books.

Eftimiades, Nicholas. 1994. *Chinese Intelligence Operations.* Annapolis, Md.: Naval Institute Press.

Elvin, Mark. 1973. *The Pattern of the Chinese Past.* Stanford, Calif.: Stanford University Press.

Endo, Masaomi, Akinori Shimizu, and Tadao Hori. 1978. "Functional Asymmetry of Visual Fields for Japanese Words in *Kana* (Syllable-Based) Writing and Random Shape Recognition in Japanese Subjects." *Neuropsychologia* 16: 291–97.

Eysenck, Hans J. 1994. "The Measurement of Creativity." In Boden, ed. (1994).

Faligot, Roger. 1996. "China's Intelligence Agency." *Politique Internationale* (Winter): 72–76.

Fallows, James. 1995. *Looking at the Sun.* New York: Vintage Books.

Fialka, John J. 1997. *War by Other Means: Economic Espionage in America.* New York: W.W. Norton.

Filin, F. P., ed. 1967. *Yazik i Myshlenie (Language and Thought).* Moscow: Akademia Nauka.

Findlay, C. Scott and Charles J. Lumsden. 1988. *The Creative Mind.* London: Academic Press.

Finke, Ronald A., Thomas B. Ward, and Steven M. Smith. 1996. *Creative Cognition: Theory, Research, and Applications.* Cambridge, Mass.: MIT Press.

Fiore, Stephen M. and Jonathan W. Schooler. 1998. "Right Hemisphere Contributions to Creative Problem Solving: Converging Evidence for Divergent Thinking." In Beeman and Chiarello, eds. (1998).

Fischer, William A. 1989. "China's Industrial Innovation: The Influence of Market Forces." In Simon and Goldman, eds. (1989).

Foss, Donald J. and David T. Hakes. 1978. *Psycholinguistics.* Englewood Cliffs, N.J.: Prentice-Hall.

Frieman, Wendy. 1989. "China's Military R&D System: Reform and Reorientation." In Simon and Goldman, eds. (1989).

Galaburda, Albert M., ed. 1989. *From Reading to Neurons.* Cambridge, Mass.: MIT Press.

Gardner, Howard. 1994. "The Creator's Pattern." In Boden, ed. (1994).

Gazzaniga, Michael S. 1992. *Nature's Mind.* New York: Basic Books.

Gelb, I. J. 1962. *A Study of Writing.* Chicago: University of Chicago Press.

Gertz, Bill. 1992. "Japanese Intelligence Network Is All Business." *Washington Times,* February 9, A6.

Gick, Mary L. and Robert S. Lockhart. 1995. "Cognition and Affective Components of Insight." In Sternberg and Davidson, eds. (1995).

Gilley, Bruce. 1999. "China's Spy Guide." *Far Eastern Economic Review* (December 23).

Gleitman, Lila R., Henry Gleitman, Barbara Landau, and Eric Wanner. 1989. "Great Expectations." In Galaburda, ed. (1989).

Gleitman, Lila R. and Paul Rozin. 1973. "Teaching Reading by Use of a Syllabary." *Reading Research Quarterly* 8, 3:494–500.

Glickman, Norman J. and Douglas P. Woodward. 1989. *The New Competitors.* New York: Basic Books.

Goody, Jack, ed. 1968. *Literacy in Traditional Societies.* Cambridge: Cambridge University Press.

———. 1986. *The Logic of Writing and the Organization of Society.* Cambridge: Cambridge University Press.

———. 1987. *The Interface Between the Written and the Oral.* Cambridge: Cambridge University Press.

Goody, Jack, and Ian Watt. 1968. "The Consequences of Literacy." In Goody ed. (1968).

Goswami, Usha and Peter Bryant. 1990. *Phonological Skills and Learning to Read.* Hillsdale, N.J.: Lawrence Erlbaum.

Gottlieb, Nanette. 1996. *Kanji Politics.* New York: Columbia University Press.

———. 2000. "Language Nationalism: Kanji on the Internet." *South Pacific Journal of Psychology* 10. Posted to <hiplab.newcastle.edu.au/pacific/gottleib.htm>.

Grant, Patricia Ellen. 1988. "Language Processing: A Neuroanatomical Primer." In de Kerckhove and Lumsden, eds. (1988).

Habein, Yaeko Sato. 1984. *The History of the Japanese Written Language.* Tokyo: University of Tokyo Press.

Halamka, John D. 1984. *Espionage in the Silicon Valley.* Berkeley, Calif.: Sybex.

Hall, Ivan P. 1998. *Cartels of the Mind: Japan's Intellectual Closed Shop.* New York: W.W. Norton.

Hannas, William C. 1997. *Asia's Orthographic Dilemma.* Honolulu: University of Hawaii Press.

Hansen, James H. 1996. *Japanese Intelligence—The Competitive Edge.* Dexter, Mich.: Thomson-Shore.

Harnad, Stevan. 1982. Metaphor and Mental Duality. In Simon and Scholes, eds. (1982).

Hashimoto Mantaro, Suzuki Takao, and Yamada Hisao. 1987. *Kanji minzoku no ketsudan: kanji no mirai ni mukete (A Decision for the Chinese Character Nation: Toward the Future of Chinese Characters).* Tokyo: Daishukan shoten.

Hatta, Takeshi. 1977. "Recognition of *Kanji* in the Left and Right Visual Fields." *Neuropsychologia* 15:685–88.

———. 1978. "Recognition of Japanese *Kanji* and *Hiragana* in the Left and Right Visual Fields." *Japanese Psychological Research* 20, 2:51–59.

Havelock, Eric. 1982. *The Literate Revolution in Greece and Its Cultural Consequences.* Princeton, N.J.: Princeton University Press.

———. 1987. "Chinese Characters and the Greek Alphabet." *Sino-Platonic Papers* 5:1–4.

———. 1991. "The Oral-Literate Equation: A Formula for the Modern Mind." In Olson and Torrance, eds. (1991).

Hayakawa, S. I. 1949/1990. *Language in Thought and Action.* New York: Harcourt.

Hellige, Joseph B. 1993. *Hemispheric Asymmetry: What's Right and What's Left.* Cambridge, Mass.: Harvard University Press.

Helman, David H., ed. 1988. *Analogical Reasoning.* Dordrecht: Kluwer Academic.

Hennessey, Beth A. and Teresa M. Amabile. 1988. "The Conditions of Creativity." In Sternberg, ed. (1988).

Herbig, Paul. 1995. *Innovation Japanese Style.* Westport, Conn.: Quorom Books.

Hesse, Mary. 1988. "Theories, Family Resemblances, and Analogy." In Helman, ed. (1986).

Heymann, Hans. 1975. *China's Approach to Technology Acquisition.* Santa Monica, Calif.: RAND Corporation.

Hirata, K. and R. Osaka. 1969. "Tachistoscopic Recognition of Japanese Letter Materials in Left and Right Visual Fields." *Neuropsychologia* 7:179–87.

Hockett, Charles. 1947/1966. "Problems of Morphemic Analysis." *Language* 23:321–43. Reprinted in Martin Joos. ed., *Readings in Linguistics I.* Chicago: University of Chicago Press.

Hofstadter, Douglas, and FARG. 1995. *Fluid Concepts and Creative Analogies.* New York: Basic Books.

Holland, John H., Keith J. Holyoak, Richard E. Nisbett, and Paul R. Thagard. 1986. *Induction: Processes of Inference, Learning, and Discovery.* Cambridge, Mass.: MIT Press.

Hong, Yunsook. 1991. *A Sociolinguistic Study of Seoul Korean.* Seoul: Research Center for Peace and Unification.

Huo Zhongwen and Wang Zongxiao. 1991. *Guófáng Kējì Qíngbàoyuán Jì Huòqǔ Jìshù* (*Sources and Methods of Obtaining National Defense Science and Technology Intelligence*). Beijing: Kexue Jishu Wenxuan Publishing Co.

Illich, Ivan. 1991. "A Plea for Research on Lay Literacy." In Olson and Torrance, eds. (1991).

Illich, Ivan and Barry Sanders. 1989. *ABC: The Alphabetization of the Popular Mind.* New York: Vintage Books.

Ingram, David. 1978. "The Role of the Syllable in Phonological Development." In Bell and Hooper, eds. (1978).

Jackendoff, Ray. 1992. *Languages of the Mind.* Cambridge, Mass.: MIT Press.

James, William. 1890/1950. *The Principles of Psychology.* New York: Dover.

Jaynes, Julian. 1976. *The Origin of Consciousness in the Breakdown of the Bicameral Mind.* Boston: Houghton Mifflin.

Ji Fengyuan (forthcoming). *Linguistic Engineering: Language and Politics During the Chinese Cultural Revolution.* Honolulu: University of Hawaii Press.

Jia, John H. and Kyna Rubin. 1997. "China's Brain Trust Abroad." Posted to <www.nafsa.org/publications/ie/spring97/chinabraintrust.html>.

Johnson, Mark. 1988. "Some Constraints on Embodied Analogical Understanding." In David H. Helman, ed. (1988).

Johnson-Laird, Philip N. 1989. "Analogy and the Exercise of Creativity." In Vosniadou and Ortony, eds. (1989).

Jones, Edward A. and Chisato Aoki. 1988. "The Processing of Japanese *Kana* and *Kanji* Characters." In de Kerckhove and Lumsden, eds. (1988).

Jurdant, Baudouin. 1988. "The Role of Vowels in Alphabetic Writing." In de Kerckhove and Lumsden, eds. (1988).

Kahaner, Larry. 1996. *Competitive Intelligence.* New York: Simon and Schuster.

Kahn, Joseph. 1996. "McDonnell Douglas's High Hopes for China Never Really Soared." *Wall Street Journal,* May 22, A1.

Kao, S. R., G. P. van Galen, and R. Hoosain, eds. 1988. *Graphonomics: Contemporary Research in Handwriting.* New York and London: Elsevier Science.

Kato Hiroki. 1979. "*Nihongo hyōkihyō no yūrisei*" (The Advantageousness of the Japanese Language's Way of Writing). *Gengo* 8, 1:66–71.

Katzenstein, Peter J. 1996. *Cultural Norms and National Security: Police and Military in Postwar Japan.* Ithaca, N.Y.: Cornell University Press.

Kavanagh, James F. and Ignatius G. Mattingly, eds. 1972. *Language by Ear and by Eye: The Relationship Between Speech and Reading.* Cambridge, Mass.: MIT Press.

Kelly, Kevin. 1994. *Out of Control: The Rise of Neo-Biological Civilization.* Reading, Mass.: Addison-Wesley.

Kennedy, George A. 1964. "The Fate of Chinese Pictographs." In *Selected Works of George A. Kennedy* Tien-yi Li, ed. New Haven, Conn.: Yale University Press.

Kess, Joseph and Tada Miyamoto. 1999. *The Japanese Mental Lexicon.* Philadelphia: John Benjamins.

Kim Min-su, ed. 1989. *Pukhan ǔi ǒhak hyǒngmyǒng* (North Korea's Linguistic Revolution). Seoul: Tosōulgwan.

Ko Yong-gun, ed. 1989. *Pukhan ǔi mal kwa kǔl* (North Korea's Language and Writing). Seoul: Ulyumunhwasa.

Koestler, Arthur. 1964. *The Act of Creation.* New York: Macmillan.

———. 1981. "The Three Domains of Creativity." In Dutton and Kransz, eds. (1981).

Kolata, Gina. 1990. "Japanese Labs in US Luring America's Computer Experts." *New York Times*, November 11, 1, 24.

Kontsevich, L. R. 1979. *Khunmin chonym (Hǔnmin Chǒng'ǔm)*. Moscow: Nauka.

Korchagina, T. I. 1977. "Osnovnye istochniki omonimii v yaponskom yazyke." (Basic Sources of Homonyms in the Japanese Language). *Voprosy yaponskoy filologii* 4: 42–50.

Kreinin, Mordechai E., ed. 1993. *International Commercial Policy: Issues for the 1990s.* Washington, D.C.: Taylor and Francis.

Kuhn, Thomas S. 1962. *The Structure of Scientific Revolutions.* Chicago: University of Chicago Press.

Kynge, James. 1999. "Warhead 'Secrets' Available on the Net, Says Beijing." *London Financial Times*, June 1.

Lafont, Robert. 1988. "Relationships Between Speech and Writing Systems in Ancient Alphabets and Syllabaries." In de Kerckhove and Lumsden, eds. (1988).

Langely, Pat and Randolph Jones. 1988. "A Computational Model of Scientific Insight." In Sternberg, ed. (1988).

Lecours, Andre. 1989. "Literacy and Acquired Aphasia." In Galaburda, ed. (1989).

Lee Ki-mun. 1977. *Geschichte der koreanische Sprache* (History of the Korean Language). Seoul.

Levine, Jonathan B., Neil Gross, and John Carey. 1989. "Is the US Selling Its High-Tech Soul to Japan?" *Business Week*, June 26, 117–18.

Leys, Simon. 1996. "One More Art" (review of *The Chinese Art of Writing* by Jean Francois Billeter). *New York Review*, April 18, 28–31.

Li, Rex. 1996. *A Theory of Conceptual Intelligence.* Westport, Conn.: Praeger.

Li Xuefen. 1999. "Why Is Chinese S&T Inferior to Others?" *Zhongguo Guoqing Guoli,* April, 23–24.

Lian Yanhua. 2000. "An Assessment of the Growth of Scientific Research Globalization." *Keyan Guanli,* July, pp 1–14.

Liberman, I. Y., D. Shankweiler, F. W. Fischer, and B. Carter. 1974. "Explicit Syllable and Phoneme Segmentation in the Young Child." *Journal of Experimental and Child Psychology* 18:201–12.

Loeb, Vernon and Walter Pincus. 1999. "China Prefers the Sand to the Moles—

Experts Say Beijing Mines Open Sources, Digging Out Secrets Grain by Grain." *Washington Post*, December 12.

Logan, Robert K. 1986. *The Alphabet Effect*. New York: William Morrow and Co.

Lucky, Robert W. 1991. *Silicon Dreams*. New York: St. Martin's Press.

Lumsden, Charles. 1988. "Gene-Culture Coevolution: Culture and Biology in Darwinian Perspective." In de Kerckhove and Lumsden, eds. (1988).

Luria, A. R. 1976. *Cognitive Development: Its Cultural and Social Foundations*. Cambridge, Mass.: Harvard University Press.

Mair, Victor H. 2001. "Language and Script." In Mair, ed., *The Columbia History of Chinese Literature*. New York: Columbia University Press.

Mandler, George. 1995. "Origins and Consequences of Novelty." In Smith, Ward, and Finke, eds. (1995).

Martin, Helmut. 1982. *Chinesische Sprachplannung* (*Chinese Language Planning*). Bochum.

Martin, Samuel E. and Young-Sook C. Lee. 1969. *Beginning Korean*. New Haven:, Conn. Yale University Press.

Martindale, Colin. 1995. "Creativity and Connectionism." In Smith, Ward, and Finke, eds. (1995).

Maskus, Keith and Christine McDaniel. 1999. "How Japan's Patent System Encourages Incremental Innovation." Available through JIAP, 2000 P Street NW, Suite 620, Washington, DC.

McGraw, Gary. 1997. "Creativity, Scientific Discovery, and AI." Lecture given in Lake Fairfax Conference Center, Reston, Va., September 23.

Mehler, Jacques. 1989. "Language at the Initial State." In Galaburda, ed. (1989).

Meyer, Herbert. 1987. *Real World Intelligence*. New York: Weidenfelt and Nicolson.

Miao, Qihao. 1993. "Technological and Industrial Intelligence in China: Development, Transition, and Perspectives." In Prescott and Gibbons, eds. (1993).

Miikkulainen, Risto. 1993. *Subsymbolic Natural Language Processing: An Integrated Model of Scripts, Lexicon, and Memory*. Cambridge, Mass.: MIT Press.

Miller, George A. 1972. "Reflections on the Conference." In Kavanagh and Mattingly, eds. (1972).

Mitchell, Melanie. 1993. *Analogy-Making as Perception*. Cambridge, Mass.: MIT Press.

Moore, Paul D. 1999. "China's Subtle Spying." *New York Times*, September 2.

Morishima, Michio. 1982. *Why Has Japan Succeeded?* Cambridge: Cambridge University Press.

Morton, John. 1989. "An Information-Processing Account of Reading Acquisition." In Galaburda, ed. (1989).

Murray, Alan and Urban C. Lehner. 1990. "What US Scientists Discover, the Japanese Convert—into Profit." *Wall Street Journal*, June 25, A1.

Nakamura, Hajime. 1964. *Ways of Thinking of Eastern Peoples*. Honolulu: East-West Center Press.

Nakayama Shigeru. 1973. "Joseph Needham, Organic Philosopher." In Nakayama Shigeru and Nathan Sivin, eds. (1973).

Nakayama Shigeru and Nathan Sivin, eds. 1973. *Chinese Science: Explorations of an Ancient Tradition.* Cambridge, Mass.: MIT Press.

Needham, Joseph. 1954. *Science and Civilisation in China.* Cambridge: Cambridge University Press.

————. 1969. *The Grand Titration: Science and Society in East and West.* Toronto: University of Toronto Press.

Nicholoson, Tom. 1982. "Japan's High-Tech Spies." *Newsweek,* July 5, 53–56.

Okimoto, Daniel I. 1989. *Between MITI and the Market: Japanese Industrial Policy for High Technology.* Stanford, Calif.: Stanford University Press.

Olson, David R. 1982. "What Is Said and What Is Meant in Speech and Writing." *Visible Language* 16, 2:151–61.

————. 1986. "Interpreting Texts and Interpreting Nature: The Effects of Literacy and Epistemology." *Visible Language* 20, 3:302–17.

————. 1991. "Literacy as Metalinguistics." In Olson and Torrance, eds. (1991).

————. 1994. *The World on Paper: The Conceptual and Cognitive Implications of Writing and Reading.* Cambridge: Cambridge University Press.

Olson, David R. and Nancy Torrance, eds. 1991. *Literacy and Orality.* Cambridge: Cambridge University Press.

Ong, Walter J. 1982. *Orality and Literacy: The Technologizing of the Word.* London: Methuen.

Orleans, Leo A. ed. 1980. *Science in Contemporary China.* Stanford, Calif.: Stanford University Press.

Paradis, Michel, Hiroko Hagiwara, and Nancy Hildebrandt. 1985. *Neurolinguistic Aspects of the Japanese Writing System.* New York: Academic Press.

Perry, Mark. 1992. *Eclipse: The Last Days of the CIA.* New York: William Morrow.

Peters, Ann M. 1983. *The Units of Language Acquisition.* Cambridge: Cambridge University Press.

Peters, Lois S. 1987. *Technical Networks Between US and Japanese Industry.* Troy, N.Y.: Center for S&T Policy, School of Management, Rensselaer Polytechnic Institute.

————. 1993. "Technology Strategies of Japanese Subsidiaries and Joint Ventures in the United States." In Kreinin, ed. (1993).

Pinker, Steven. 1994. *The Language Instinct.* New York: William Morrow.

Pirsig, Robert. 1974. *Zen and the Art of Motorcycle Maintenance.* New York: Bantam Books.

————. 1991. *Lila: An Inquiry into Morals.* New York: Bantam Books.

Platt, Kevin. 2000. "China Answers Critics with a Book of Nuke Web Sites." *Christian Science Monitor,* July 7.

Poincaré, Henri. 1913/1982. *The Foundations of Science: Science and Hypothesis, the Value of Science, Science and Method.* Lancaster, Pa.: Science Press.

Porter, Michael E. 1990. *The Competitive Advantage of Nations.* New York: Free Press.

Prescott, John E. and Patrick T. Gibbons, eds. 1993. *Global Perspectives on Competitive Intelligence.* Alexandria, Va.: Society of Competitive Intelligence Professionals.

Prestowitz, Clyde V. 1988. *Trading Places.* New York: Basic Books.

Qi Liang and Wang Xiangsui. 1999. *Chāoxiàn Zhàn* (*Unrestricted Warfare*) Beijing: PLA Literary Publishing Co.

Qian Wen-yuan. 1985. *The Great Inertia: Scientific Stagnation in Traditional China.* London, Croom Helm.

Quinn, John F. 1998. "Commercial Intelligence Gathering: JETRO and the Japanese Experience." Posted to <www.ccnet.com/~suntzu75 /jindesp.htm>.

Rakic, Pasco. 1989. "Competitive Interactions During Neuronal and Synaptic Development." In Galaburda, ed. (1989).

Rauch R. 1977. "Cognitive Strategies in Patients with Unilateral Temporal Lobe Excisions." *Neuropsychologia* 15:385–96.

Raymond, James C., ed. 1982. *Literacy as a Human Problem.* Mobile: University of Alabama Press.

Read, C. A, Y. Zhang, H. Nie, and B. Ding. 1986. "The Ability to Manipulate Speech Sounds Depends on Knowing Alphabetic Reading." *Cognition* 24:31–44.

Reber, Arthur S. and Don L. Scarborough, eds. 1977. *Toward a Psychology of Reading.* Hillsdale, N.J.: Lawrence Erlbaum.

Reid, Proctor P. and Alan Schriesheim, eds. 1996. *Foreign Participation in U.S. Research and Development: Asset or Liability?.* Washington, D.C.: National Academy Press.

Renaud, Young-Key Kim, ed. 1997. *The Korean Alphabet: Its History and Structure.* Honolulu: University of Hawaii Press.

Ridley, Matt. 2000. *Genome.* New York: Harper Collins.

Rosch, Eleanor and Barbara B. Lloyd, eds. 1978. *Cognition and Categorization.* Hillsdale, N.J.: Lawrence Erlbaum.

Rosenberg, Nathan, Ralph Landau, and David Mowery, eds. 1992. *Technology and the Wealth of Nations.* Stanford, Calif.: Stanford University Press.

Rosenberg, Nathan and W. Edward Steinmueller. 1988. "Why Are Americans Such Poor Imitators?" *American Economic Review* (May): 229–34.

Rothenberg, Albert. 1979. *The Emerging Goddess: The Creative Process in Art, Science, and Other Fields.* Chicago: University of Chicago Press.

Rothenberg, Albert and Carl R. Hausman, eds. 1976. *The Creativity Question.* Durham, N.C.: Duke University Press.

Roukis, George S., Hugh Conway, and Bruce H. Charnov, eds. 1990. *Global Corporate Intelligence.* New York: Quorum Books.

Russell, Bertrand. 1922/1993. *The Problem of China.* Philadelphia: Coronet Books.

Sachs, Oliver. 1989/1990. *Seeing Voices.* New York: Quality Paperback Book Club.

Saenger, Paul. 1991. "The Separation of Words and the Physiology of Reading." In Olson and Torrance, eds. (1991).

———. 1997. *Space Between Words: The Origins of Silent Reading.* Stanford, Calif.: Stanford University Press.

Sakakibara Kiyonori and D. Eleanor Westney. 1992. "Japan's Management of Global Innovation: Technology Management and Crossing Borders." In Rosenberg et al., eds. (1992).

Samuels, Richard J. 1994. *Rich Nation, Strong Army: National Security and the Technological Transformation of Japan.* Ithaca, N.Y.: Cornell University Press.

Sansom, George. 1928. *An Historical Grammar of Japanese.* London: Oxford University Press.

Schnepp. Otto 1989. "The Impact of Returning Scholars on Chinese Science and Technology." In Simon and Goldman, eds. (1989).

Scholes, Robert J. and Brenda J. Willis. 1991. "Linguistics, Literacy, and Marshall McLuhan." In Olson and Torrance, eds. (1991).

Schooler, Jonathan W. and Joseph Melcher. 1995. "The Ineffability of Insight." In Smith, Ward, and Finke, eds. (1995).

Schooler, Jonathan W., Stellan Ohlsson, and Kevin Brooks. 1993 "Thoughts Beyond Words: When Language Overshadows Insight." *Journal of American Experimental Psychology: General* 122, 2:166–83.

Schwartz, Benjamin. 1964. *In Search of Wealth and Power.* New York: Harper and Row.

Schweizer, Peter. 1993. *Friendly Spies.* New York: Atlantic Monthly Press.

Scinto, Leonard F. M. 1986. *Written Language and Psychological Development.* New York: Academic Press.

Scribner, Sylvia and Michael Cole. 1981. *The Psychology of Literacy.* Cambridge, Mass.: Harvard University Press.

Seifert, Colleen M., David E. Meyer, Natalie Davidson, Andrea L. Patalano, and Ilan Yaniv. 1995. "Demystification of Cognitive Insight: Opportunistic Assimilation and the Prepared-Mind Perspective." In Sternberg and Davidson, eds. (1995).

Seybolt, Peter J. and Gregory K. Chiang, eds. 1978. *Language Reform in China.* New York: M. E. Sharpe.

Shlain, Leonard. 1999. *The Alphabet Versus the Goddess.* New York: Penguin Putnam.

Sigurdson, Jon. 1980. *Technology and Science in the People's Republic of China.* Oxford: Pergamon Press.

Simon, Denis Fred. 1989. "Technology Transfer and China's Emerging Role in the World Economy." In Simon and Goldman, eds. (1989).

Simon, Denis Fred and Merle Goldman, eds. 1989. *Science and Technology in Post-Mao China.* Cambridge, Mass.: Council on East Asian Studies, Harvard University.

Simon, Thomas W. and Robert J. Scholes, eds. 1982. *Language, Mind, and Brain.* Hillsdale, N.J.: Lawrence Erlbaum.

Simonton, Dean Keith. 1988a. "Creativity, Leadership, and Chance." In Sternberg, ed. (1988).

———. 1988b. "Evolution and Creativity." In Findlay and Lumsden (1988).

———. 1995. "Foresight in Insight? A Darwinian Answer." In Sternberg and Davidson, eds. (1995).

Sivin, Nathan, ed. 1977. *Science and Technology in East Asia.* New York: Science History Publications.

———. 1980. "Science in China's Past." In Orleans, ed. (1980).

———. 1982. "Why the Scientific Revolution Did Not Take Place in China or Didn't It?" *Chinese Science* 5:45–66.

Smith, Steven M., Thomas B. Ward, and Ronald A. Finke, eds. 1995. *The Creative Cognitive Approach.* Cambridge, Mass.: MIT Press.

Sokolov, A. N. 1972. *Inner Speech and Thought.* New York: Plenum Press.

Spencer, Linda M. 1991. *Foreign Investment in the United States: Unencumbered Access.* Washington D.C.: Economic Strategy Institute.

Springer, Sally P. and Georg Deutsch. 1998. *Left Brain Right Brain: Perspectives from Cognitive Neuroscience.* New York: W.H. Freeman.

Steinberg, Danny D. and Jun Yamada. 1978–1979a. "Are Whole Word Kanji Easier to Learn Than Syllable Kana?" *Reading Research Quarterly* 14, 1:88–99.

————. 1978–1979b. "Pigs Will Be Chickens: Reply to Tzeng and Singer." *Reading Research Quarterly* 14, 4:668–71.

Sternberg, Robert J., ed. 1988. *The Nature of Creativity.* Cambridge: Cambridge University Press.

Sternberg, Robert J. and Janet E. Davidson, eds. 1995. *The Nature of Insight.* Cambridge, Mass.: MIT Press.

St. George, M., M. Kutas, A. Martinez and M. I. Sereno. 1999. "Semantic Integration in Reading: Engagement of the Right Hemisphere During Discourse Processing." *Brain* 122:1317–25.

Stock, Brian. 1983. *The Implications of Literacy: Written Language and Models of Interpretation in the Eleventh and Twelfth Centuries.* Princeton, N.J.: Princeton University Press.

Suttmeir, Richard P. 1989. "Science, Technology, and China's Political Future—A Framework for Analysis." In Simon and Goldman, eds. (1989).

Suzuki Takao. 1975. "On the Twofold Phonetic Realization of Basic Concepts: In Defense of Chinese Characters in Japanese." In Fred C. C. Peng, ed., *Language in Japanese Society.* Tokyo.

Tan Po. 1997. "Spy Headquarters Behind the Shrubs." *Cheng Ming,* March 1, 34–37.

Tang, Tong B. 1984. *Science and Technology in China.* London: Longman.

Taylor, Insup and David Olson, eds. 1995. *Scripts and Literacy.* Dordrecht: Kluwer Academic.

Taylor, Insup and M. Martin Taylor. 1995. *Writing and Literacy in Chinese, Korean, and Japanese.* Philadelphia: John Benjamins.

Taylor, M. Martin. 1988. "The Bilateral Cooperative Model of Reading." In de Kerckhove and Lumsden, eds. (1988).

Teece, David J., ed. 1987. *The Competitive Challenge: Strategies for Industrial Innovation and Renewal.* Cambridge, Mass.: Ballinger.

Turner, Mark. 1988. "Categories and Analogies." In Helman, ed. (1988).

Tzeng, Ovid J. L. and Daisy L. Hung. 1988. "Orthography, Reading, and Cerebral Functions." In de Kerckhove and Lumsden, eds. (1988).

Tzeng, Ovid J. L., D. L. Hung, S. Chen, J. Wu, and M. S. Hsi. 1986. "Processing Chinese Logographs by Chinese Brain-Damaged Patients." In Kao, van Galen, and Hoosain, eds. (1986).

Tzeng, Ovid J. L., Daisy L. Hung, Bill Cotton, and William S.-Y. Wang. 1979. "Visual Lateralization Effect in Reading Chinese Characters." *Nature* 282:499–501.

Tzeng, Ovid J. L., Daisy L. Hung, and Linda Garro. 1978. "Reading the Chinese Characters: An Information Processing View." *Journal of Chinese Linguistics* 6:287–305.

Tzeng, Ovid J. L., Daisy L. Hung, and William S.-Y. Wang. 1977. "Speech Recoding in Reading Chinese Characters." *Journal of Experimental Psychology: Human Learning and Memory* 3, 6:621–30.

Unger, J. Marshal. 1987. *The Fifth Generation Fallacy.* Oxford: Oxford University Press.

van Wolferen, Karel. 1989. *The Enigma of Japanese Power.* New York: Alfred A. Knopf.

Vosniadou, Stella and Andrew Ortony. 1989a. "Similarity and Analogical Reasoning: A Synthesis." In Vosniadou and Ortony, eds. (1989).

———, eds. 1989b. *Similarity and Analogical Reasoning.* Cambridge: Cambridge University Press.

Vygotsky, L. S. 1962. *Thought and Language.* Cambridge, Mass.: MIT Press.

Ward, Thomas. 1995. "What's Old About New Ideas." In Smith, Ward, and Fink, eds. (1995).

Ward, Thomas B., Ronald A. Fink, and Steven M. Smith. 1995. *Creativity and the Mind.* New York: Plenum Press.

Ward, Thomas B., Steven M. Smith, and Jyotsna Vaid, eds. 1997. *Creative Thought.* Washington, D.C.,: American Psychological Association.

Weidenbaum, Murray and Samuel Hughes. 1996. *The Bamboo Network.* New York: Free Press.

Weisberg, Robert W. 1993. *Creativity: Beyond the Myth of Genius.* New York: W. H. Freeman.

———. 1995. "Prolegomena to Theories of Insight on Problem Solving: A Taxonomy of Problems." In Sternberg and Davidson, eds. (1995).

Weiskrantz, L. ed. 1988. *Thought Without Language.* Oxford: Clarendon Press.

West, Bruce and Jonas Salk. 1988. "Creativity As a Distributed Function." In Findlay and Lumsden (1988).

Wrostad, Merald E. 1976. "A Manifesto for Visible Language." *Visible Language* 10, 1:5–40.

Wu Duanmin. 1997. "The 21st Century: The Time When China Will Snatch Nobel Prizes." *21 Shiji,* June 13.

Xu Hongying. 1996. "Research on the Collection and Rational Distribution of Foreign Sci-Tech Journals in China." Paper read at the 62nd IFLA General Conference in Beijing, August 25–31, 1996. Posted to <ifla.org/IV/ifla62/62-honx.htm>.

Yoder, Stephen K. and Eduardo Lachica. 1988. "US Tries Once Again to Persuade Japan to Overhaul 'Unfair' Patent Procedures." *Wall Street Journal,* August 26, 8.

Yukawa, Hideki. 1973. *Creativity and Intuition.* Tokyo: Kodansha.

Index

Acknowledgments

I am amused that this book on creativity fulfills Koestler's (1964) definition of creativity by "bisociating" two separate fields of inquiry: the so-called gray aspects of technology transfer and the psycholinguistics of writing. People whose advice I have sought in the one field, however, are unlikely to know or care much for those who helped me understand problems in the other. And given the sensitivity of some of these issues, I'm not sure all contributors would relish the notoriety. So let me simply acknowledge a few people who helped bring this book into print.

Victor Mair was a constant source of inspiration. His research on Chinese language and writing has had a tremendous impact on my thinking in this field. John DeFrancis also was instrumental in shaping my views toward East Asian orthography.

Richard Bloom, an expert in political psychology, and Derrick de Kerckhove, who has written extensively on the social and psychological effects of alphabetic writing, were kind enough to review early chapters and provide criticism. Patricia Crosby, Owen Lock, Thomas Pierson, and John Rohsenow read the entire manuscript and offered many useful suggestions.

I benefited from consultations with specialists in trade, applied linguistics, and East Asian affairs, especially Stephen F. Argubright, Jr., Marc Damashek and his colleagues, Nicholas Eftimiades, Hollis C. Hebbel, Lee Livingston, Stephen C. Mercado, Sydney A. Seiler, and Sharon Y. Thanks are also due William H. Calvin for his early encouragement; Elayne R. for latitude and forbearance; Thomas Howell, Rachel Howe, and their team for encouragement and support; Peter Agree, Alison Anderson, and Walda Metcalf for guiding the manuscript through the publishing process.

My debt to my parents, Carl and Iva Hannas, is enormous. I also wish to thank my Asian language teachers for their patience and dedication. Finally, I thank my wife, Jennifer Thu Hannas, whose love and good sense have been the foundation for everything.

I should add that the opinions expressed here are mine alone and do not necessarily reflect the views of any of these individuals or the institutions and organizations with which I am or have been associated.